BEAUTY AND · THE BEAST OF PARADISE LOST

1

KAORI YUKI

La belle et la bête du paradis perdu

Table des matières

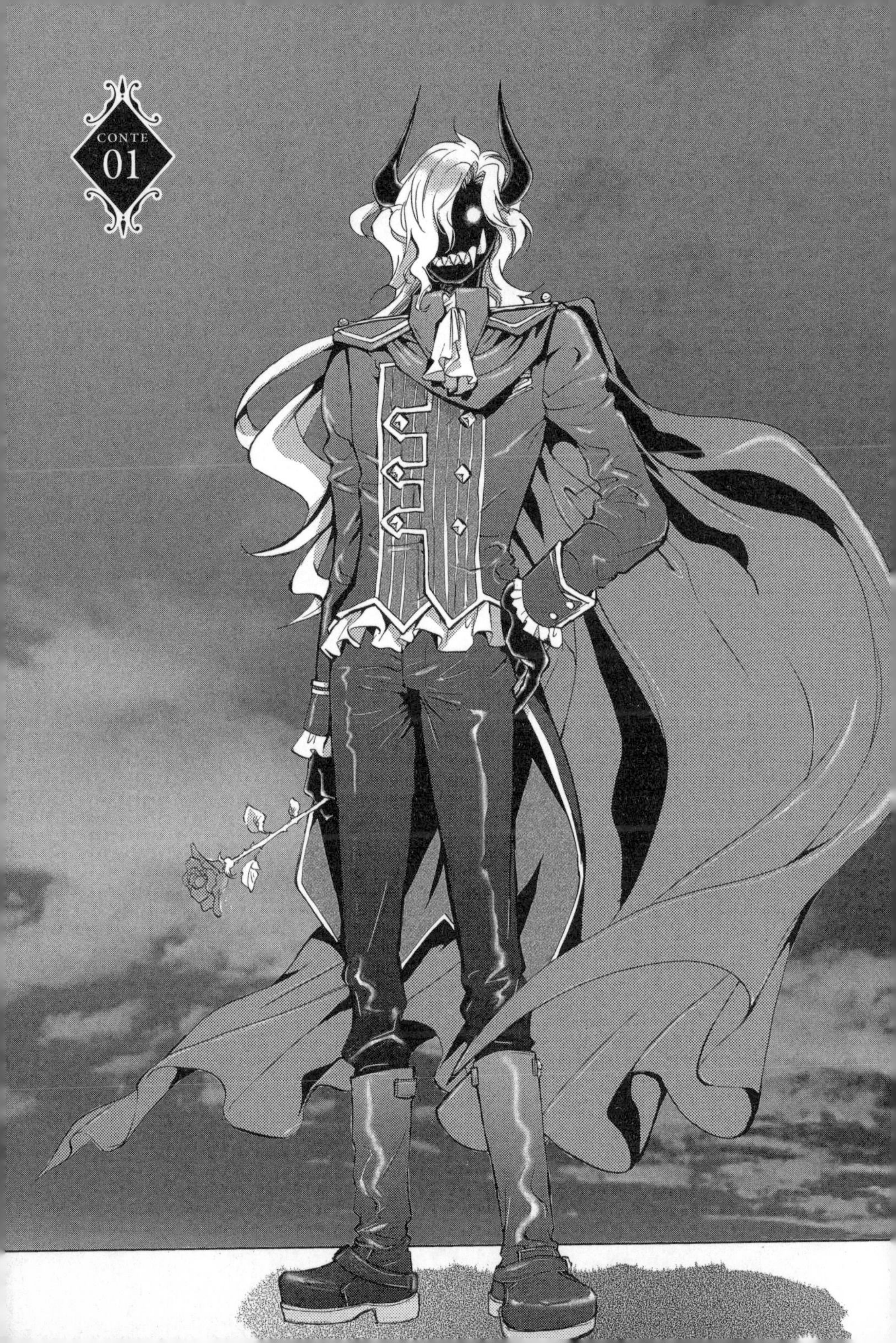
CONTE
01

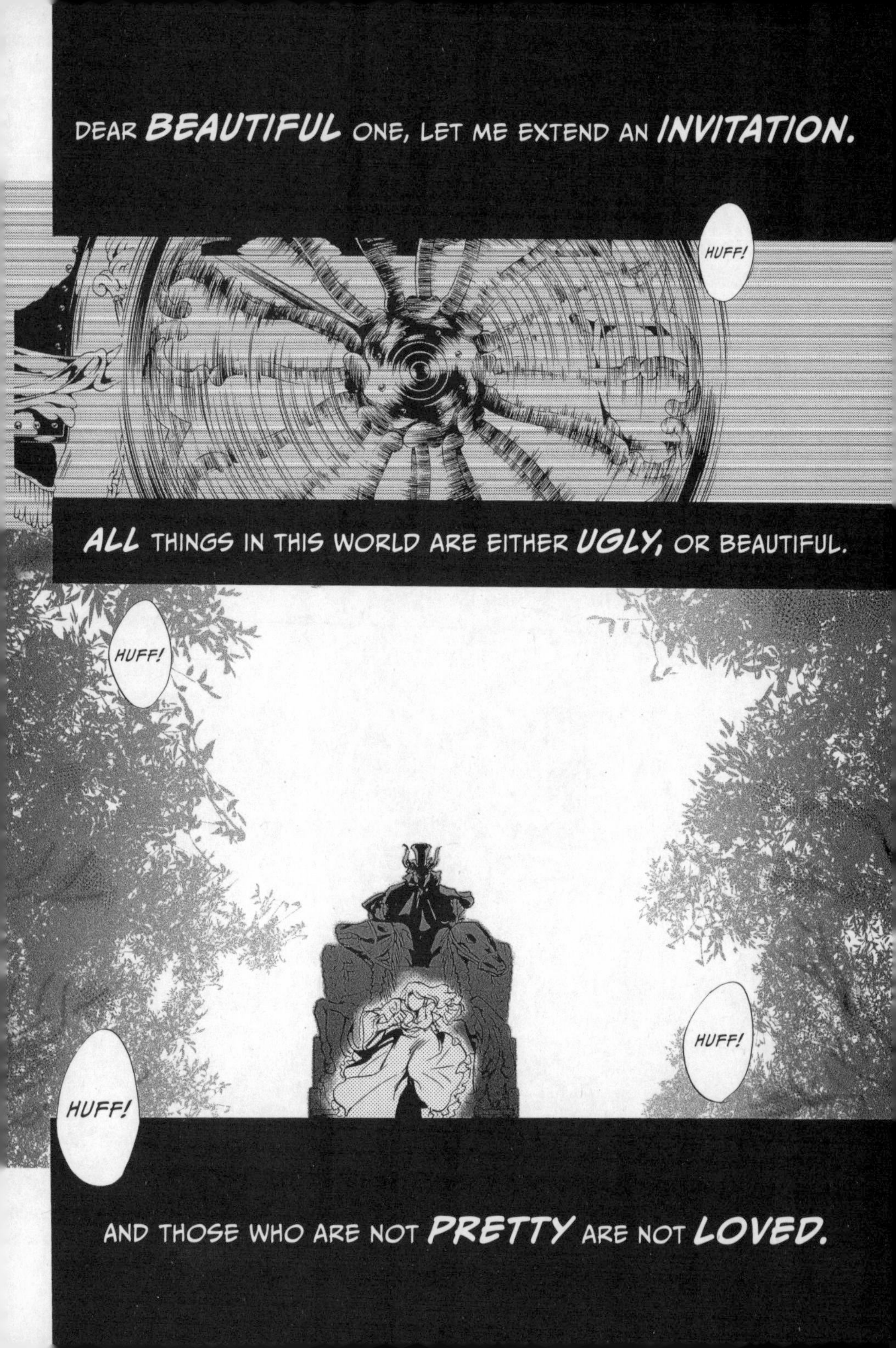
DEAR BEAUTIFUL ONE, LET ME EXTEND AN INVITATION.
HUFF!
ALL THINGS IN THIS WORLD ARE EITHER UGLY, OR BEAUTIFUL.
HUFF!
HUFF!
HUFF!
AND THOSE WHO ARE NOT PRETTY ARE NOT LOVED.

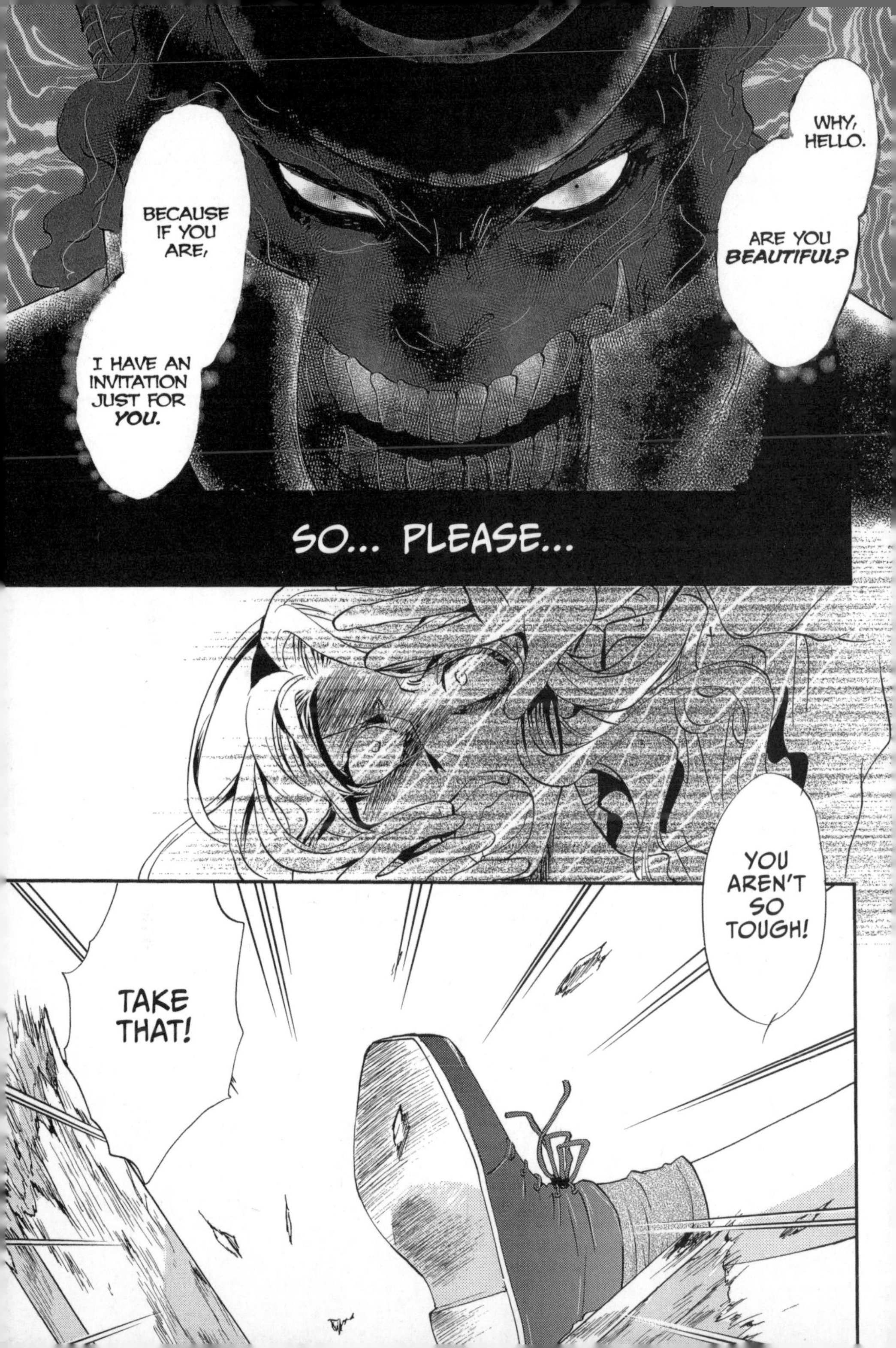
WHY, HELLO.
ARE YOU BEAUTIFUL?
BECAUSE IF YOU ARE,
I HAVE AN INVITATION JUST FOR YOU.
SO... PLEASE...
YOU AREN'T SO TOUGH!
TAKE THAT!

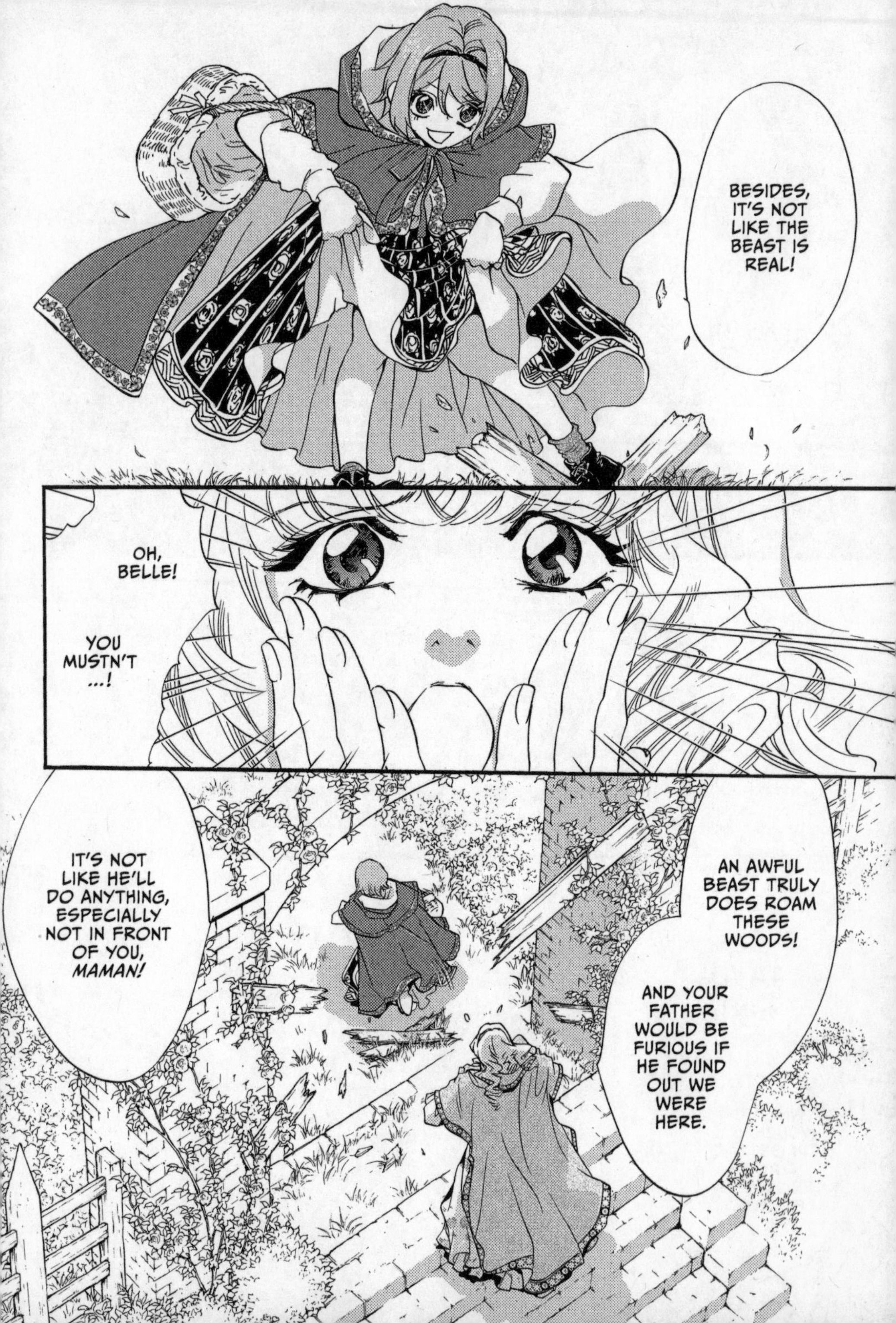
BESIDES, IT'S NOT LIKE THE BEAST IS REAL!
OH, BELLE!
YOU MUSTN'T ...!
AN AWFUL BEAST TRULY DOES ROAM THESE WOODS!
AND YOUR FATHER WOULD BE FURIOUS IF HE FOUND OUT WE WERE HERE.
IT'S NOT LIKE HE'LL DO ANYTHING, ESPECIALLY NOT IN FRONT OF YOU, *MAMAN!*

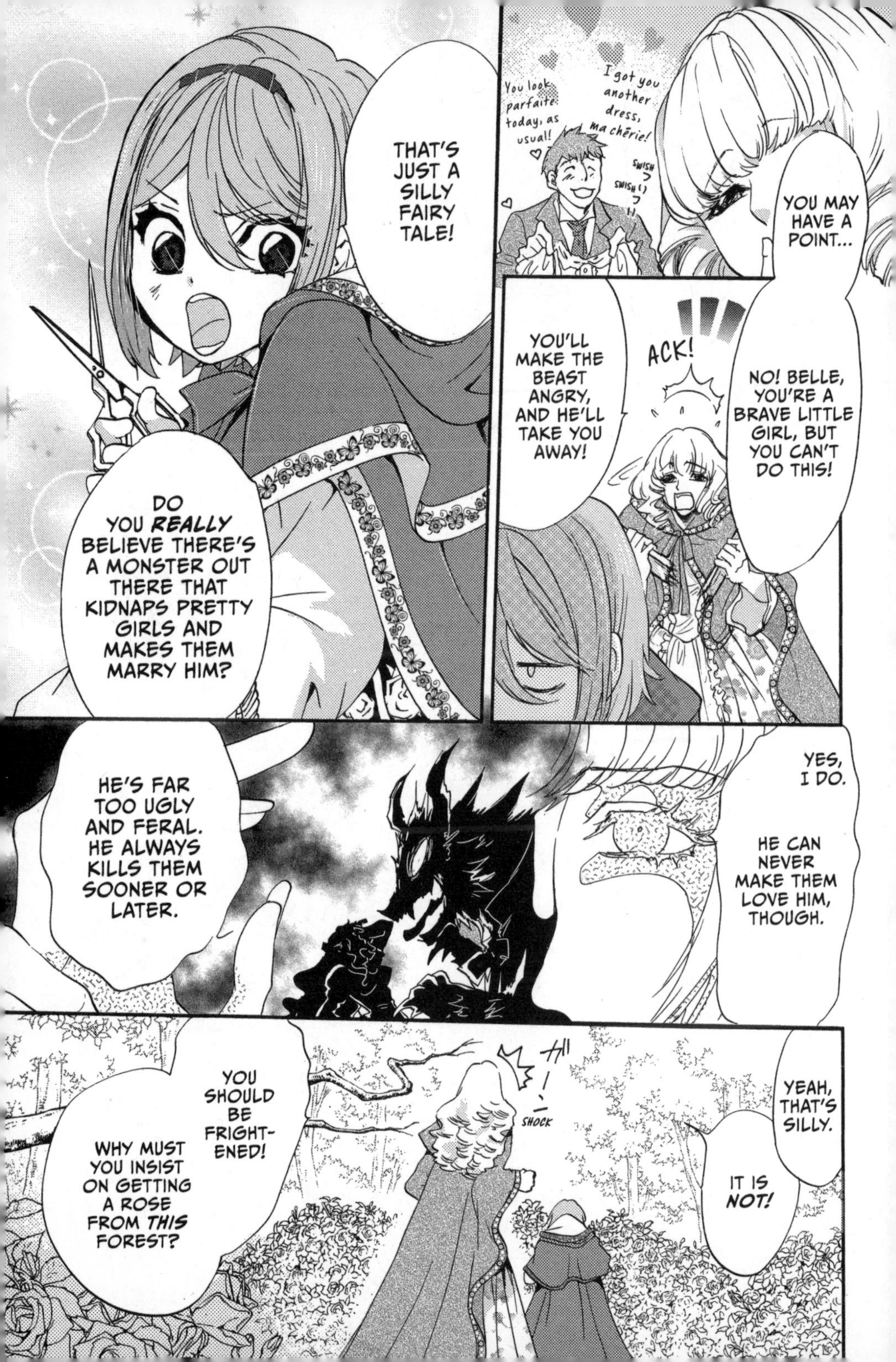
YOU MAY HAVE A POINT...
I got you another dress, ma chérie!
You look parfaite today, as usual!
SWISH
SWISH
NO! BELLE, YOU'RE A BRAVE LITTLE GIRL, BUT YOU CAN'T DO THIS!
ACK!
YOU'LL MAKE THE BEAST ANGRY, AND HE'LL TAKE YOU AWAY!
THAT'S JUST A SILLY FAIRY TALE!
DO YOU ***REALLY*** BELIEVE THERE'S A MONSTER OUT THERE THAT KIDNAPS PRETTY GIRLS AND MAKES THEM MARRY HIM?
YES, I DO.
HE CAN NEVER MAKE THEM LOVE HIM, THOUGH.
HE'S FAR TOO UGLY AND FERAL. HE ALWAYS KILLS THEM SOONER OR LATER.
YEAH, THAT'S SILLY.
IT IS ***NOT!***
SHOCK
YOU SHOULD BE FRIGHT-ENED!
WHY MUST YOU INSIST ON GETTING A ROSE FROM ***THIS*** FOREST?

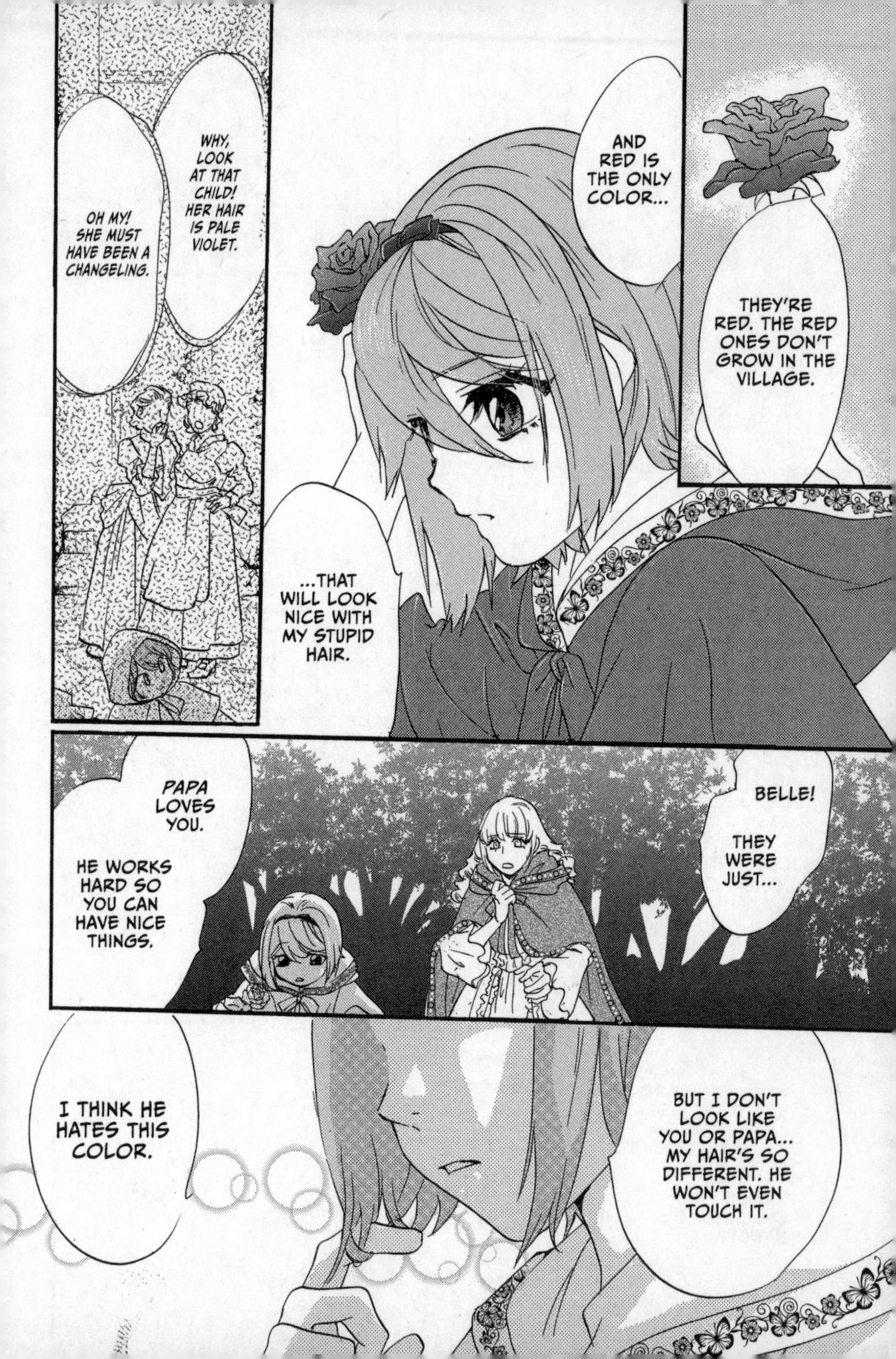
THEY'RE RED. THE RED ONES DON'T GROW IN THE VILLAGE.
AND RED IS THE ONLY COLOR...
...THAT WILL LOOK NICE WITH MY STUPID HAIR.
WHY, LOOK AT THAT CHILD! HER HAIR IS PALE VIOLET.
OH MY! SHE MUST HAVE BEEN A CHANGELING.
BELLE!
THEY WERE JUST...
PAPA LOVES YOU.
HE WORKS HARD SO YOU CAN HAVE NICE THINGS.
BUT I DON'T LOOK LIKE YOU OR PAPA... MY HAIR'S SO DIFFERENT. HE WON'T EVEN TOUCH IT.
I THINK HE HATES THIS COLOR.

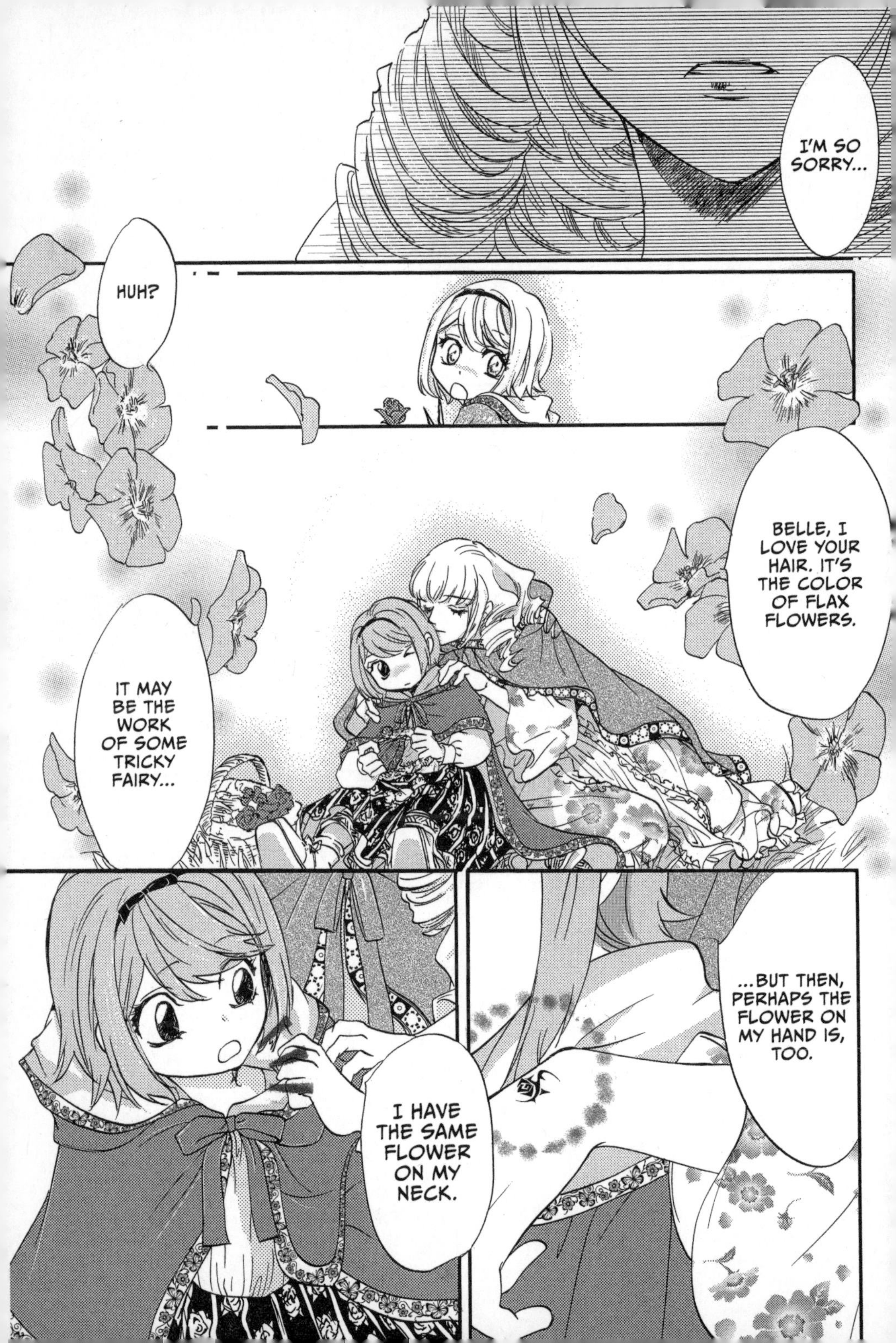
I'M SO SORRY...
HUH?
BELLE, I LOVE YOUR HAIR. IT'S THE COLOR OF FLAX FLOWERS.
IT MAY BE THE WORK OF SOME TRICKY FAIRY...
...BUT THEN, PERHAPS THE FLOWER ON MY HAND IS, TOO.
I HAVE THE SAME FLOWER ON MY NECK.

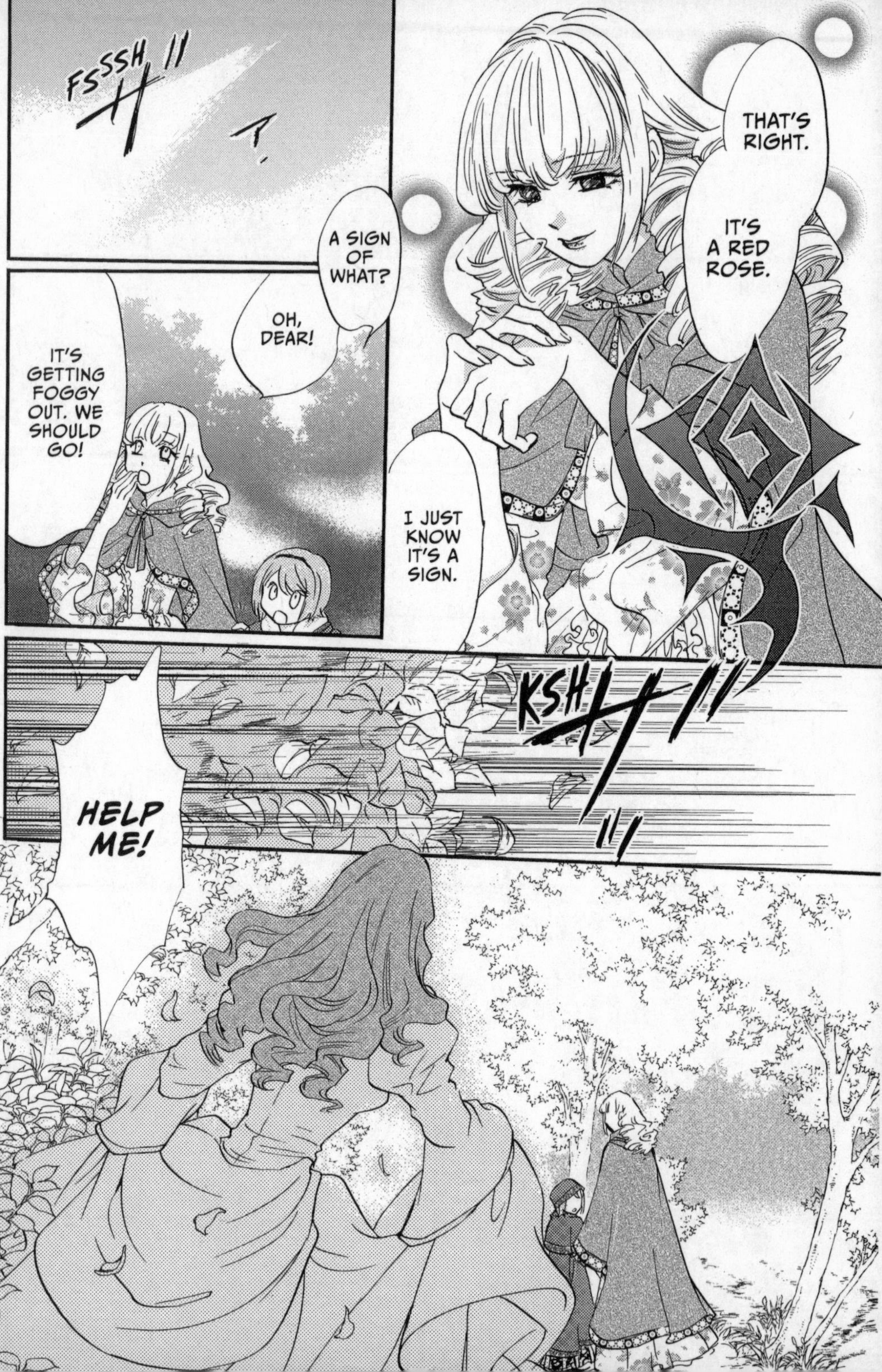
THAT'S RIGHT.
IT'S A RED ROSE.
A SIGN OF WHAT?
I JUST KNOW IT'S A SIGN.
FSSSHH
ア
OH, DEAR!
IT'S GETTING FOGGY OUT. WE SHOULD GO!
KSHH
HELP ME!

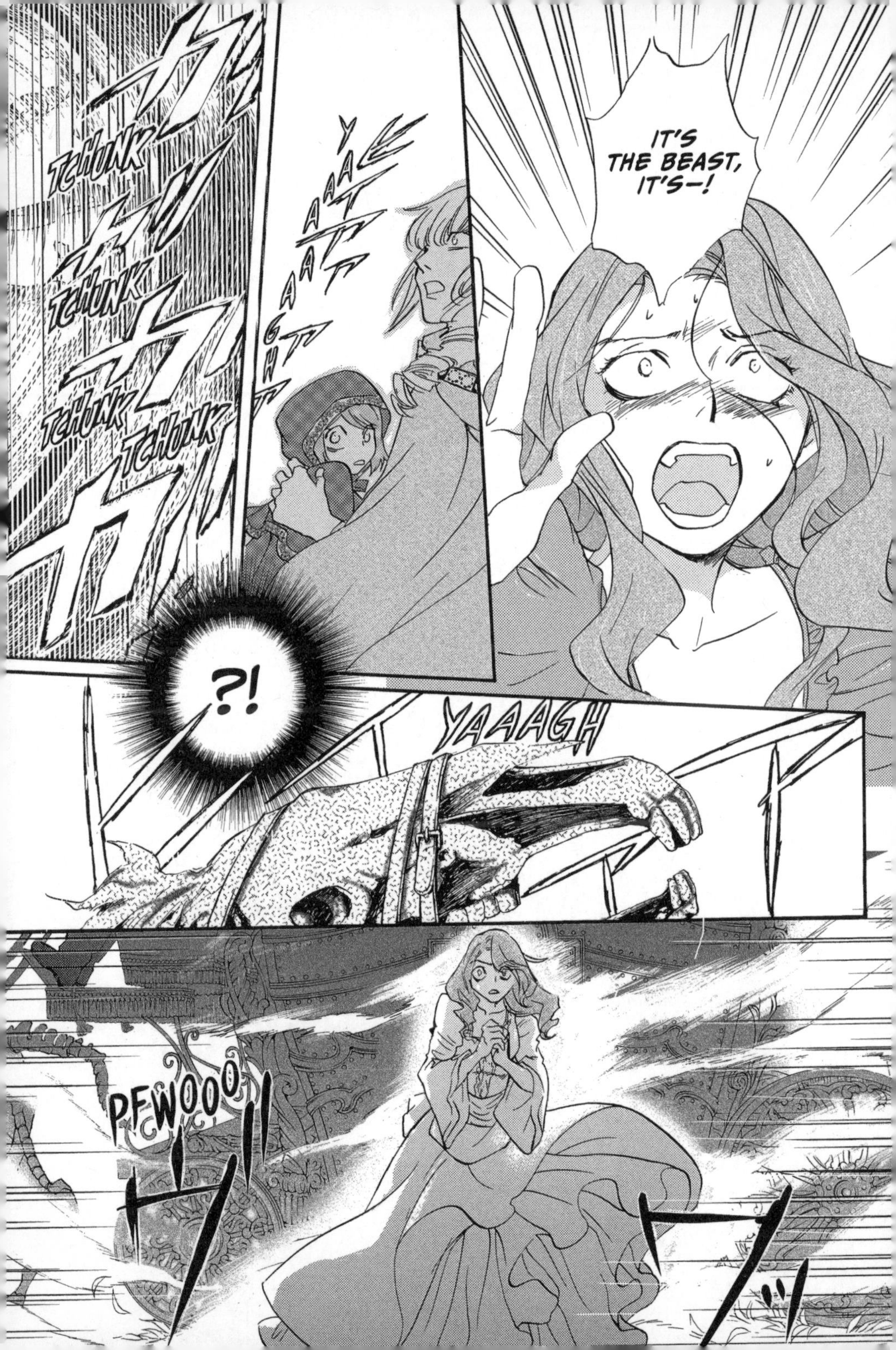
IT'S THE BEAST, IT'S—!
YAAAAAAGHT
TCHUNK
TCHUNK
TCHUNK
TCHUNK
?!
YAAAGH
PFWOOO

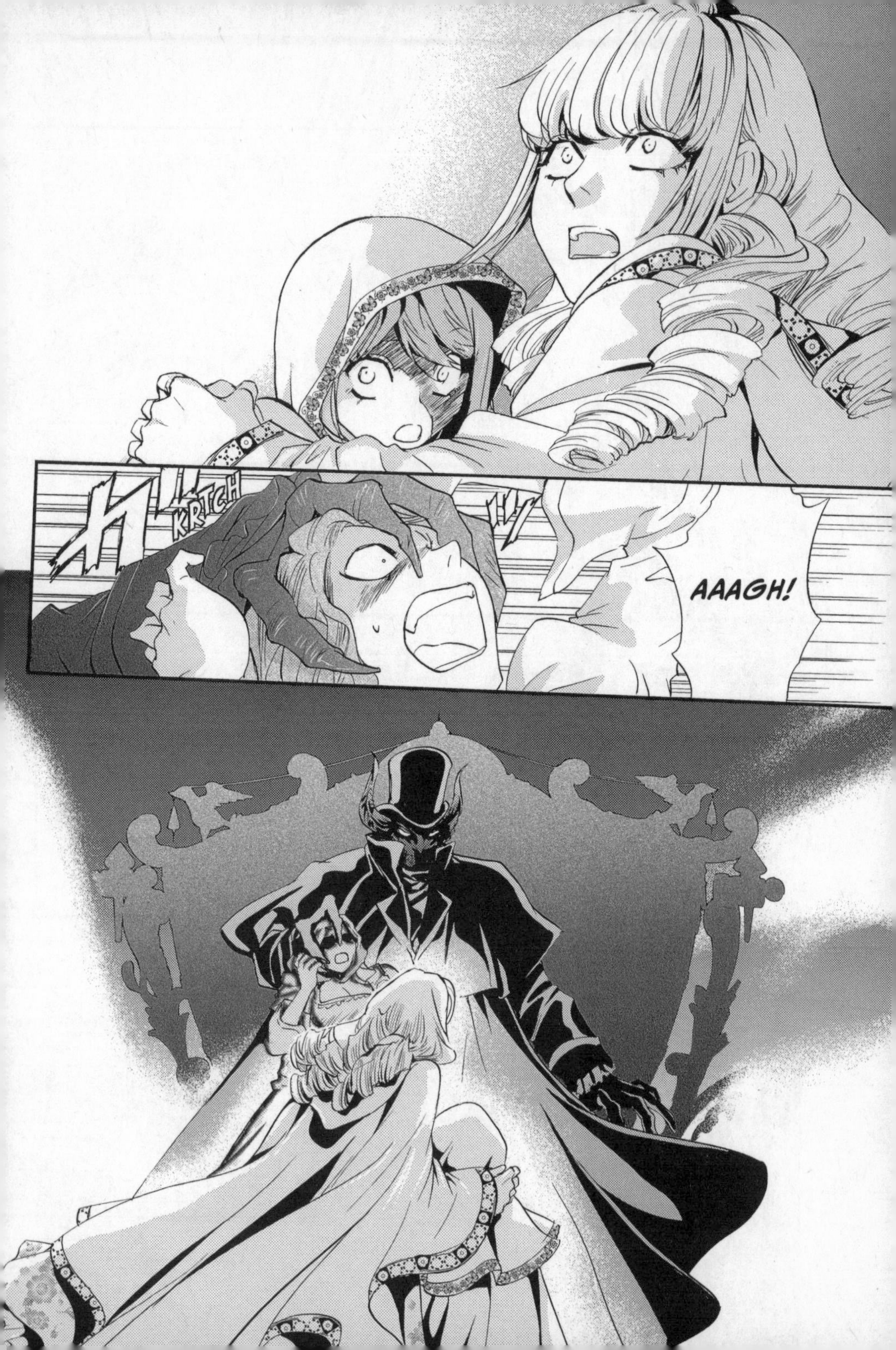
KRTCH
AAAGH!

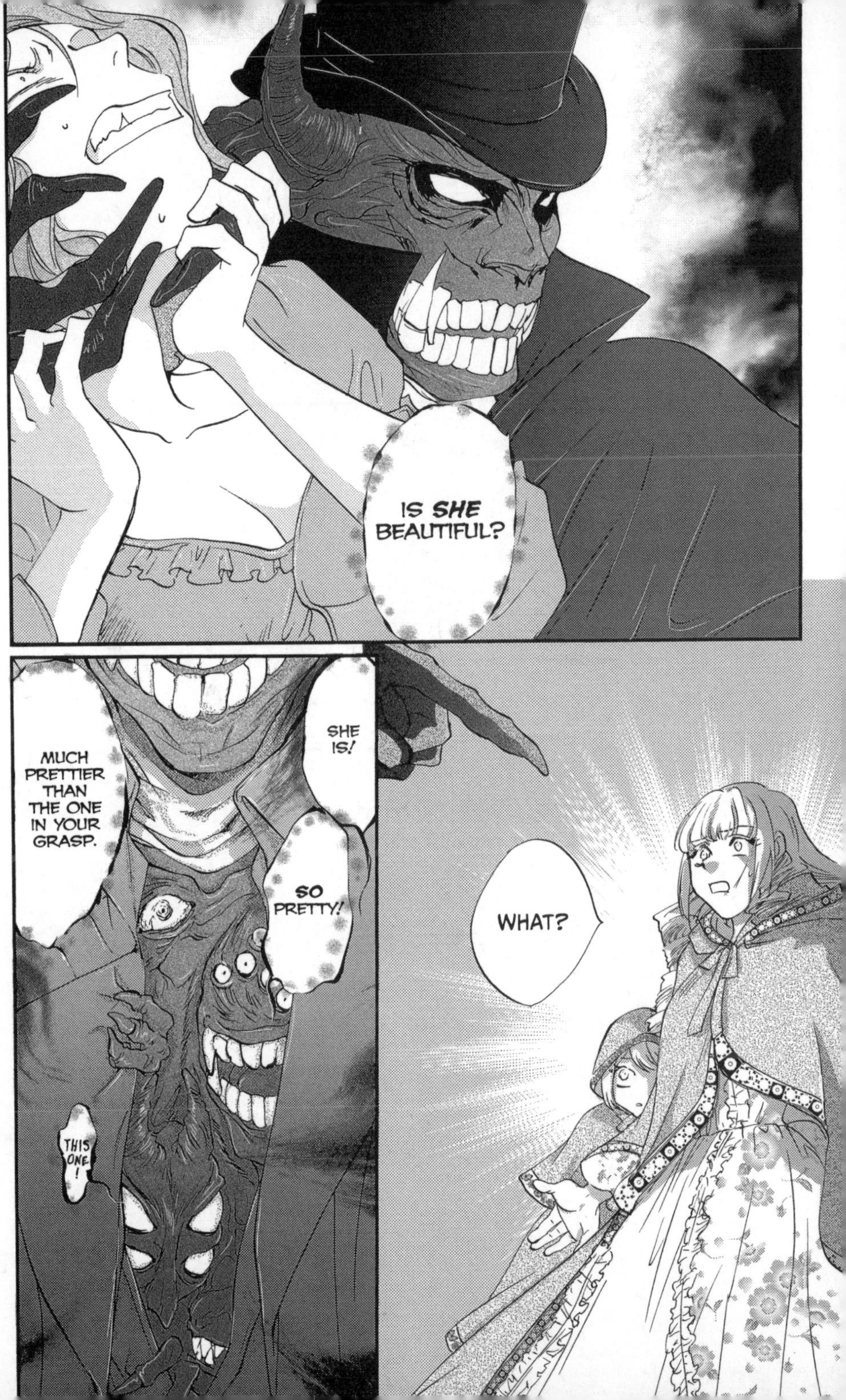
IS SHE BEAUTIFUL?
WHAT?
SHE IS!
MUCH PRETTIER THAN THE ONE IN YOUR GRASP.
SO PRETTY!
THIS ONE!

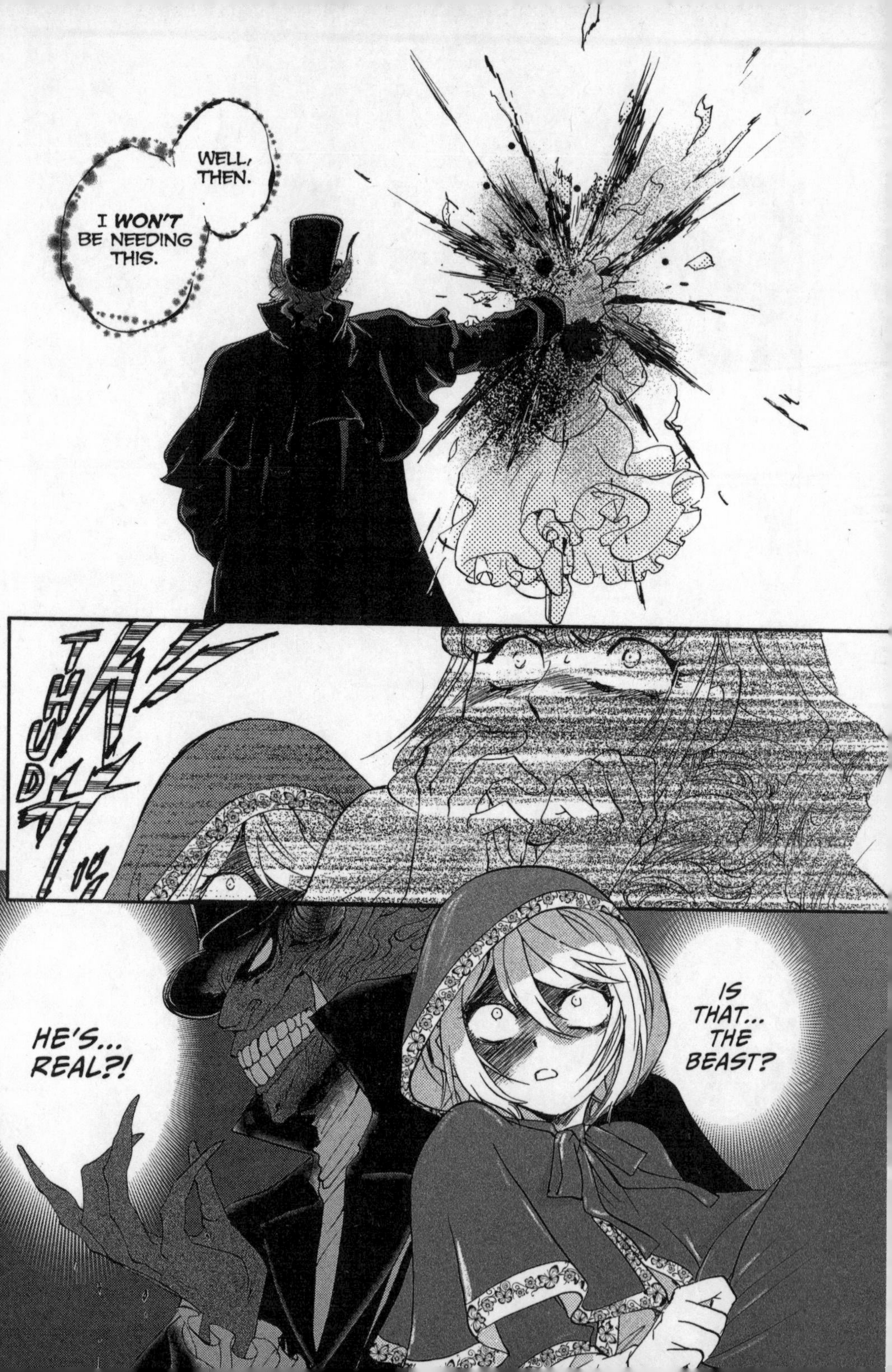
WELL, THEN.
I WON'T BE NEEDING THIS.
THUDD
IS THAT... THE BEAST?
HE'S... REAL?!

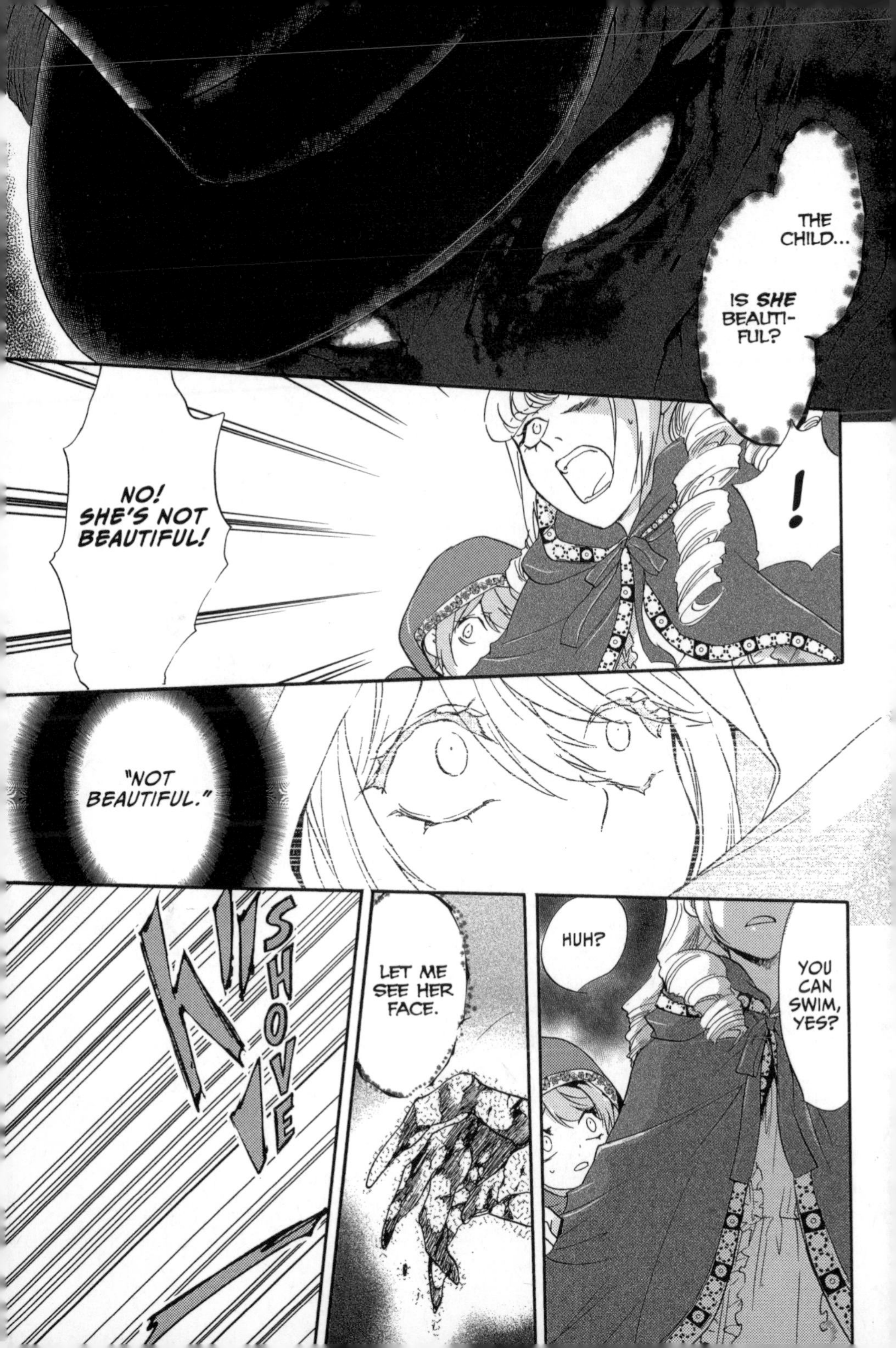
THE CHILD...
IS **SHE** BEAUTIFUL?
!
NO! SHE'S NOT BEAUTIFUL!
"NOT BEAUTIFUL."
YOU CAN SWIM, YES?
HUH?
LET ME SEE HER FACE.
SHOVE

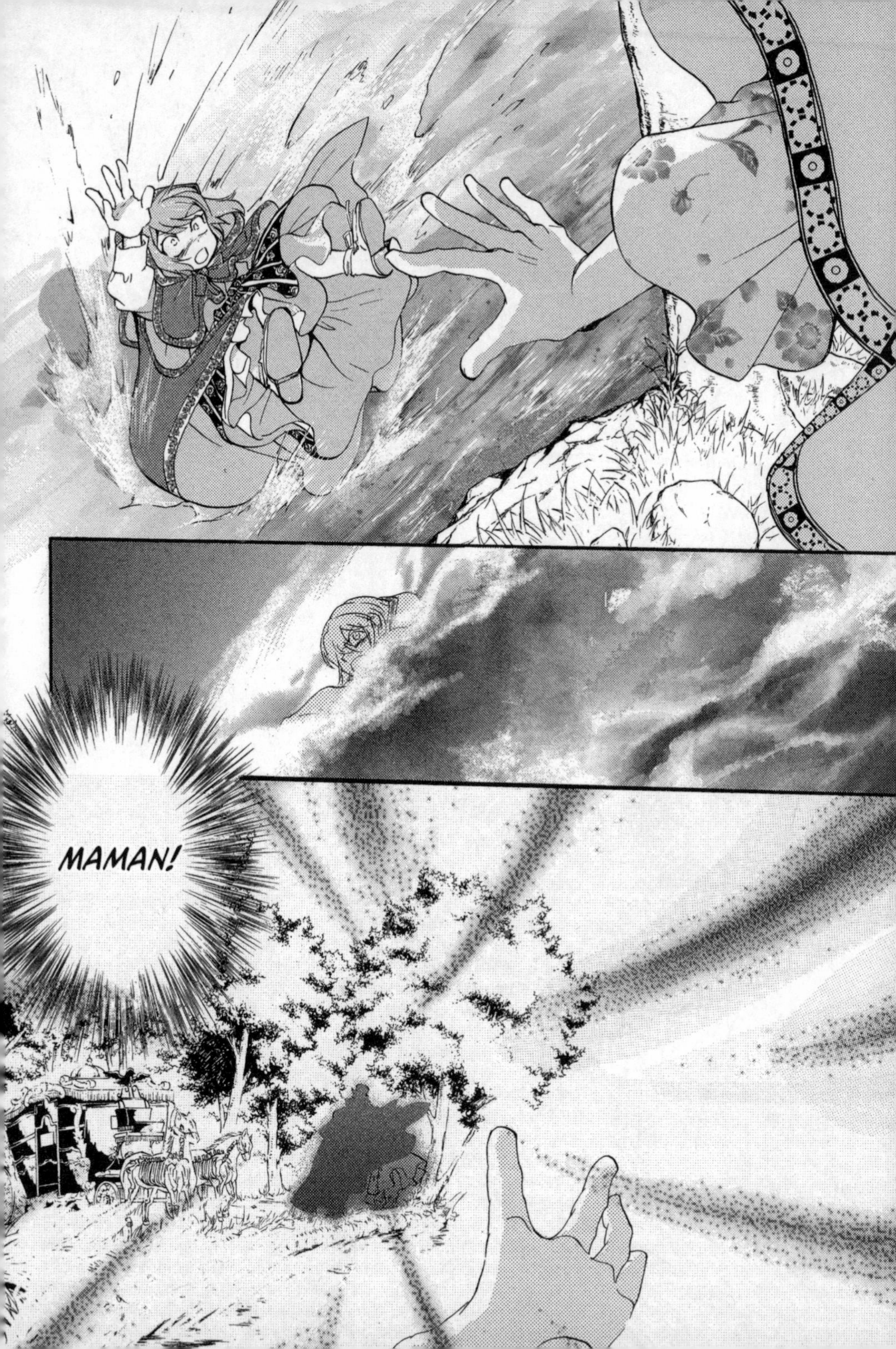
MAMAN!

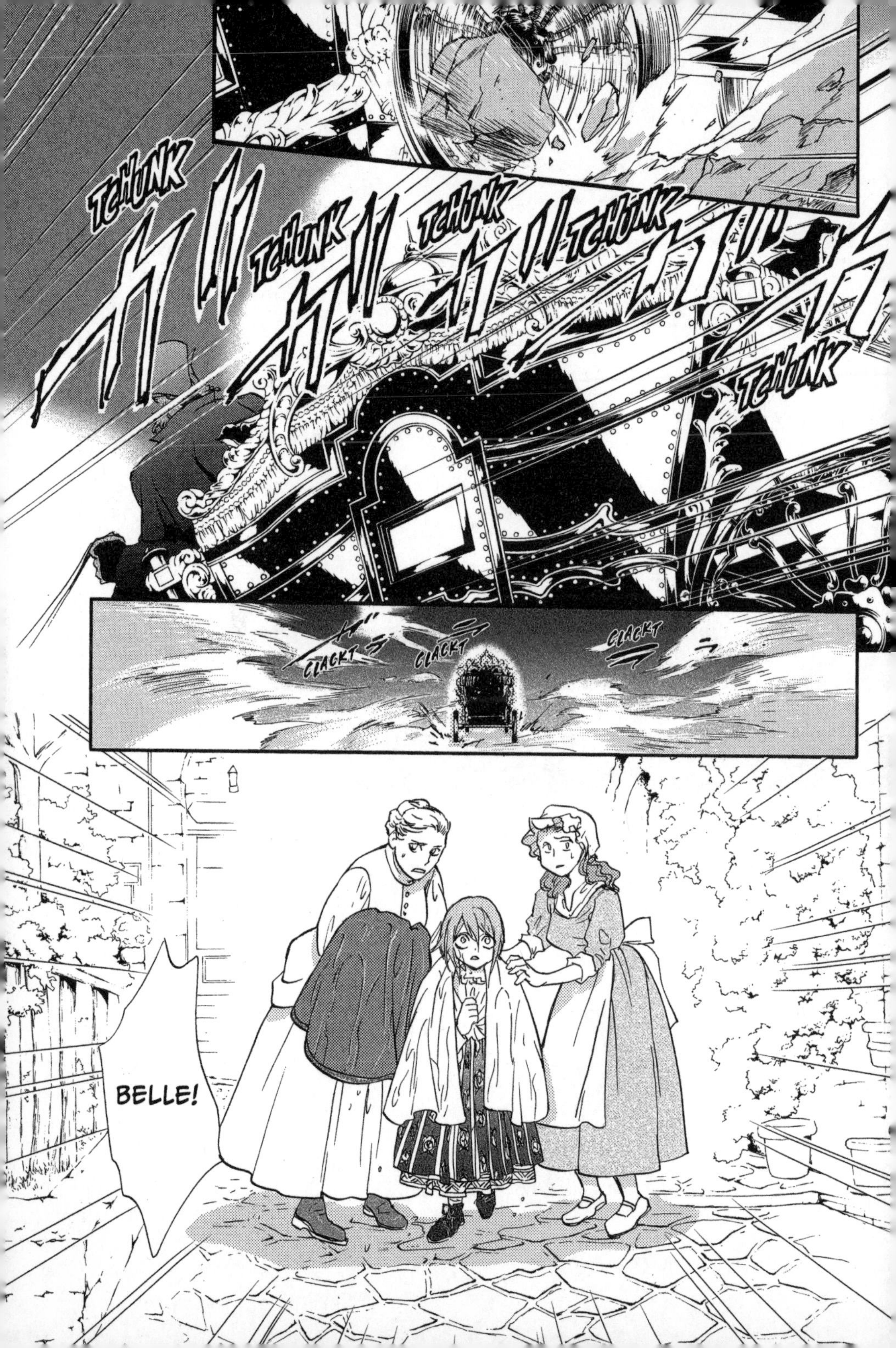
TCHUNK
TCHUNK
TCHUNK
TCHUNK
TCHUNK
CLACKT
CLACKT
CLACKT
BELLE!

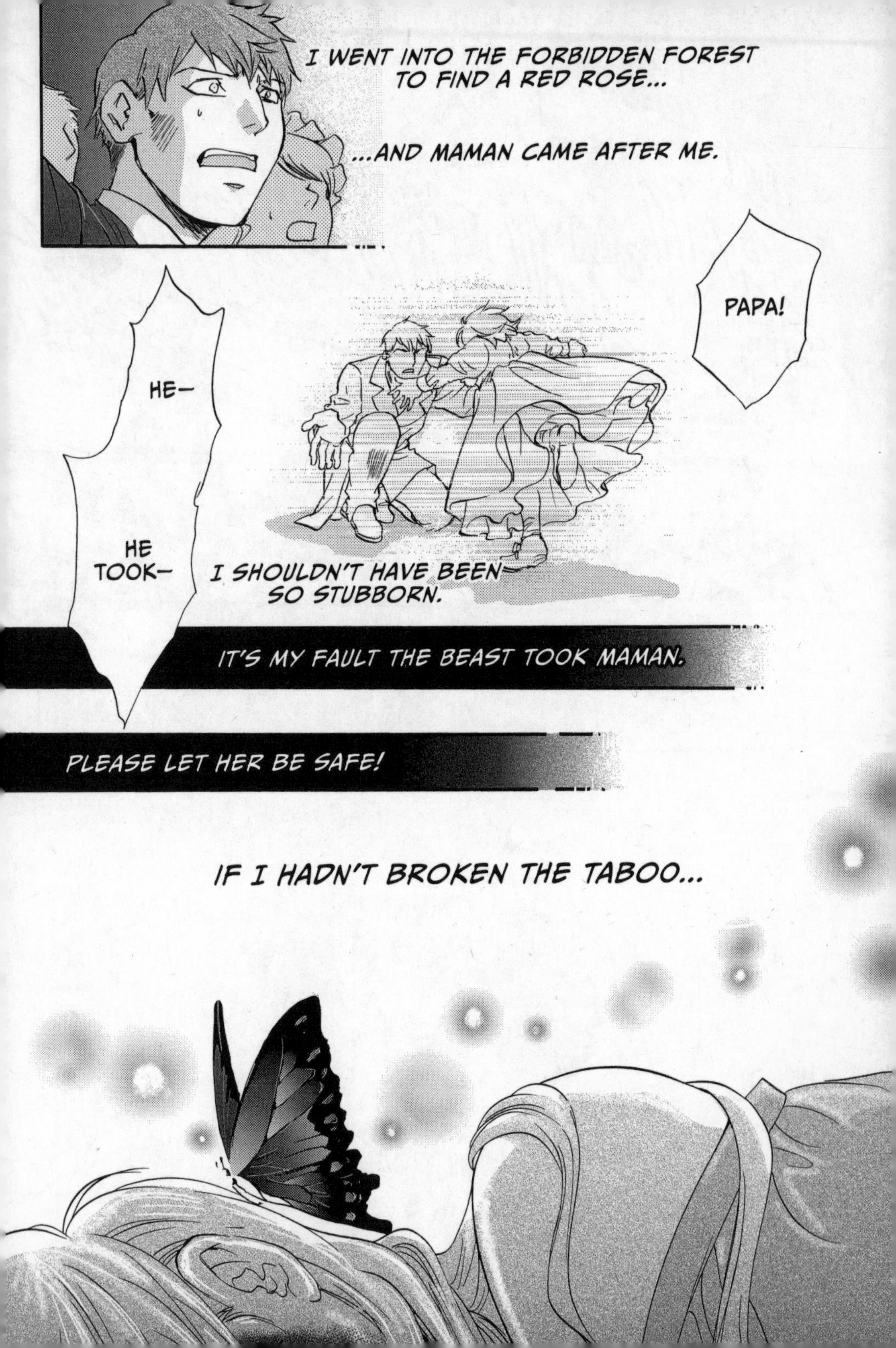
I WENT INTO THE FORBIDDEN FOREST TO FIND A RED ROSE...
...AND MAMAN CAME AFTER ME.
PAPA!
HE—
HE TOOK—
I SHOULDN'T HAVE BEEN SO STUBBORN.
IT'S MY FAULT THE BEAST TOOK MAMAN.
PLEASE LET HER BE SAFE!
IF I HADN'T BROKEN THE TABOO...

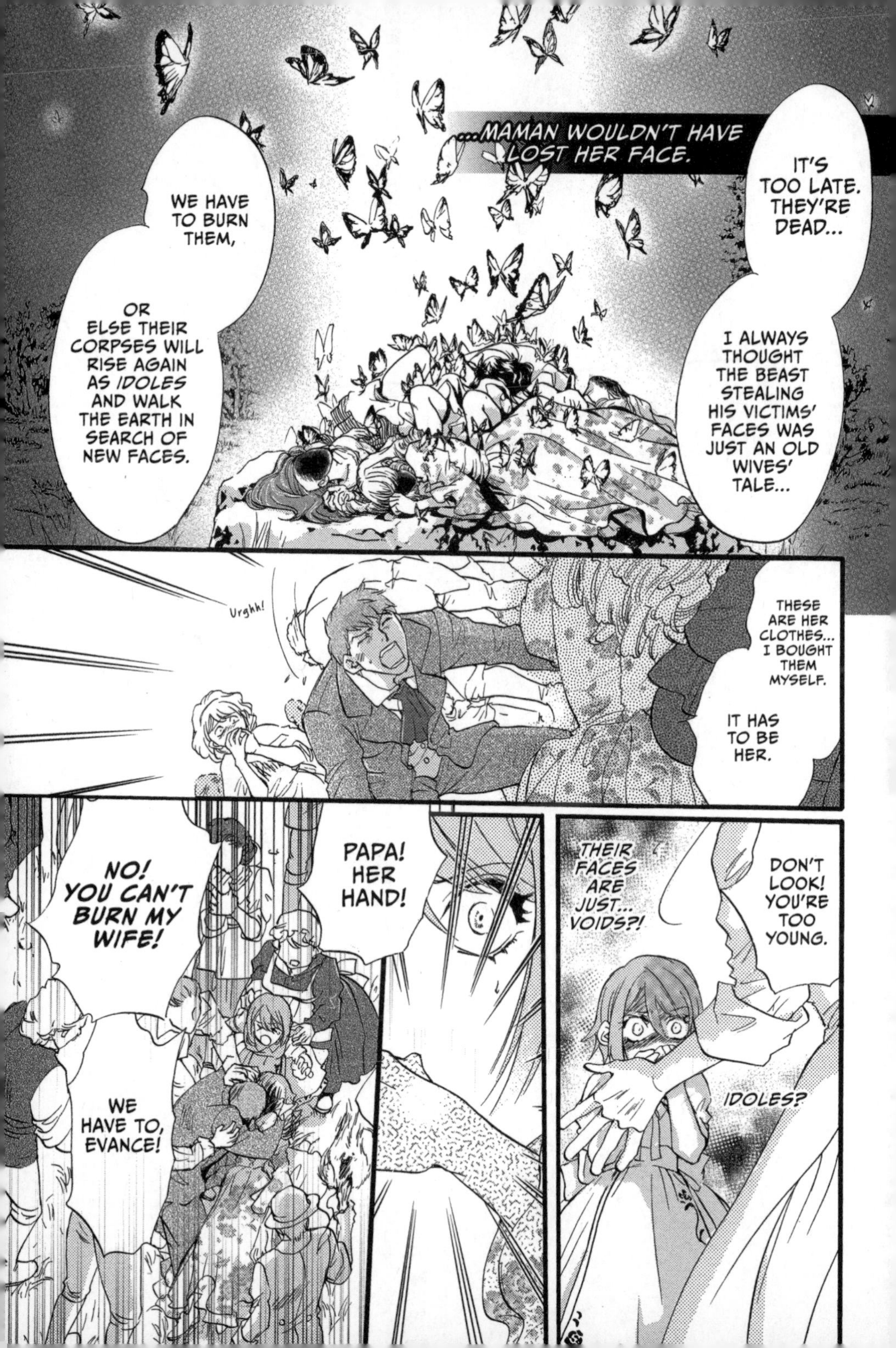
IT'S TOO LATE. THEY'RE DEAD...
...MAMAN WOULDN'T HAVE LOST HER FACE.
I ALWAYS THOUGHT THE BEAST STEALING HIS VICTIMS' FACES WAS JUST AN OLD WIVES' TALE...
WE HAVE TO BURN THEM,
OR ELSE THEIR CORPSES WILL RISE AGAIN AS *IDOLES* AND WALK THE EARTH IN SEARCH OF NEW FACES.
THESE ARE HER CLOTHES... I BOUGHT THEM MYSELF.
IT HAS TO BE HER.
Urghh!
DON'T LOOK! YOU'RE TOO YOUNG.
THEIR FACES ARE JUST... VOIDS?!
IDOLES?
PAPA! HER HAND!
NO! YOU CAN'T BURN MY WIFE!
WE HAVE TO, EVANCE!

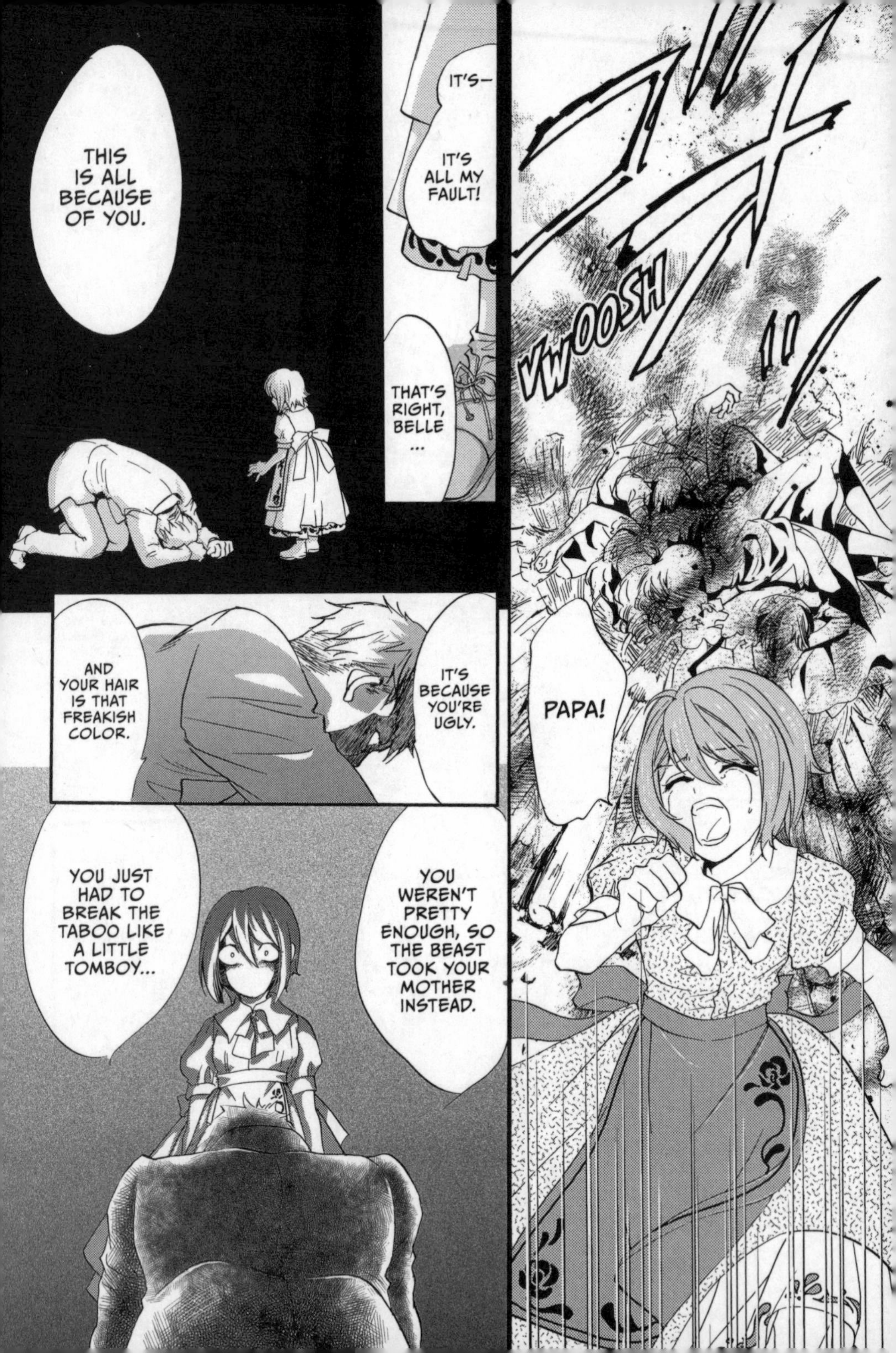
VWOOSH
PAPA!
IT'S—
IT'S ALL MY FAULT!
THAT'S RIGHT, BELLE ...
THIS IS ALL BECAUSE OF YOU.
IT'S BECAUSE YOU'RE UGLY.
AND YOUR HAIR IS THAT FREAKISH COLOR.
YOU WEREN'T PRETTY ENOUGH, SO THE BEAST TOOK YOUR MOTHER INSTEAD.
YOU JUST HAD TO BREAK THE TABOO LIKE A LITTLE TOMBOY...

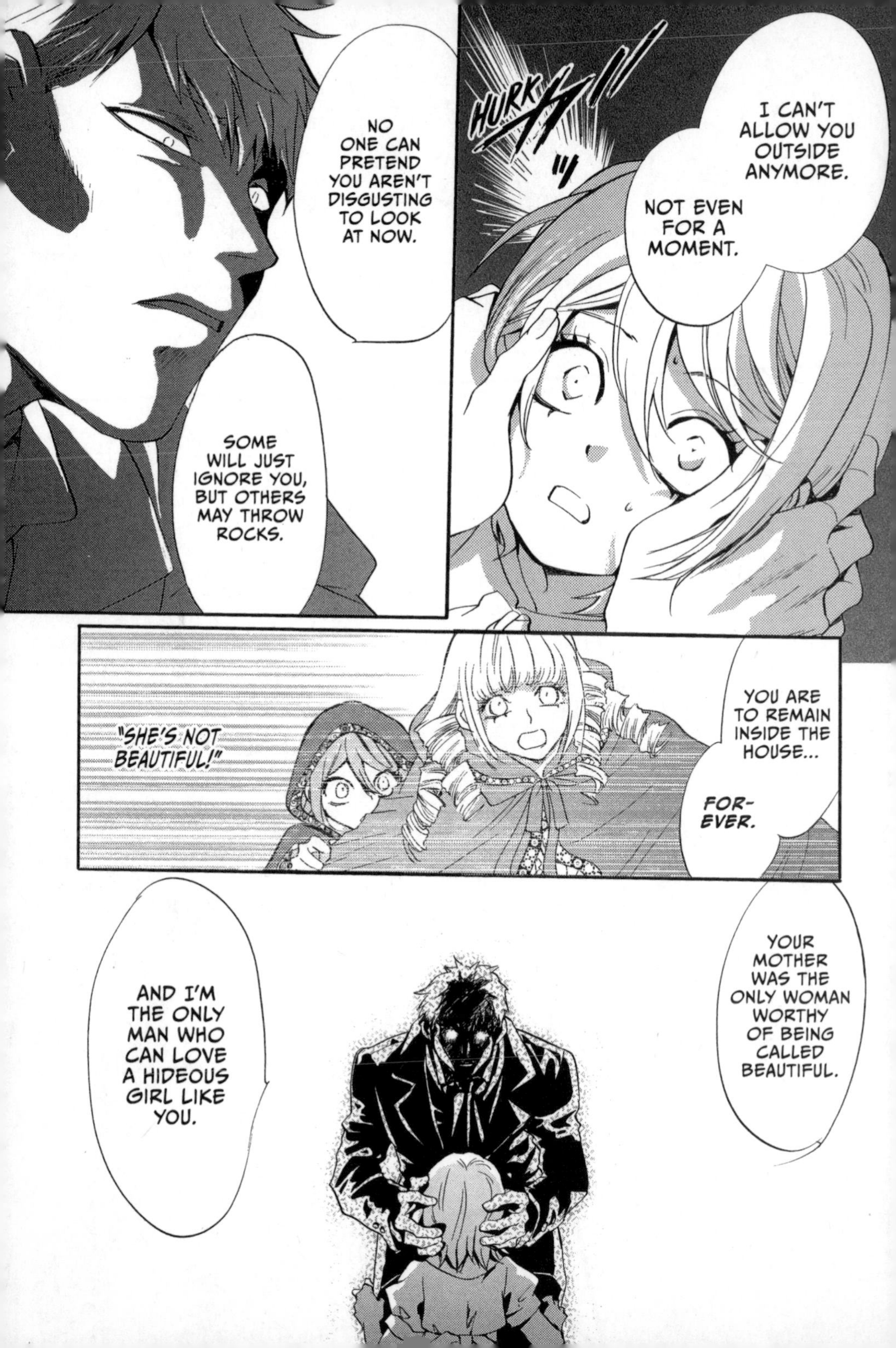
I CAN'T ALLOW YOU OUTSIDE ANYMORE.
NOT EVEN FOR A MOMENT.
HURK
NO ONE CAN PRETEND YOU AREN'T DISGUSTING TO LOOK AT NOW.
SOME WILL JUST IGNORE YOU, BUT OTHERS MAY THROW ROCKS.
YOU ARE TO REMAIN INSIDE THE HOUSE...
FOR-EVER.
"SHE'S NOT BEAUTIFUL!"
YOUR MOTHER WAS THE ONLY WOMAN WORTHY OF BEING CALLED BEAUTIFUL.
AND I'M THE ONLY MAN WHO CAN LOVE A HIDEOUS GIRL LIKE YOU.

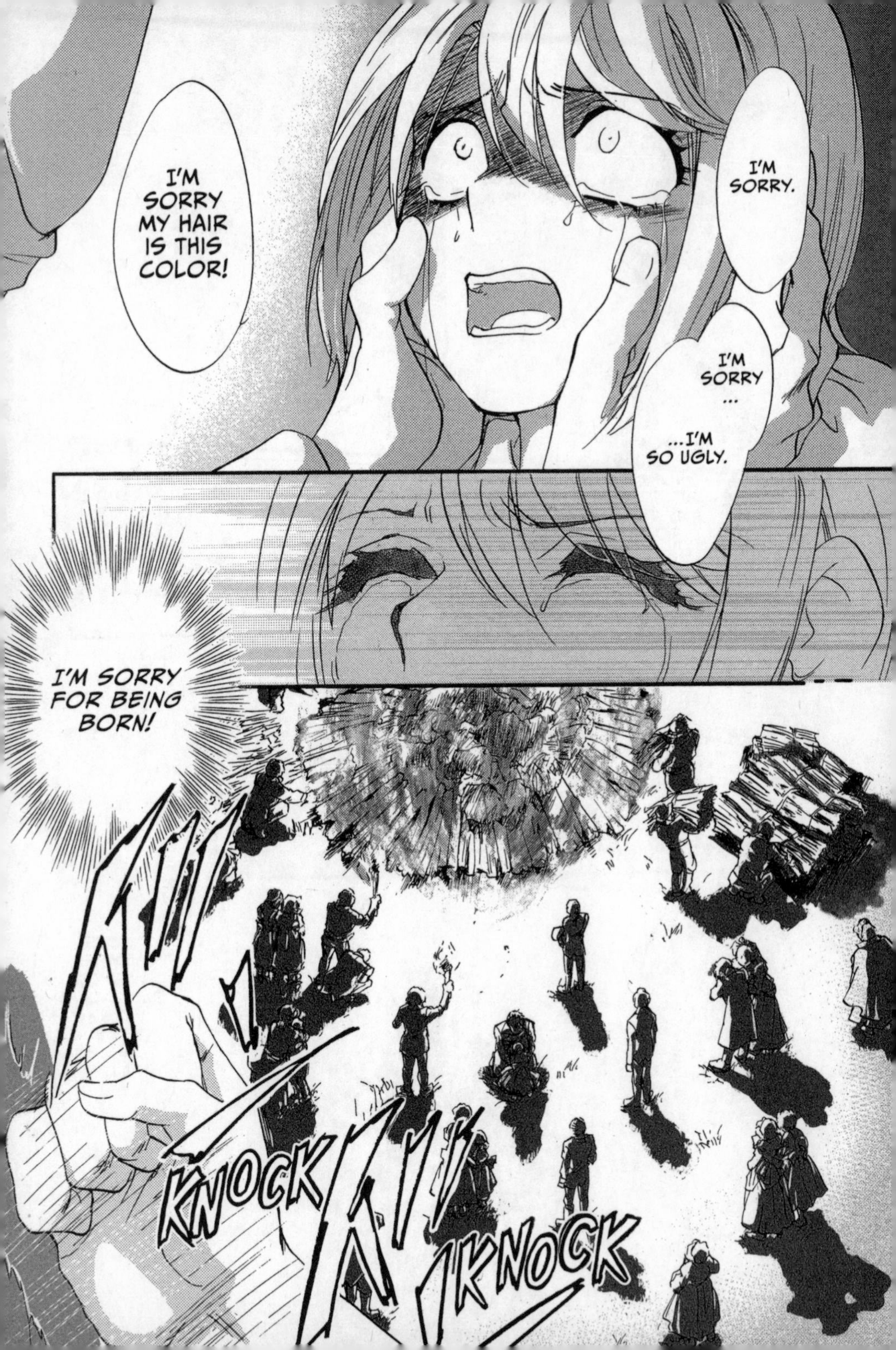
I'M SORRY.
I'M SORRY MY HAIR IS THIS COLOR!
I'M SORRY ...
...I'M SO UGLY.
I'M SORRY FOR BEING BORN!
KNOCK
KNOCK

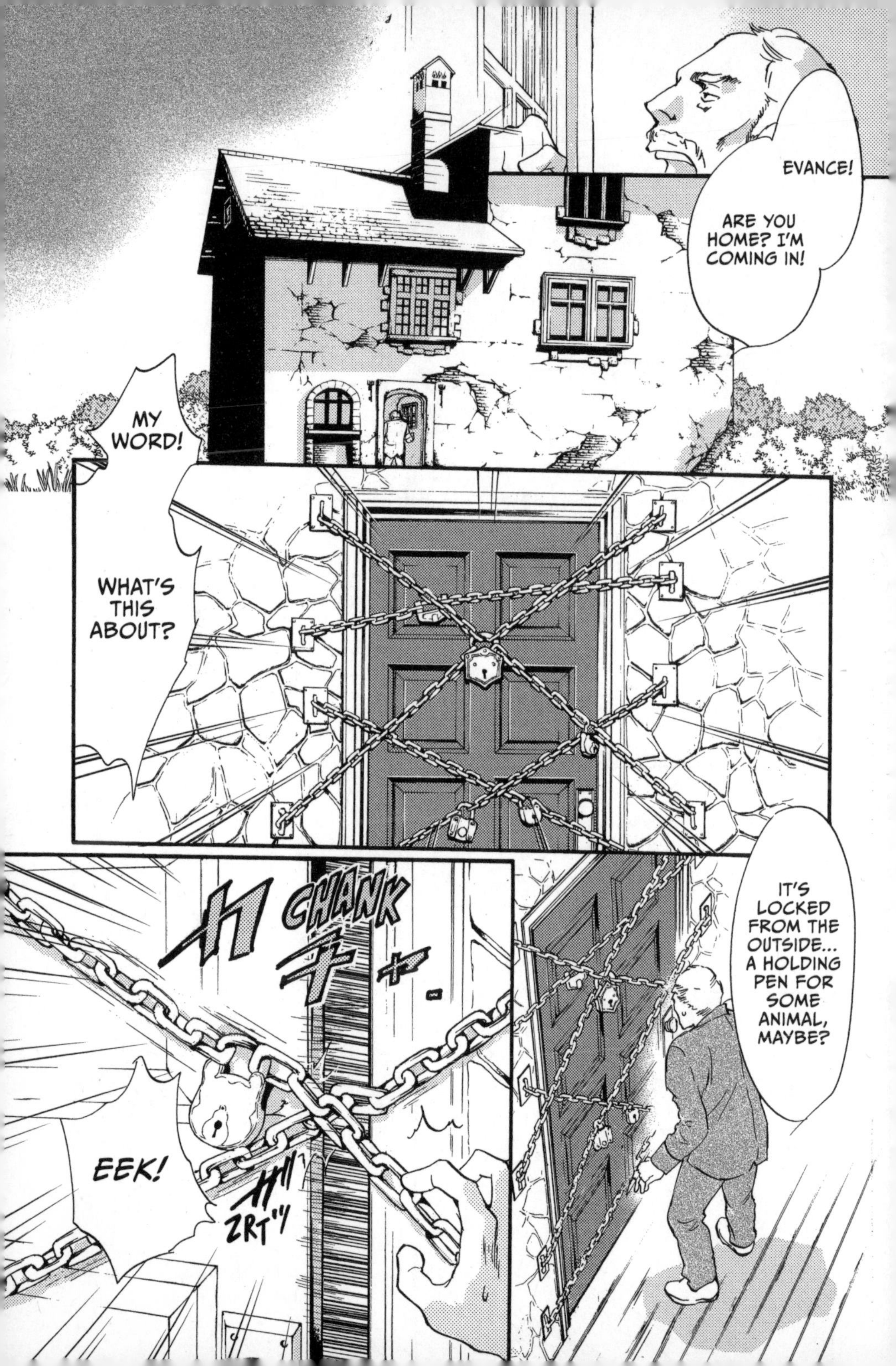
EVANCE!
ARE YOU HOME? I'M COMING IN!
MY WORD!
WHAT'S THIS ABOUT?
IT'S LOCKED FROM THE OUTSIDE... A HOLDING PEN FOR SOME ANIMAL, MAYBE?
CHANK
EEK!
ZRT

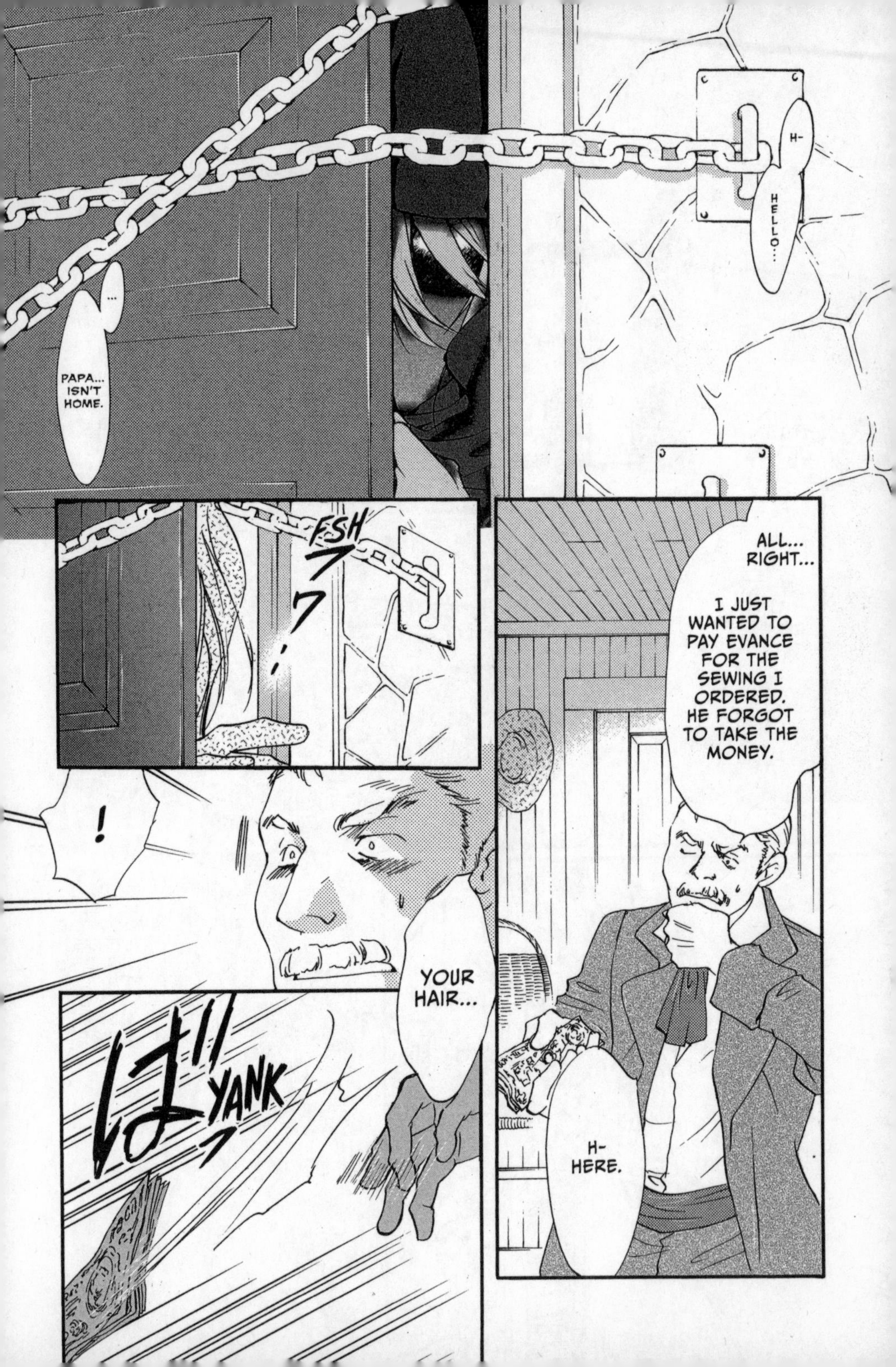
H-
HELLO...
...
PAPA... ISN'T HOME.
ALL... RIGHT...
I JUST WANTED TO PAY EVANCE FOR THE SEWING I ORDERED. HE FORGOT TO TAKE THE MONEY.
H- HERE.
FSH
!
YOUR HAIR...
は YANK

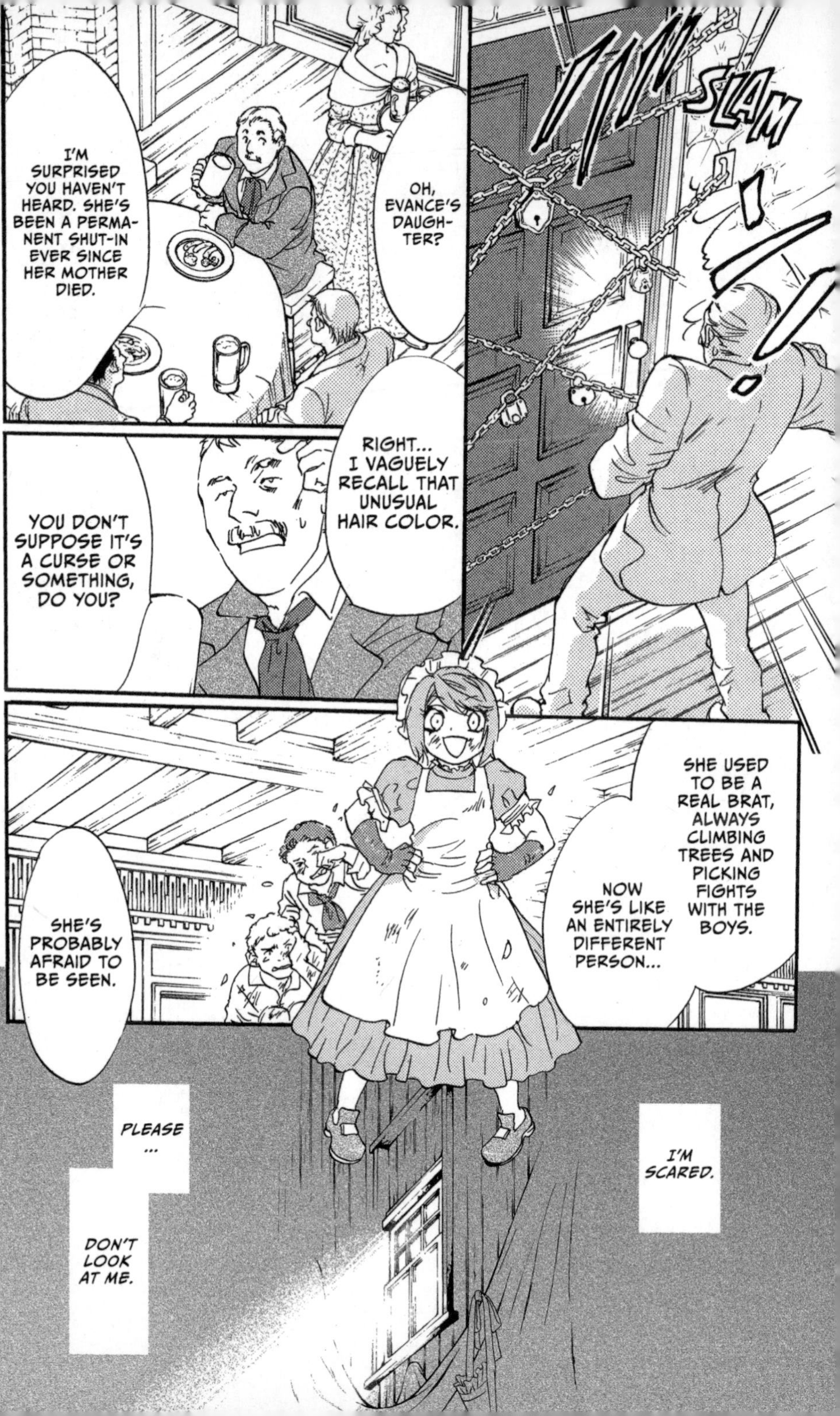
SLAM
OH, EVANCE'S DAUGHTER?
I'M SURPRISED YOU HAVEN'T HEARD. SHE'S BEEN A PERMANENT SHUT-IN EVER SINCE HER MOTHER DIED.
RIGHT... I VAGUELY RECALL THAT UNUSUAL HAIR COLOR.
YOU DON'T SUPPOSE IT'S A CURSE OR SOMETHING, DO YOU?
SHE USED TO BE A REAL BRAT, ALWAYS CLIMBING TREES AND PICKING FIGHTS WITH THE BOYS.
NOW SHE'S LIKE AN ENTIRELY DIFFERENT PERSON...
SHE'S PROBABLY AFRAID TO BE SEEN.
I'M SCARED.
PLEASE...
DON'T LOOK AT ME.

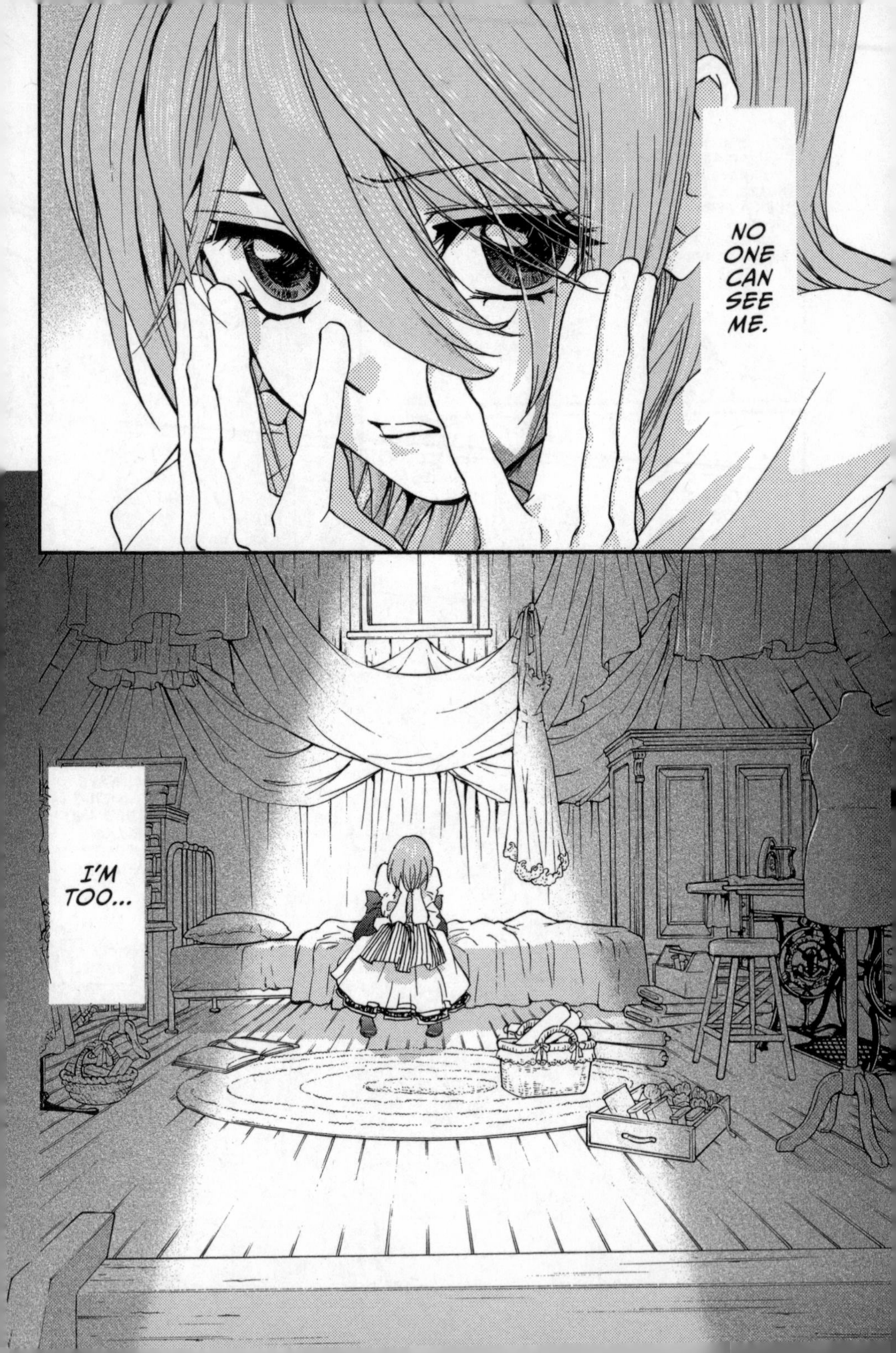

NO ONE CAN SEE ME.
I'M TOO...

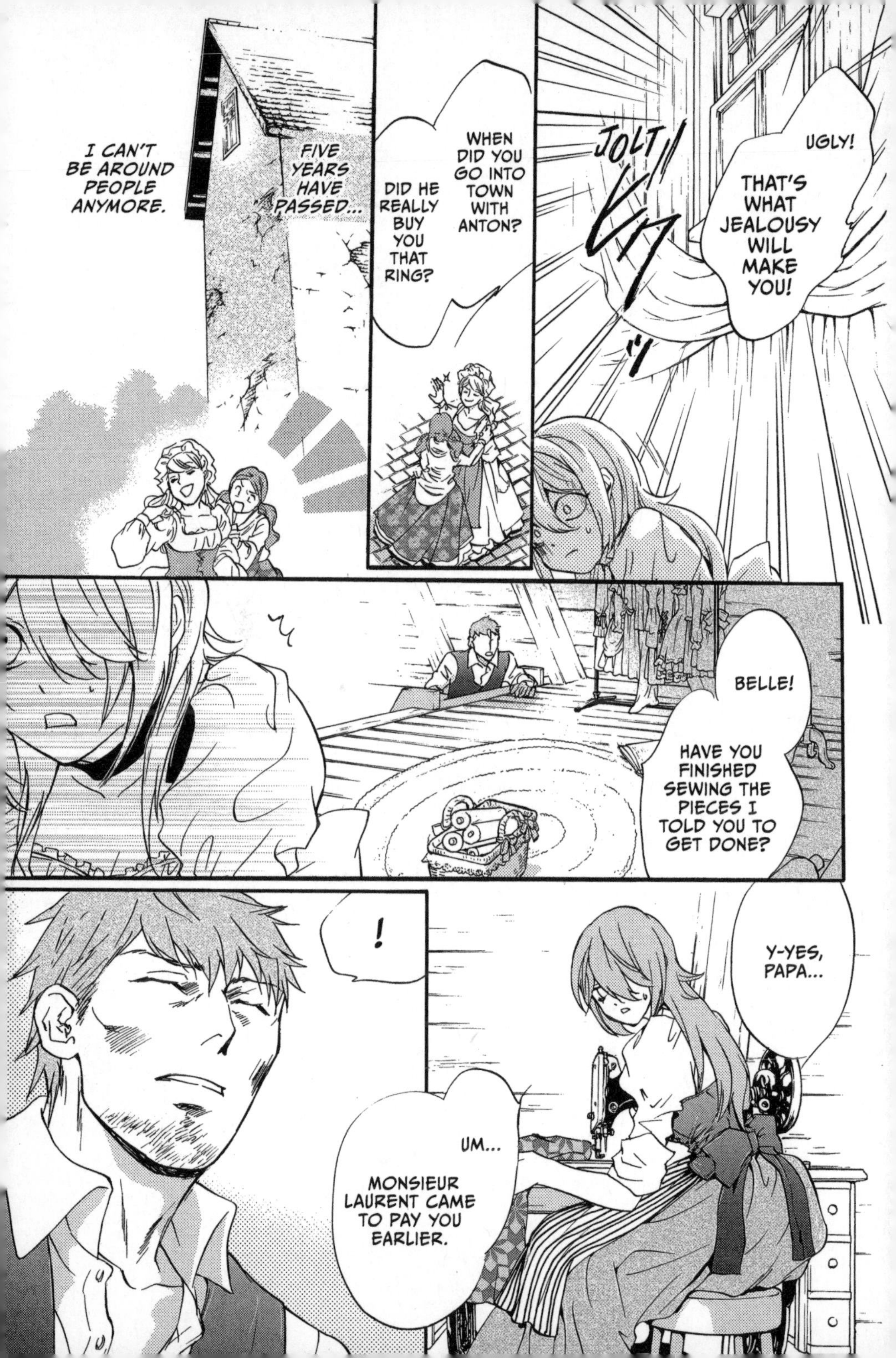
UGLY!
THAT'S WHAT JEALOUSY WILL MAKE YOU!
JOLT
WHEN DID YOU GO INTO TOWN WITH ANTON?
DID HE REALLY BUY YOU THAT RING?
FIVE YEARS HAVE PASSED...
I CAN'T BE AROUND PEOPLE ANYMORE.
BELLE!
HAVE YOU FINISHED SEWING THE PIECES I TOLD YOU TO GET DONE?
Y-YES, PAPA...
UM...
MONSIEUR LAURENT CAME TO PAY YOU EARLIER.
!

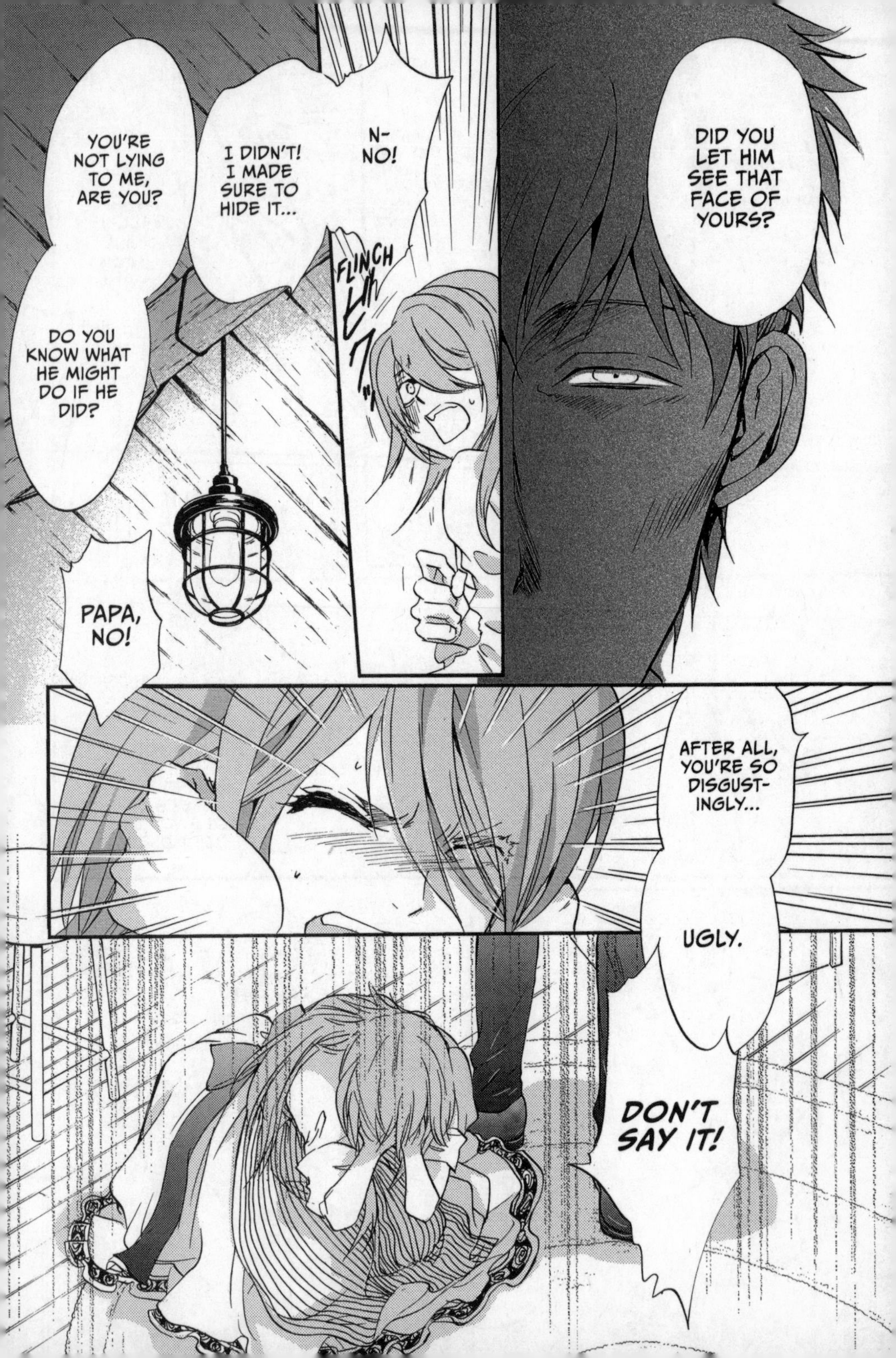
DID YOU LET HIM SEE THAT FACE OF YOURS?
N-NO!
FLINCH
I DIDN'T! I MADE SURE TO HIDE IT...
YOU'RE NOT LYING TO ME, ARE YOU?
DO YOU KNOW WHAT HE MIGHT DO IF HE DID?
PAPA, NO!
AFTER ALL, YOU'RE SO DISGUST-INGLY...
UGLY.
DON'T SAY IT!

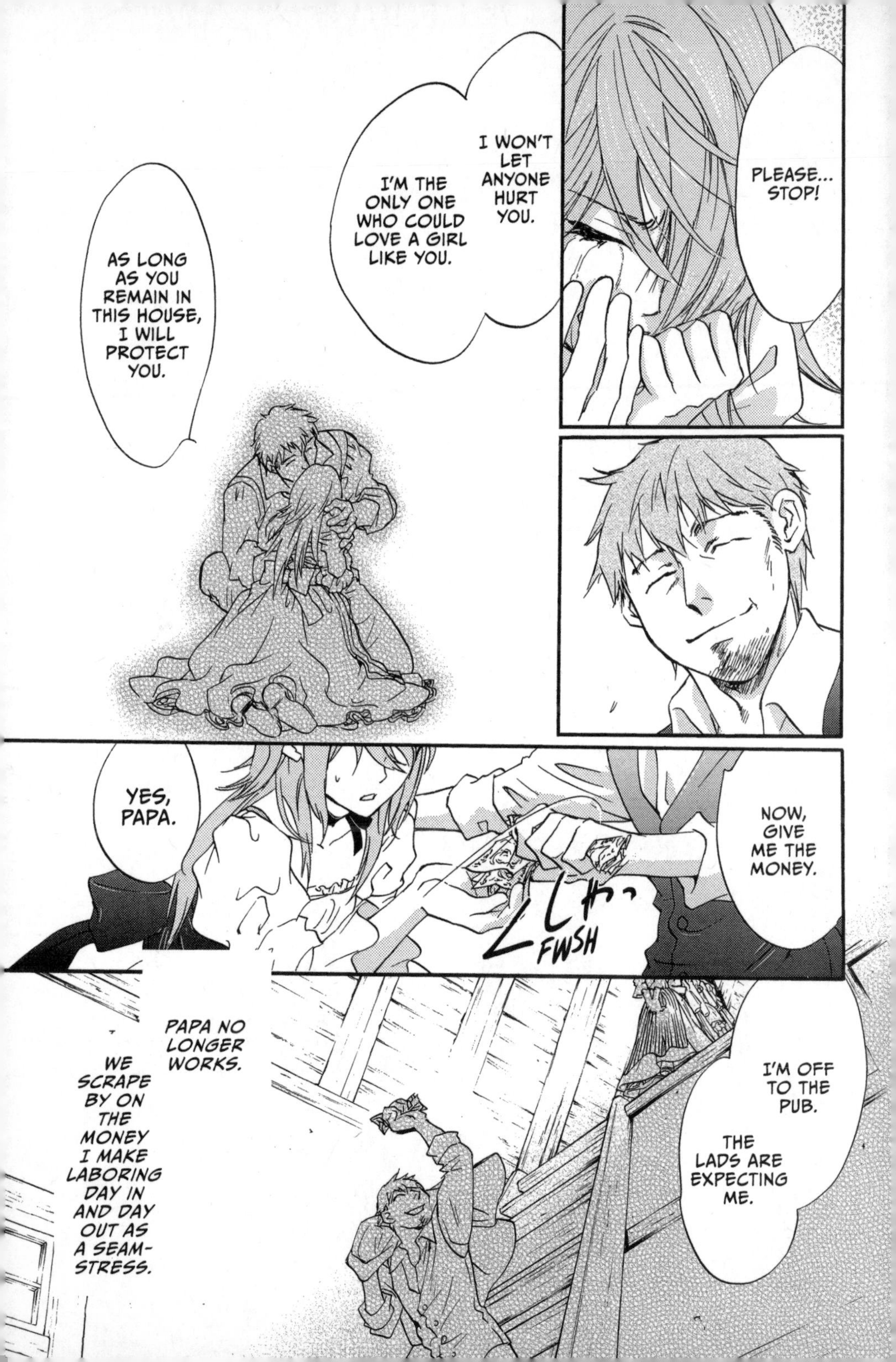
PLEASE... STOP!
I WON'T LET ANYONE HURT YOU.
I'M THE ONLY ONE WHO COULD LOVE A GIRL LIKE YOU.
AS LONG AS YOU REMAIN IN THIS HOUSE, I WILL PROTECT YOU.
NOW, GIVE ME THE MONEY.
FWSH
YES, PAPA.
I'M OFF TO THE PUB.
THE LADS ARE EXPECTING ME.
PAPA NO LONGER WORKS.
WE SCRAPE BY ON THE MONEY I MAKE LABORING DAY IN AND DAY OUT AS A SEAM-STRESS.

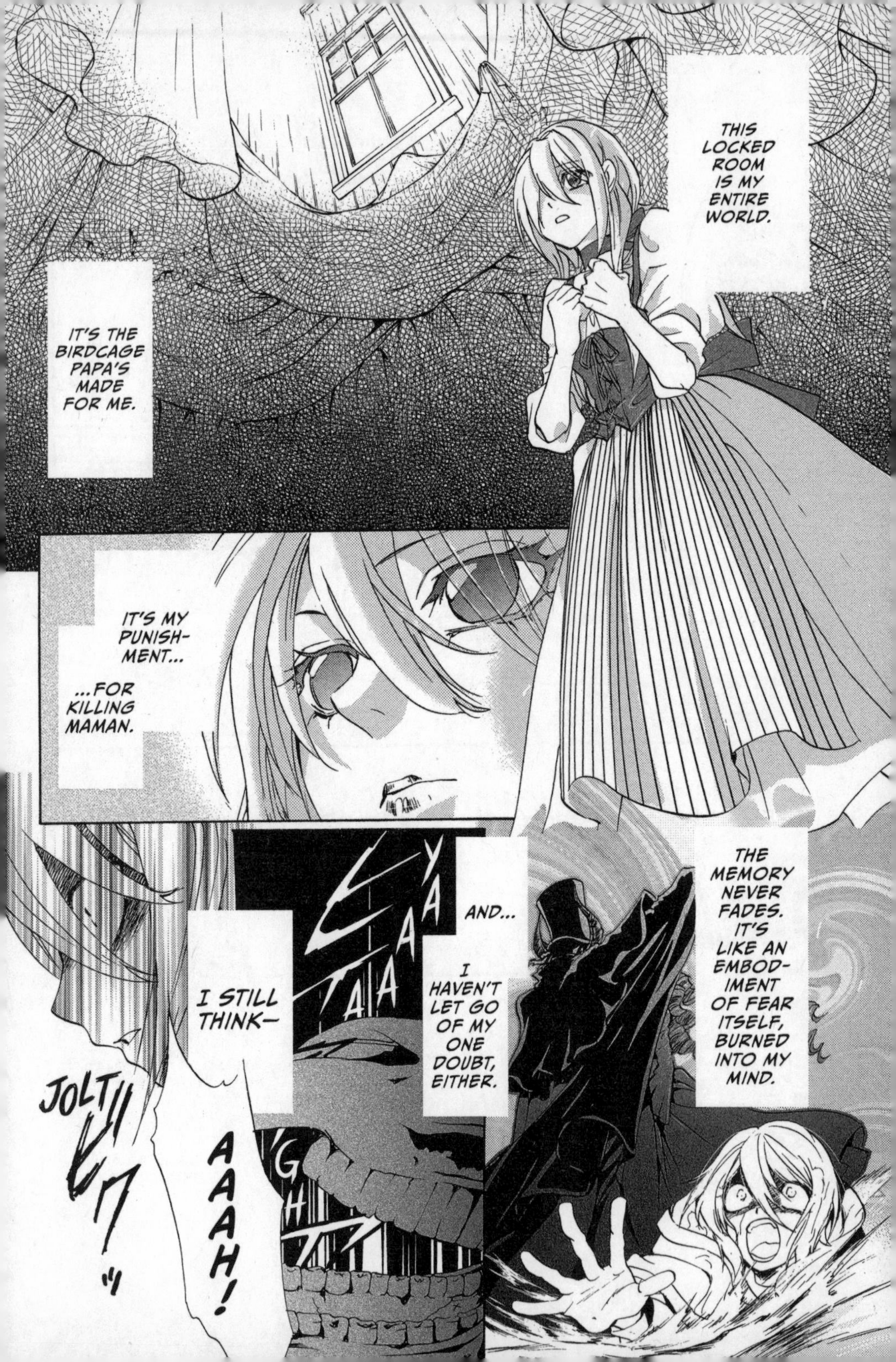
THIS LOCKED ROOM IS MY ENTIRE WORLD.
IT'S THE BIRDCAGE PAPA'S MADE FOR ME.
IT'S MY PUNISHMENT...
...FOR KILLING MAMAN.
THE MEMORY NEVER FADES. IT'S LIKE AN EMBODIMENT OF FEAR ITSELF, BURNED INTO MY MIND.
AND...
I HAVEN'T LET GO OF MY ONE DOUBT, EITHER.
YAAAAA
AAAAH!
I STILL THINK—
JOLT!!

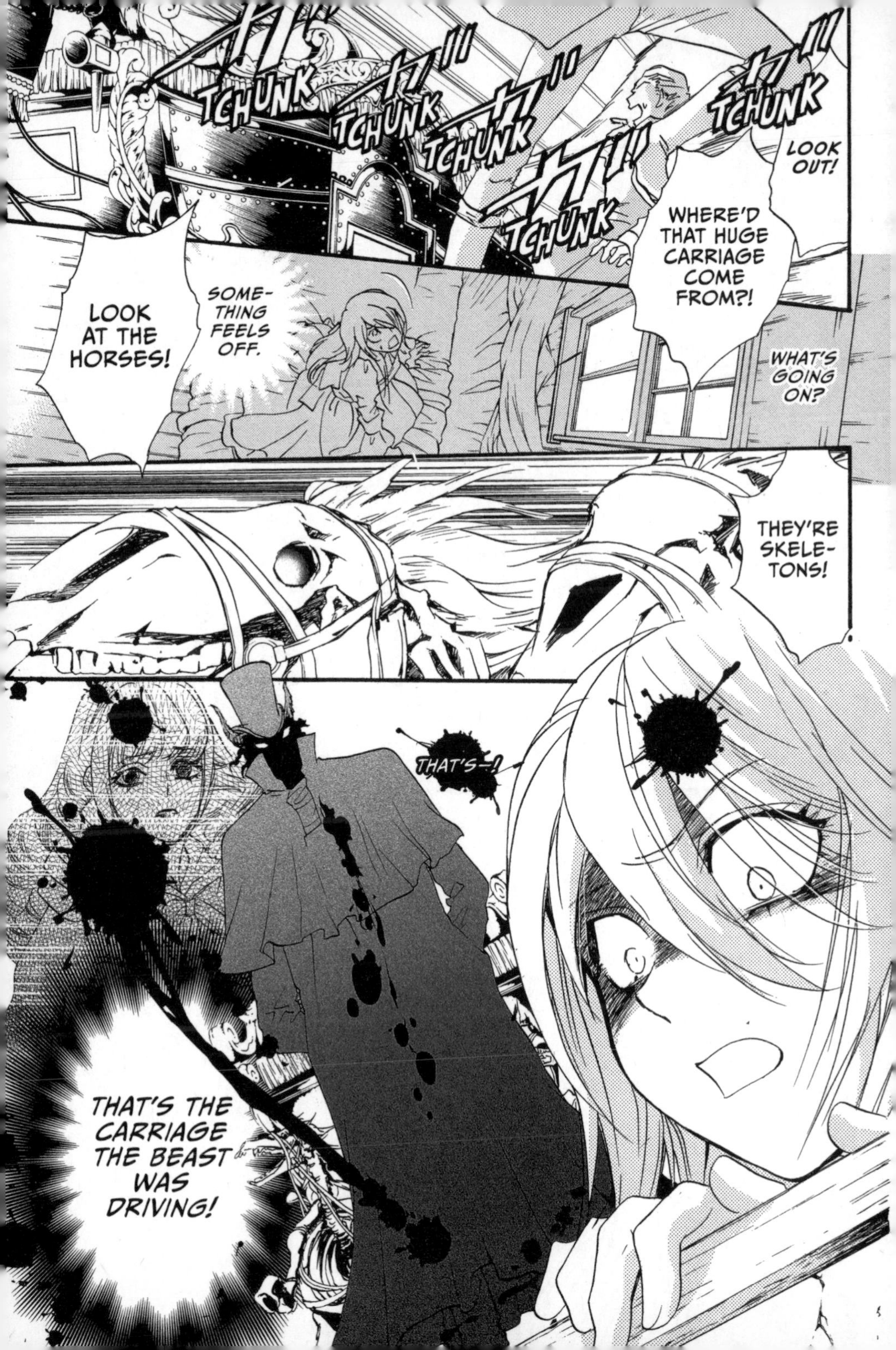
TCHUNK
LOOK OUT!
TCHUNK
TCHUNK
TCHUNK
TCHUNK
WHERE'D THAT HUGE CARRIAGE COME FROM?!
WHAT'S GOING ON?
SOME-THING FEELS OFF.
LOOK AT THE HORSES!
THEY'RE SKELE-TONS!
THAT'S—!
THAT'S THE CARRIAGE THE BEAST WAS DRIVING!

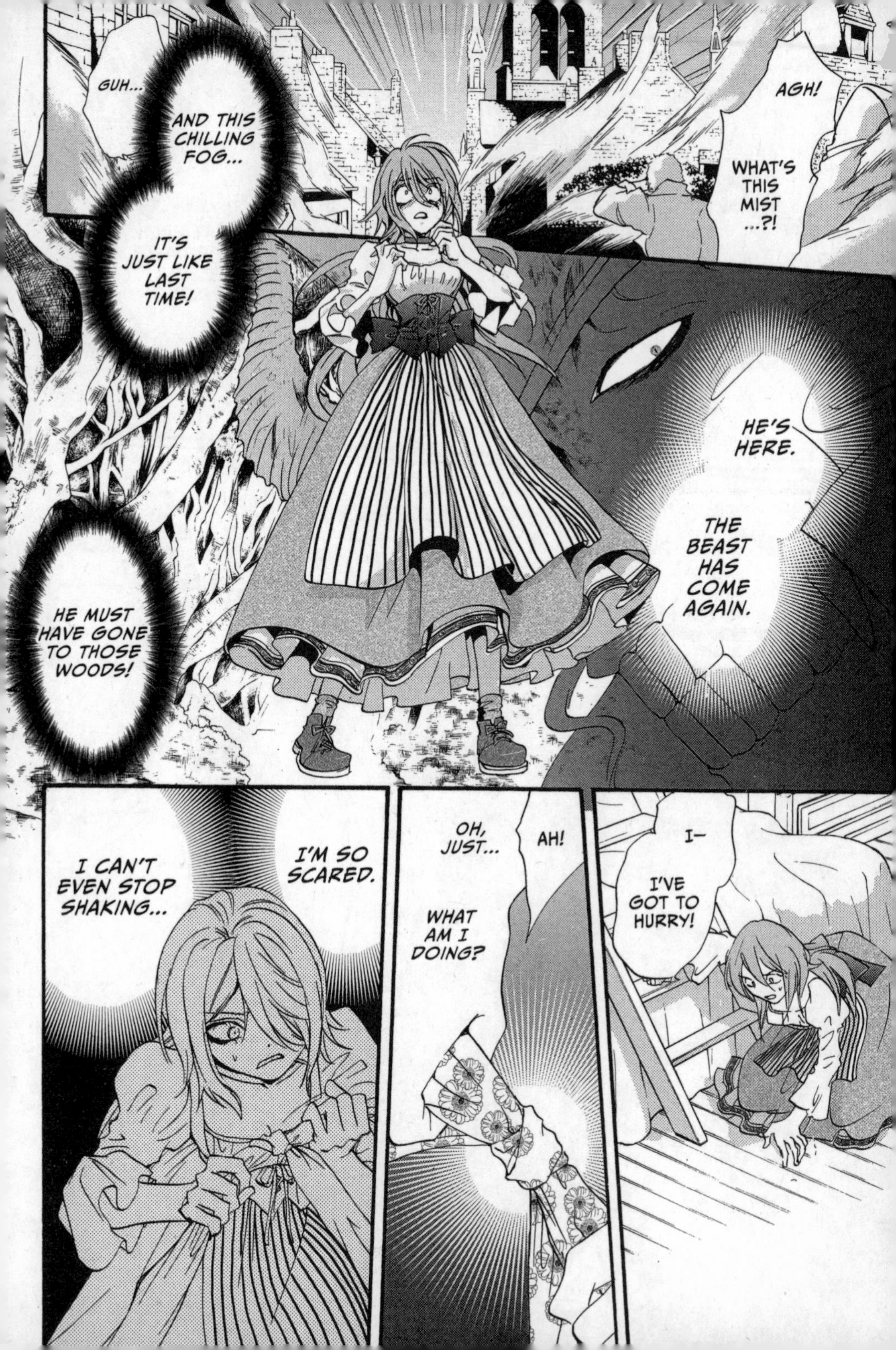
AGH!
WHAT'S THIS MIST ...?!
GUH...
AND THIS CHILLING FOG...
IT'S JUST LIKE LAST TIME!
HE'S HERE.
THE BEAST HAS COME AGAIN.
HE MUST HAVE GONE TO THOSE WOODS!
I—
I'VE GOT TO HURRY!
AH!
OH, JUST...
WHAT AM I DOING?
I'M SO SCARED.
I CAN'T EVEN STOP SHAKING...

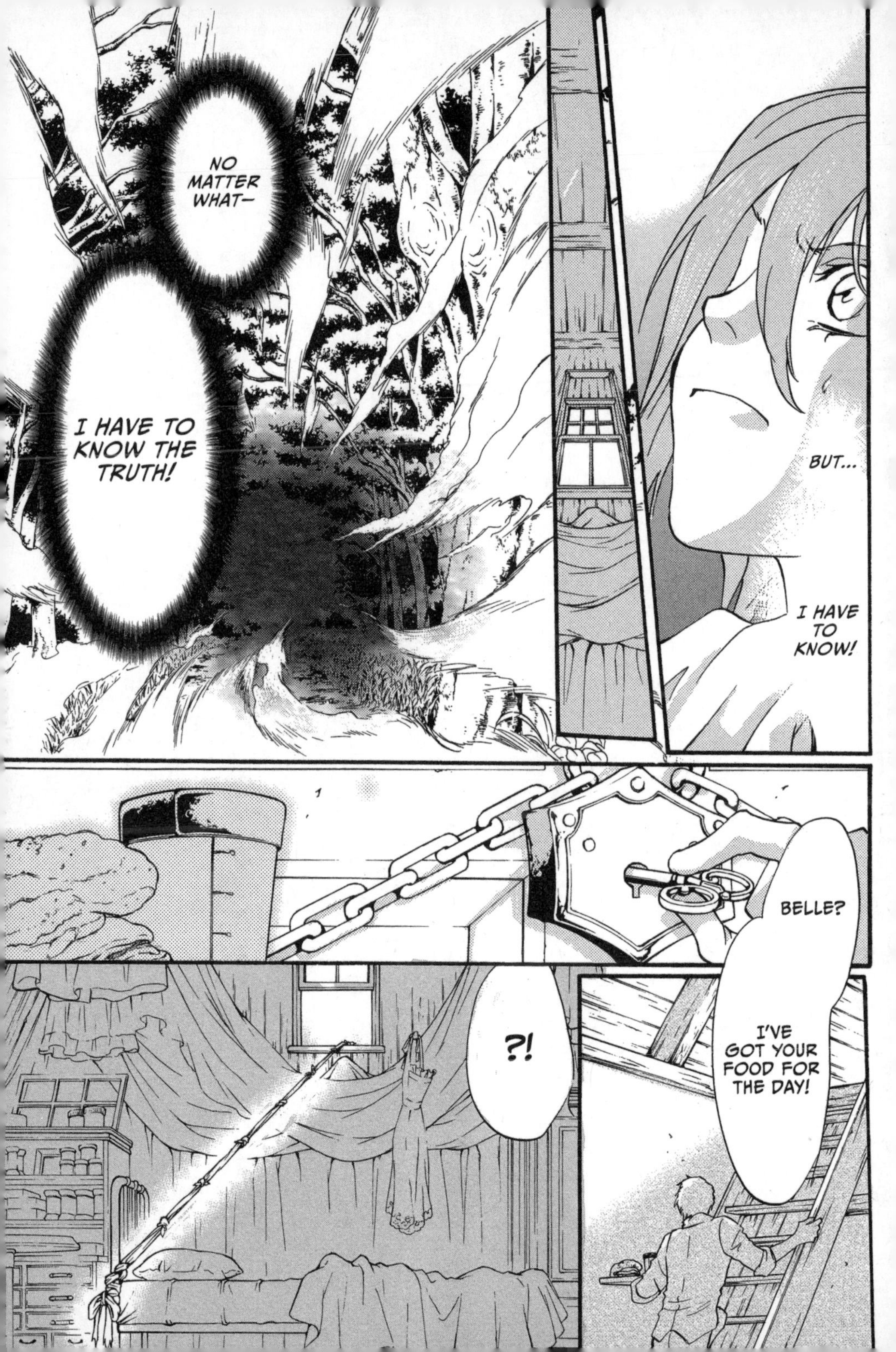
BUT...
I HAVE TO KNOW!
NO MATTER WHAT—
I HAVE TO KNOW THE TRUTH!
BELLE?
I'VE GOT YOUR FOOD FOR THE DAY!
?!

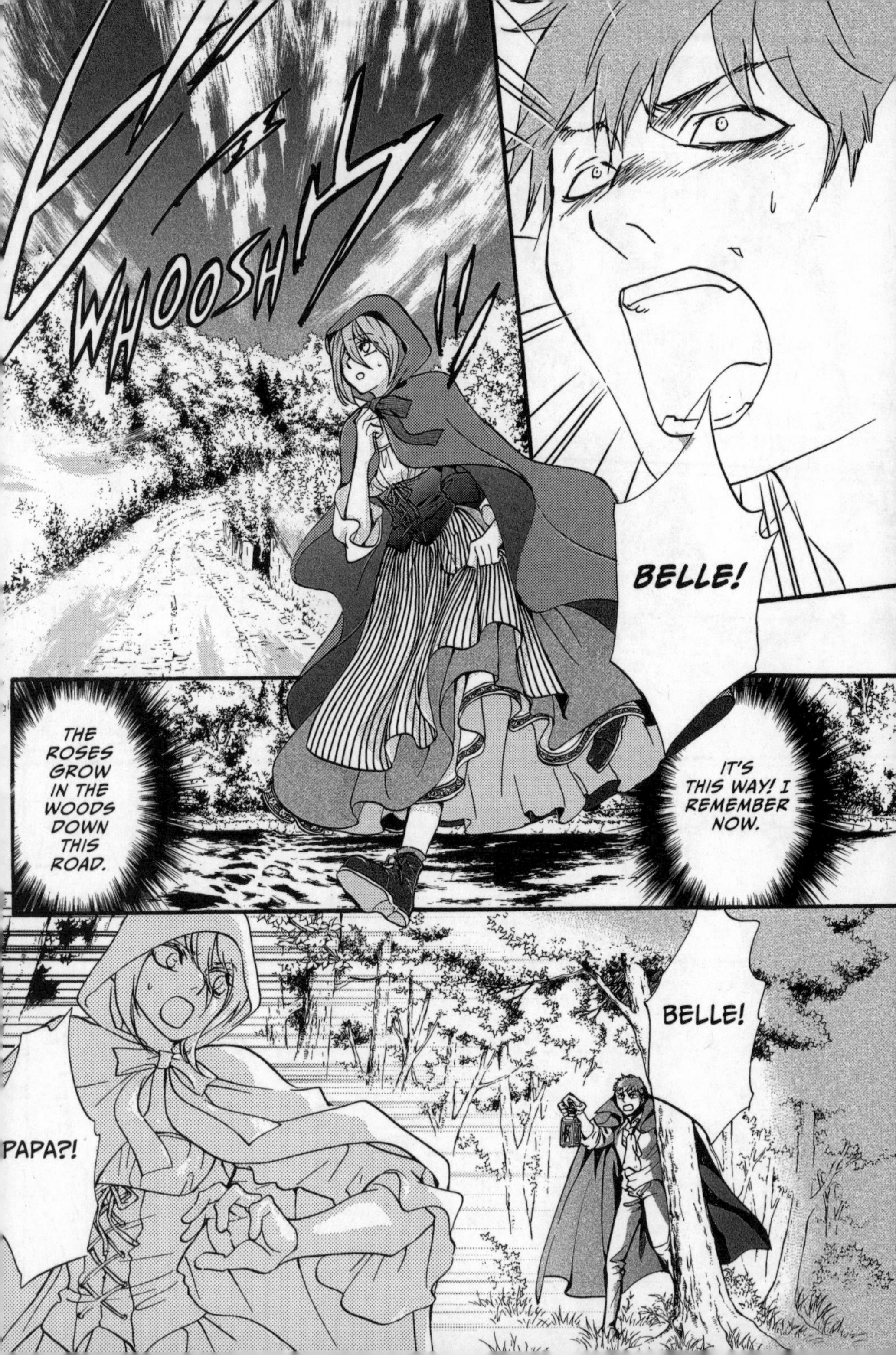
BELLE!
WHOOSH
IT'S THIS WAY! I REMEMBER NOW.
THE ROSES GROW IN THE WOODS DOWN THIS ROAD.
BELLE!
PAPA?!

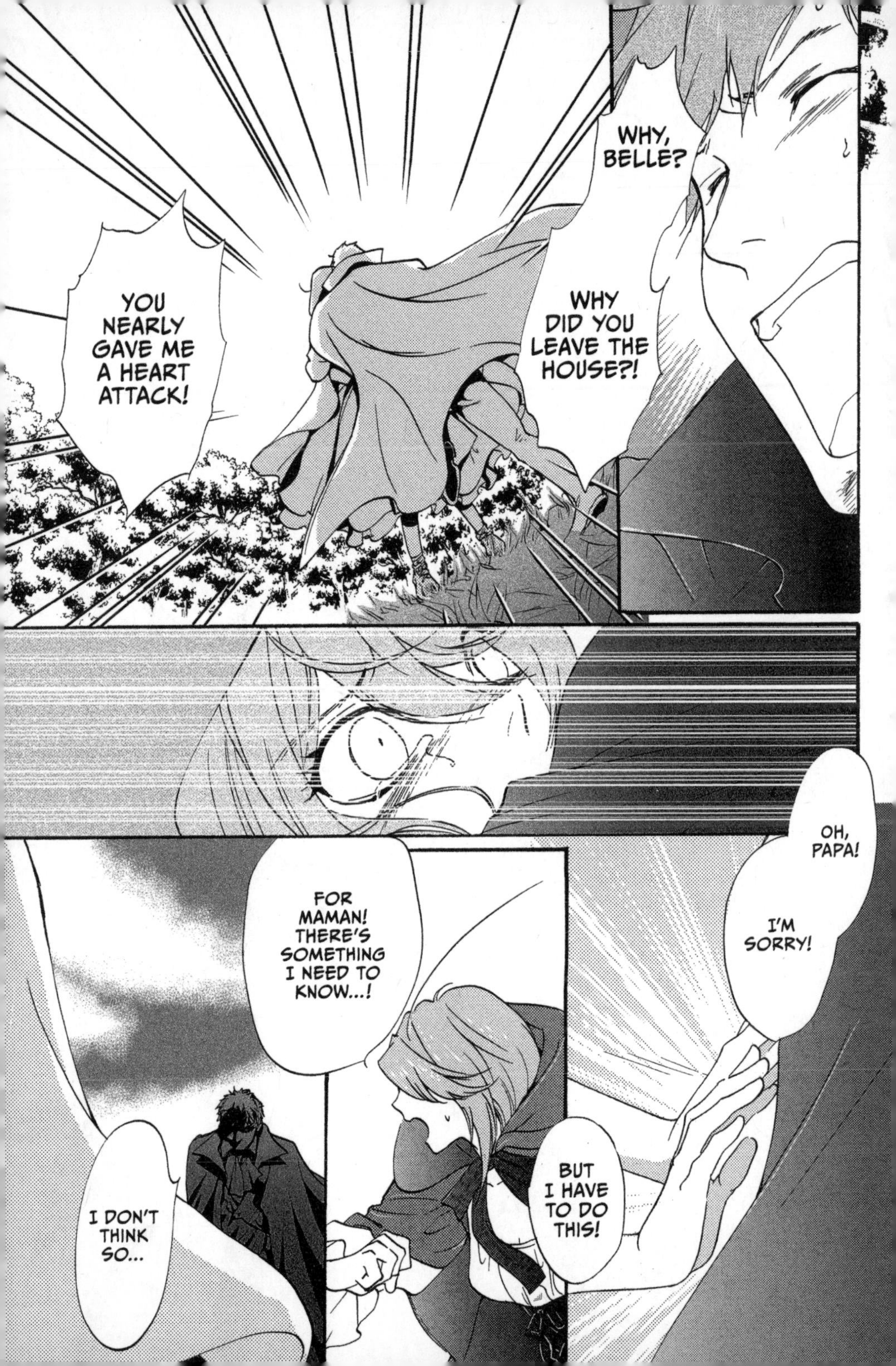
WHY, BELLE?
WHY DID YOU LEAVE THE HOUSE?!
YOU NEARLY GAVE ME A HEART ATTACK!
OH, PAPA!
I'M SORRY!
BUT I HAVE TO DO THIS!
FOR MAMAN! THERE'S SOMETHING I NEED TO KNOW...!
I DON'T THINK SO...

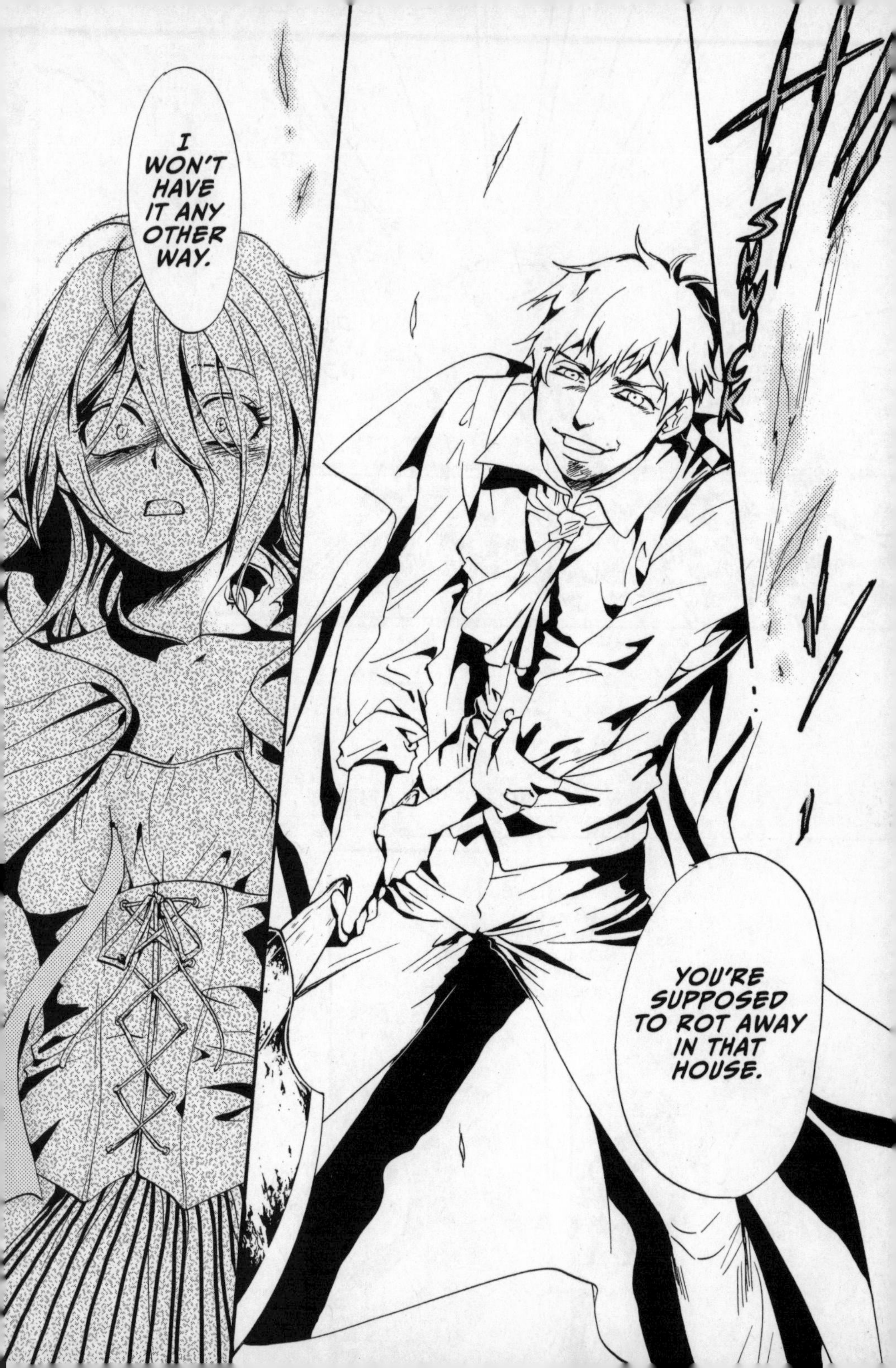
SHWUCK
YOU'RE SUPPOSED TO ROT AWAY IN THAT HOUSE.
I WON'T HAVE IT ANY OTHER WAY.

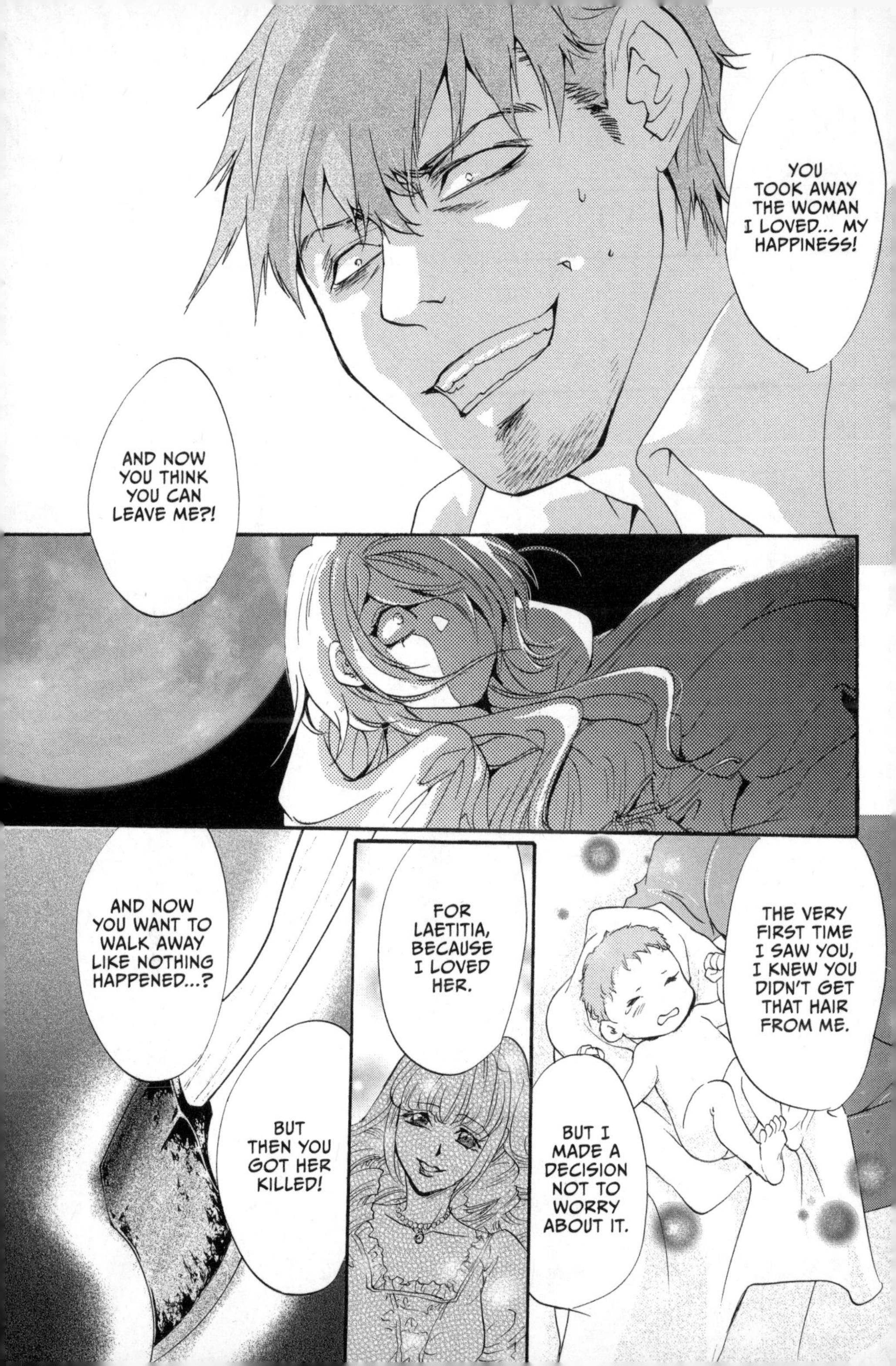
YOU TOOK AWAY THE WOMAN I LOVED... MY HAPPINESS!
AND NOW YOU THINK YOU CAN LEAVE ME?!
THE VERY FIRST TIME I SAW YOU, I KNEW YOU DIDN'T GET THAT HAIR FROM ME.
BUT I MADE A DECISION NOT TO WORRY ABOUT IT.
FOR LAETITIA, BECAUSE I LOVED HER.
BUT THEN YOU GOT HER KILLED!
AND NOW YOU WANT TO WALK AWAY LIKE NOTHING HAPPENED...?

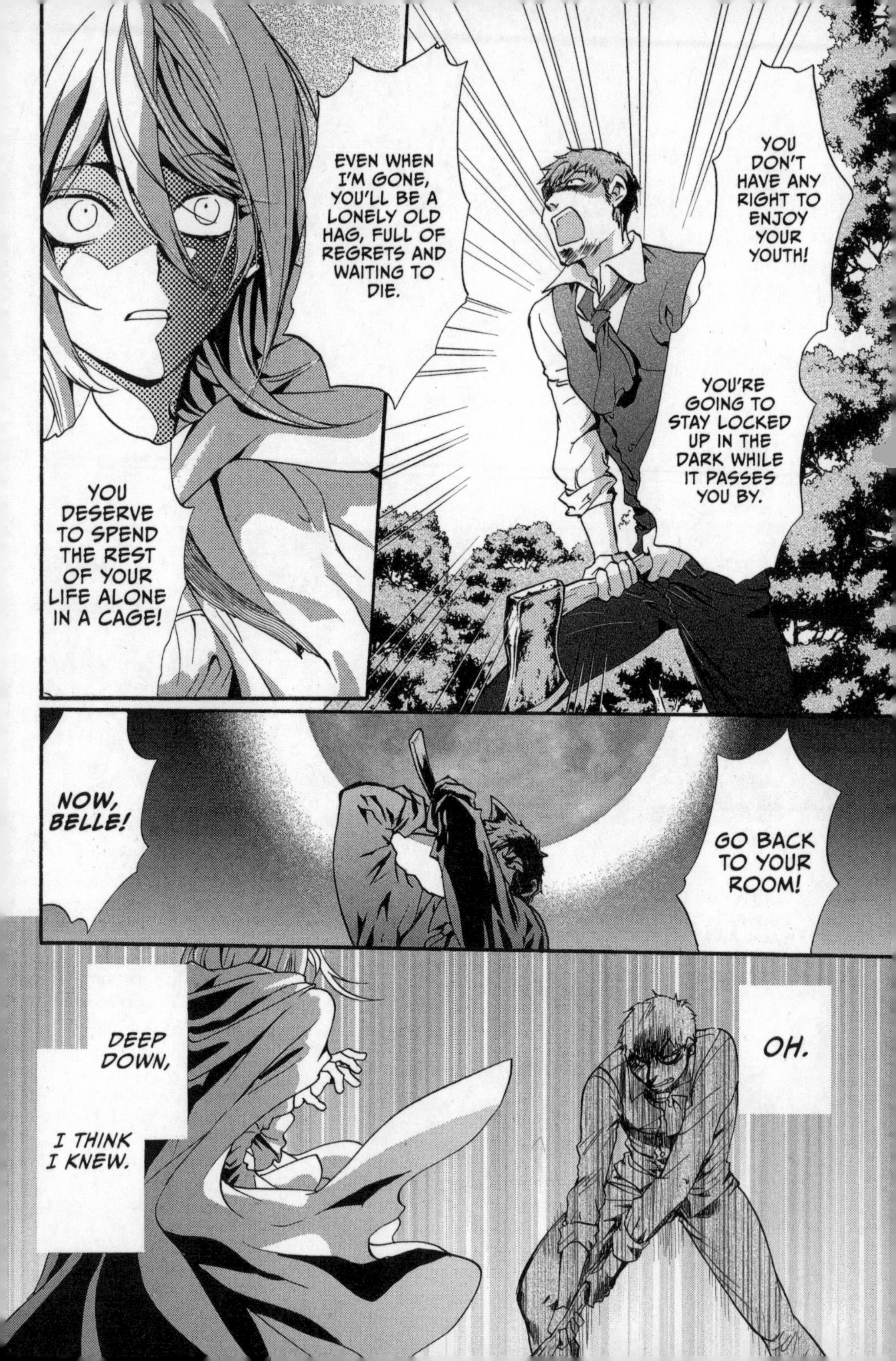
YOU DON'T HAVE ANY RIGHT TO ENJOY YOUR YOUTH!
YOU'RE GOING TO STAY LOCKED UP IN THE DARK WHILE IT PASSES YOU BY.
EVEN WHEN I'M GONE, YOU'LL BE A LONELY OLD HAG, FULL OF REGRETS AND WAITING TO DIE.
YOU DESERVE TO SPEND THE REST OF YOUR LIFE ALONE IN A CAGE!
GO BACK TO YOUR ROOM!
NOW, BELLE!
OH.
DEEP DOWN,
I THINK I KNEW.

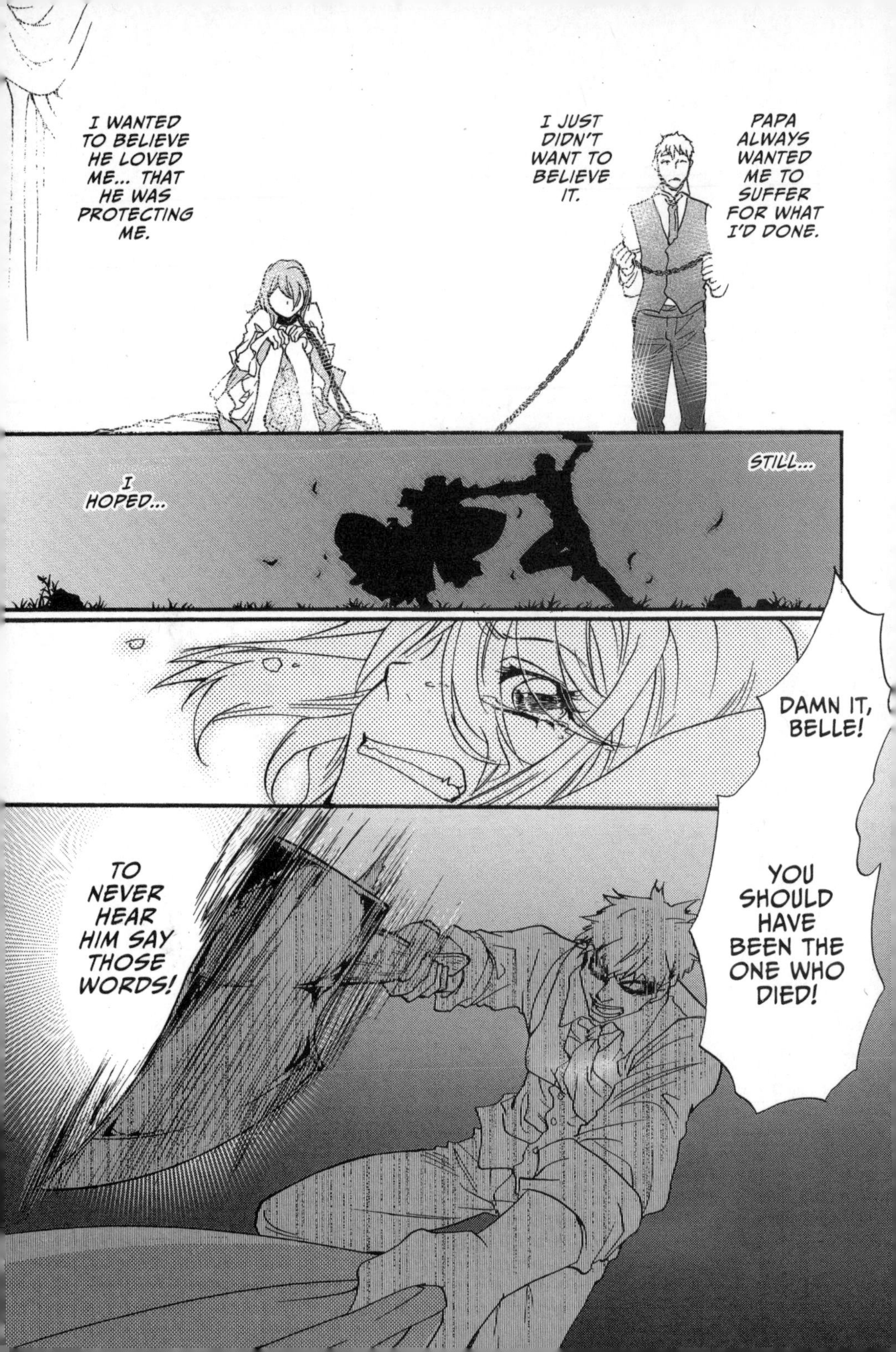
PAPA ALWAYS WANTED ME TO SUFFER FOR WHAT I'D DONE.
I JUST DIDN'T WANT TO BELIEVE IT.
I WANTED TO BELIEVE HE LOVED ME... THAT HE WAS PROTECTING ME.
STILL...
I HOPED...
DAMN IT, BELLE!
YOU SHOULD HAVE BEEN THE ONE WHO DIED!
TO NEVER HEAR HIM SAY THOSE WORDS!

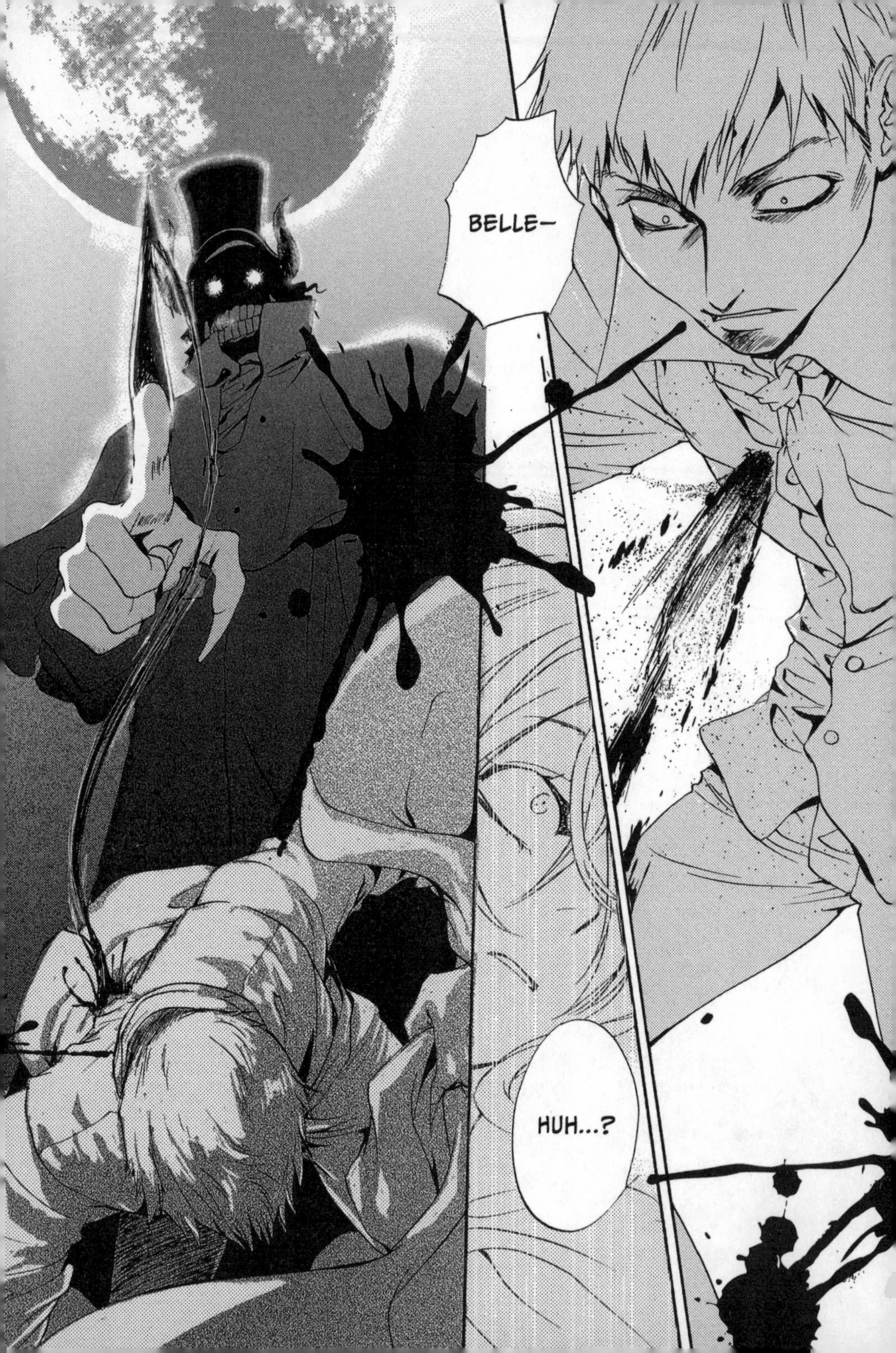
BELLE—
HUH...?

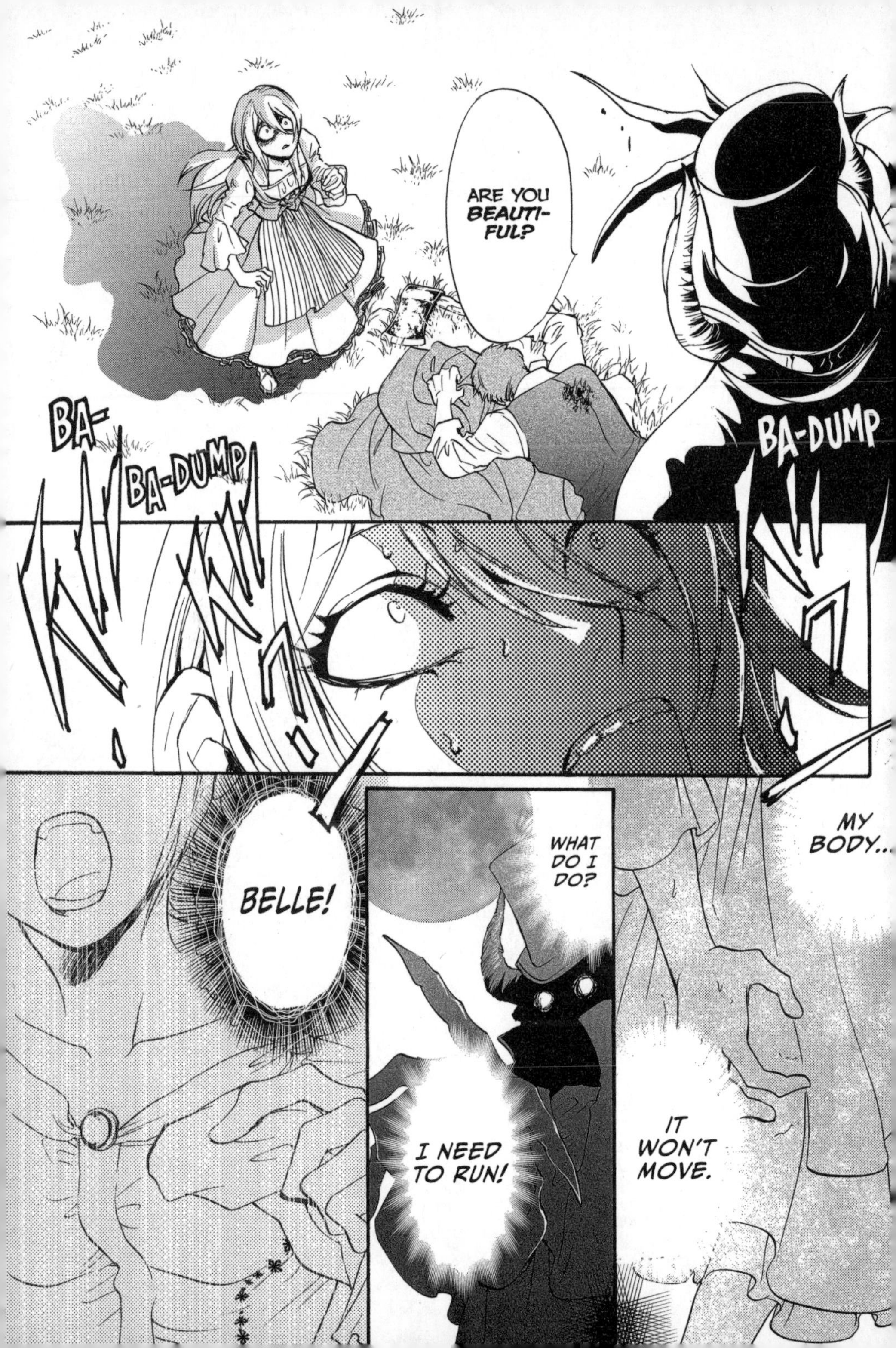

ARE YOU BEAUTI-FUL?
BA-DUMP
BA-BA-DUMP
MY BODY...
IT WON'T MOVE.
WHAT DO I DO?
I NEED TO RUN!
BELLE!

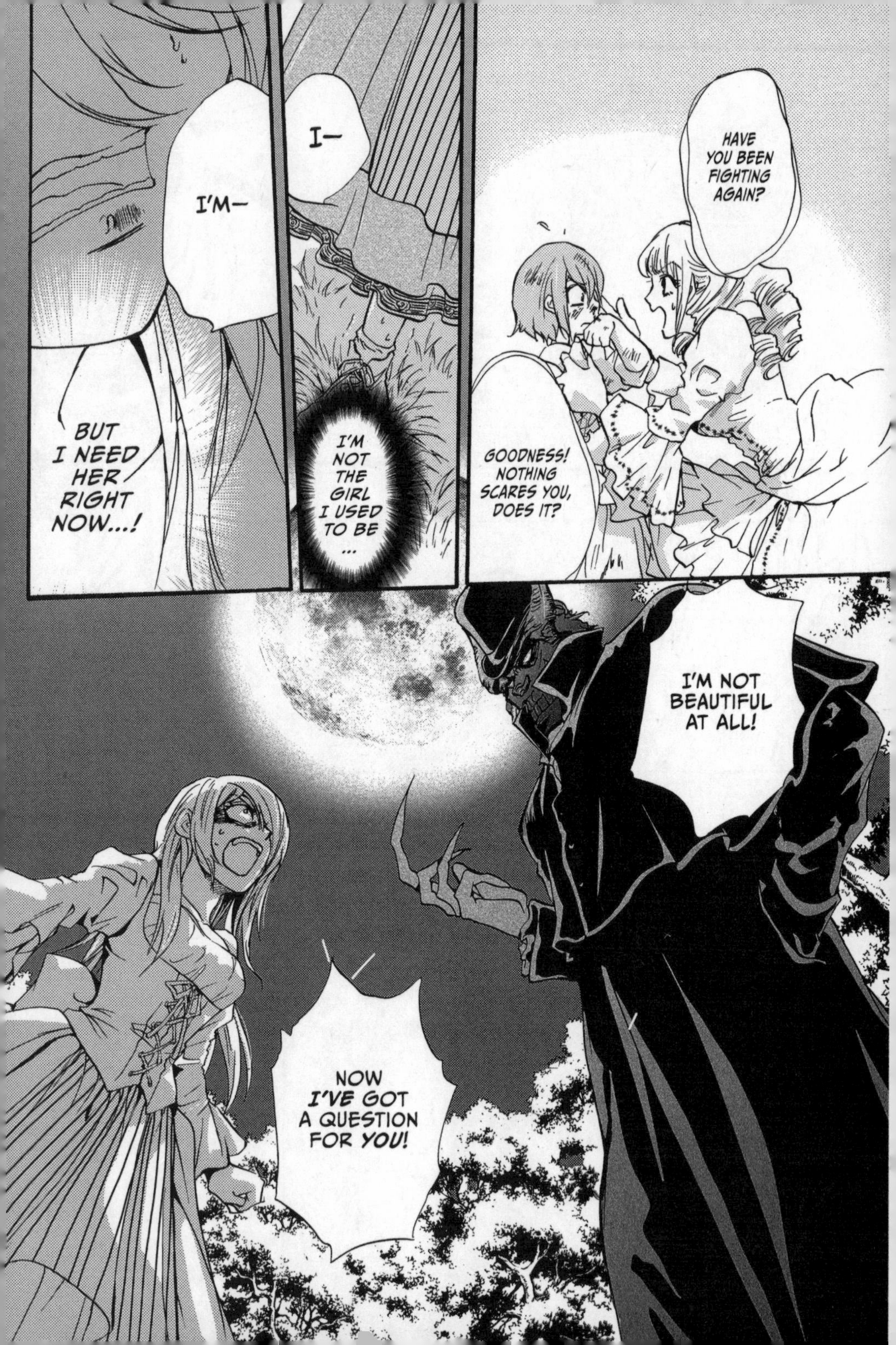
HAVE YOU BEEN FIGHTING AGAIN?
GOODNESS! NOTHING SCARES YOU, DOES IT?
I—
I'M NOT THE GIRL I USED TO BE ...
I'M—
BUT I NEED HER RIGHT NOW...!
I'M NOT BEAUTIFUL AT ALL!
NOW I'VE GOT A QUESTION FOR YOU!

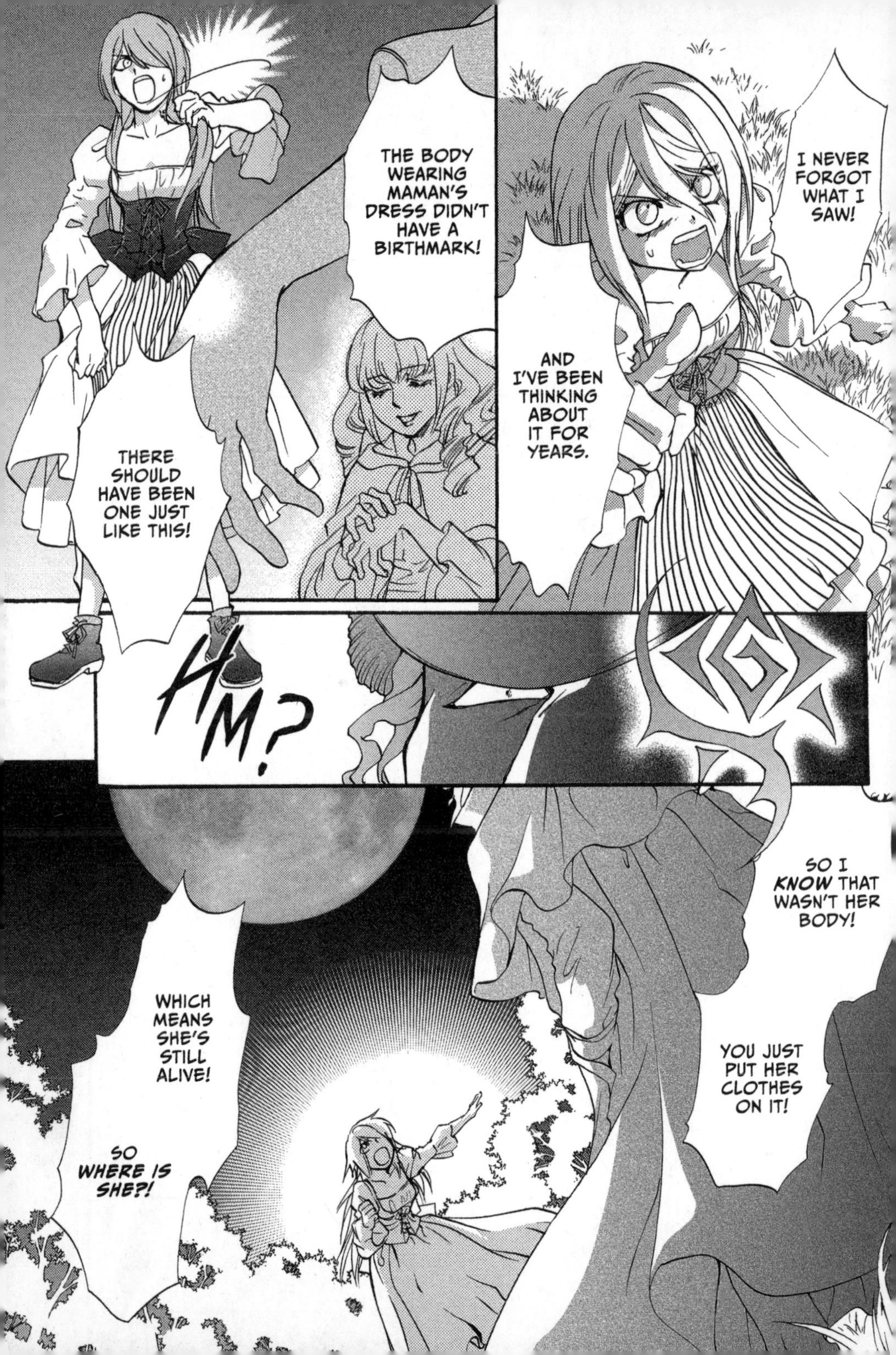
I NEVER FORGOT WHAT I SAW!
AND I'VE BEEN THINKING ABOUT IT FOR YEARS.
THE BODY WEARING MAMAN'S DRESS DIDN'T HAVE A BIRTHMARK!
THERE SHOULD HAVE BEEN ONE JUST LIKE THIS!
HM?
SO I ***KNOW*** THAT WASN'T HER BODY!
YOU JUST PUT HER CLOTHES ON IT!
WHICH MEANS SHE'S STILL ALIVE!
SO ***WHERE IS SHE?!***

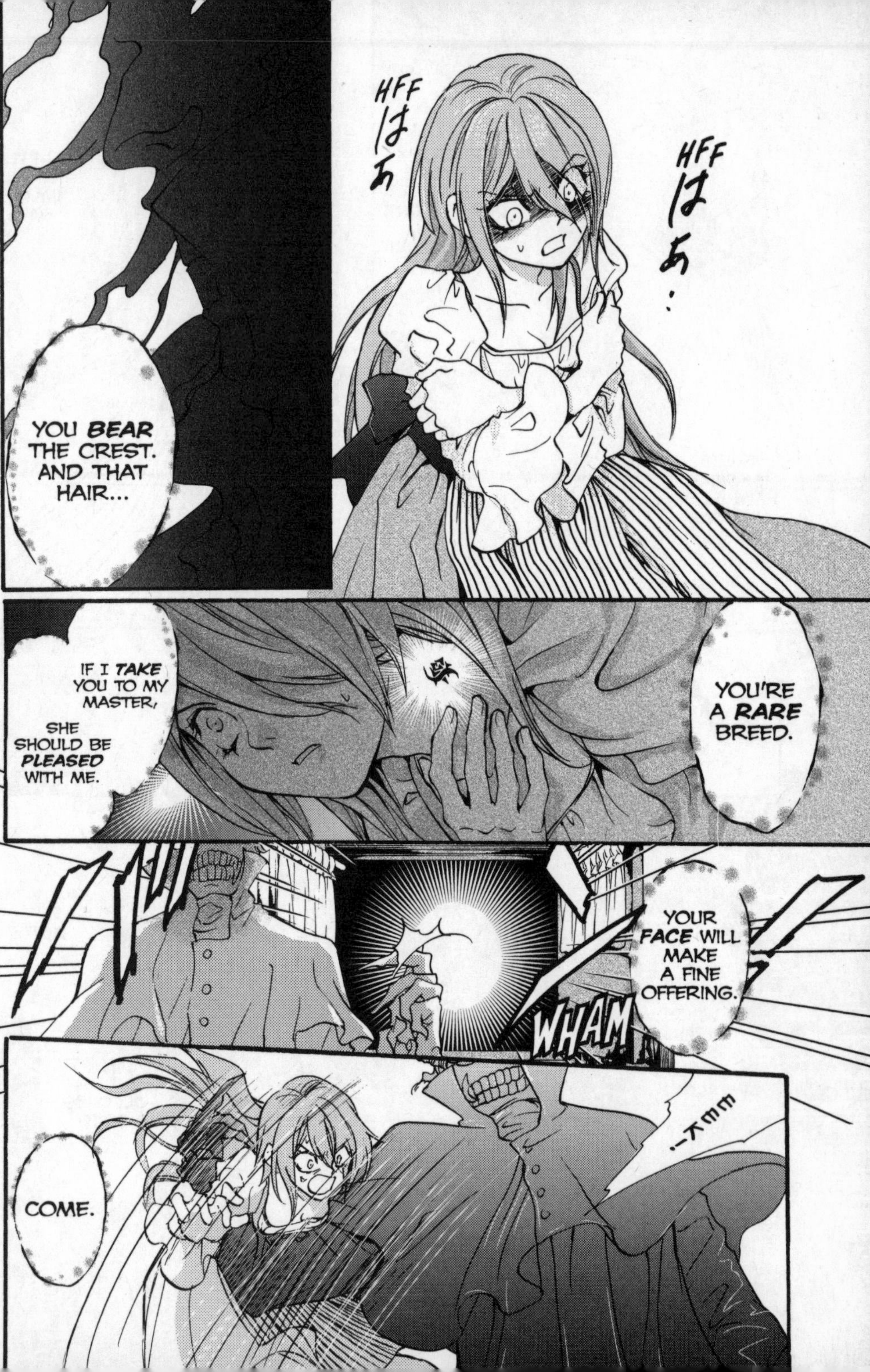
HFF はぁ
HFF はぁ…
YOU BEAR THE CREST. AND THAT HAIR...
YOU'RE A RARE BREED.
IF I TAKE YOU TO MY MASTER,
SHE SHOULD BE PLEASED WITH ME.
YOUR FACE WILL MAKE A FINE OFFERING.
WHAM
MMK-!
COME.

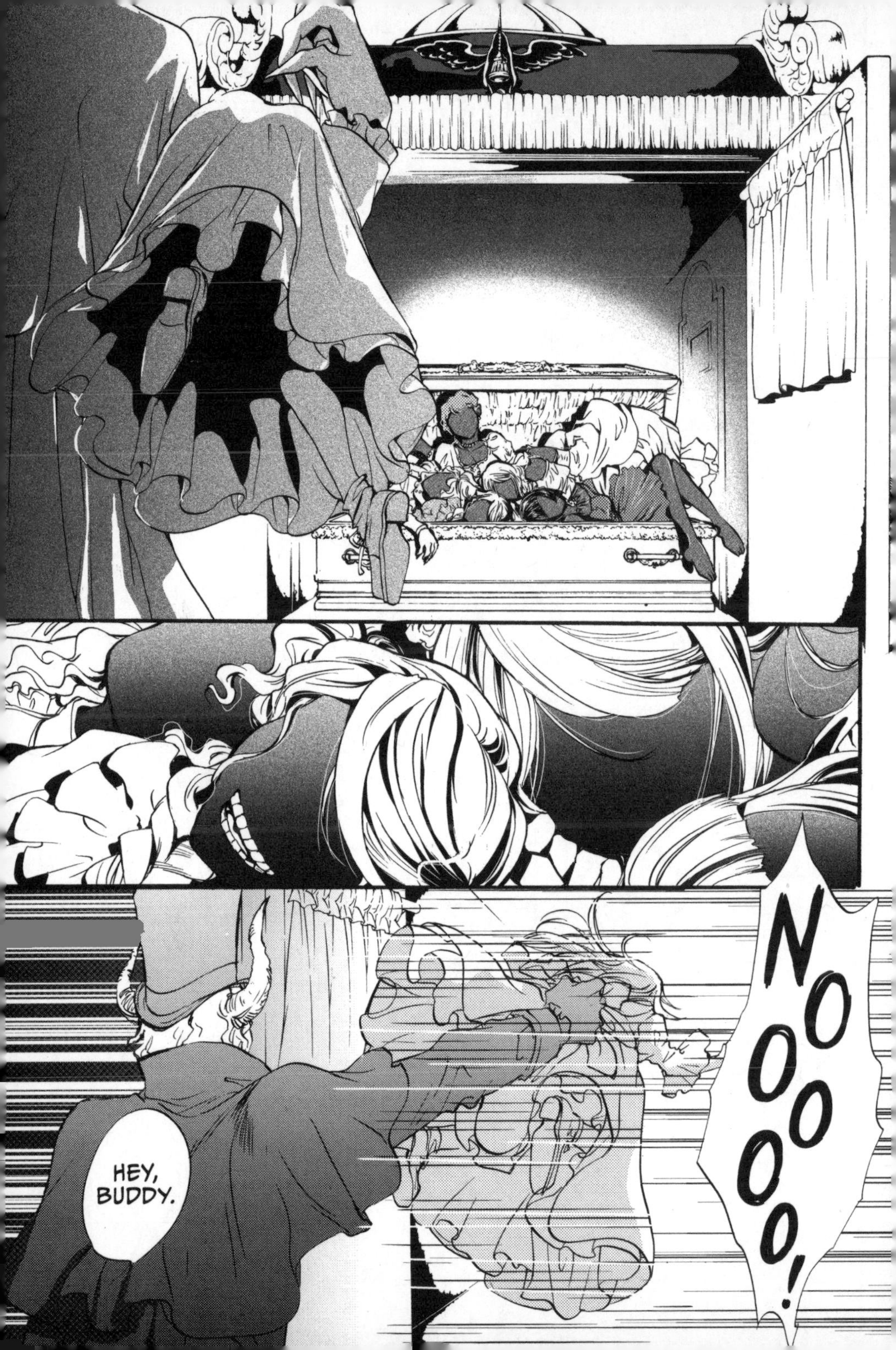
NOOOOO!
HEY, BUDDY.

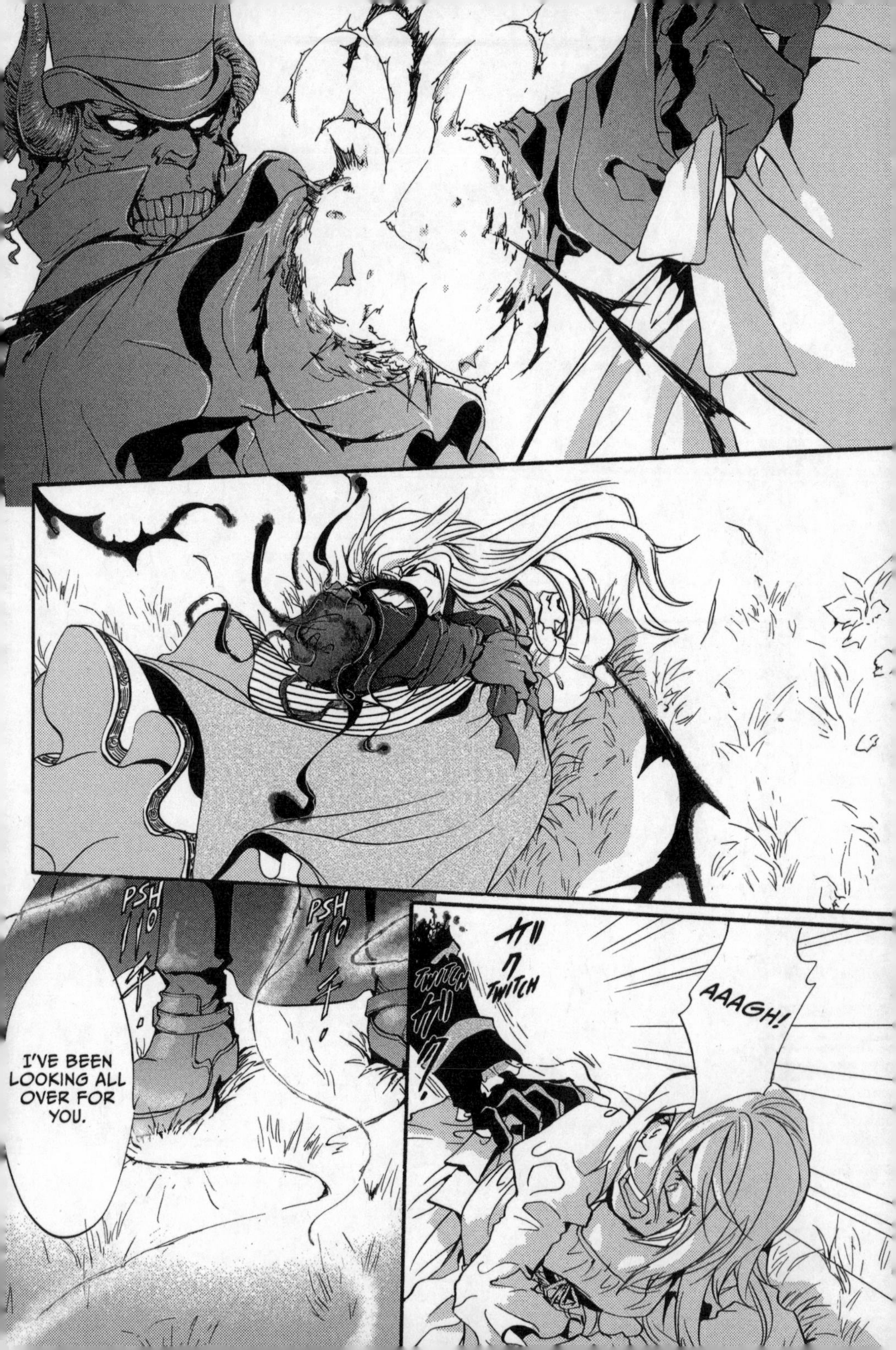
TWITCH
TWITCH
AAAGH!
PSH
PSH
I'VE BEEN LOOKING ALL OVER FOR YOU.

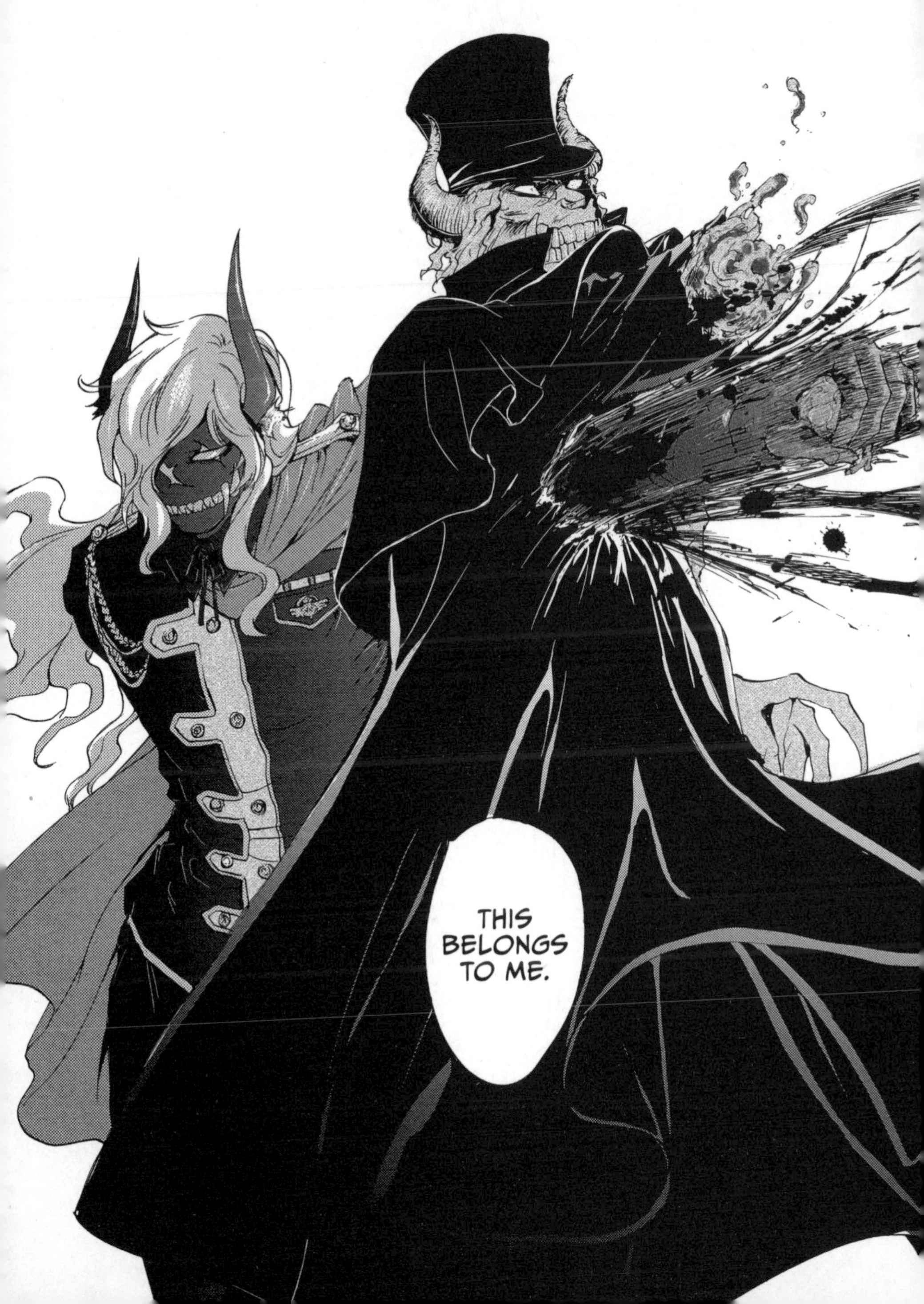
THIS BELONGS TO ME.

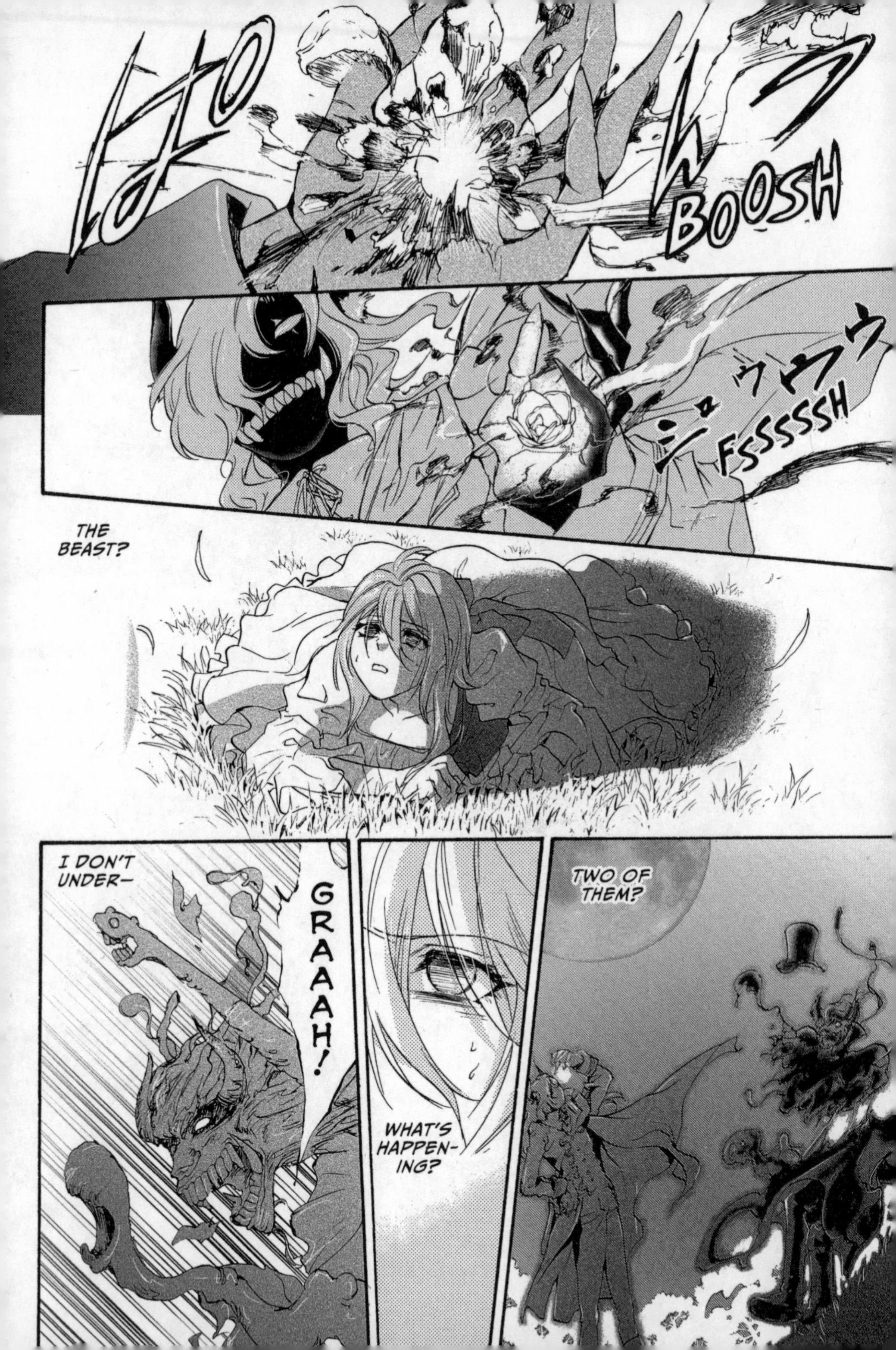
BOOSH
FSSSSH
THE BEAST?
TWO OF THEM?
WHAT'S HAPPEN-ING?
I DON'T UNDER—
GRAAAH!

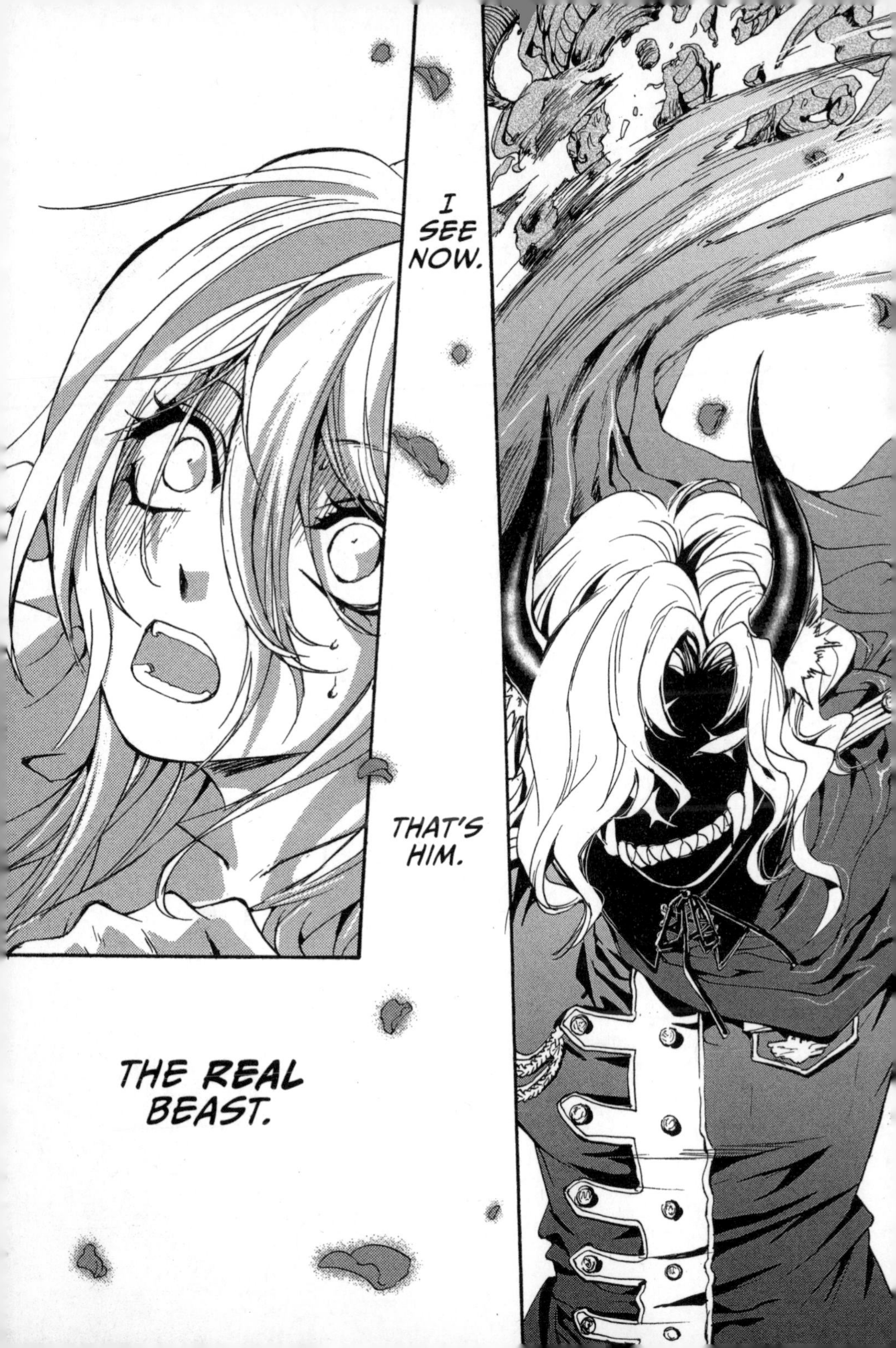
I SEE NOW.
THAT'S HIM.
THE REAL BEAST.

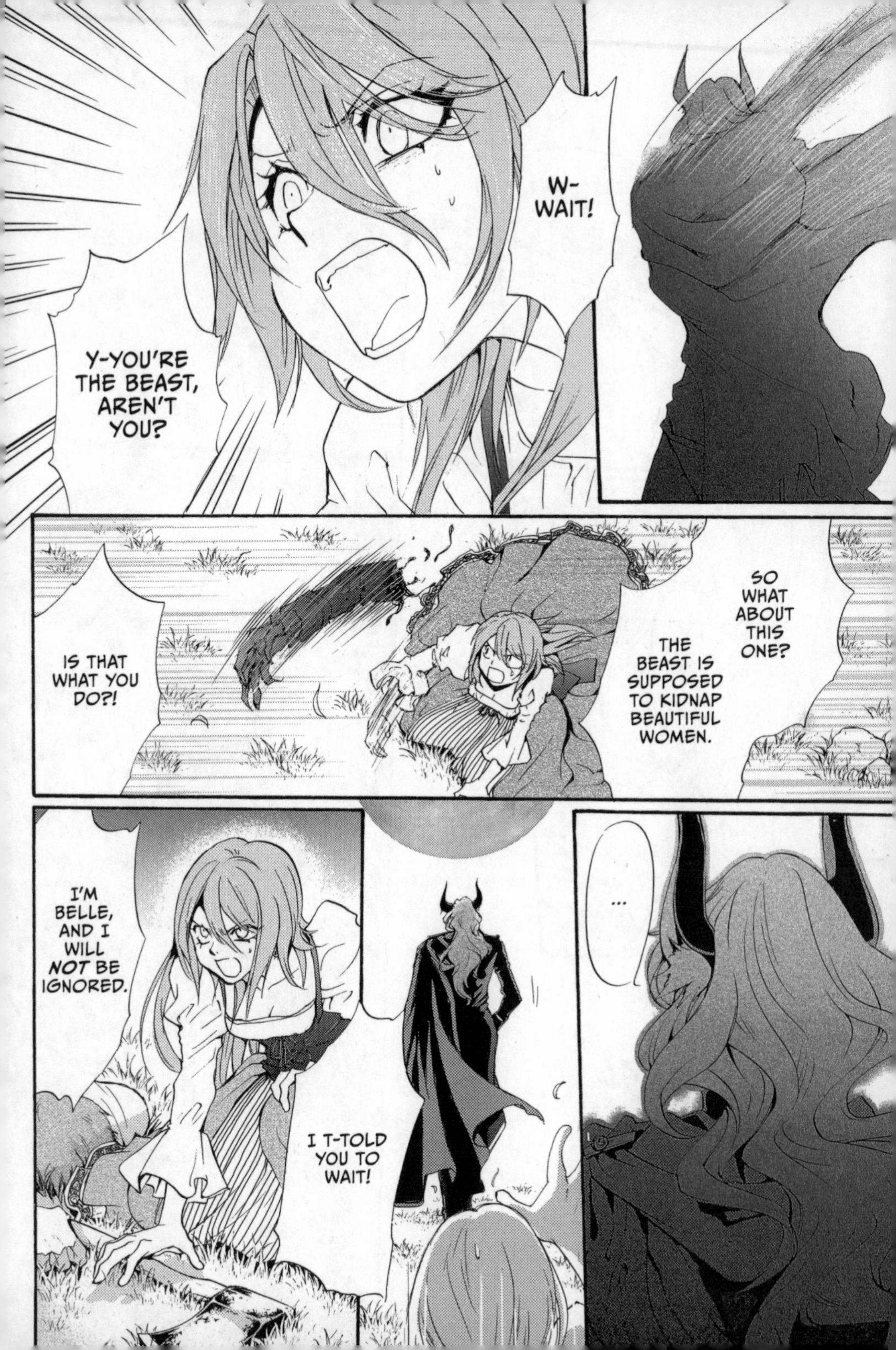
W-WAIT!
Y-YOU'RE THE BEAST, AREN'T YOU?
SO WHAT ABOUT THIS ONE?
THE BEAST IS SUPPOSED TO KIDNAP BEAUTIFUL WOMEN.
IS THAT WHAT YOU DO?!
...
I'M BELLE, AND I WILL *NOT* BE IGNORED.
I T-TOLD YOU TO WAIT!

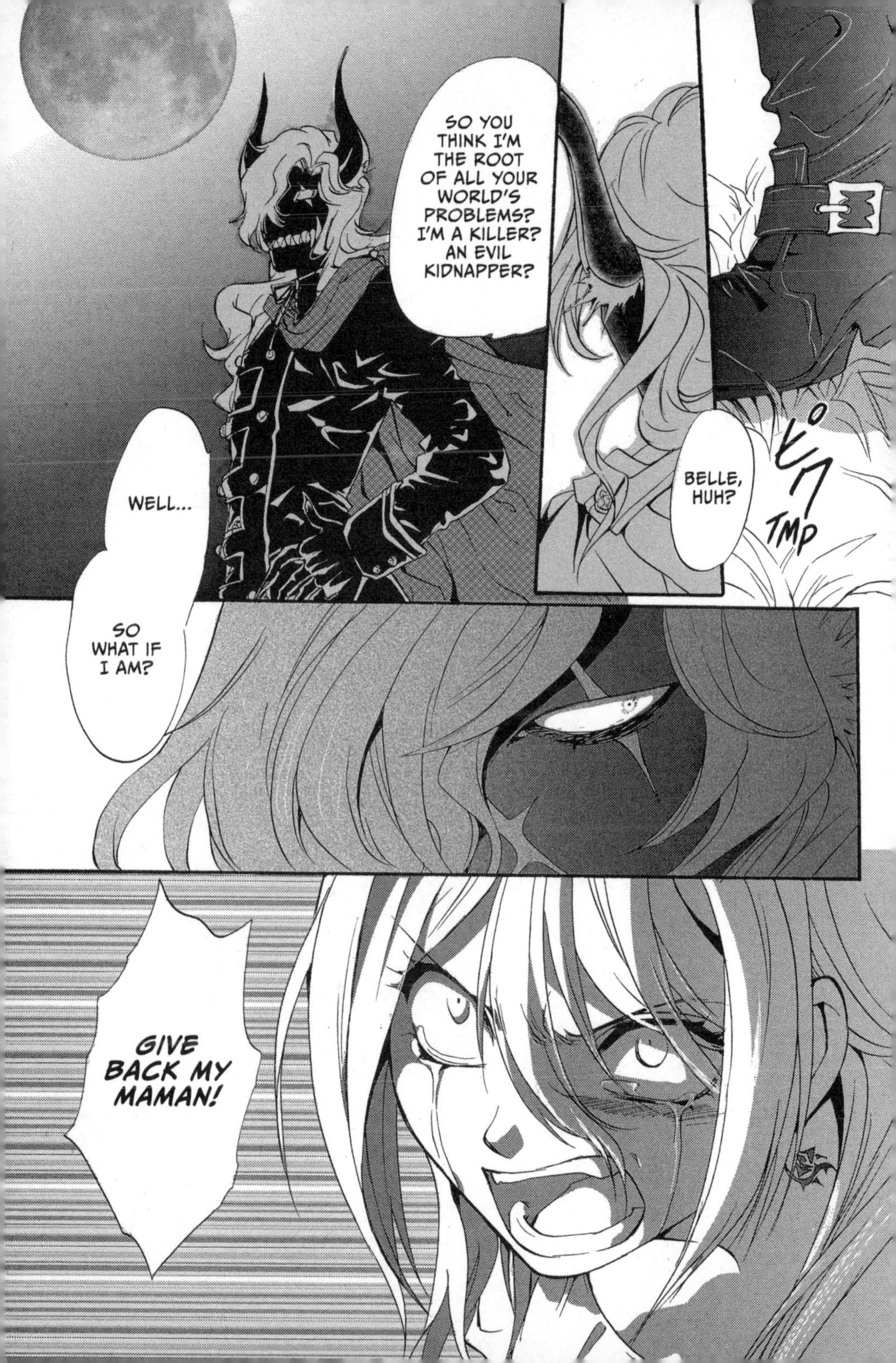
ピク
TMP
BELLE, HUH?
SO YOU THINK I'M THE ROOT OF ALL YOUR WORLD'S PROBLEMS? I'M A KILLER? AN EVIL KIDNAPPER?
WELL...
SO WHAT IF I AM?
GIVE BACK MY MAMAN!

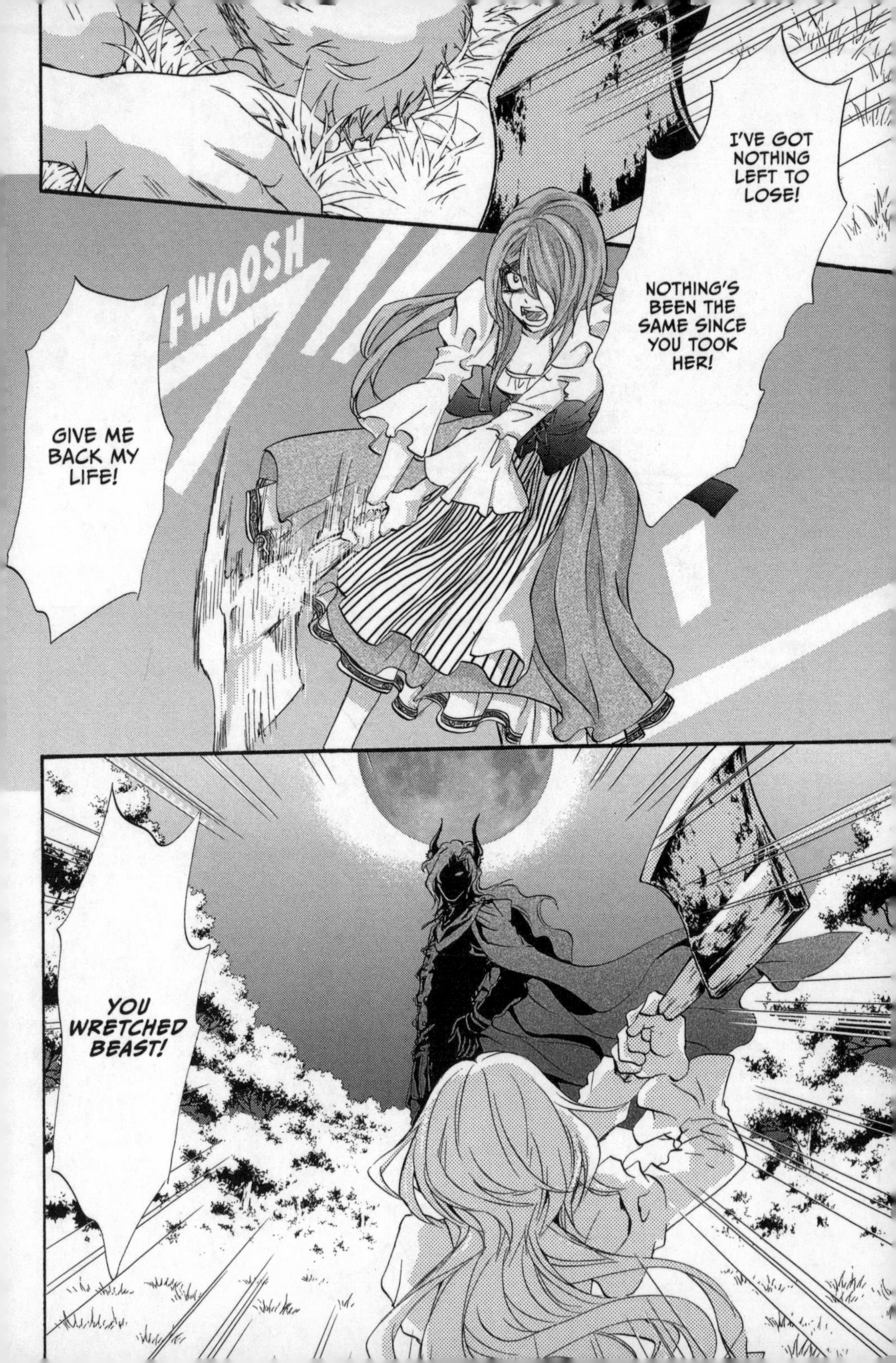
I'VE GOT NOTHING LEFT TO LOSE!
NOTHING'S BEEN THE SAME SINCE YOU TOOK HER!
FWOOSH
GIVE ME BACK MY LIFE!
YOU WRETCHED BEAST!

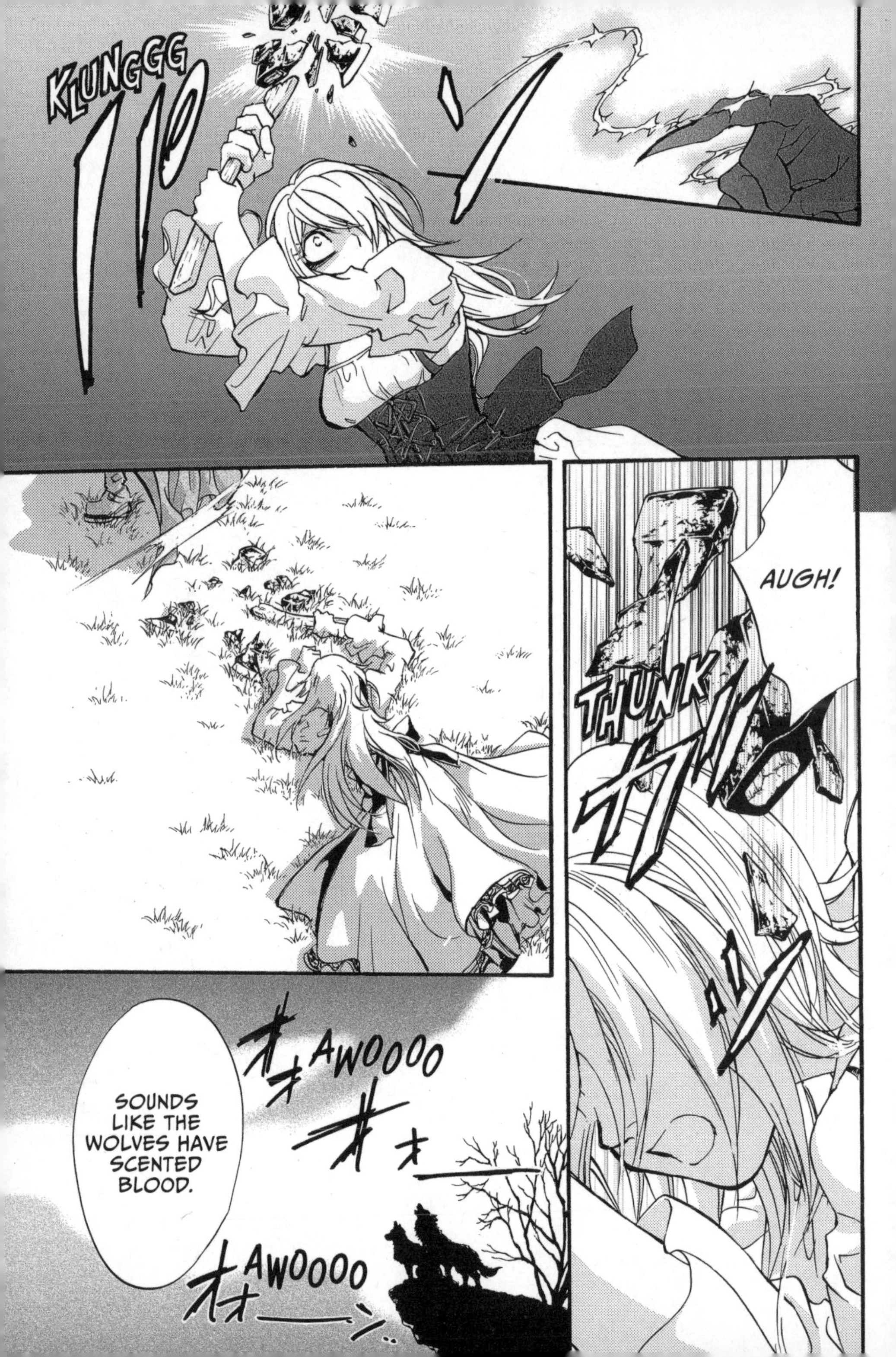
KLUNGGG
THUNK
AUGH!
AWOOOO
SOUNDS LIKE THE WOLVES HAVE SCENTED BLOOD.
AWOOOO

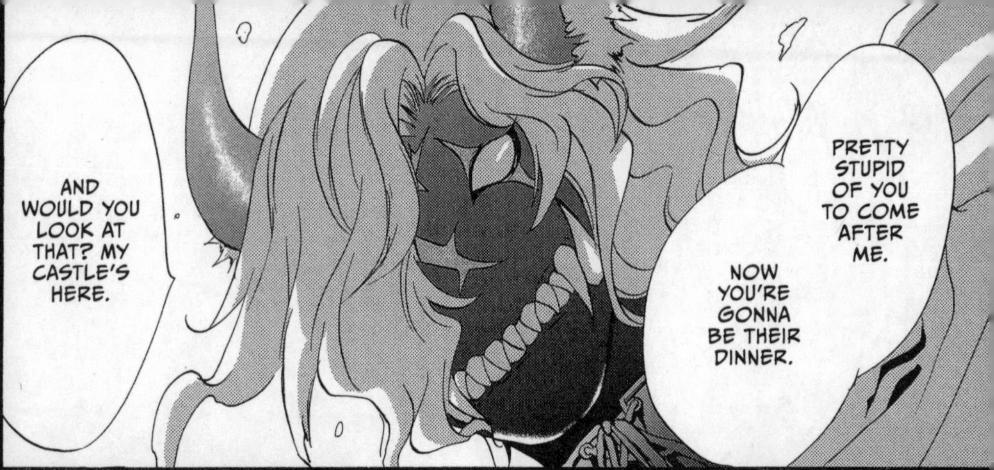
PRETTY STUPID OF YOU TO COME AFTER ME.
NOW YOU'RE GONNA BE THEIR DINNER.
AND WOULD YOU LOOK AT THAT? MY CASTLE'S HERE.

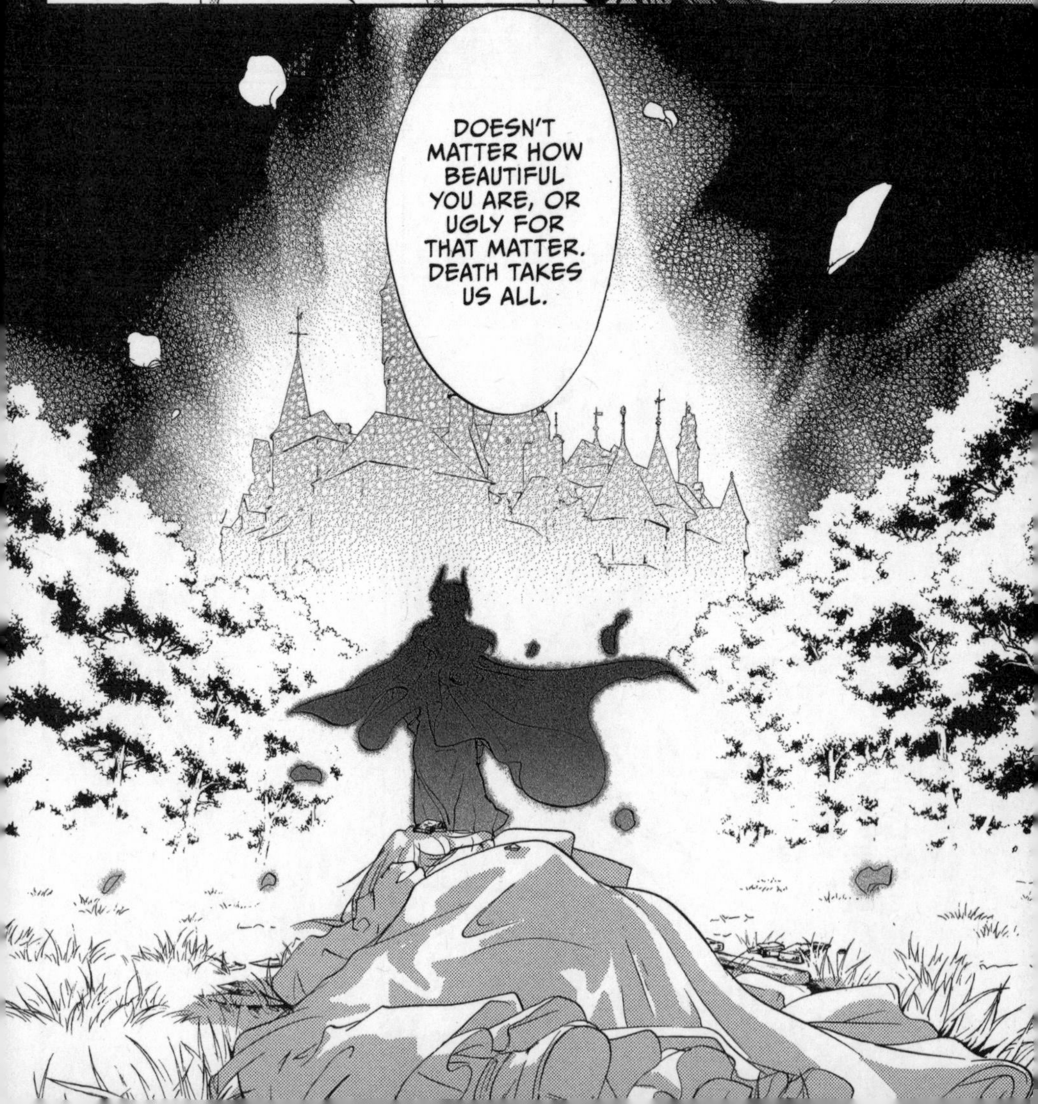
DOESN'T MATTER HOW BEAUTIFUL YOU ARE, OR UGLY FOR THAT MATTER. DEATH TAKES US ALL.

LA BELLE ET LA BÊTE

DU PARADIS PERDU

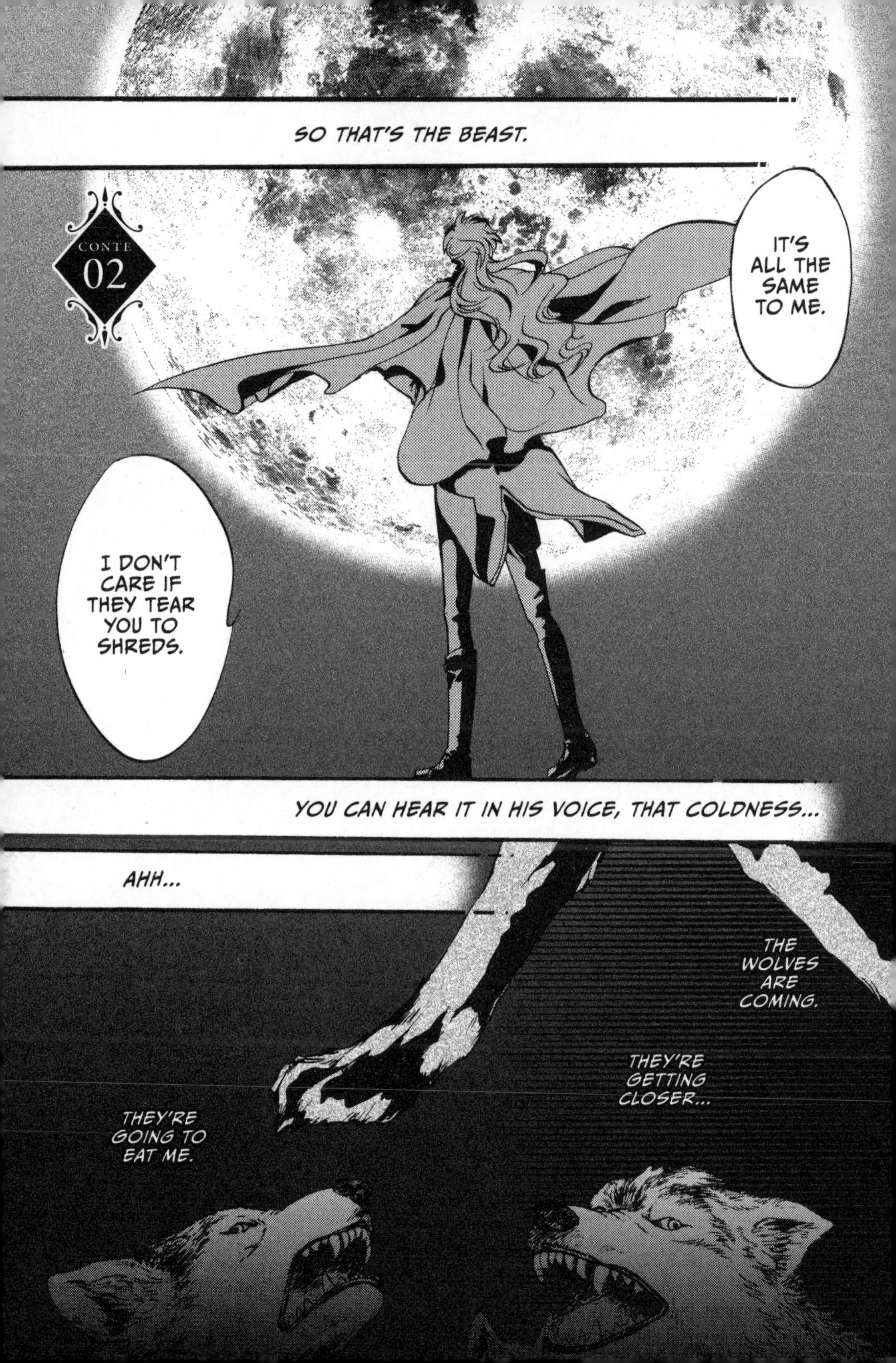
SO THAT'S THE BEAST.
CONTE 02
IT'S ALL THE SAME TO ME.
I DON'T CARE IF THEY TEAR YOU TO SHREDS.
YOU CAN HEAR IT IN HIS VOICE, THAT COLDNESS...
AHH...
THE WOLVES ARE COMING.
THEY'RE GETTING CLOSER...
THEY'RE GOING TO EAT ME.

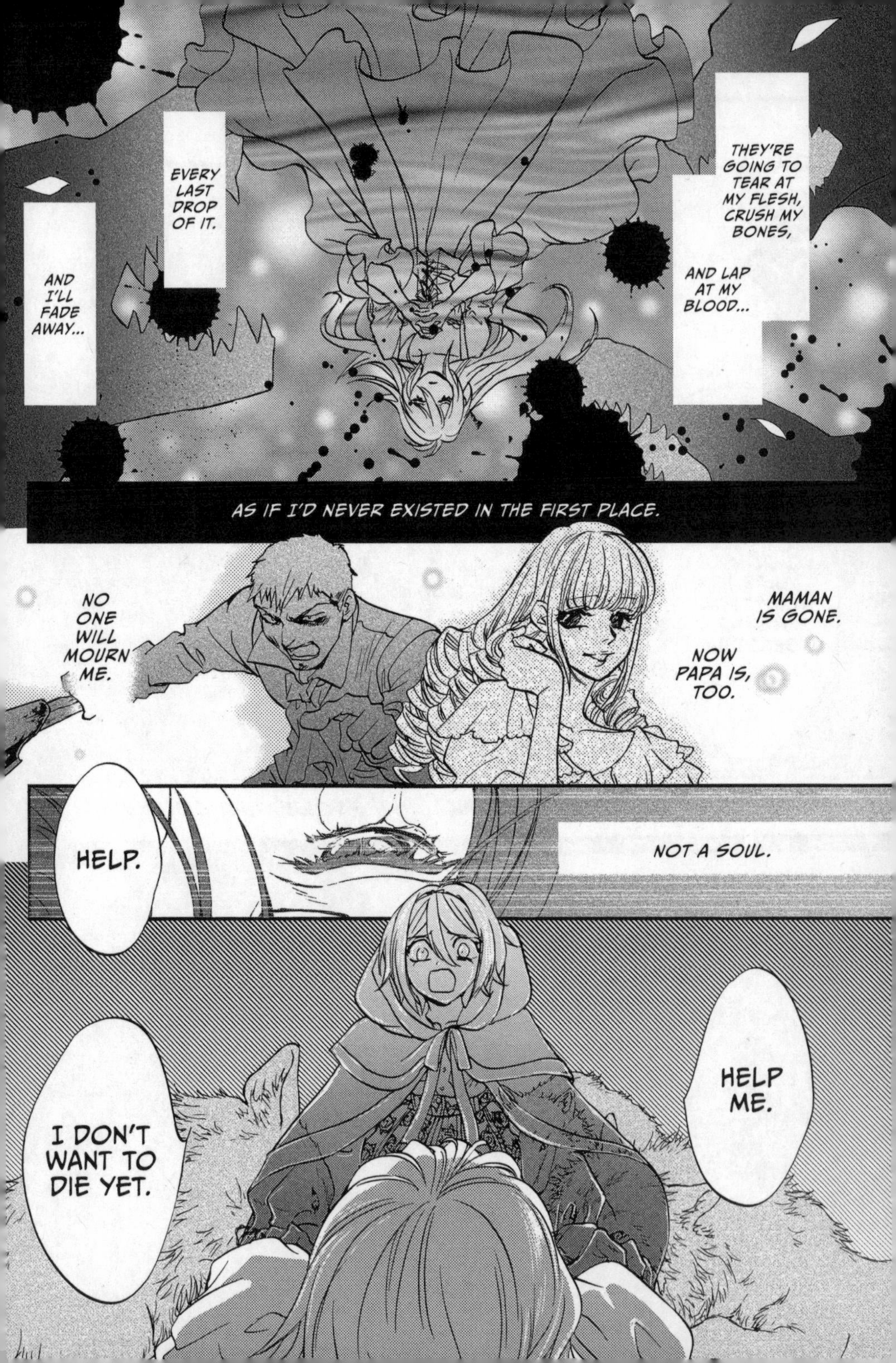
THEY'RE GOING TO TEAR AT MY FLESH, CRUSH MY BONES,
AND LAP AT MY BLOOD...
EVERY LAST DROP OF IT.
AND I'LL FADE AWAY...
AS IF I'D NEVER EXISTED IN THE FIRST PLACE.
MAMAN IS GONE.
NOW PAPA IS, TOO.
NO ONE WILL MOURN ME.
NOT A SOUL.
HELP.
HELP ME.
I DON'T WANT TO DIE YET.

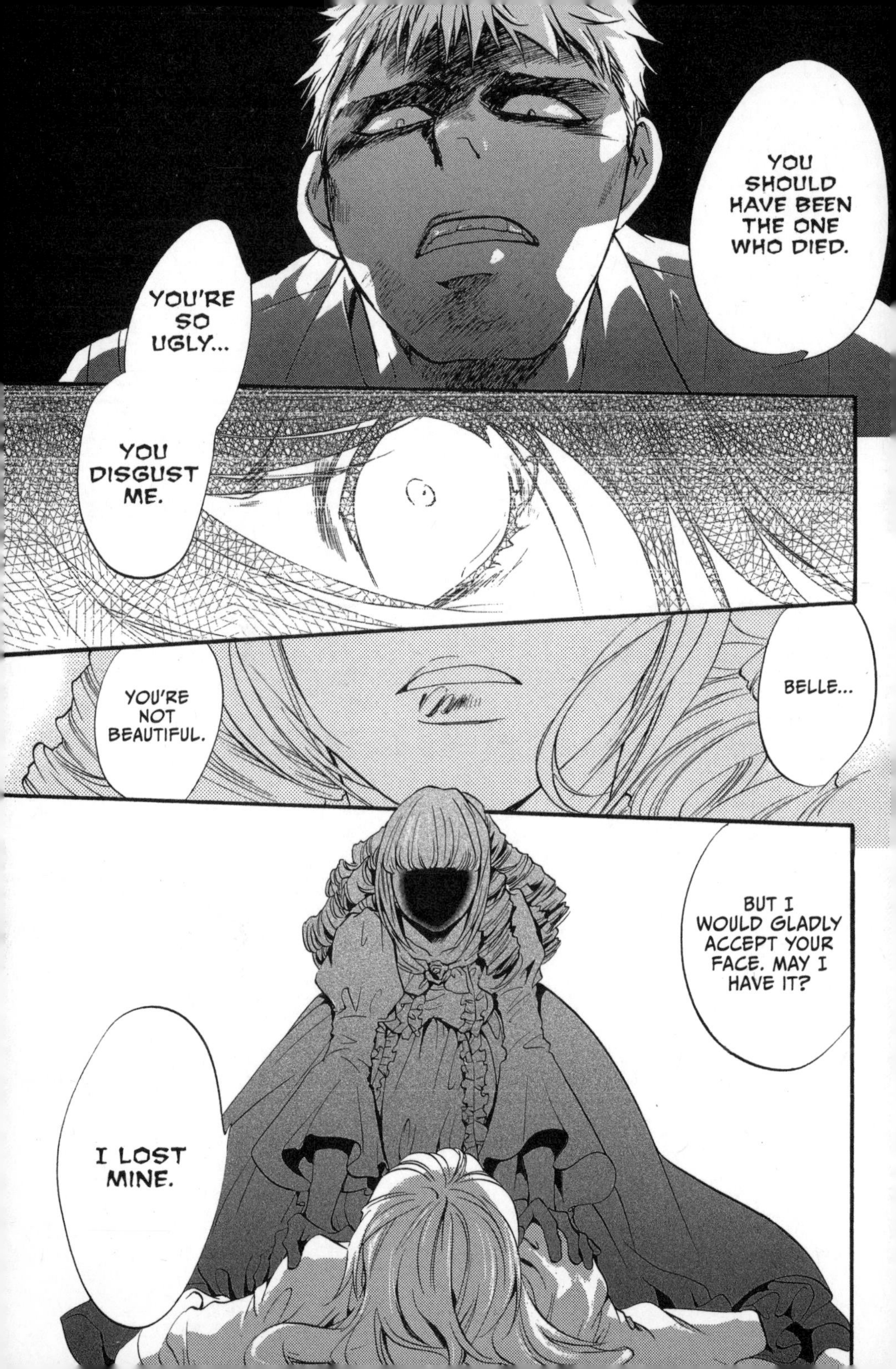
YOU SHOULD HAVE BEEN THE ONE WHO DIED.
YOU'RE SO UGLY...
YOU DISGUST ME.
BELLE...
YOU'RE NOT BEAUTIFUL.
BUT I WOULD GLADLY ACCEPT YOUR FACE. MAY I HAVE IT?
I LOST MINE.

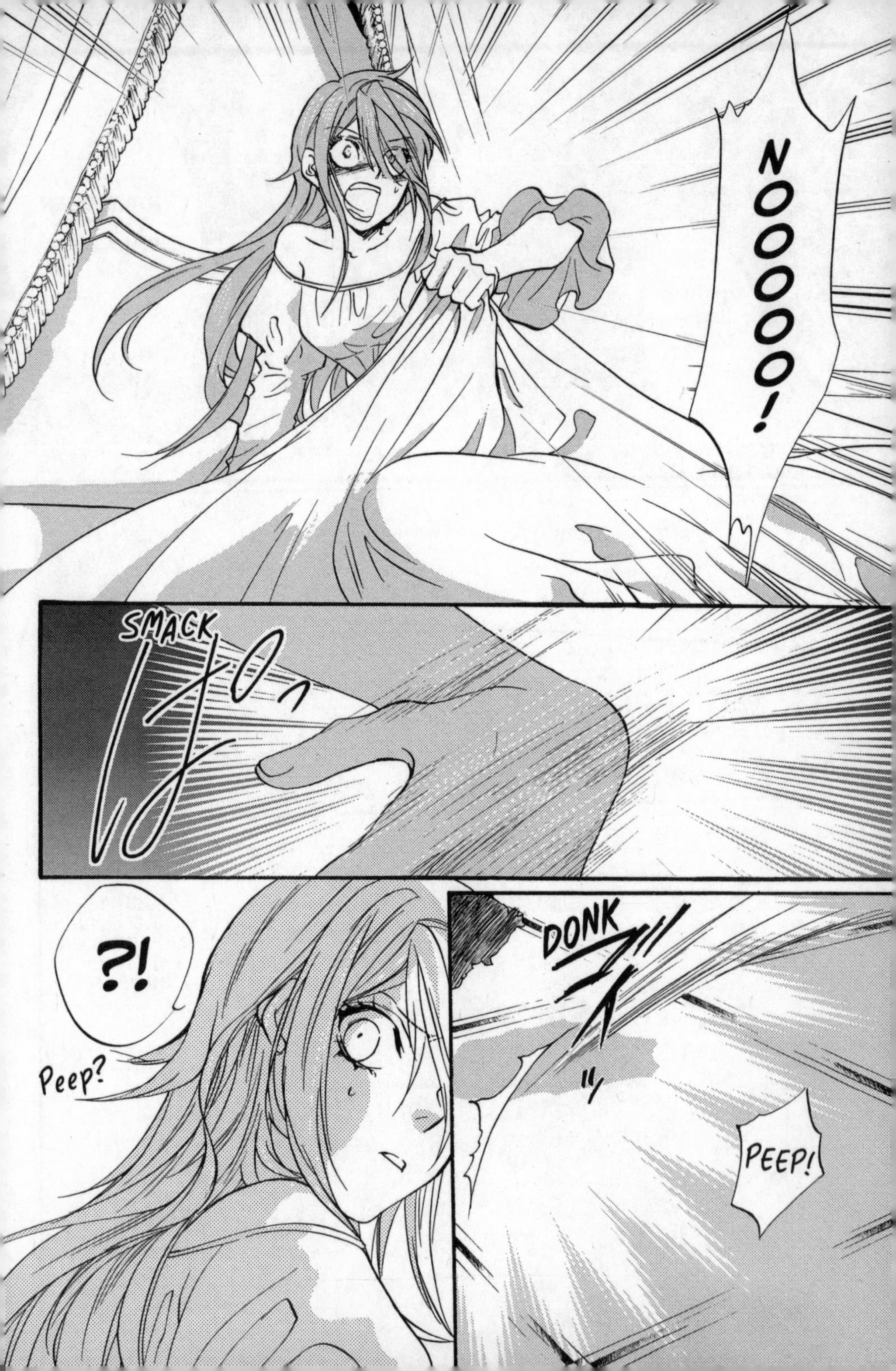
NOOOOOO!
SMACK
DONK
PEEP!
?!
Peep?

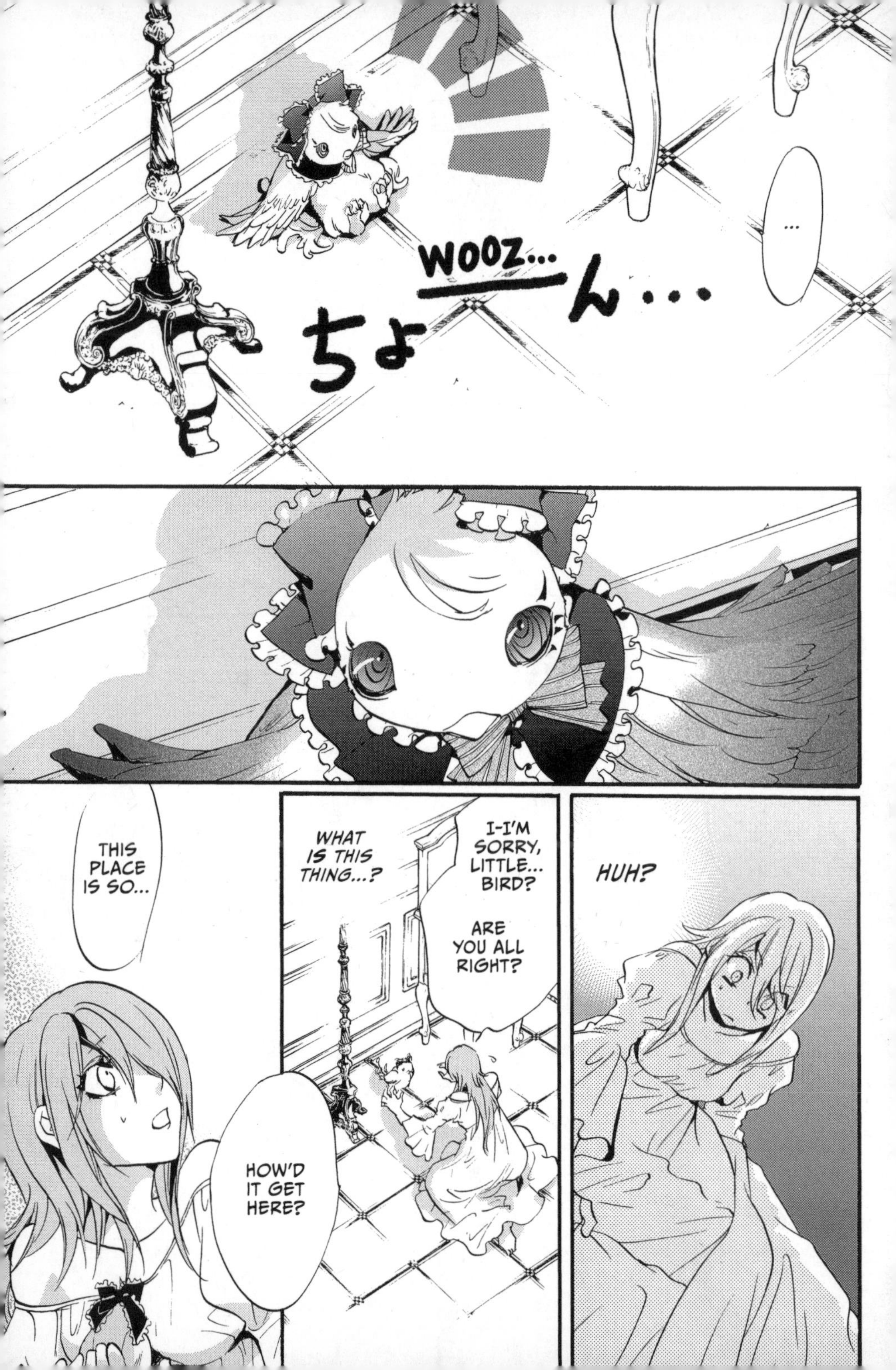
...
WOOZ...
ちょーん...
HUH?
I-I'M SORRY, LITTLE... BIRD?
ARE YOU ALL RIGHT?
WHAT IS THIS THING...?
THIS PLACE IS SO...
HOW'D IT GET HERE?

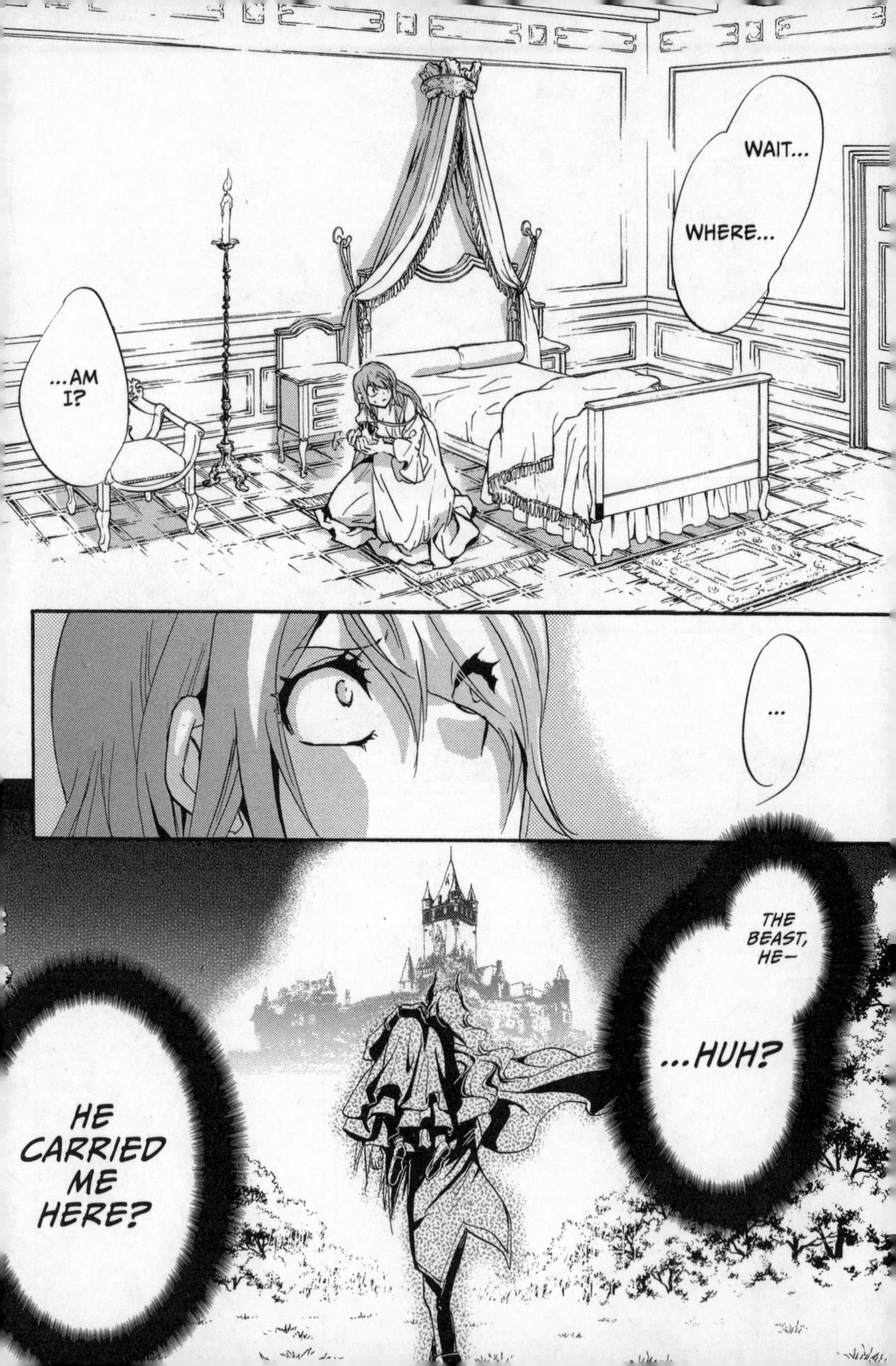
WAIT... WHERE...
...AM I?
...
THE BEAST, HE—
...HUH?
HE CARRIED ME HERE?

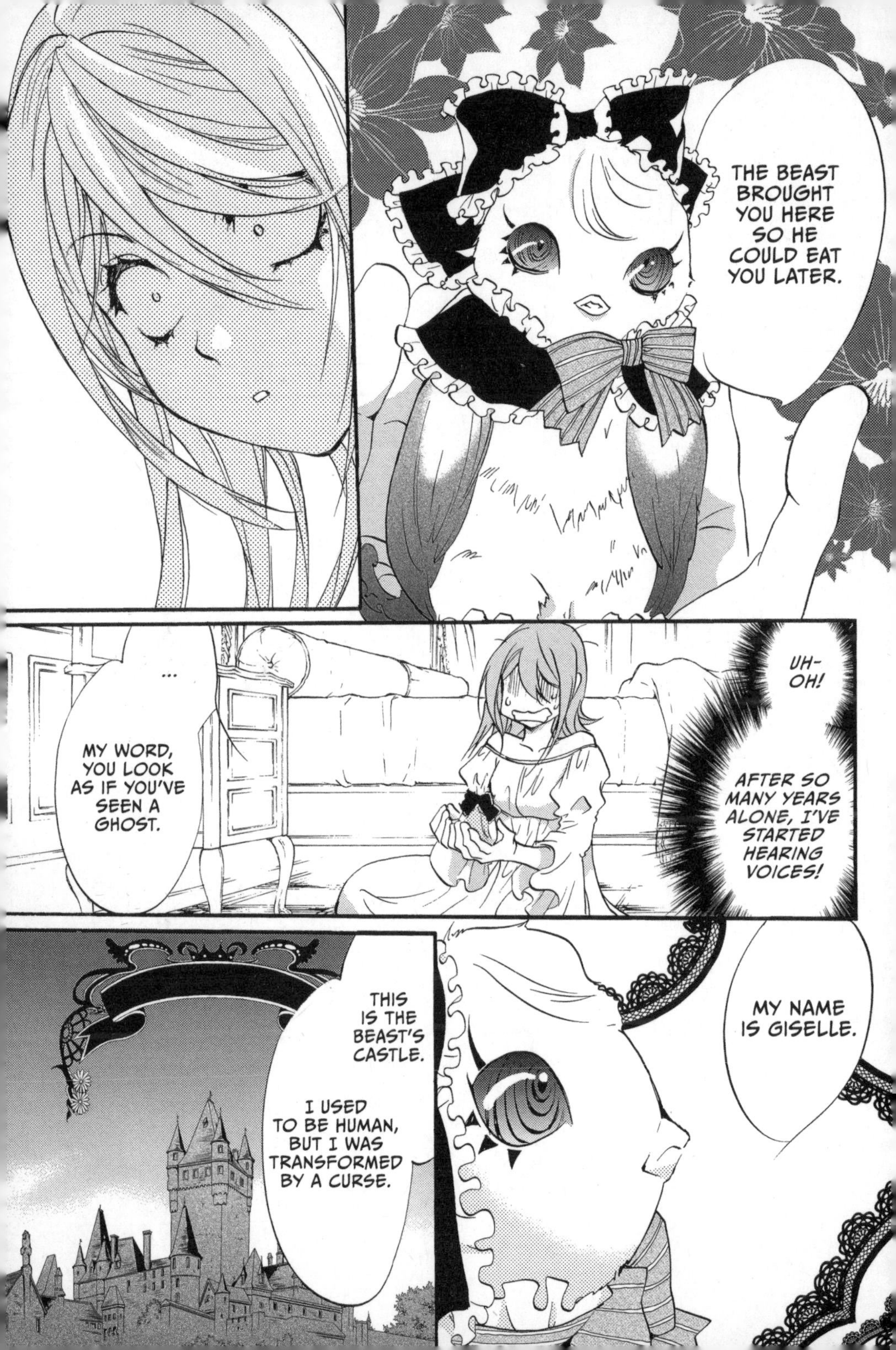
THE BEAST BROUGHT YOU HERE SO HE COULD EAT YOU LATER.
UH-OH!
AFTER SO MANY YEARS ALONE, I'VE STARTED HEARING VOICES!
...
MY WORD, YOU LOOK AS IF YOU'VE SEEN A GHOST.
MY NAME IS GISELLE.
THIS IS THE BEAST'S CASTLE.
I USED TO BE HUMAN, BUT I WAS TRANSFORMED BY A CURSE.

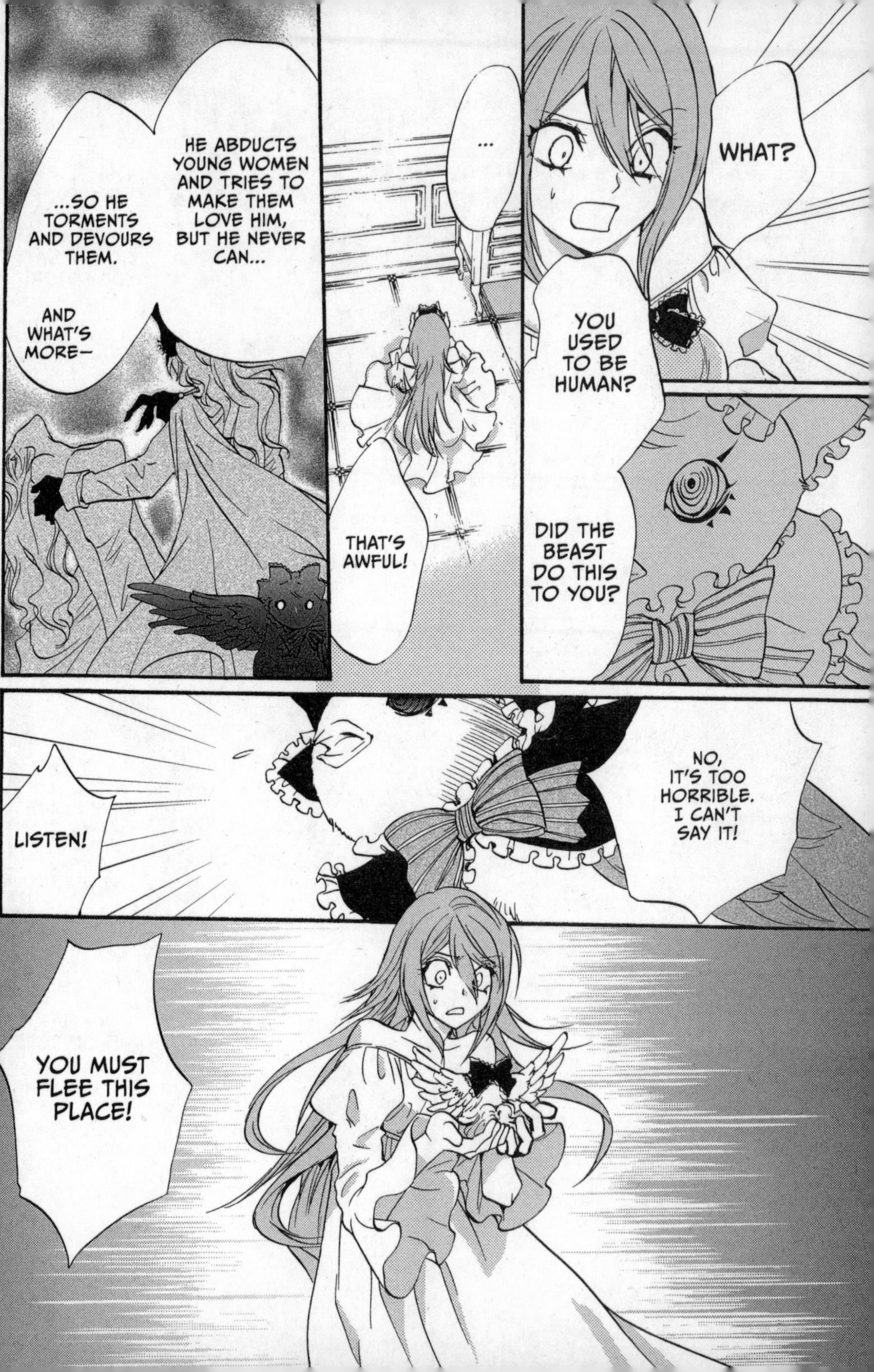
WHAT?
YOU USED TO BE HUMAN?
DID THE BEAST DO THIS TO YOU?
...
THAT'S AWFUL!
HE ABDUCTS YOUNG WOMEN AND TRIES TO MAKE THEM LOVE HIM, BUT HE NEVER CAN...
...SO HE TORMENTS AND DEVOURS THEM.
AND WHAT'S MORE—
NO, IT'S TOO HORRIBLE. I CAN'T SAY IT!
LISTEN!
YOU MUST FLEE THIS PLACE!

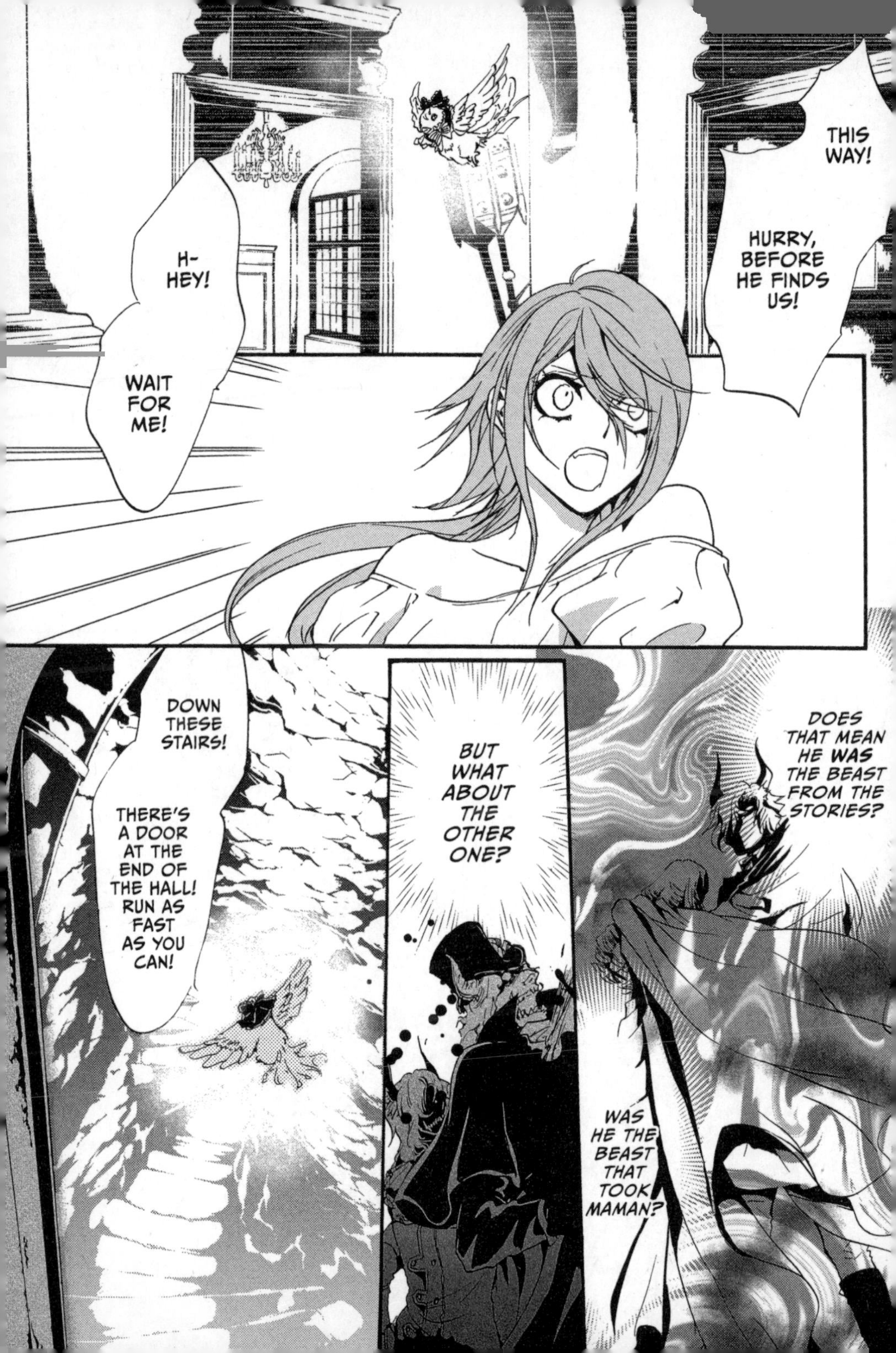
THIS WAY!
HURRY, BEFORE HE FINDS US!
H- HEY!
WAIT FOR ME!
DOES THAT MEAN HE **WAS** THE BEAST FROM THE STORIES?
WAS HE THE BEAST THAT TOOK MAMAN?
BUT WHAT ABOUT THE OTHER ONE?
DOWN THESE STAIRS!
THERE'S A DOOR AT THE END OF THE HALL! RUN AS FAST AS YOU CAN!

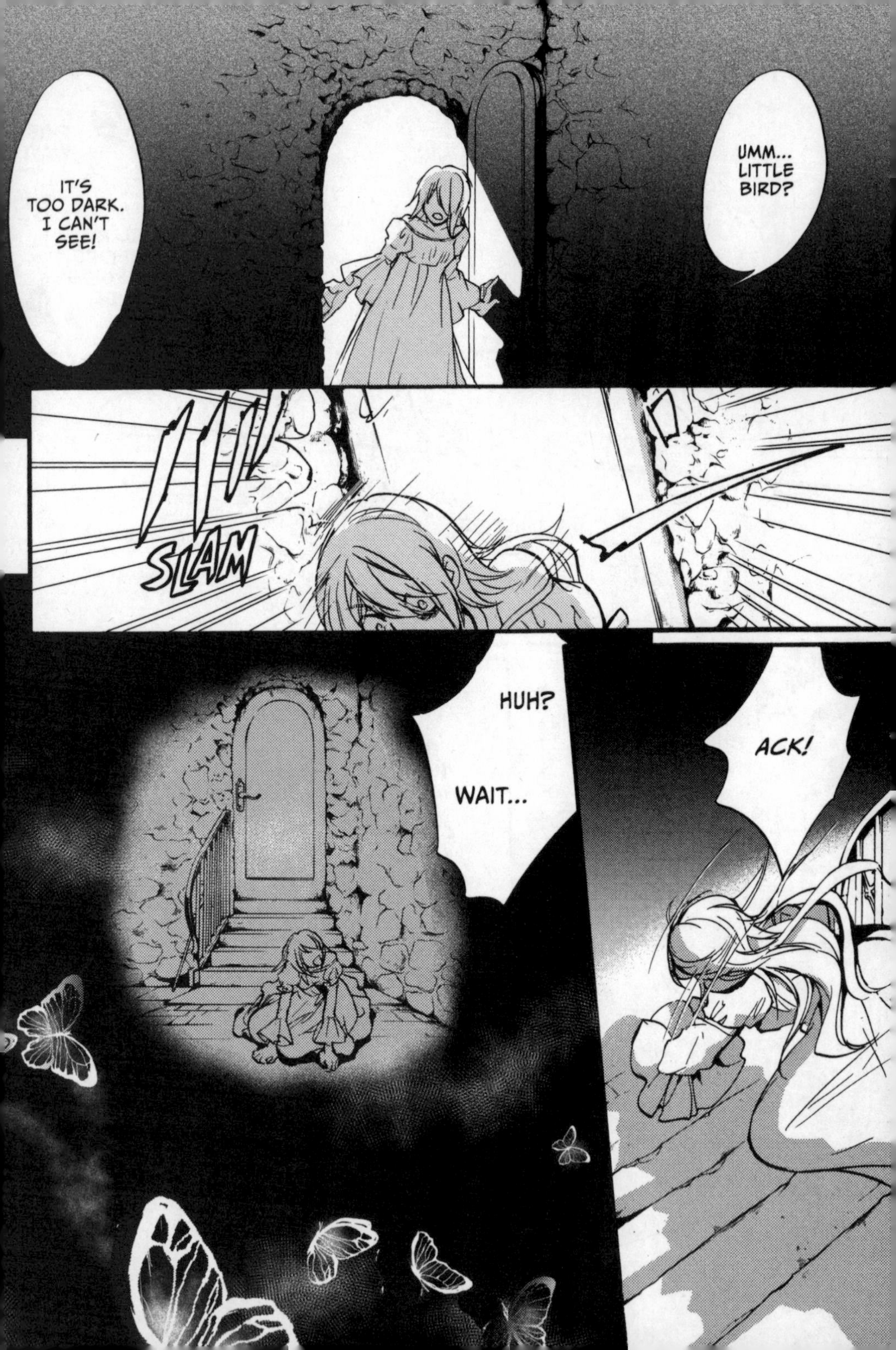
UMM... LITTLE BIRD?
IT'S TOO DARK. I CAN'T SEE!
SLAM
ACK!
HUH?
WAIT...

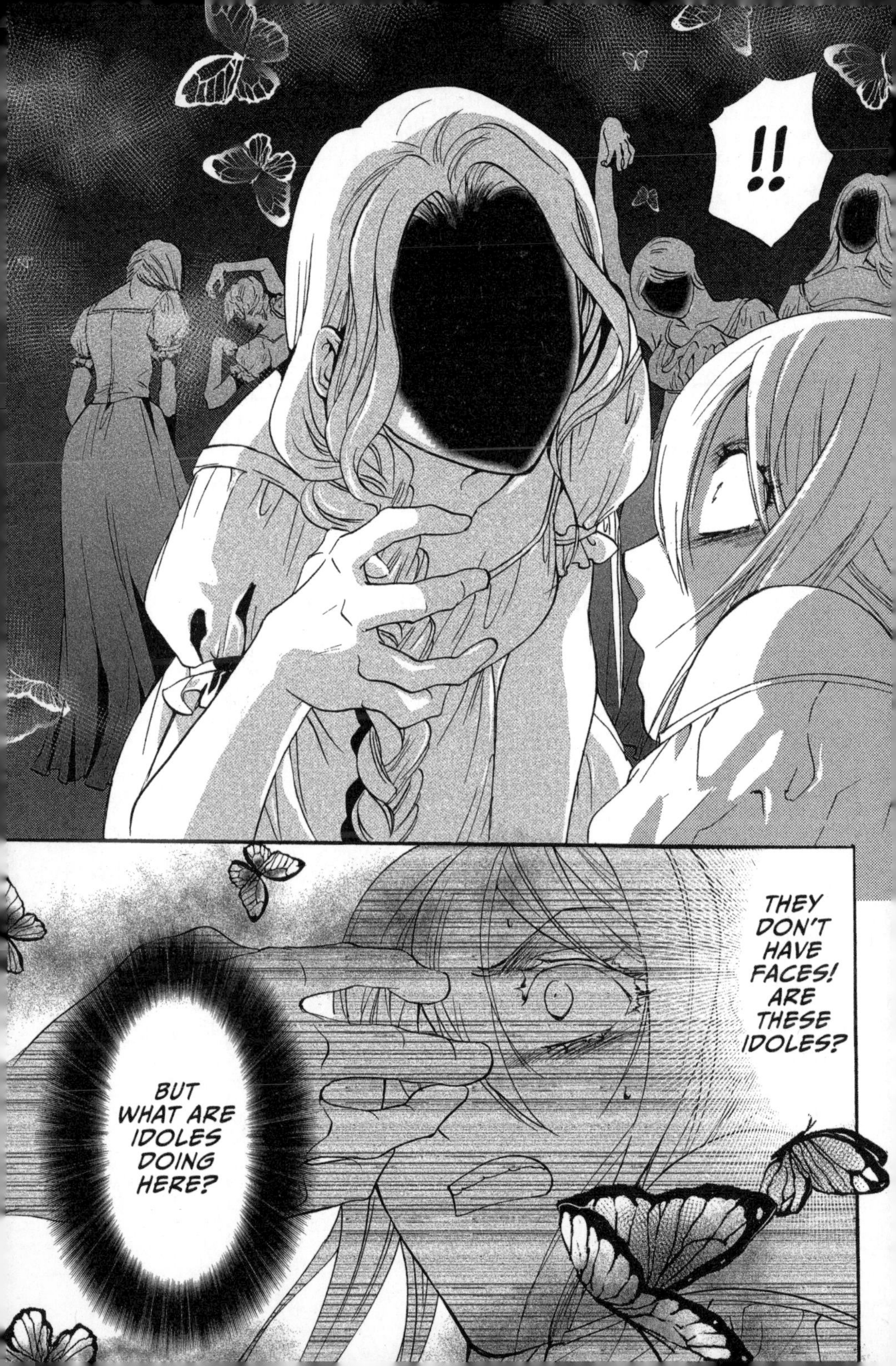
!!
THEY DON'T HAVE FACES! ARE THESE IDOLES?
BUT WHAT ARE IDOLES DOING HERE?

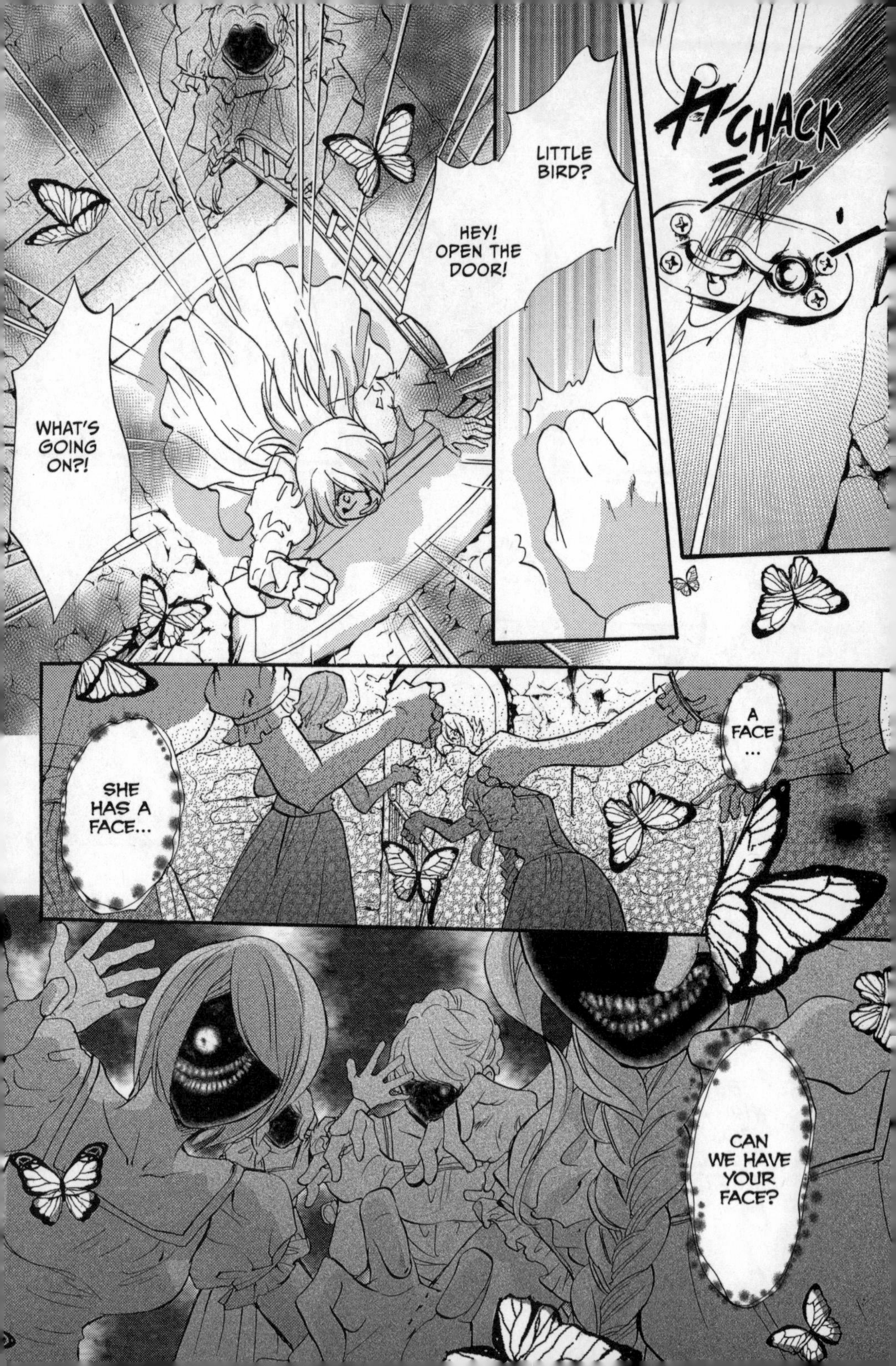
KA-CHACK
LITTLE BIRD?
HEY! OPEN THE DOOR!
WHAT'S GOING ON?!
A FACE ...
SHE HAS A FACE...
CAN WE HAVE YOUR FACE?

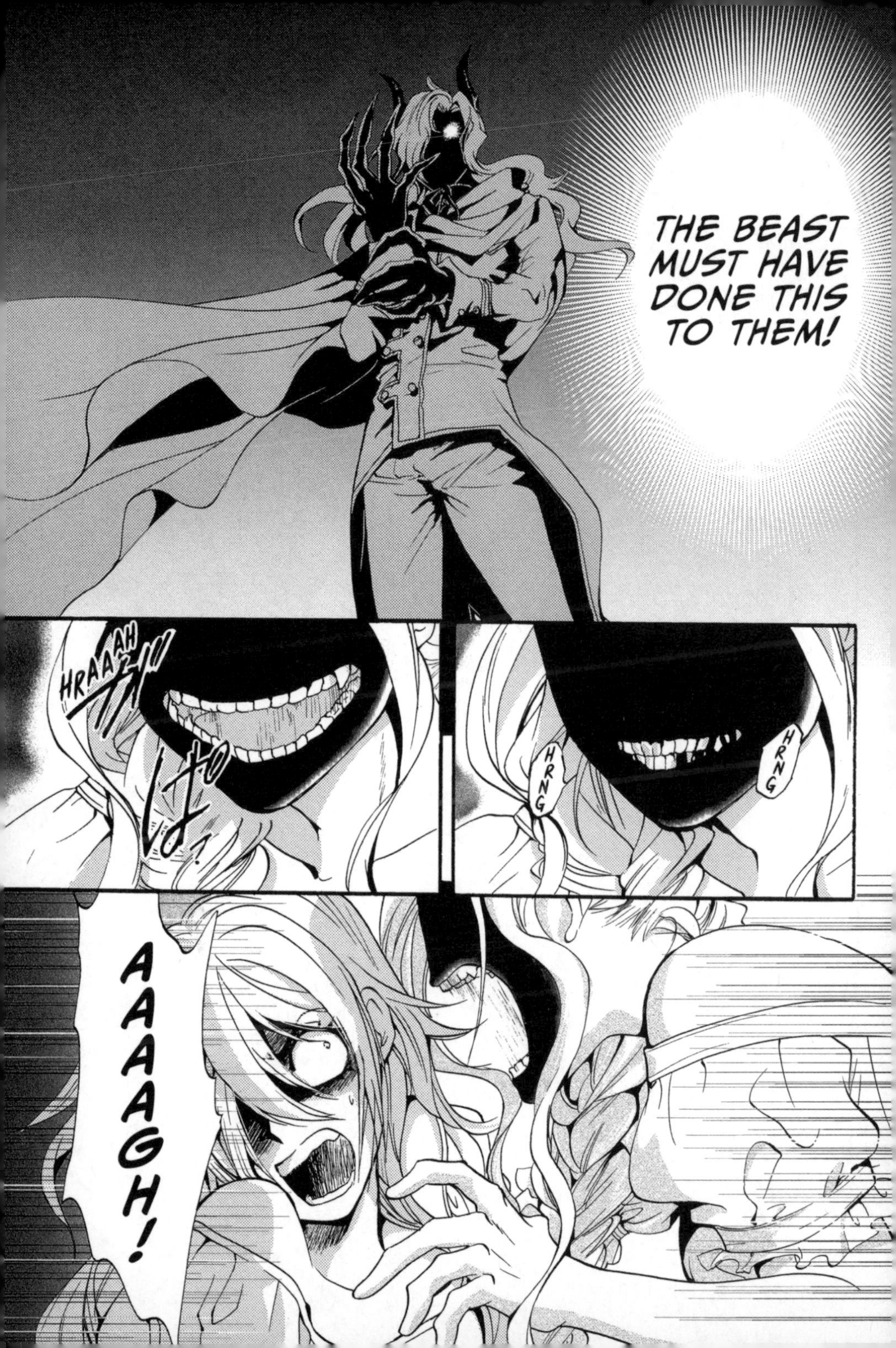
THE BEAST MUST HAVE DONE THIS TO THEM!
HRNG
HRNG
HRAAAH
AAAAAGH!

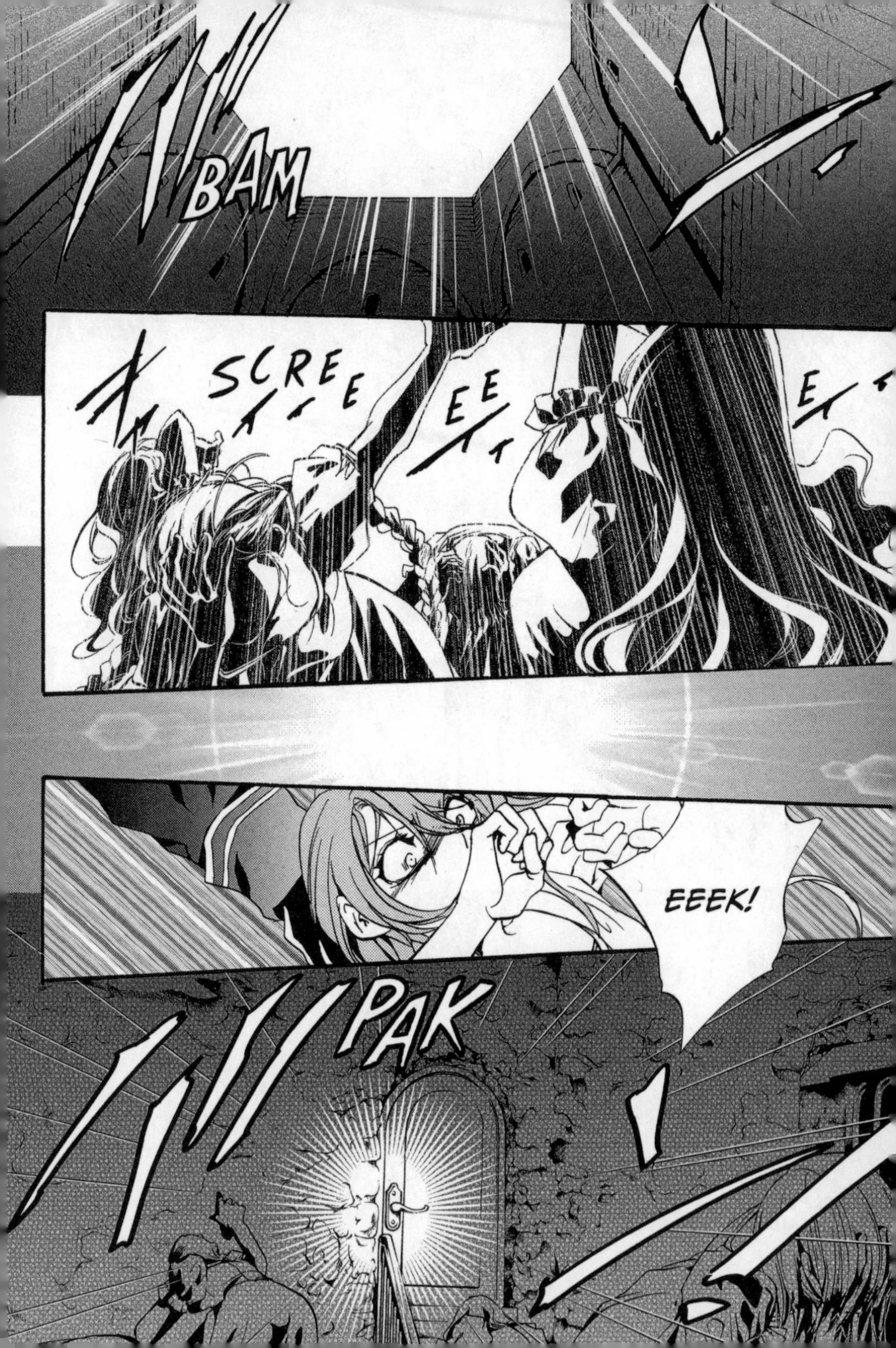
BAM
SCREEEEE
EEEK!
PAK

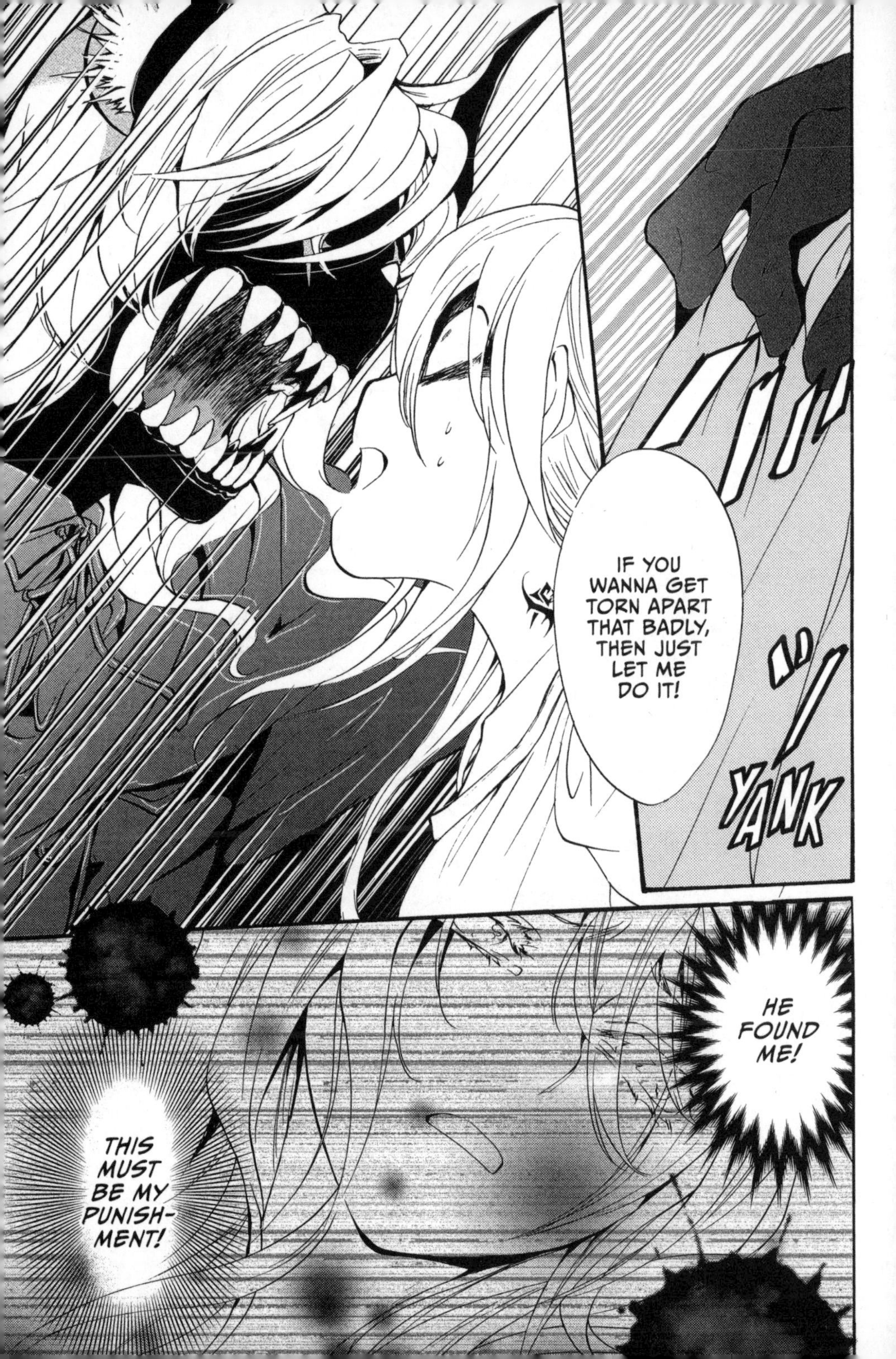
YANK
IF YOU WANNA GET TORN APART THAT BADLY, THEN JUST LET ME DO IT!
HE FOUND ME!
THIS MUST BE MY PUNISH-MENT!

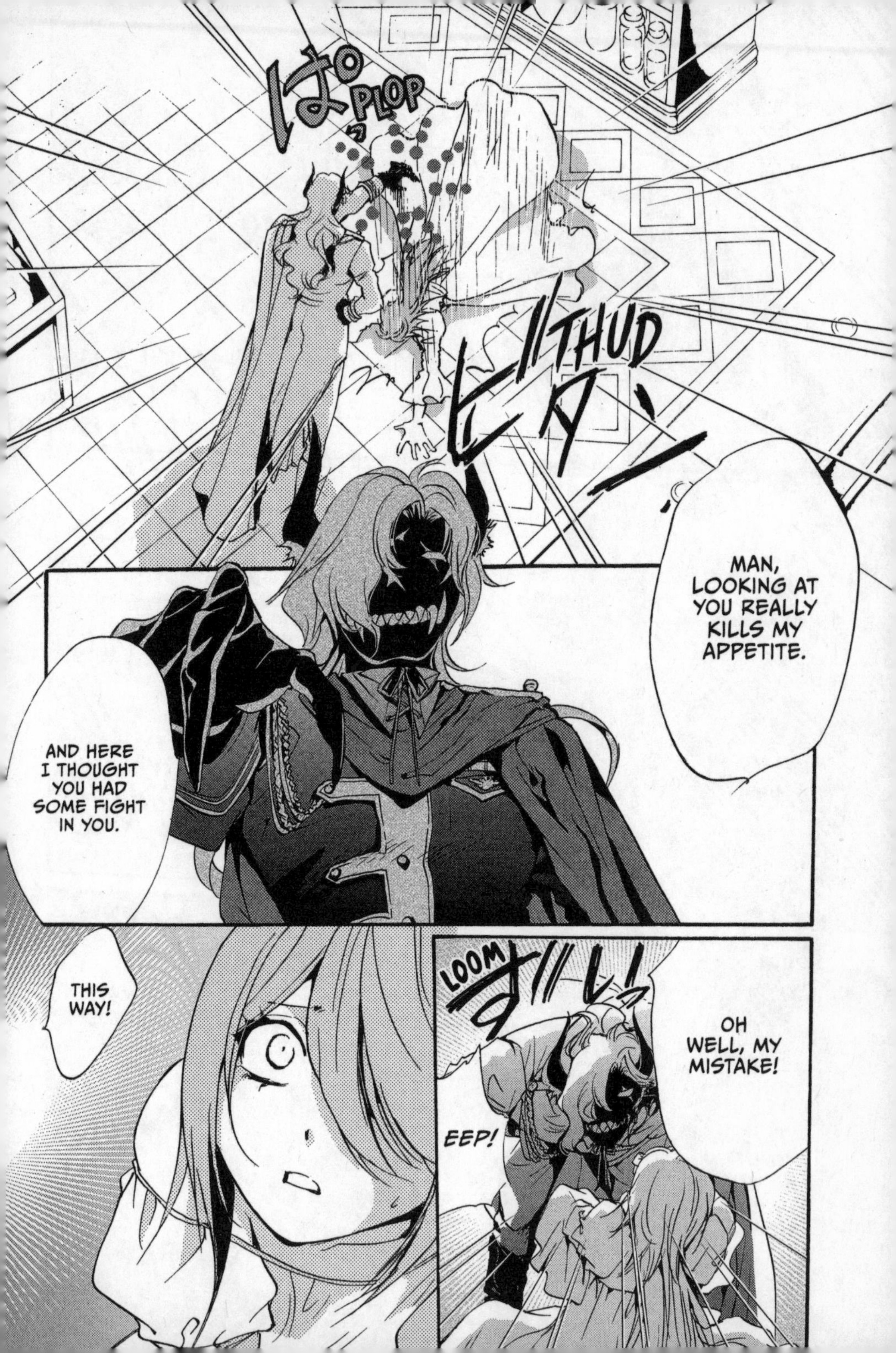
PLOP
THUD
MAN, LOOKING AT YOU REALLY KILLS MY APPETITE.
AND HERE I THOUGHT YOU HAD SOME FIGHT IN YOU.
LOOM
OH WELL, MY MISTAKE!
EEP!
THIS WAY!

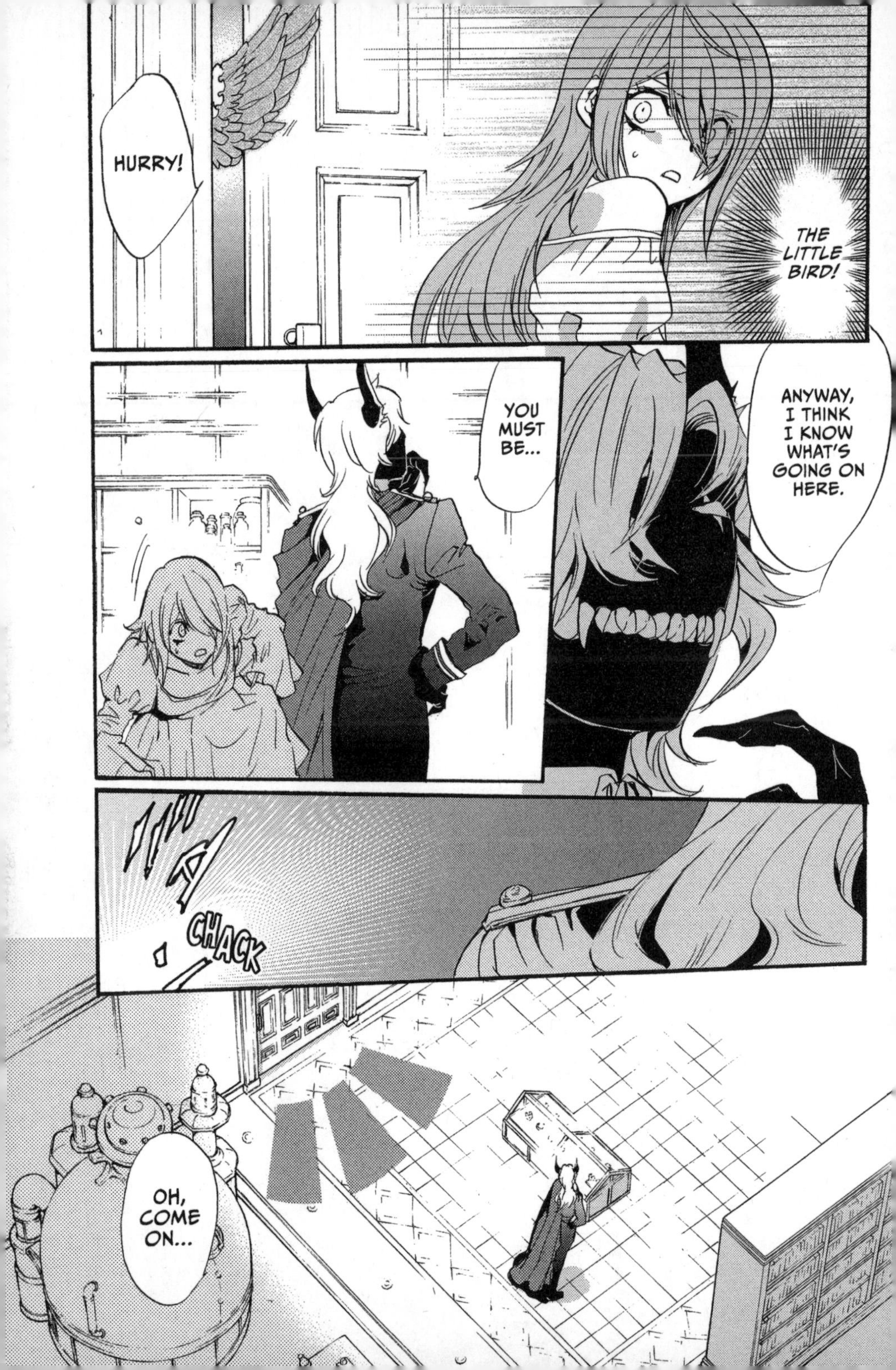
THE LITTLE BIRD!
HURRY!
ANYWAY, I THINK I KNOW WHAT'S GOING ON HERE.
YOU MUST BE...
CHACK
OH, COME ON...

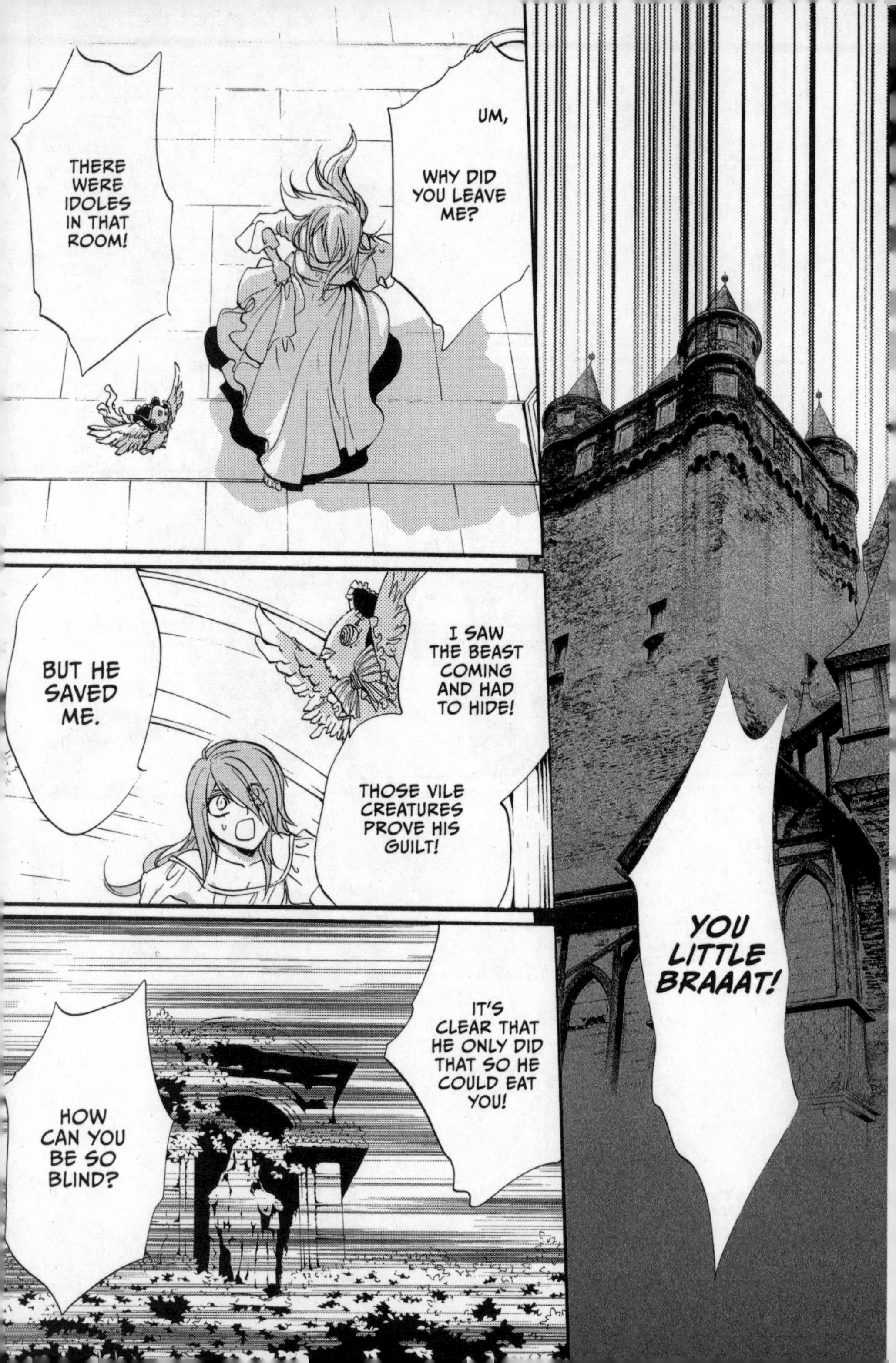
YOU LITTLE BRAAAT!
UM,
WHY DID YOU LEAVE ME?
THERE WERE IDOLES IN THAT ROOM!
I SAW THE BEAST COMING AND HAD TO HIDE!
THOSE VILE CREATURES PROVE HIS GUILT!
BUT HE SAVED ME.
IT'S CLEAR THAT HE ONLY DID THAT SO HE COULD EAT YOU!
HOW CAN YOU BE SO BLIND?

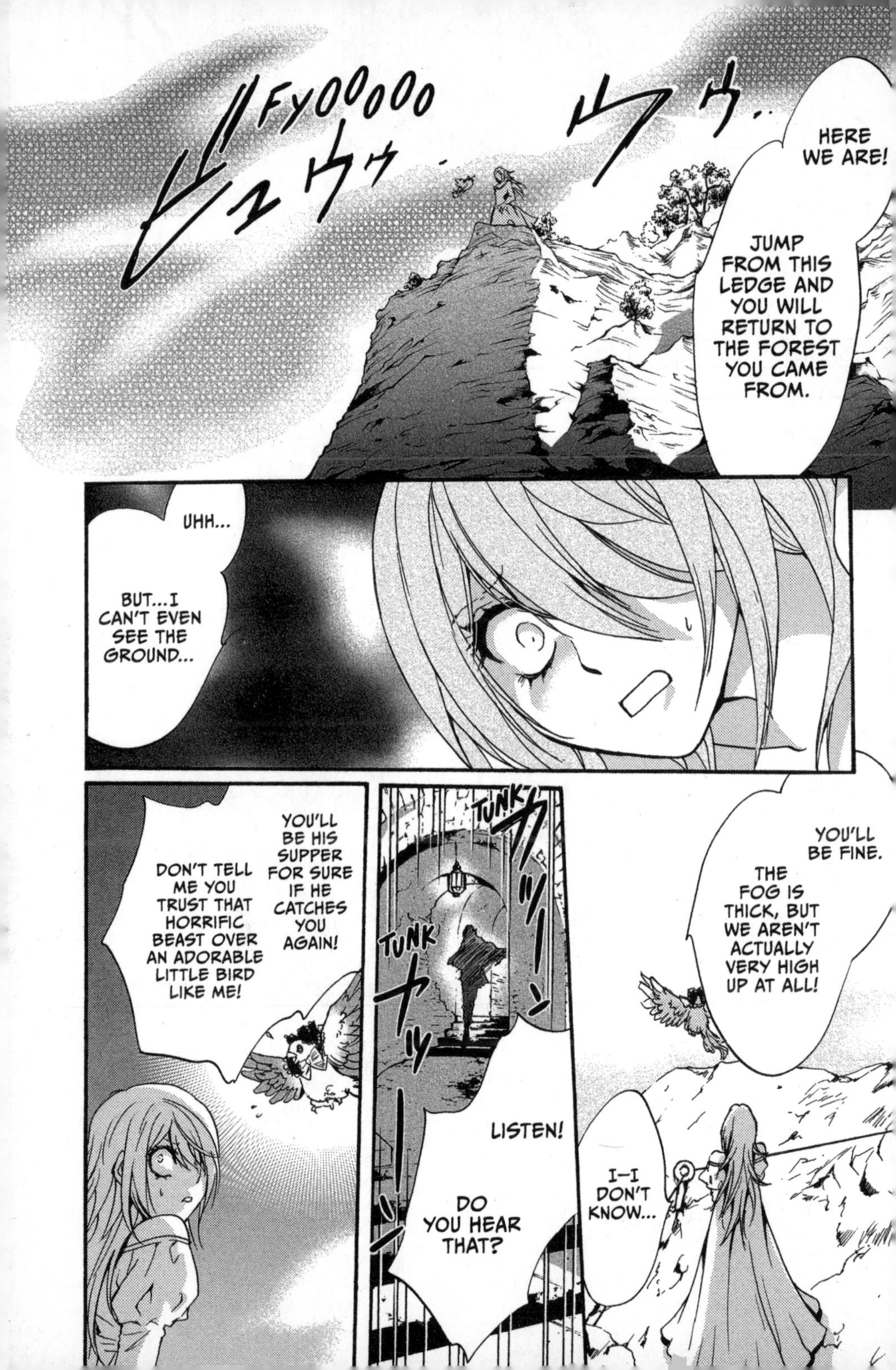
HERE WE ARE!
JUMP FROM THIS LEDGE AND YOU WILL RETURN TO THE FOREST YOU CAME FROM.
FYOOOOOO
UHH...
BUT...I CAN'T EVEN SEE THE GROUND...
YOU'LL BE FINE.
THE FOG IS THICK, BUT WE AREN'T ACTUALLY VERY HIGH UP AT ALL!
I-I DON'T KNOW...
TUNK
TUNK
LISTEN!
DO YOU HEAR THAT?
YOU'LL BE HIS SUPPER FOR SURE IF HE CATCHES YOU AGAIN!
DON'T TELL ME YOU TRUST THAT HORRIFIC BEAST OVER AN ADORABLE LITTLE BIRD LIKE ME!

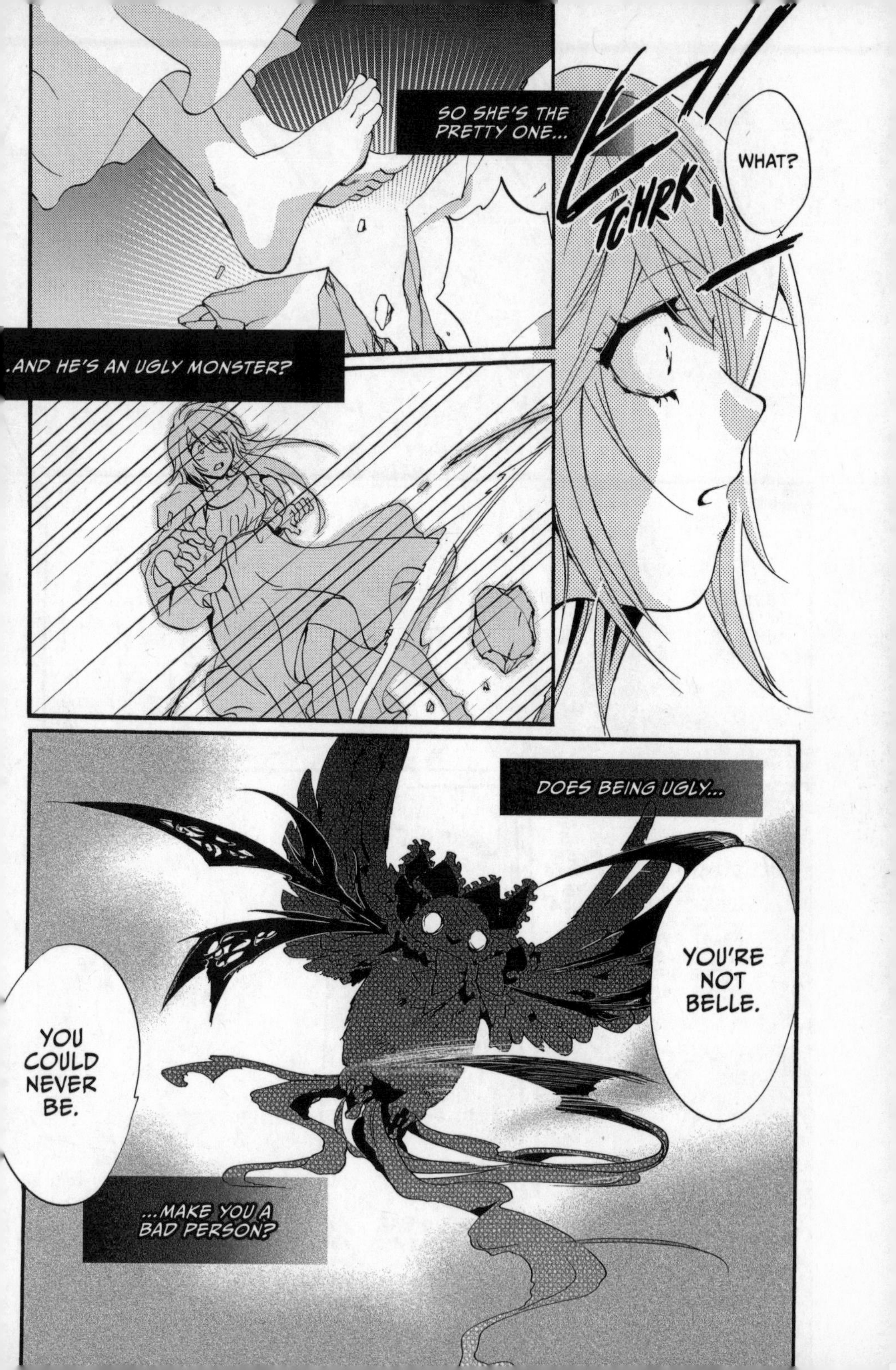
WHAT?
TCHRK
SO SHE'S THE PRETTY ONE...
.AND HE'S AN UGLY MONSTER?
DOES BEING UGLY...
YOU'RE NOT BELLE.
YOU COULD NEVER BE.
...MAKE YOU A BAD PERSON?

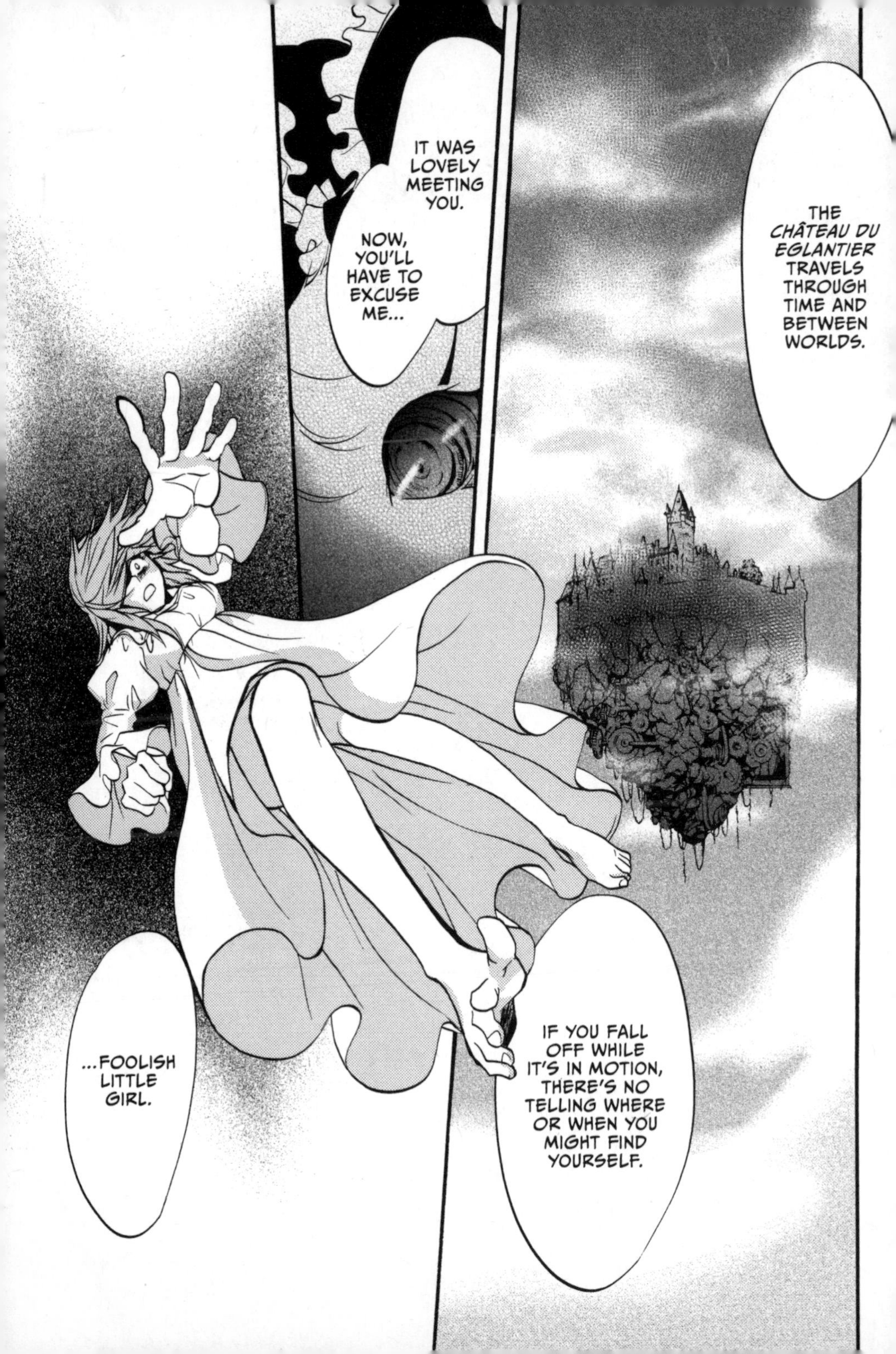
THE CHÂTEAU DU EGLANTIER TRAVELS THROUGH TIME AND BETWEEN WORLDS.
IT WAS LOVELY MEETING YOU.
NOW, YOU'LL HAVE TO EXCUSE ME...
IF YOU FALL OFF WHILE IT'S IN MOTION, THERE'S NO TELLING WHERE OR WHEN YOU MIGHT FIND YOURSELF.
...FOOLISH LITTLE GIRL.

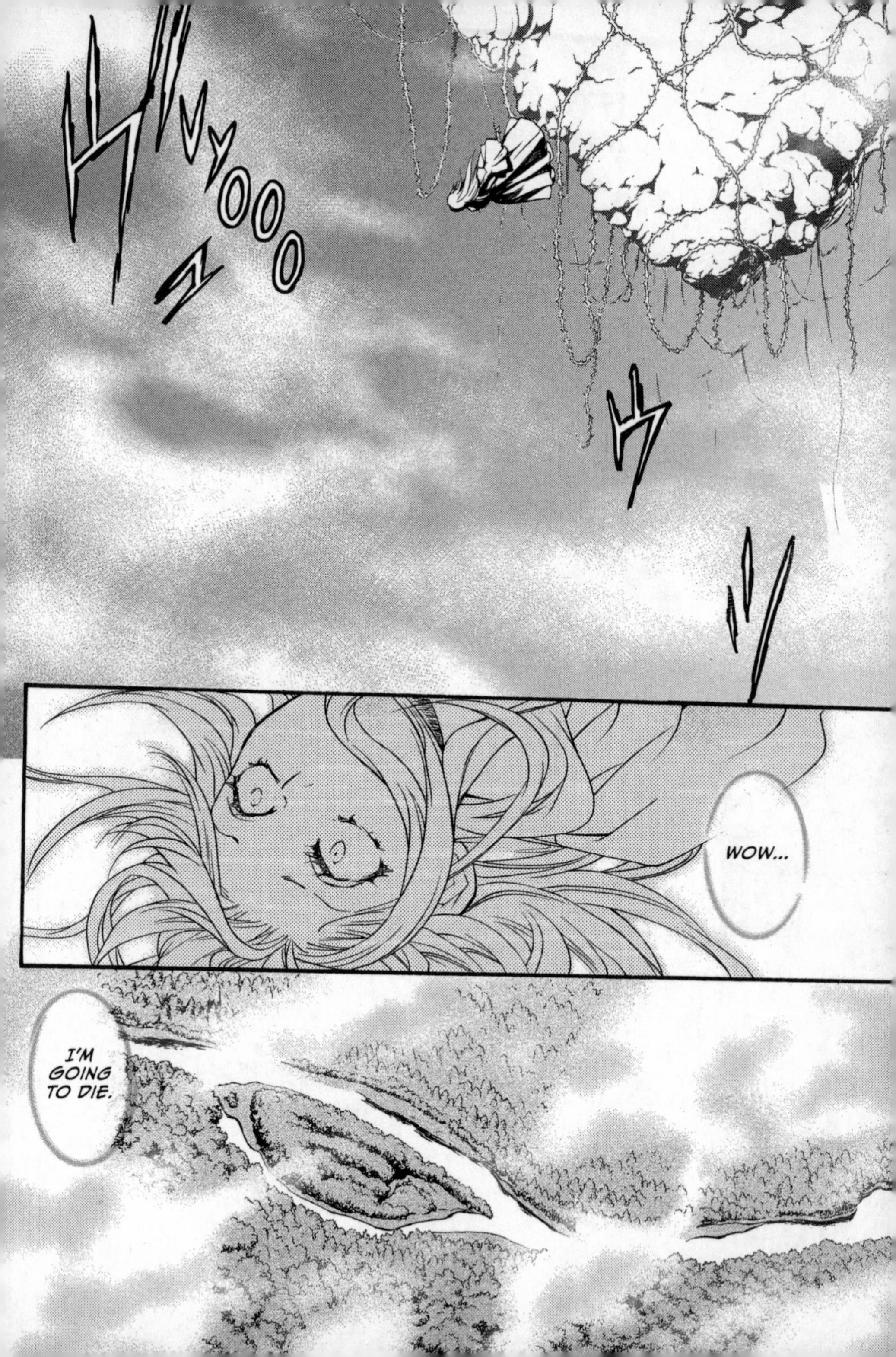
VYOOO
WOW...
I'M GOING TO DIE.

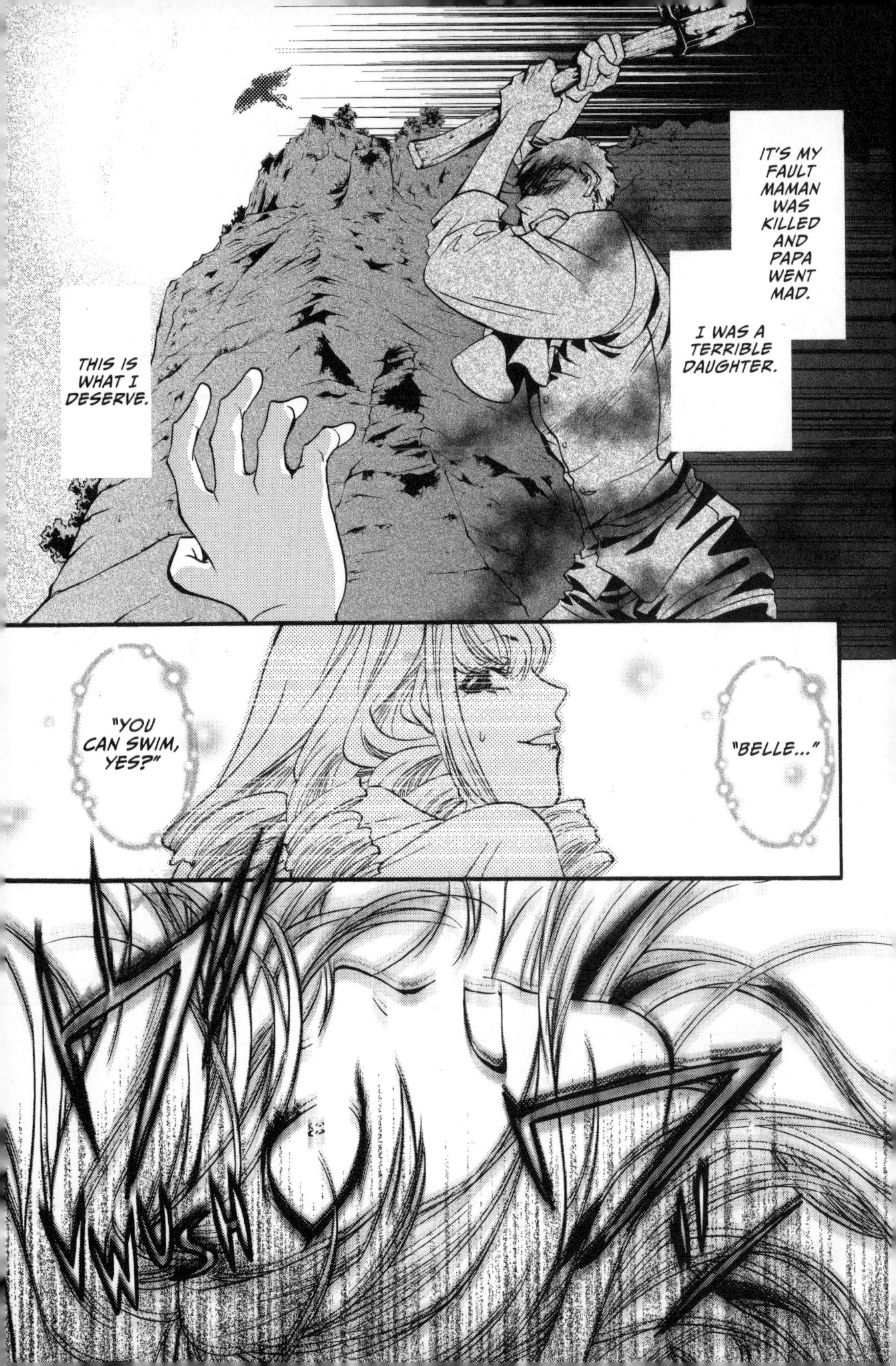
IT'S MY FAULT MAMAN WAS KILLED AND PAPA WENT MAD.
I WAS A TERRIBLE DAUGHTER.
THIS IS WHAT I DESERVE.
"BELLE..."
"YOU CAN SWIM, YES?"

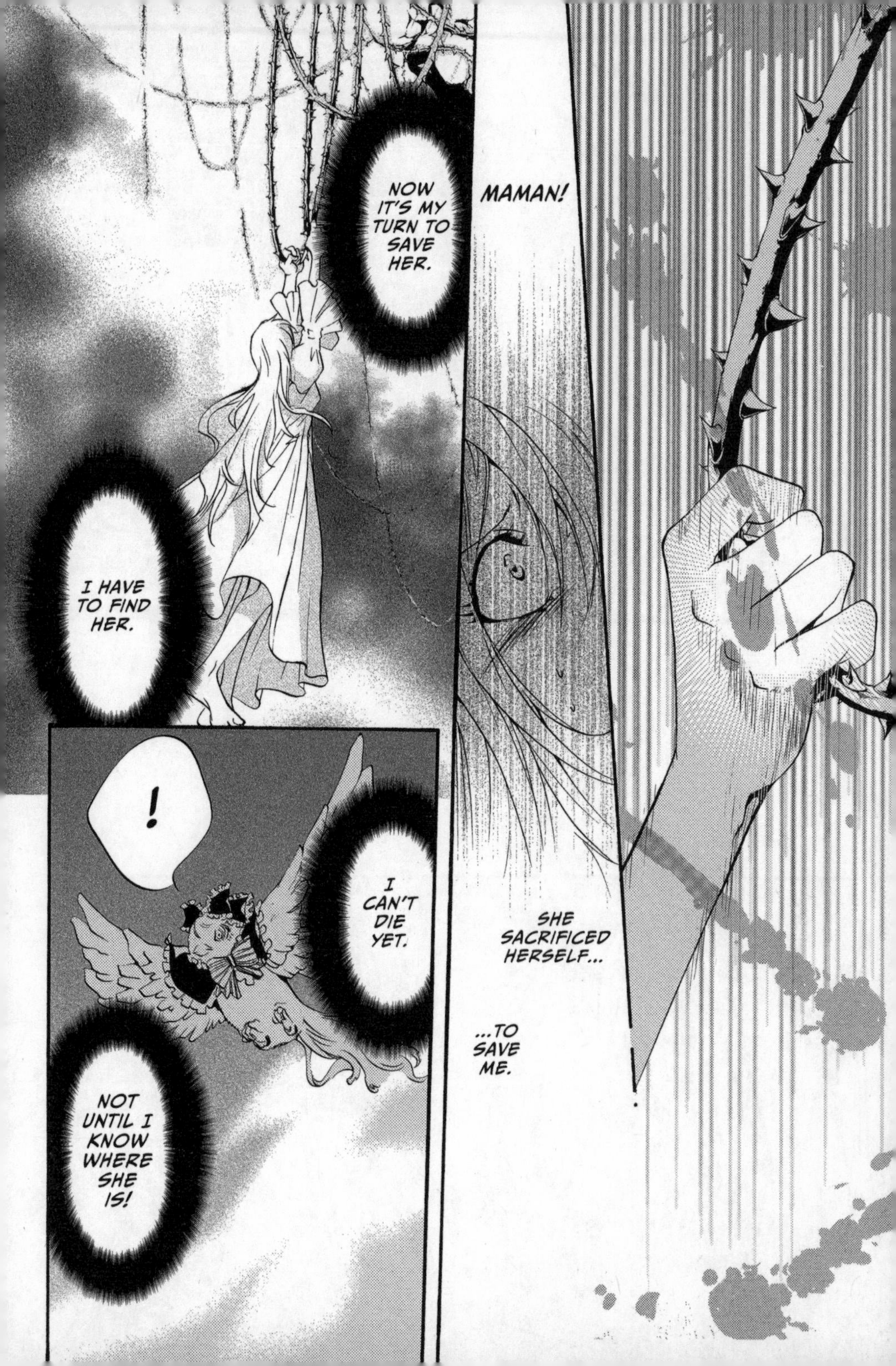
MAMAN!
SHE SACRIFICED HERSELF...
...TO SAVE ME.
NOW IT'S MY TURN TO SAVE HER.
I HAVE TO FIND HER.
!
I CAN'T DIE YET.
NOT UNTIL I KNOW WHERE SHE IS!

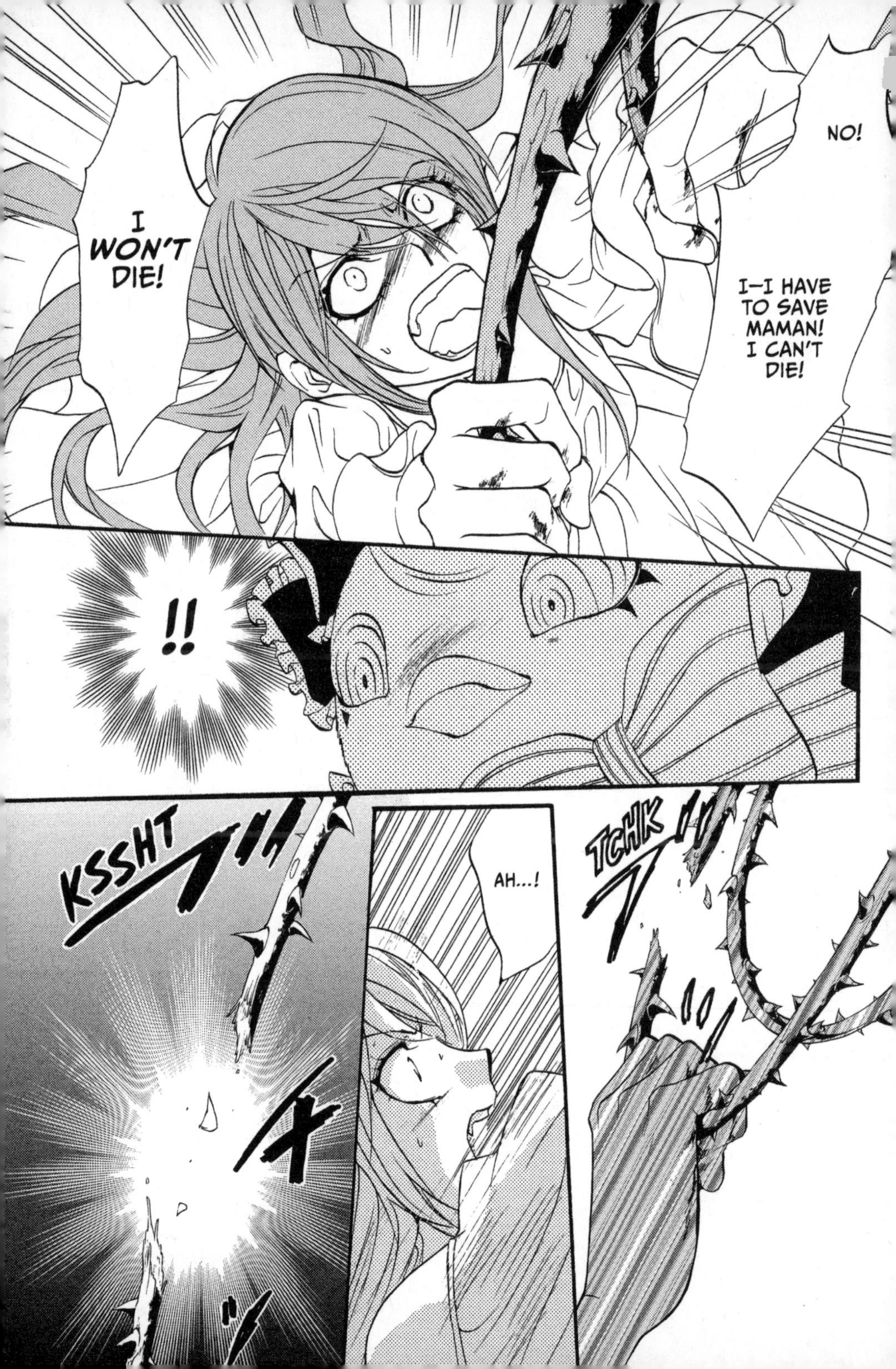
NO!
I—I HAVE TO SAVE MAMAN! I CAN'T DIE!
I WON'T DIE!
!!
TCHK
AH...!
KSSHT

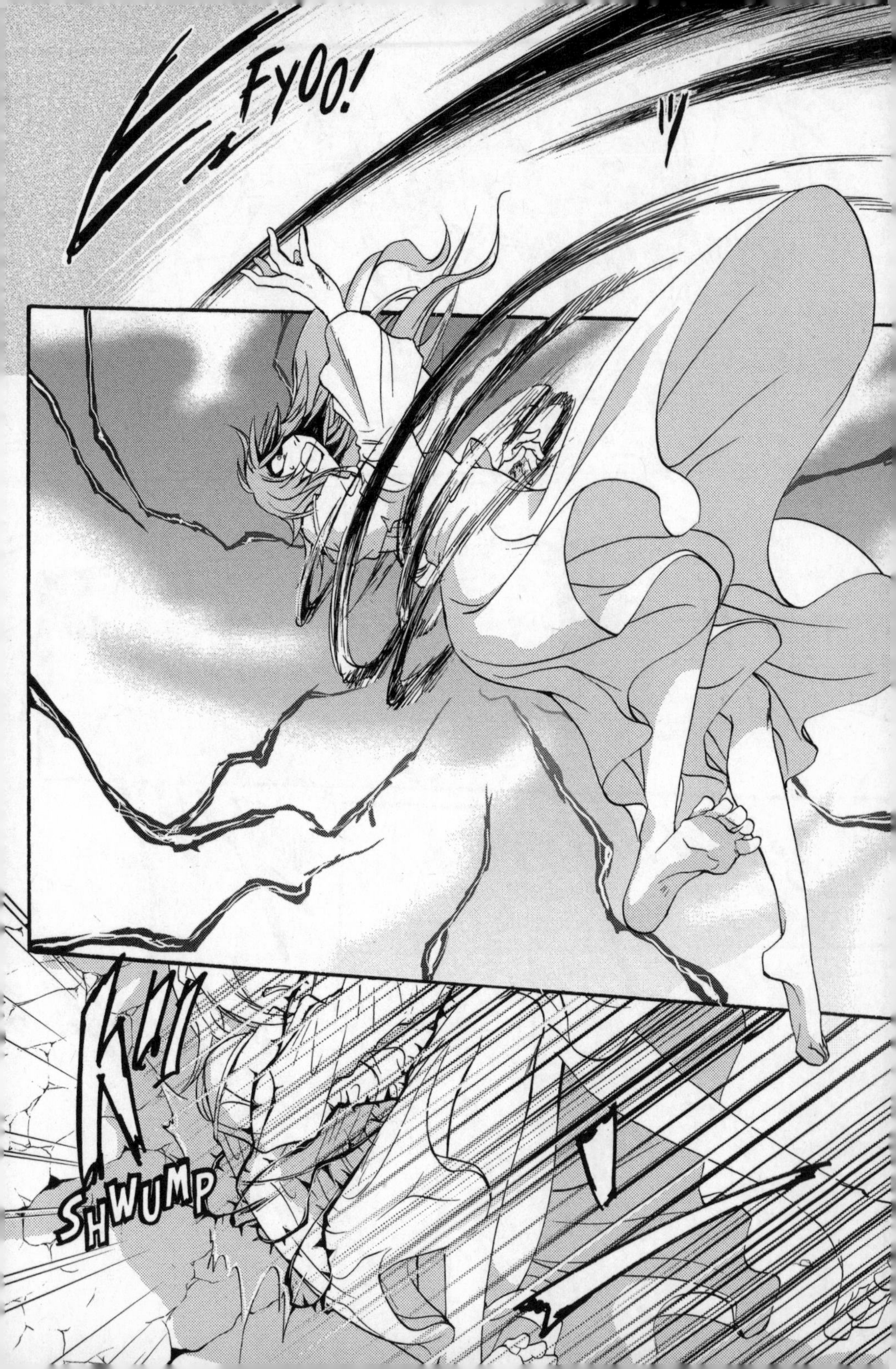
FYOO!
SHWUMP

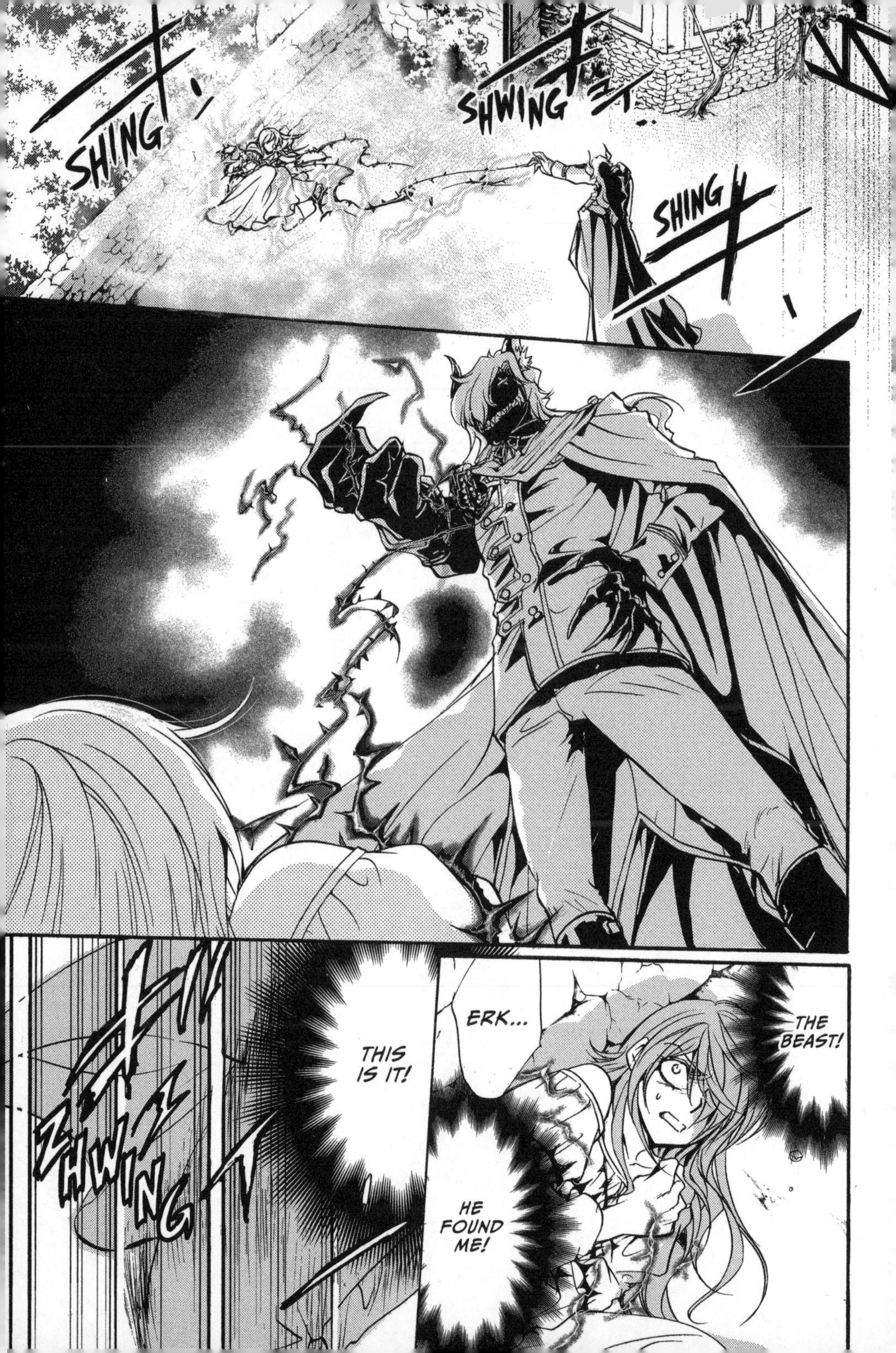
SHWING
SHING
SHING
THE BEAST!
HE FOUND ME!
ERK...
THIS IS IT!
ZHWING

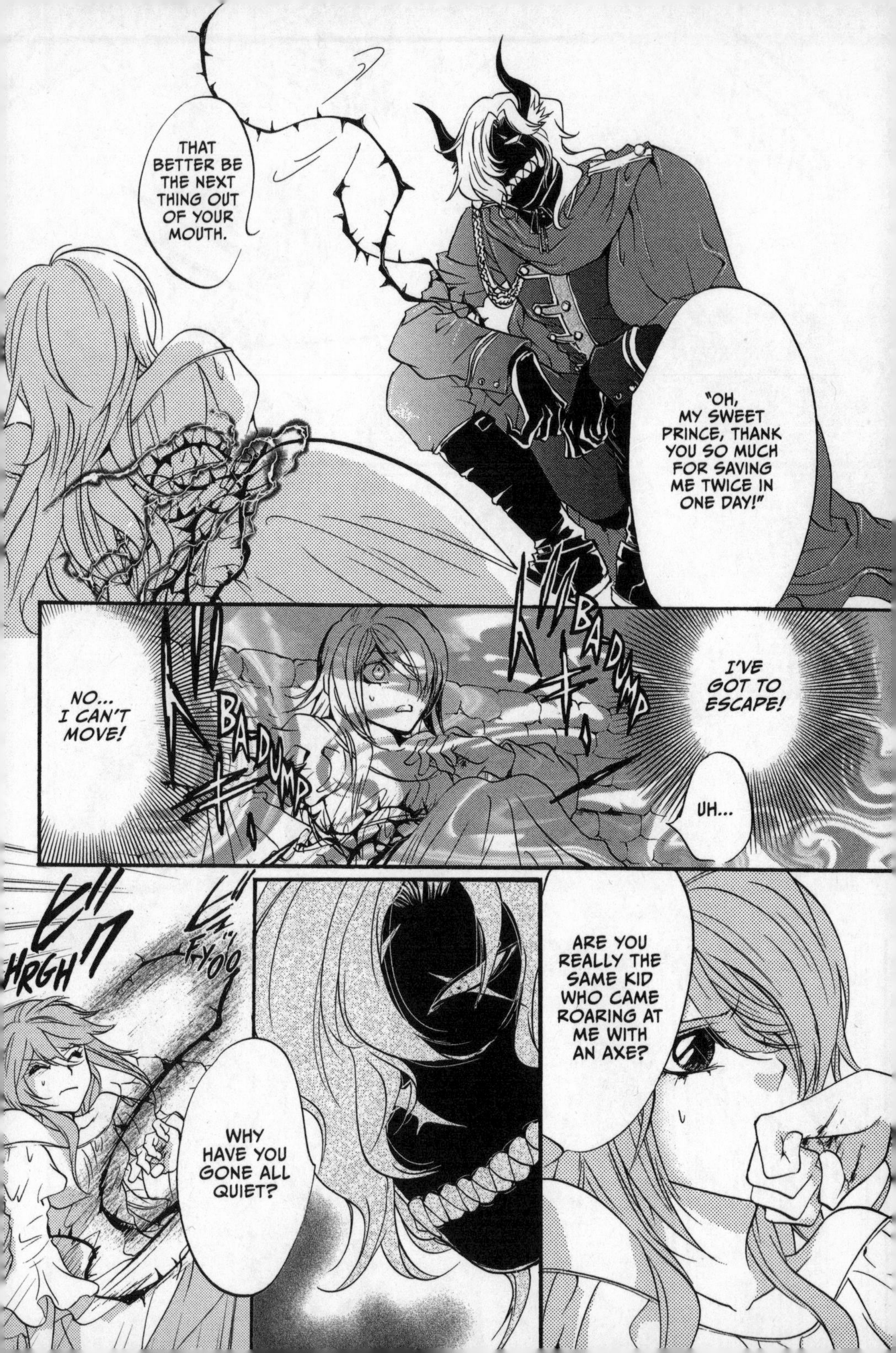
"OH, MY SWEET PRINCE, THANK YOU SO MUCH FOR SAVING ME TWICE IN ONE DAY!"
THAT BETTER BE THE NEXT THING OUT OF YOUR MOUTH.
I'VE GOT TO ESCAPE!
BA-DUMP
UH...
BA-DUMP
NO... I CAN'T MOVE!
ARE YOU REALLY THE SAME KID WHO CAME ROARING AT ME WITH AN AXE?
WHY HAVE YOU GONE ALL QUIET?
FYOO
HRGH

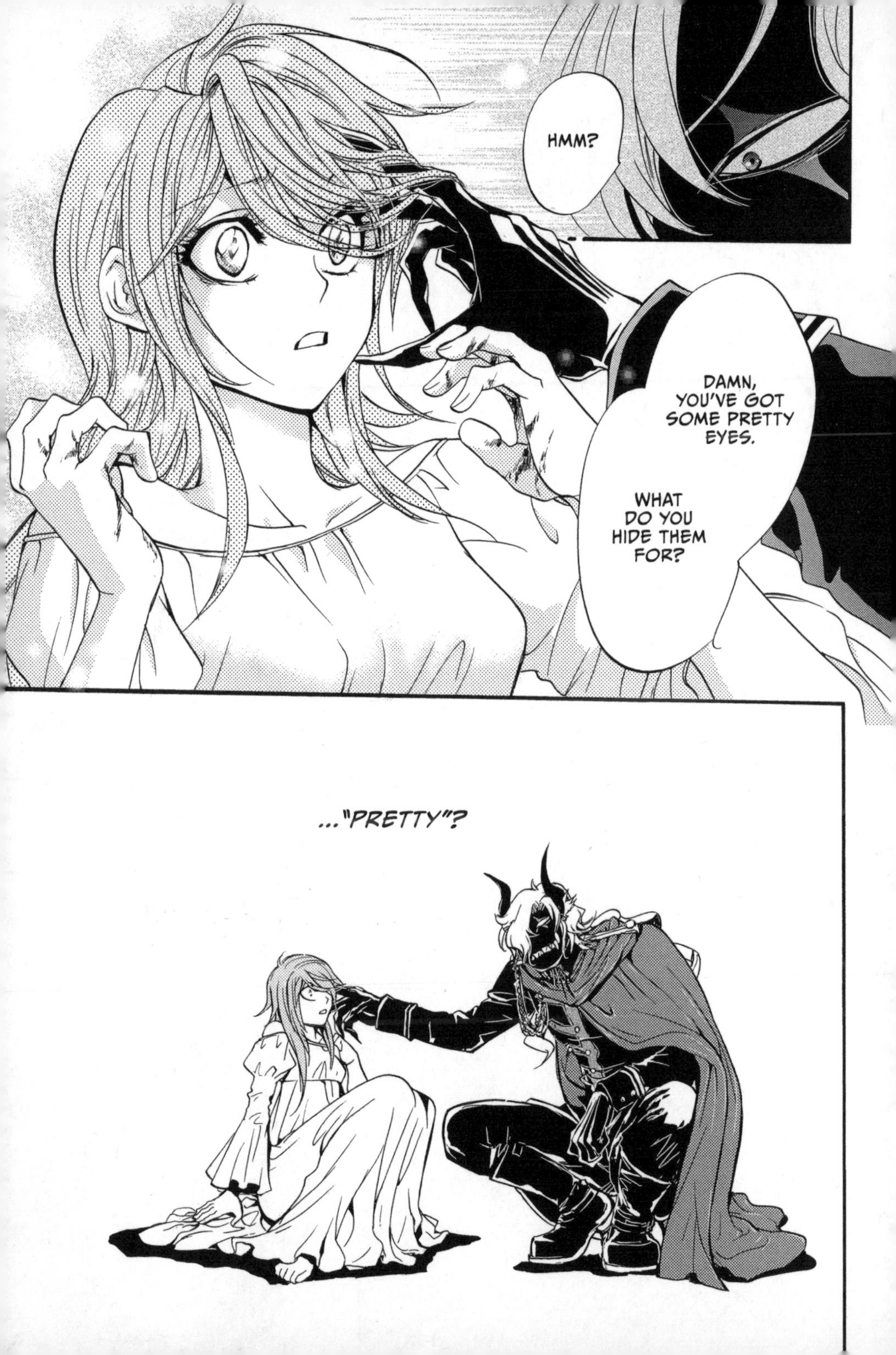
HMM?
DAMN, YOU'VE GOT SOME PRETTY EYES.
WHAT DO YOU HIDE THEM FOR?
..."PRETTY"?

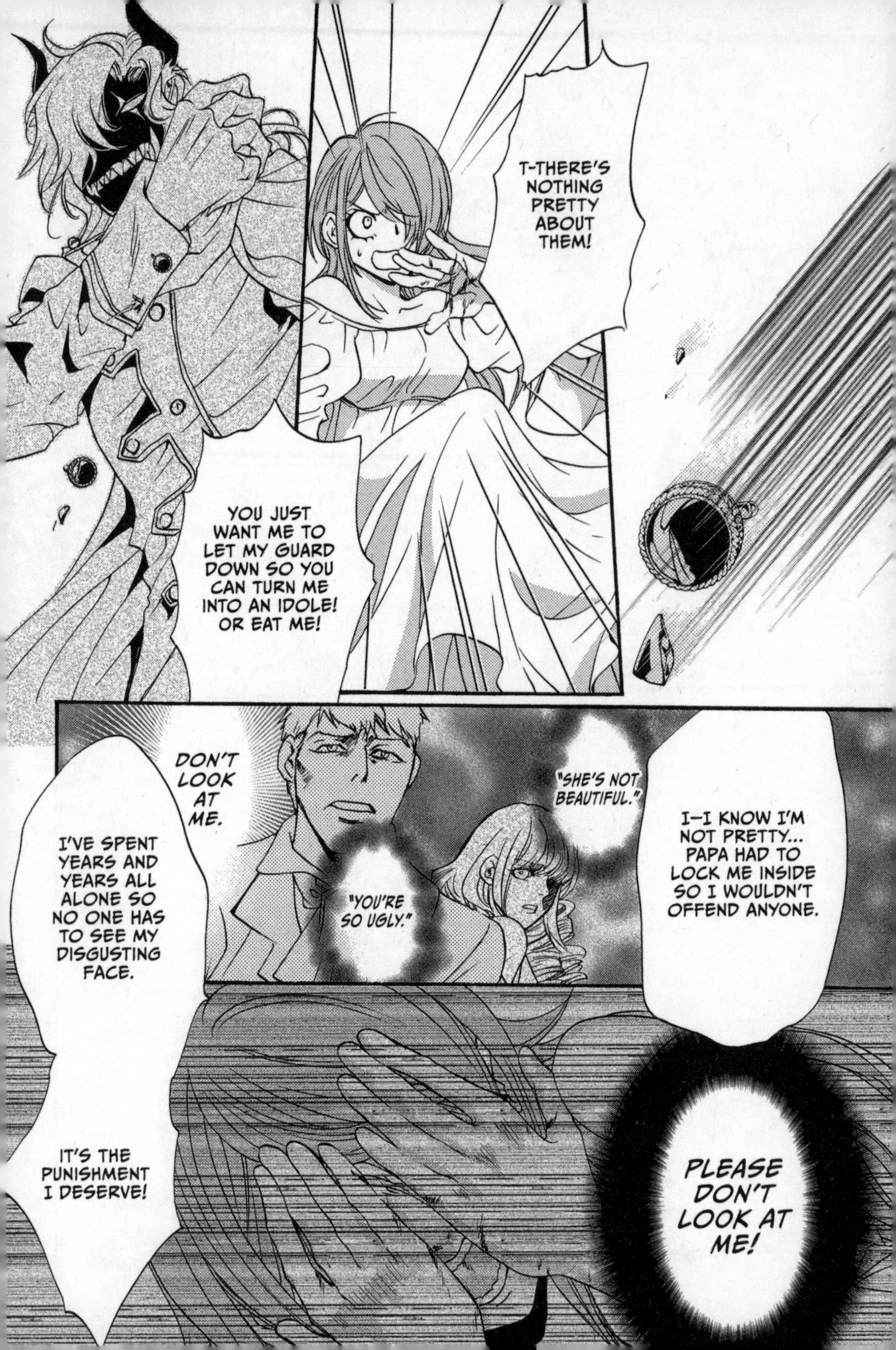
T-THERE'S NOTHING PRETTY ABOUT THEM!
YOU JUST WANT ME TO LET MY GUARD DOWN SO YOU CAN TURN ME INTO AN IDOLE! OR EAT ME!
I—I KNOW I'M NOT PRETTY... PAPA HAD TO LOCK ME INSIDE SO I WOULDN'T OFFEND ANYONE.
"SHE'S NOT BEAUTIFUL."
"YOU'RE SO UGLY."
DON'T LOOK AT ME.
I'VE SPENT YEARS AND YEARS ALL ALONE SO NO ONE HAS TO SEE MY DISGUSTING FACE.
PLEASE DON'T LOOK AT ME!
IT'S THE PUNISHMENT I DESERVE!

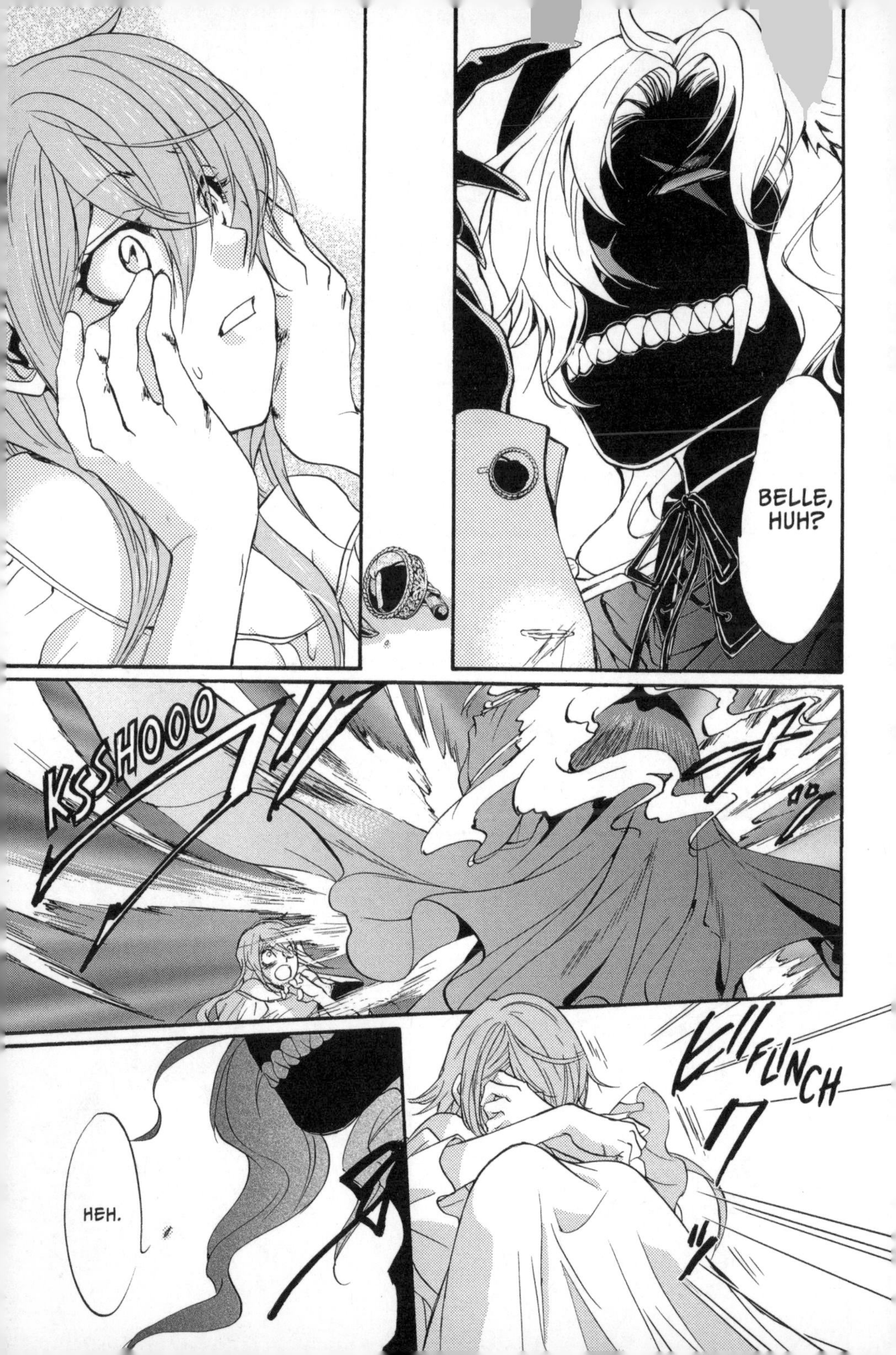
BELLE, HUH?
KSSHOOO
FLINCH
HEH.

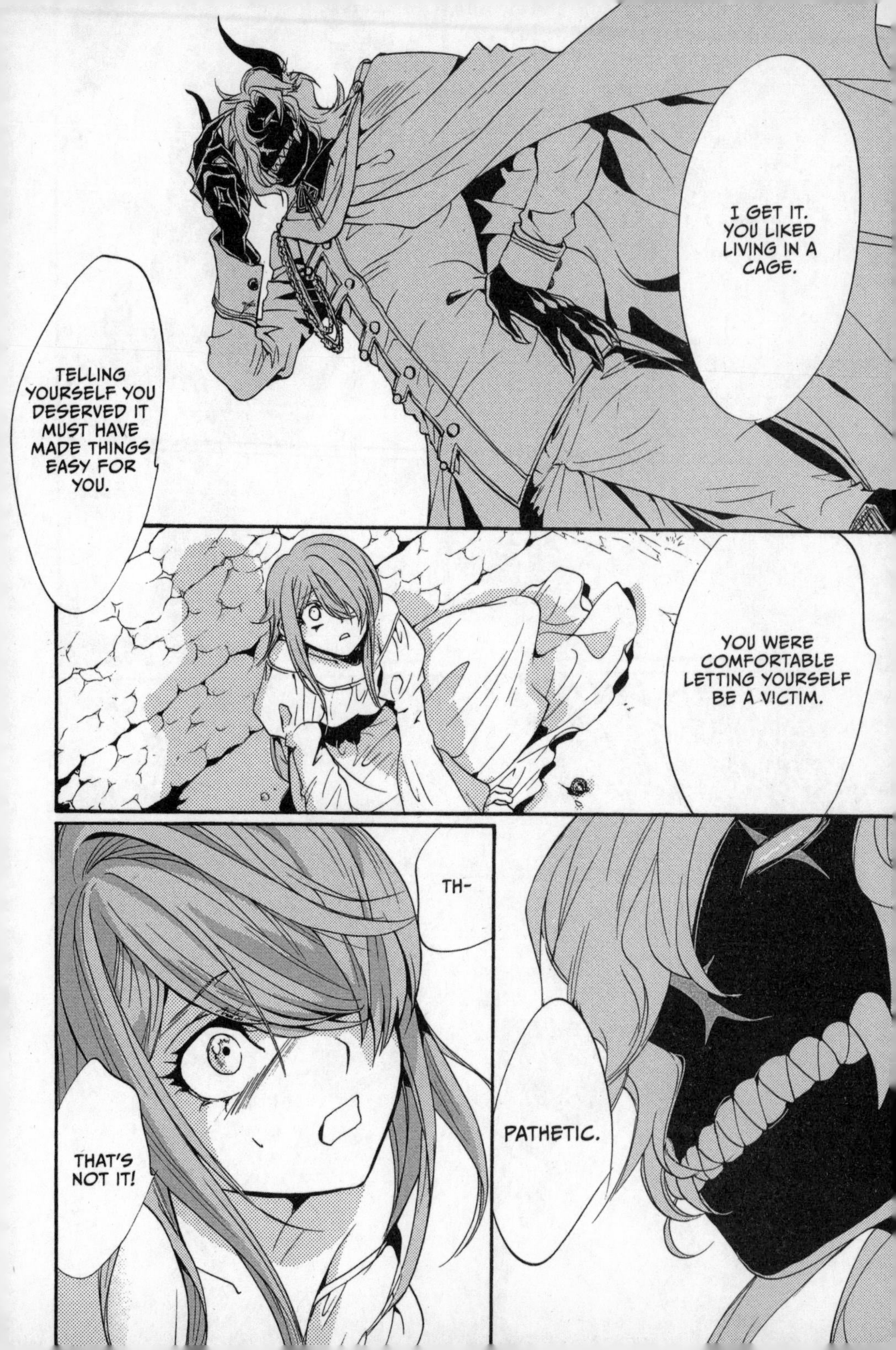
I GET IT. YOU LIKED LIVING IN A CAGE.
TELLING YOURSELF YOU DESERVED IT MUST HAVE MADE THINGS EASY FOR YOU.
YOU WERE COMFORTABLE LETTING YOURSELF BE A VICTIM.
PATHETIC.
TH-
THAT'S NOT IT!

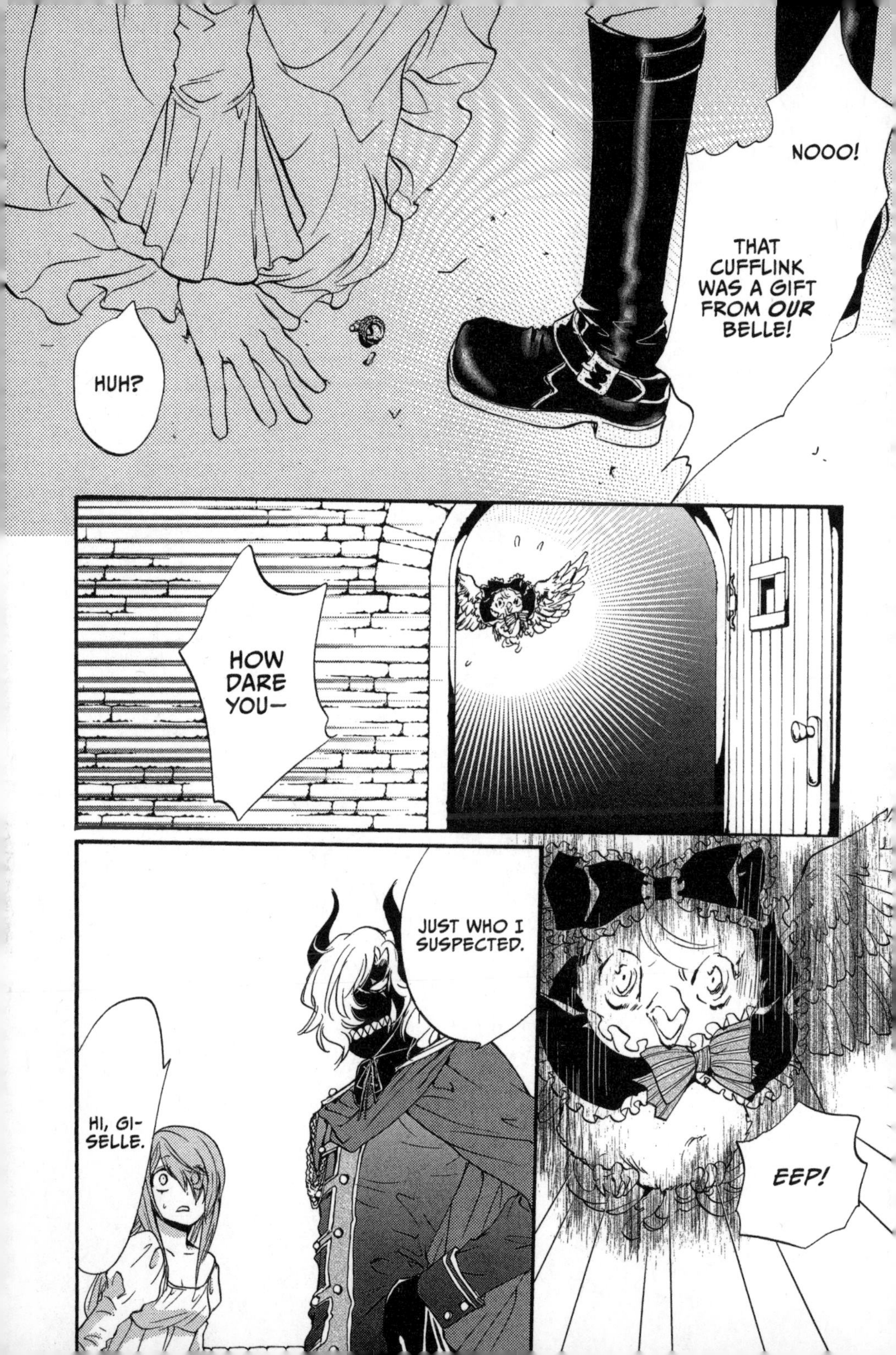
NOOO!
THAT CUFFLINK WAS A GIFT FROM *OUR* BELLE!
HUH?
HOW DARE YOU—
EEP!
JUST WHO I SUSPECTED.
HI, GI-SELLE.

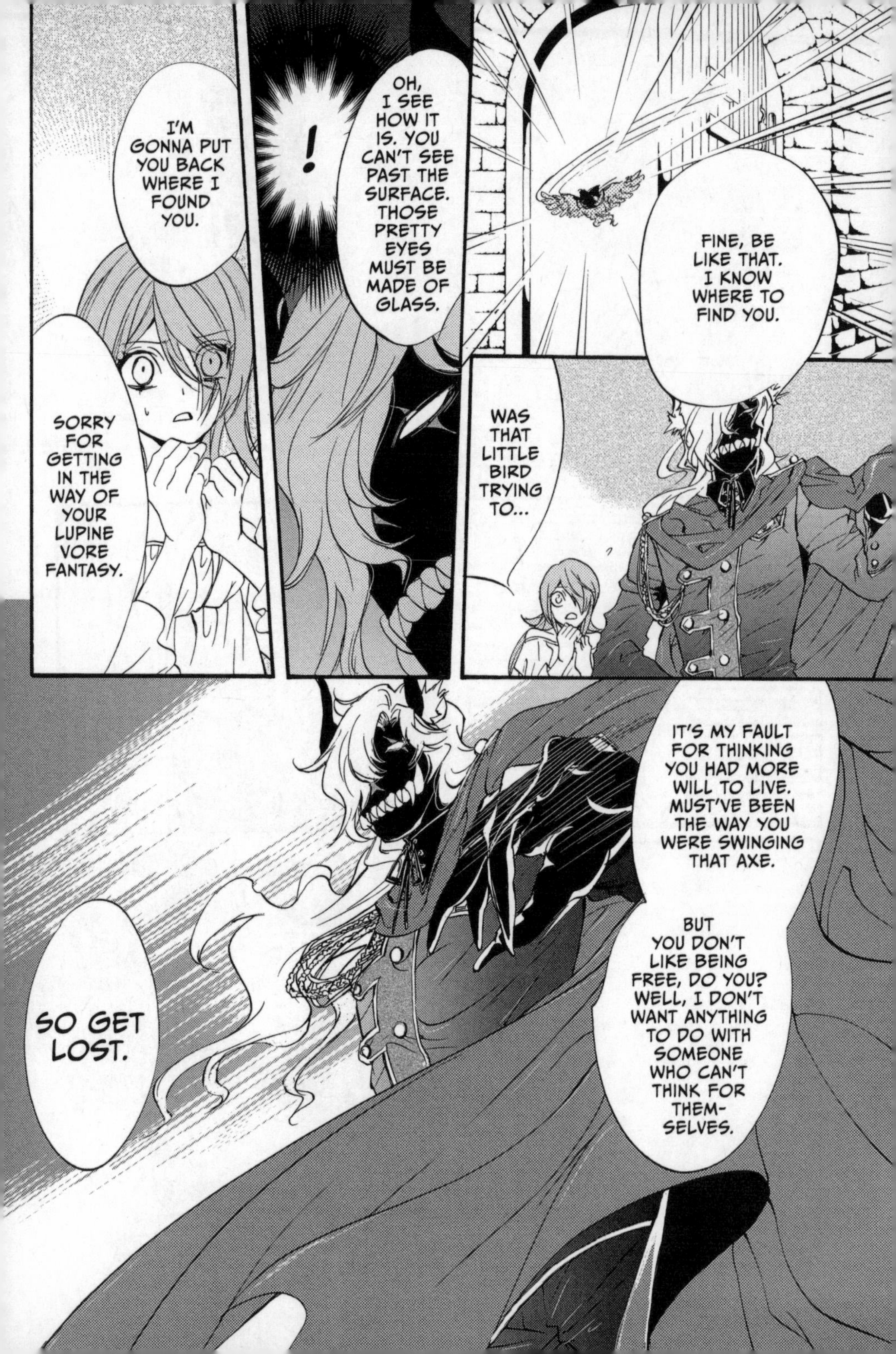
FINE, BE LIKE THAT. I KNOW WHERE TO FIND YOU.
WAS THAT LITTLE BIRD TRYING TO...
OH, I SEE HOW IT IS. YOU CAN'T SEE PAST THE SURFACE. THOSE PRETTY EYES MUST BE MADE OF GLASS.
!
I'M GONNA PUT YOU BACK WHERE I FOUND YOU.
SORRY FOR GETTING IN THE WAY OF YOUR LUPINE VORE FANTASY.
IT'S MY FAULT FOR THINKING YOU HAD MORE WILL TO LIVE. MUST'VE BEEN THE WAY YOU WERE SWINGING THAT AXE.
BUT YOU DON'T LIKE BEING FREE, DO YOU? WELL, I DON'T WANT ANYTHING TO DO WITH SOMEONE WHO CAN'T THINK FOR THEM-SELVES.
SO GET LOST.

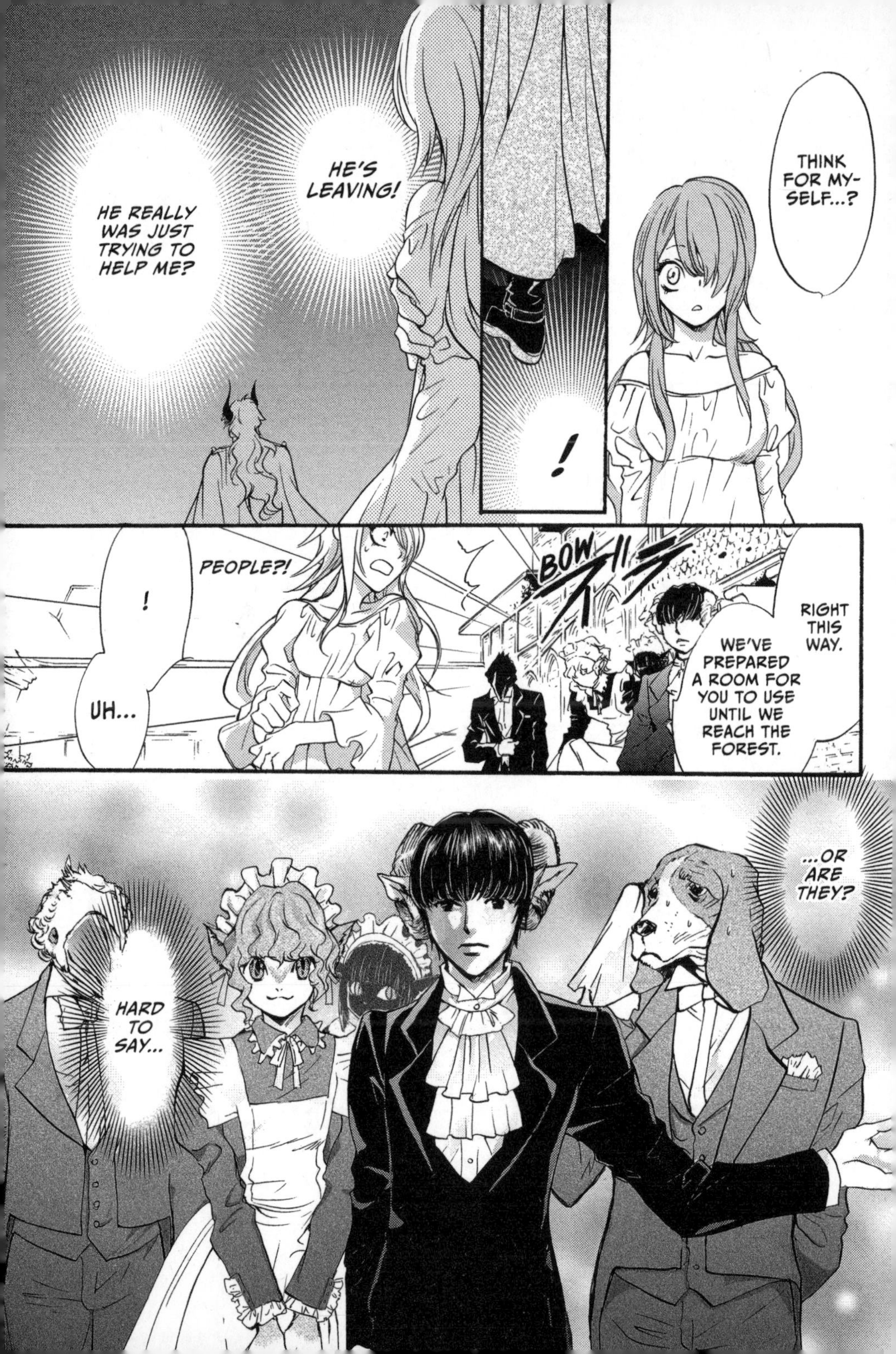
THINK FOR MY-SELF...?
!
HE'S LEAVING!
HE REALLY WAS JUST TRYING TO HELP ME?
RIGHT THIS WAY.
WE'VE PREPARED A ROOM FOR YOU TO USE UNTIL WE REACH THE FOREST.
BOW
!
PEOPLE?!
UH...
...OR ARE THEY?
HARD TO SAY...

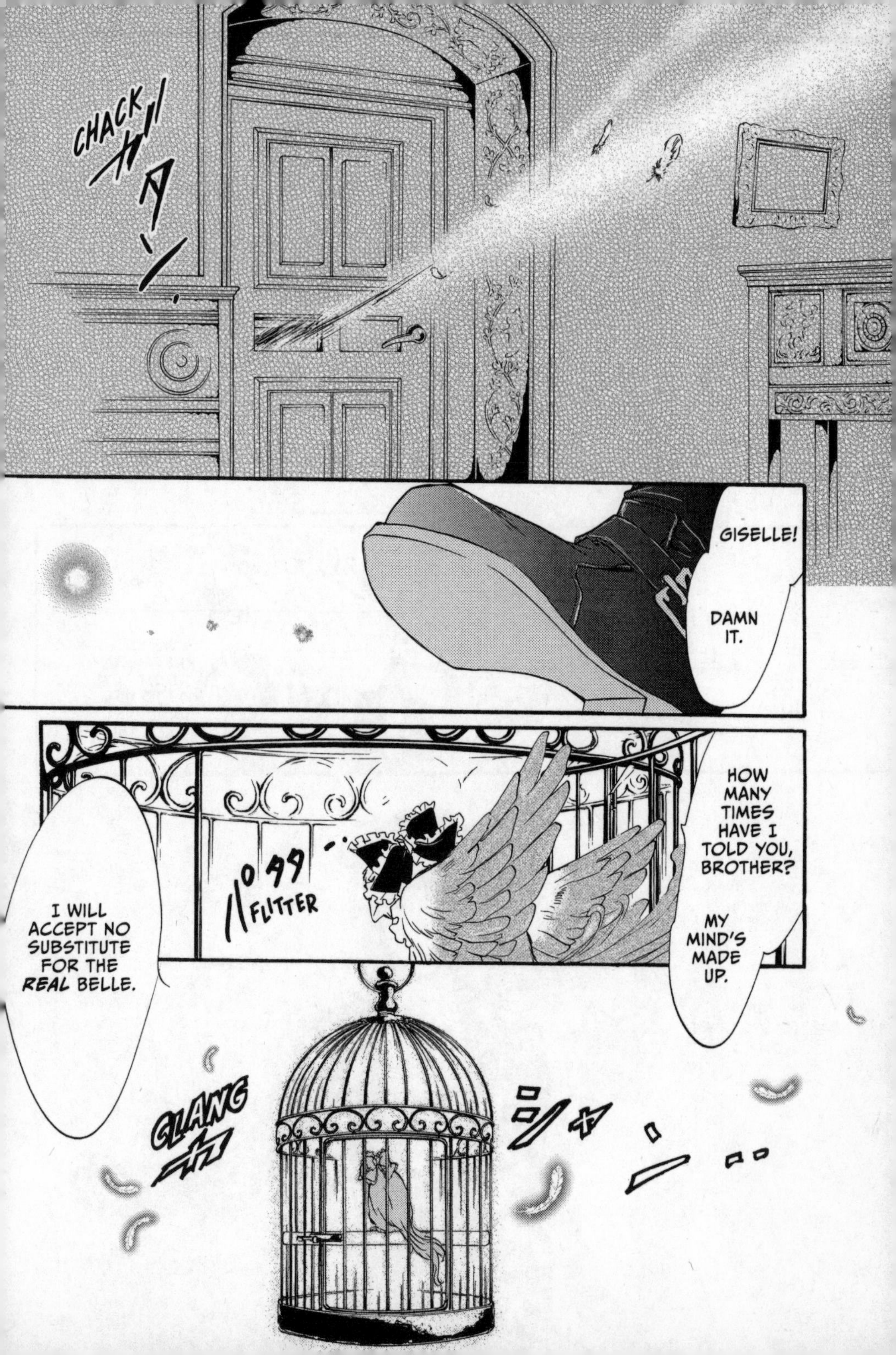
CHACK
GISELLE!
DAMN IT.
HOW MANY TIMES HAVE I TOLD YOU, BROTHER?
MY MIND'S MADE UP.
FLITTER
I WILL ACCEPT NO SUBSTITUTE FOR THE REAL BELLE.
CLANG

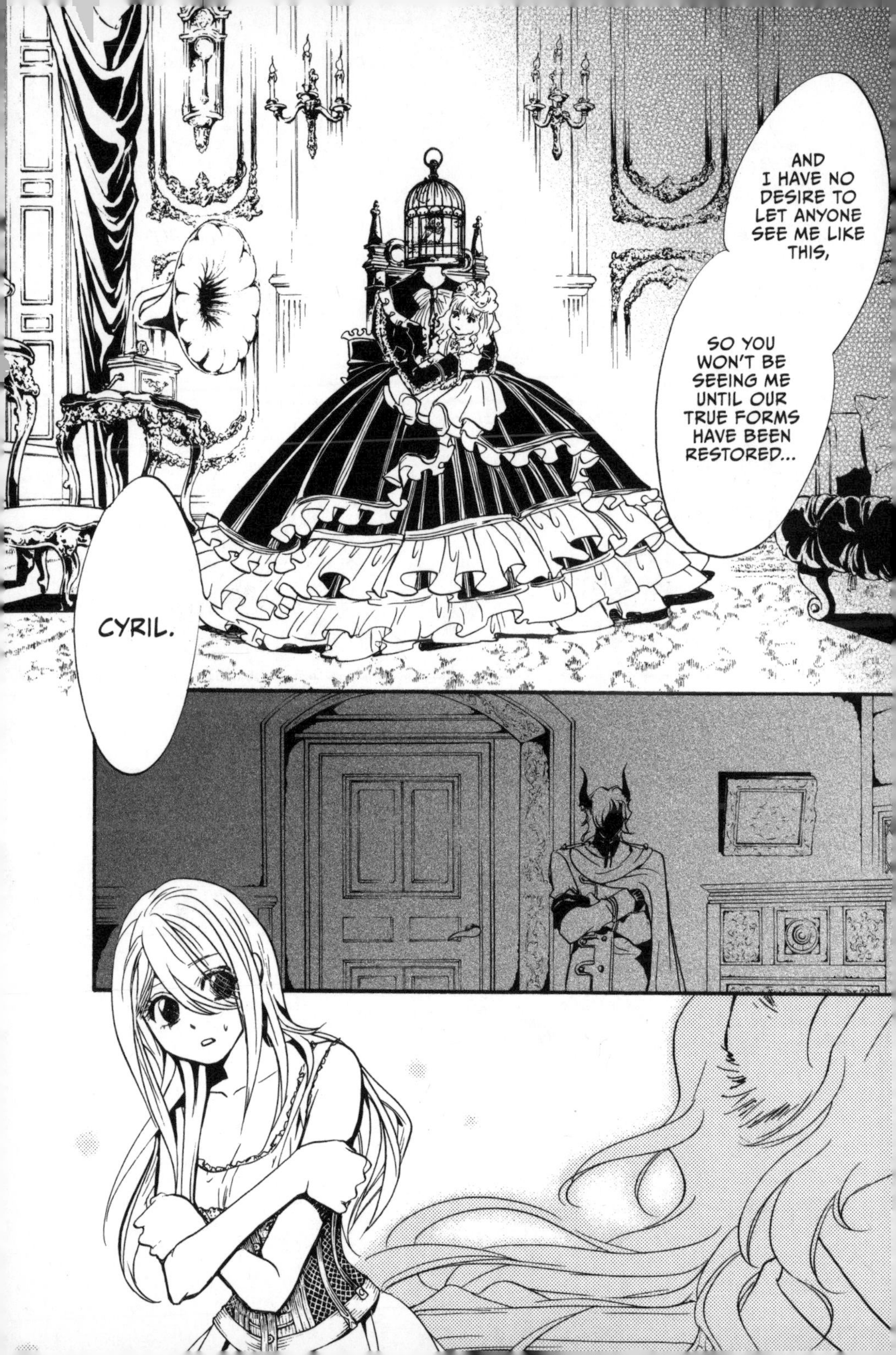
AND I HAVE NO DESIRE TO LET ANYONE SEE ME LIKE THIS,
SO YOU WON'T BE SEEING ME UNTIL OUR TRUE FORMS HAVE BEEN RESTORED...
CYRIL.

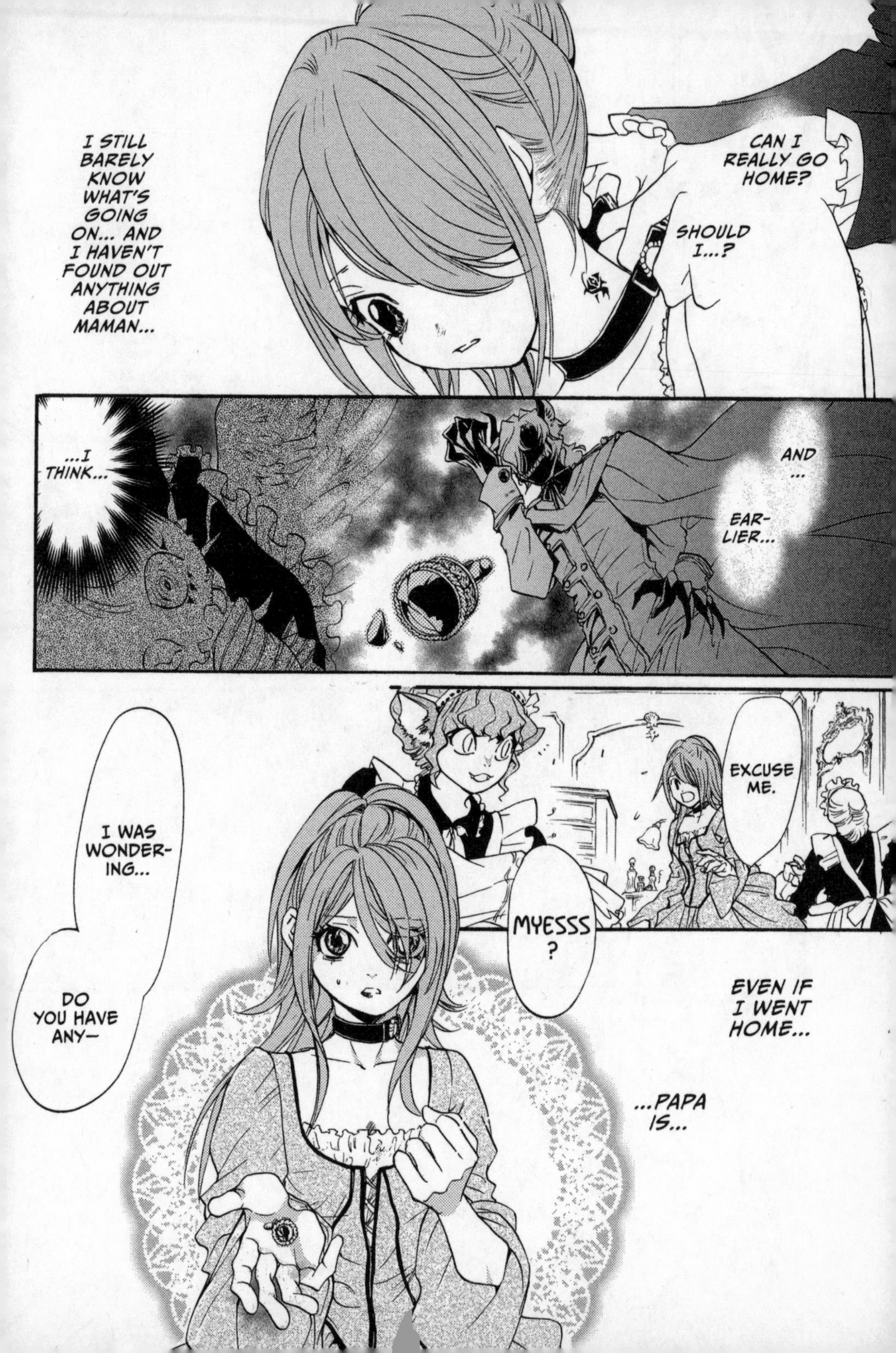
CAN I REALLY GO HOME?
SHOULD I...?
I STILL BARELY KNOW WHAT'S GOING ON... AND I HAVEN'T FOUND OUT ANYTHING ABOUT MAMAN...
AND ...
EAR-LIER...
...I THINK...
EXCUSE ME.
MYESSS ?
EVEN IF I WENT HOME...
...PAPA IS...
I WAS WONDER-ING...
DO YOU HAVE ANY—

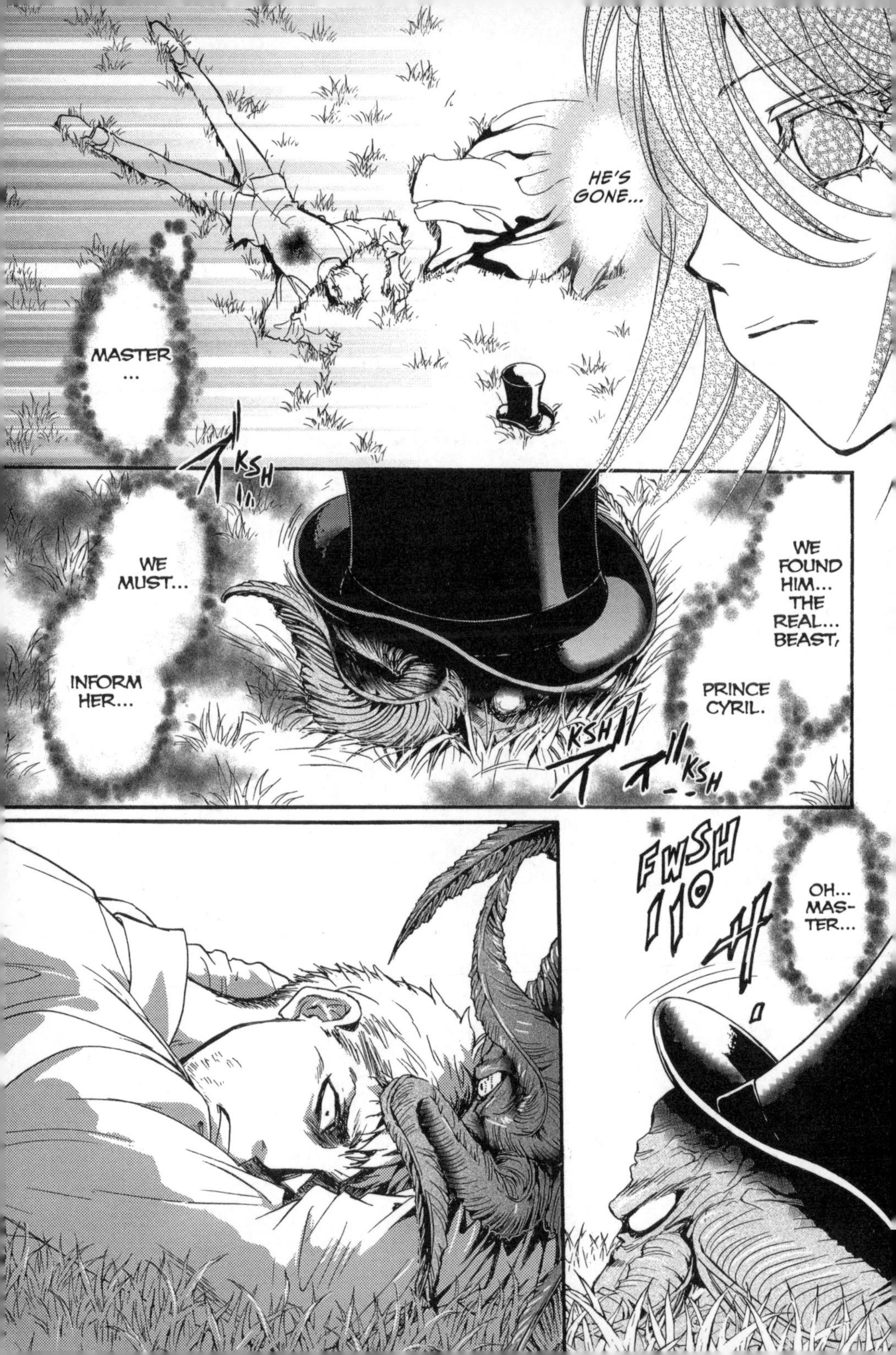
HE'S GONE...
MASTER ...
KSH
WE FOUND HIM... THE REAL... BEAST,
PRINCE CYRIL.
KSH
KSH
WE MUST...
INFORM HER...
OH... MAS-TER...
FWSH

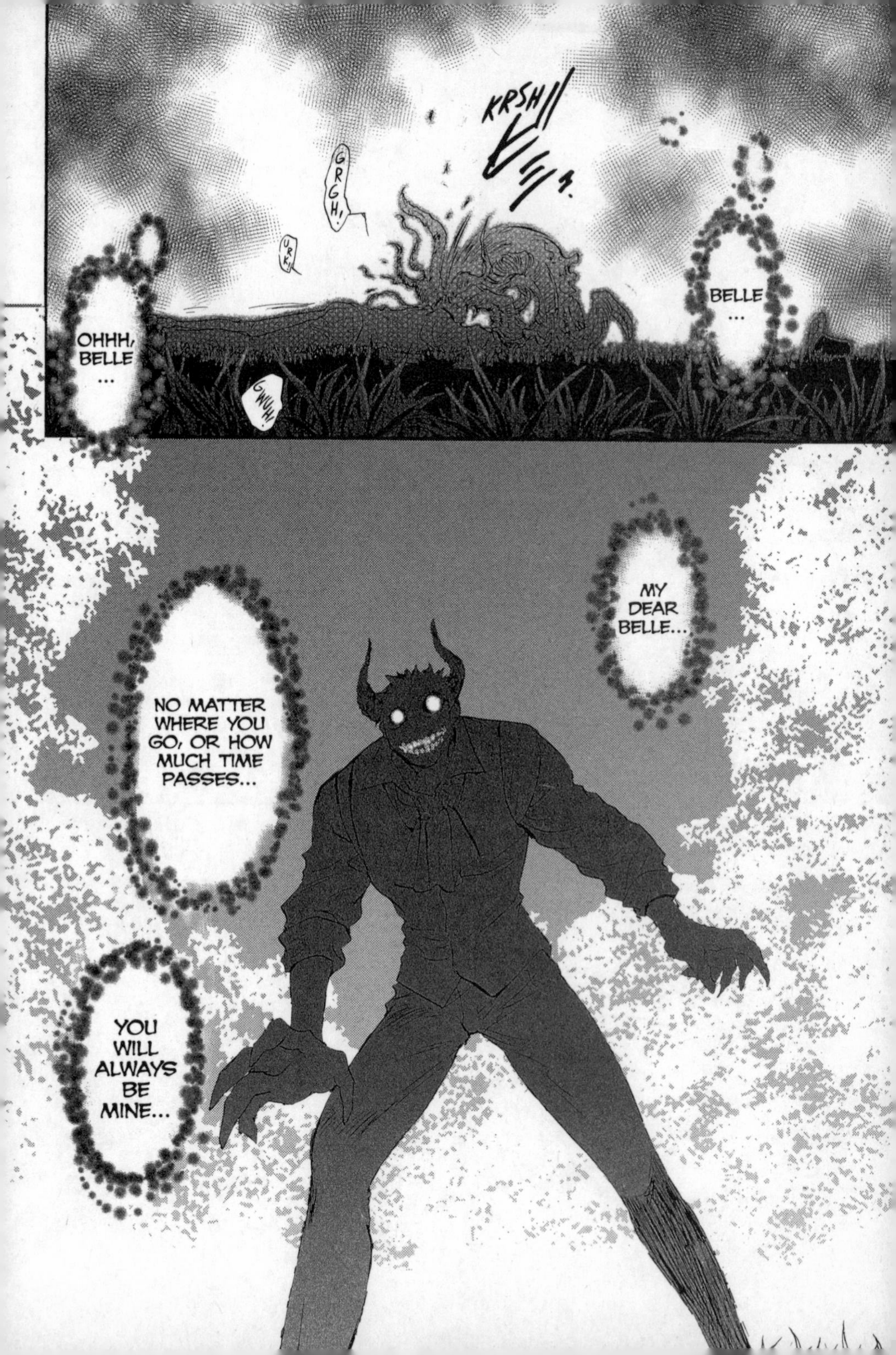
BELLE ...
KRSH
GRGH!
URK!
OHHH, BELLE ...
GWUH!
MY DEAR BELLE...
NO MATTER WHERE YOU GO, OR HOW MUCH TIME PASSES...
YOU WILL ALWAYS BE MINE...

LA BELLE ET LA BÊTE
DU PARADIS PERDU

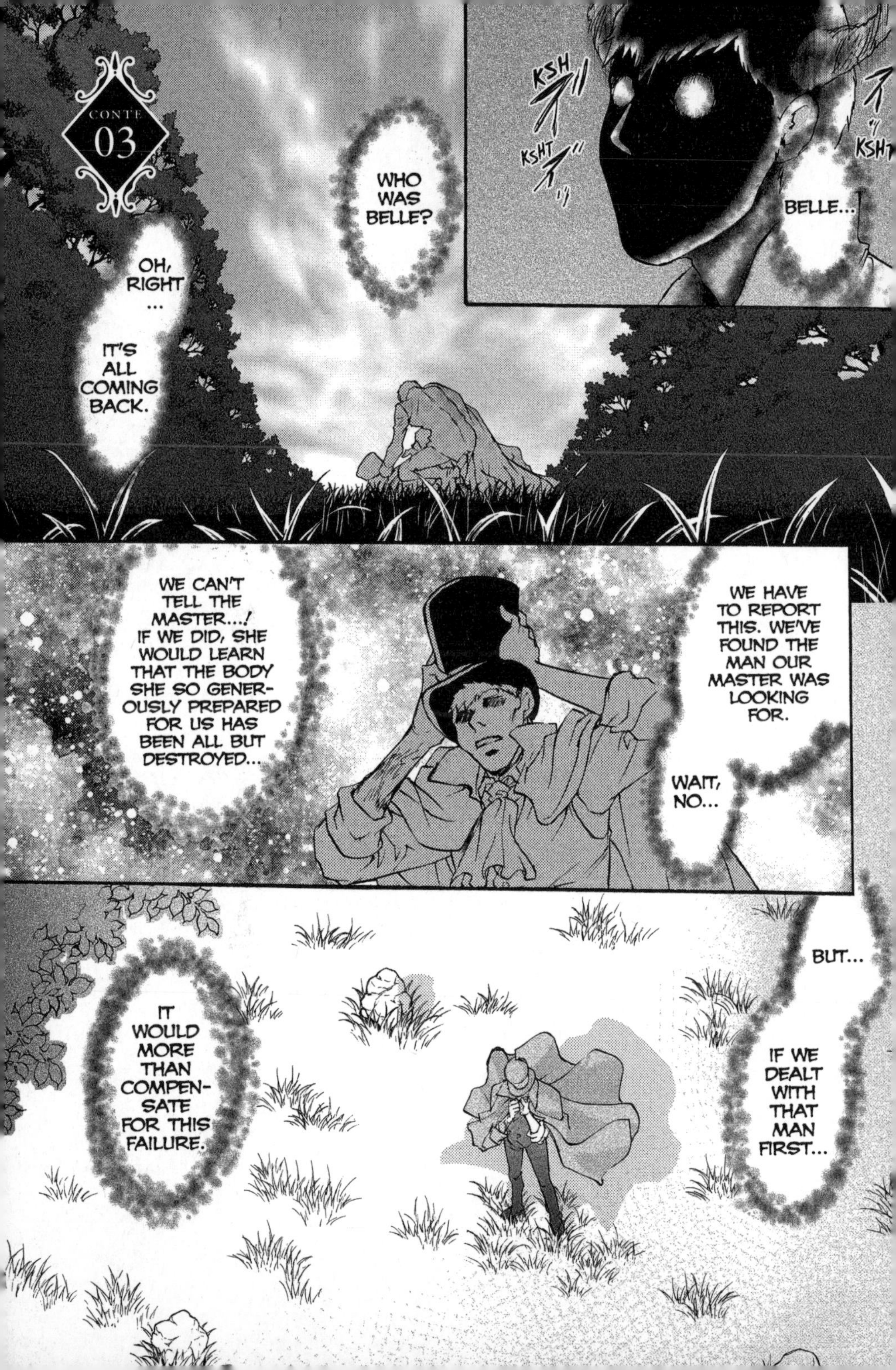
KSH
KSHT
KSHT
BELLE...
CONTE 03
WHO WAS BELLE?
OH, RIGHT ...
IT'S ALL COMING BACK.
WE HAVE TO REPORT THIS. WE'VE FOUND THE MAN OUR MASTER WAS LOOKING FOR.
WAIT, NO...
WE CAN'T TELL THE MASTER...! IF WE DID, SHE WOULD LEARN THAT THE BODY SHE SO GENER-OUSLY PREPARED FOR US HAS BEEN ALL BUT DESTROYED...
BUT...
IF WE DEALT WITH THAT MAN FIRST...
IT WOULD MORE THAN COMPEN-SATE FOR THIS FAILURE.

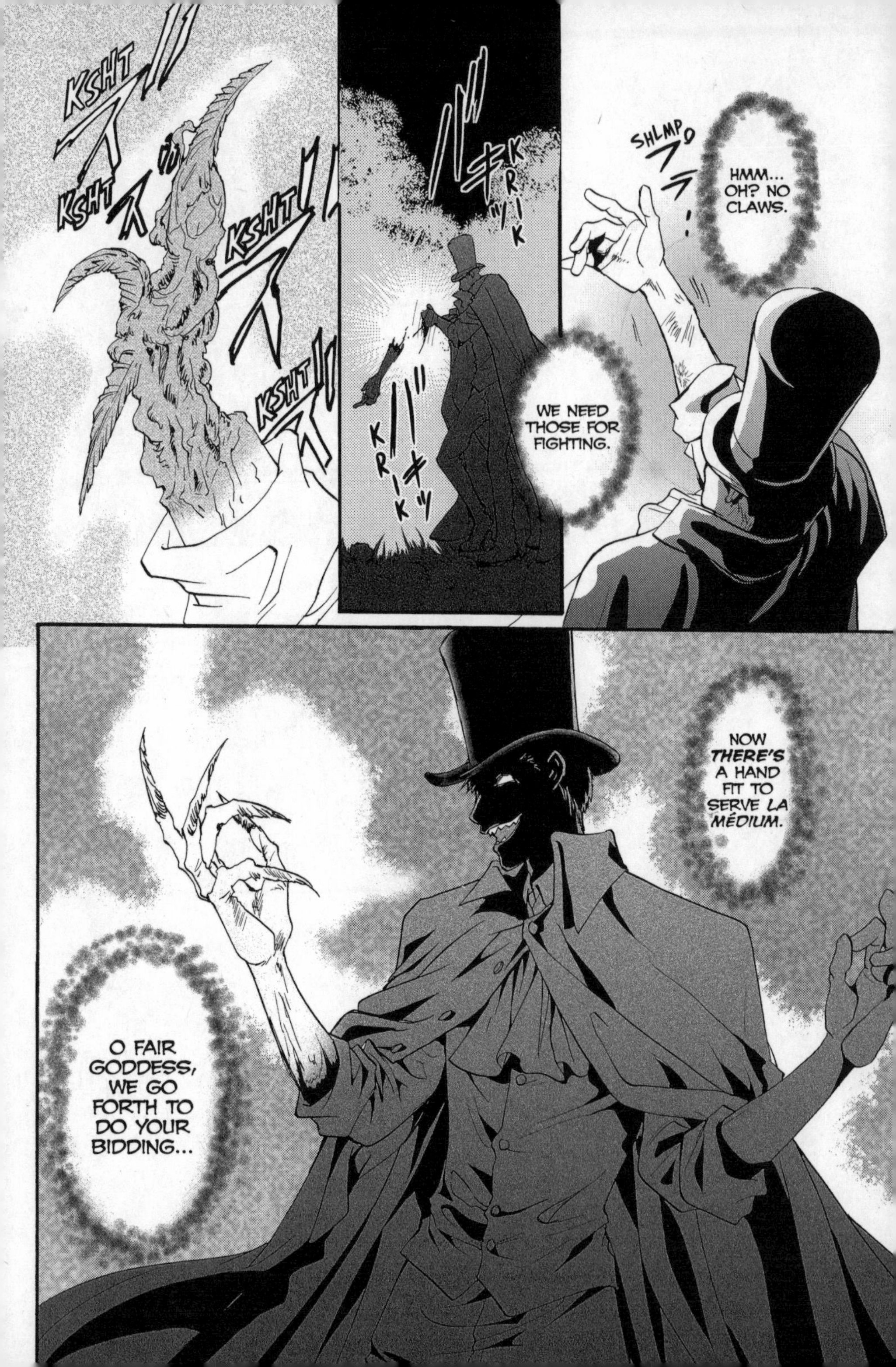
SHLMP
HMM... OH? NO CLAWS.
KRIK
WE NEED THOSE FOR FIGHTING.
KRIK
KSHT
KSHT
KSHT
KSHT
NOW *THERE'S* A HAND FIT TO SERVE *LA MÉDIUM.*
O FAIR GODDESS, WE GO FORTH TO DO YOUR BIDDING...

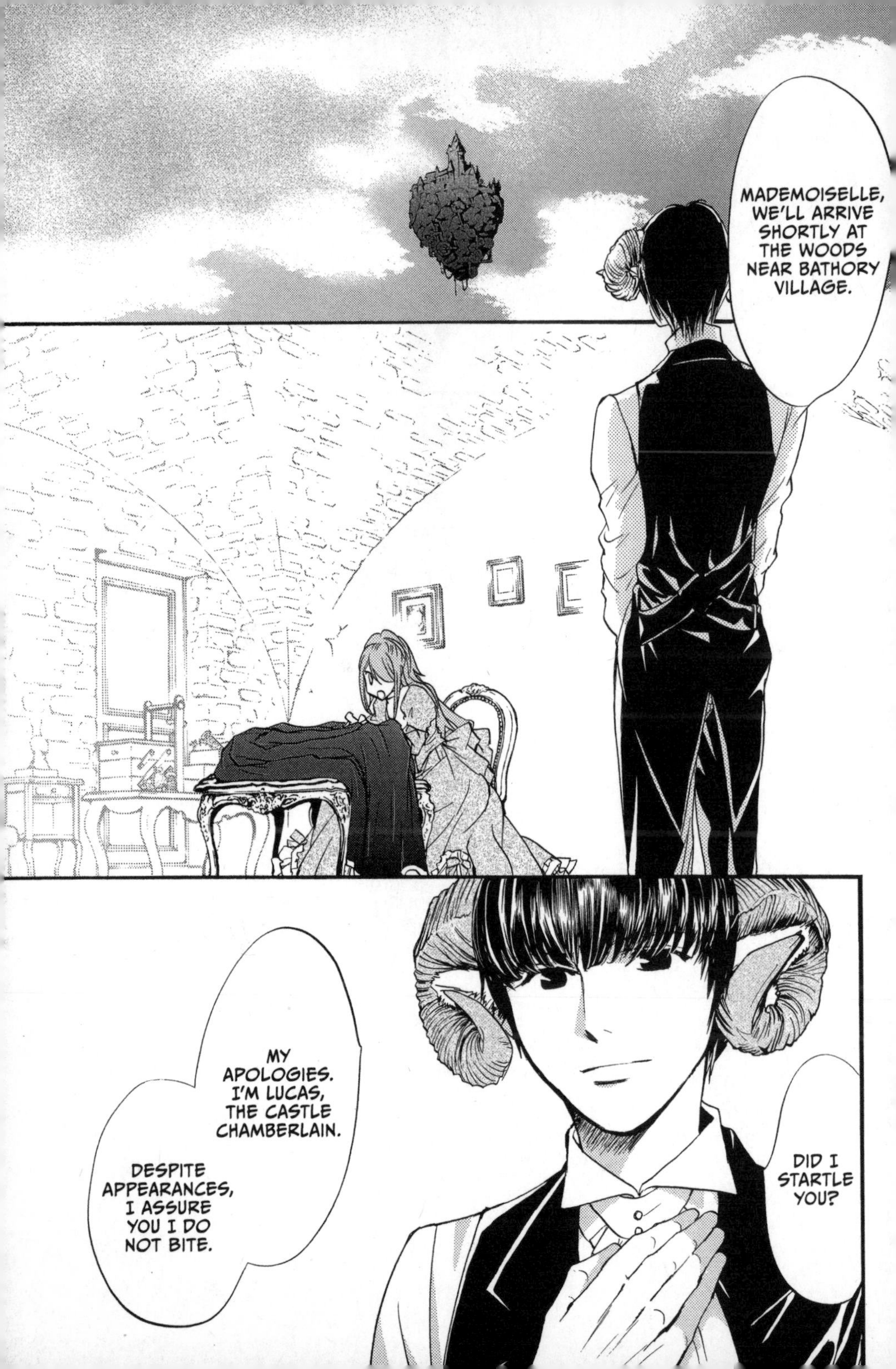
MADEMOISELLE, WE'LL ARRIVE SHORTLY AT THE WOODS NEAR BATHORY VILLAGE.
DID I STARTLE YOU?
MY APOLOGIES. I'M LUCAS, THE CASTLE CHAMBERLAIN.
DESPITE APPEARANCES, I ASSURE YOU I DO NOT BITE.

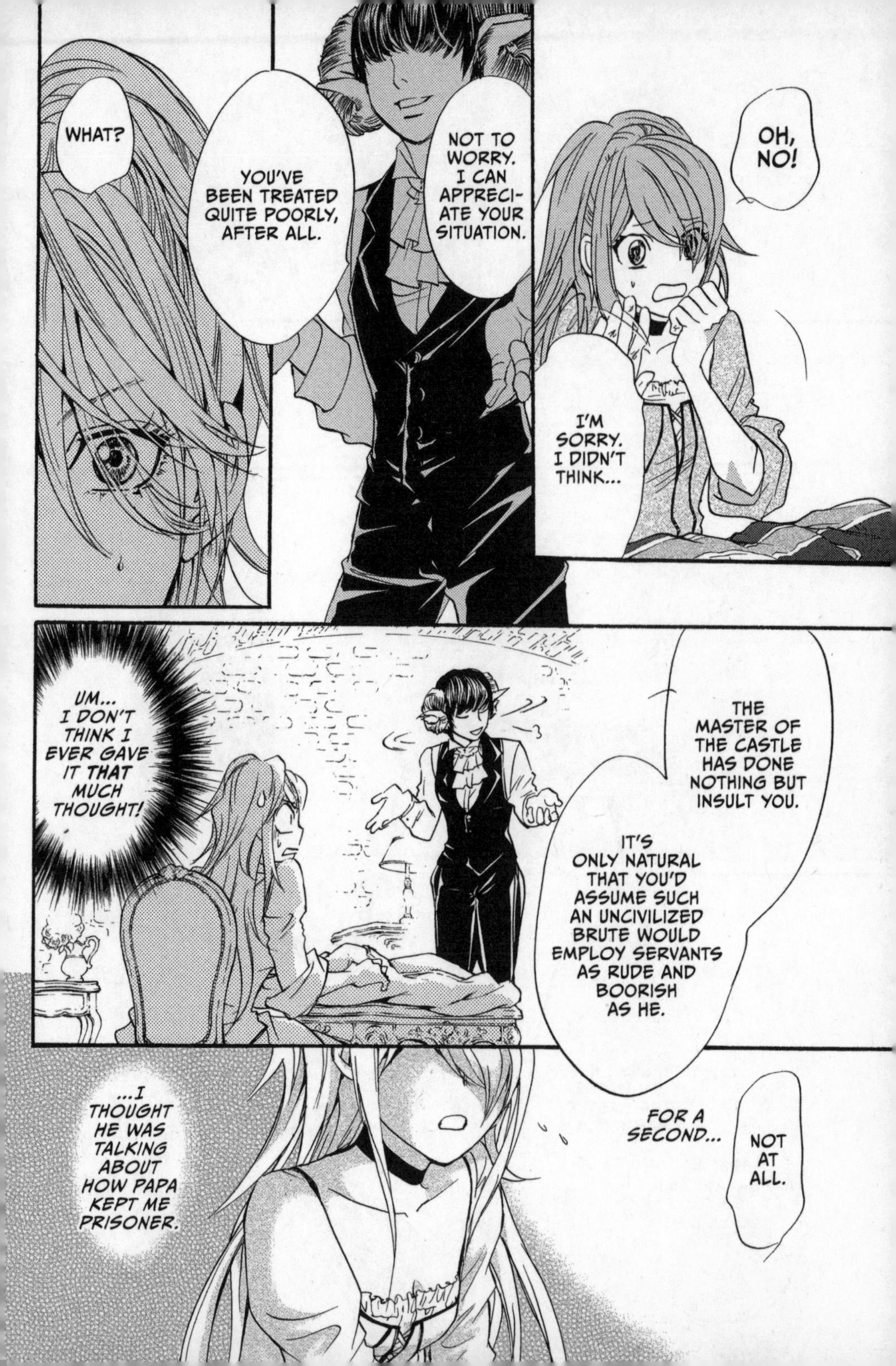
OH, NO!
I'M SORRY. I DIDN'T THINK...
NOT TO WORRY. I CAN APPRECI-ATE YOUR SITUATION.
YOU'VE BEEN TREATED QUITE POORLY, AFTER ALL.
WHAT?
THE MASTER OF THE CASTLE HAS DONE NOTHING BUT INSULT YOU.
IT'S ONLY NATURAL THAT YOU'D ASSUME SUCH AN UNCIVILIZED BRUTE WOULD EMPLOY SERVANTS AS RUDE AND BOORISH AS HE.
UM... I DON'T THINK I EVER GAVE IT THAT MUCH THOUGHT!
NOT AT ALL.
FOR A SECOND...
...I THOUGHT HE WAS TALKING ABOUT HOW PAPA KEPT ME PRISONER.

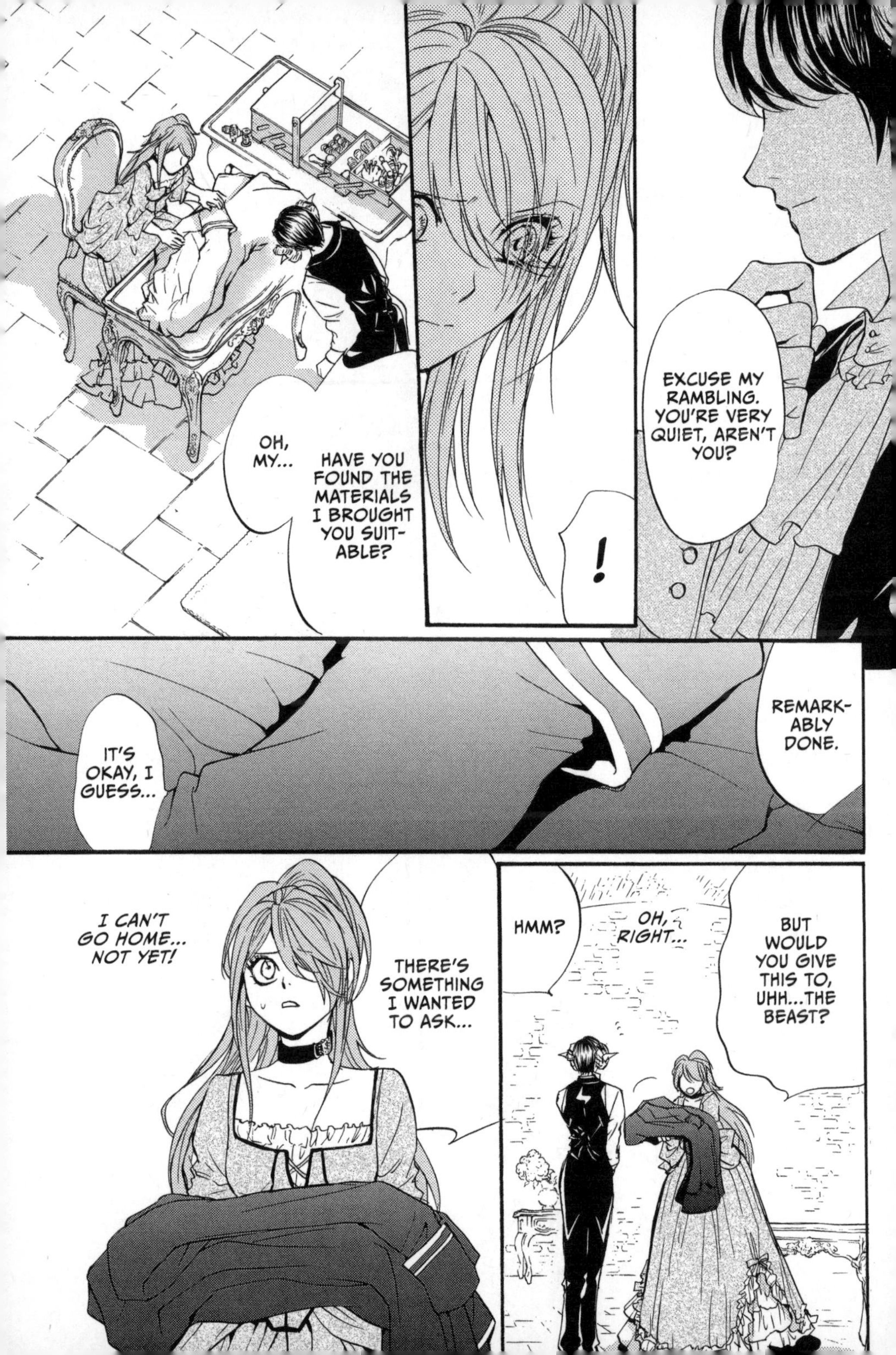
EXCUSE MY RAMBLING. YOU'RE VERY QUIET, AREN'T YOU?
!
OH, MY... HAVE YOU FOUND THE MATERIALS I BROUGHT YOU SUIT-ABLE?
REMARK-ABLY DONE.
IT'S OKAY, I GUESS...
BUT WOULD YOU GIVE THIS TO, UHH...THE BEAST?
OH, RIGHT...
HMM?
THERE'S SOMETHING I WANTED TO ASK...
I CAN'T GO HOME... NOT YET!

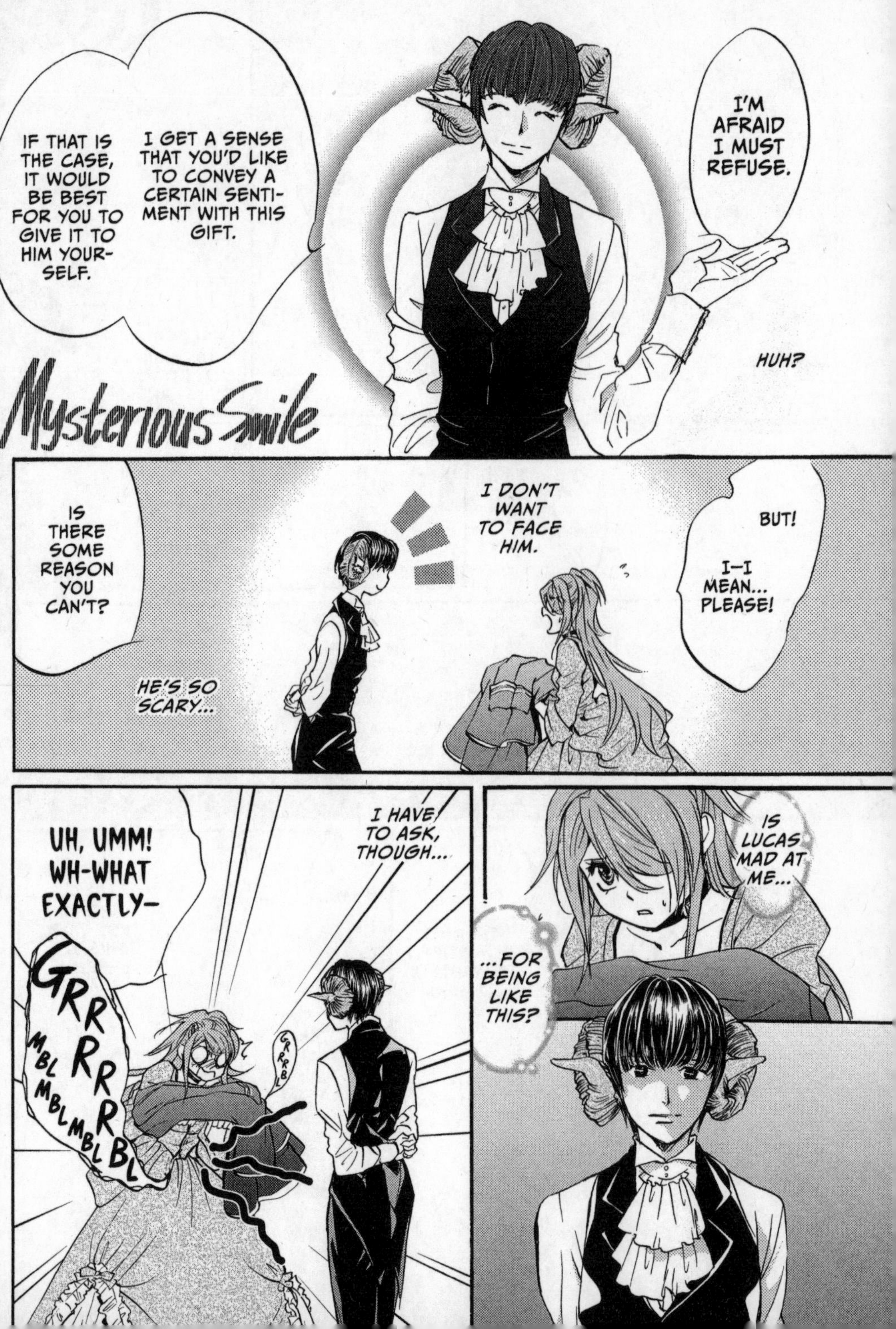
I'M AFRAID I MUST REFUSE.
I GET A SENSE THAT YOU'D LIKE TO CONVEY A CERTAIN SENTI-MENT WITH THIS GIFT.
IF THAT IS THE CASE, IT WOULD BE BEST FOR YOU TO GIVE IT TO HIM YOUR-SELF.
HUH?
Mysterious Smile
BUT!
I—I MEAN... PLEASE!
I DON'T WANT TO FACE HIM.
IS THERE SOME REASON YOU CAN'T?
HE'S SO SCARY...
IS LUCAS MAD AT ME...
...FOR BEING LIKE THIS?
I HAVE TO ASK, THOUGH...
UH, UMM! WH-WHAT EXACTLY—
GRRRRRBL MBL MBLMBLMBL
GRRRBL

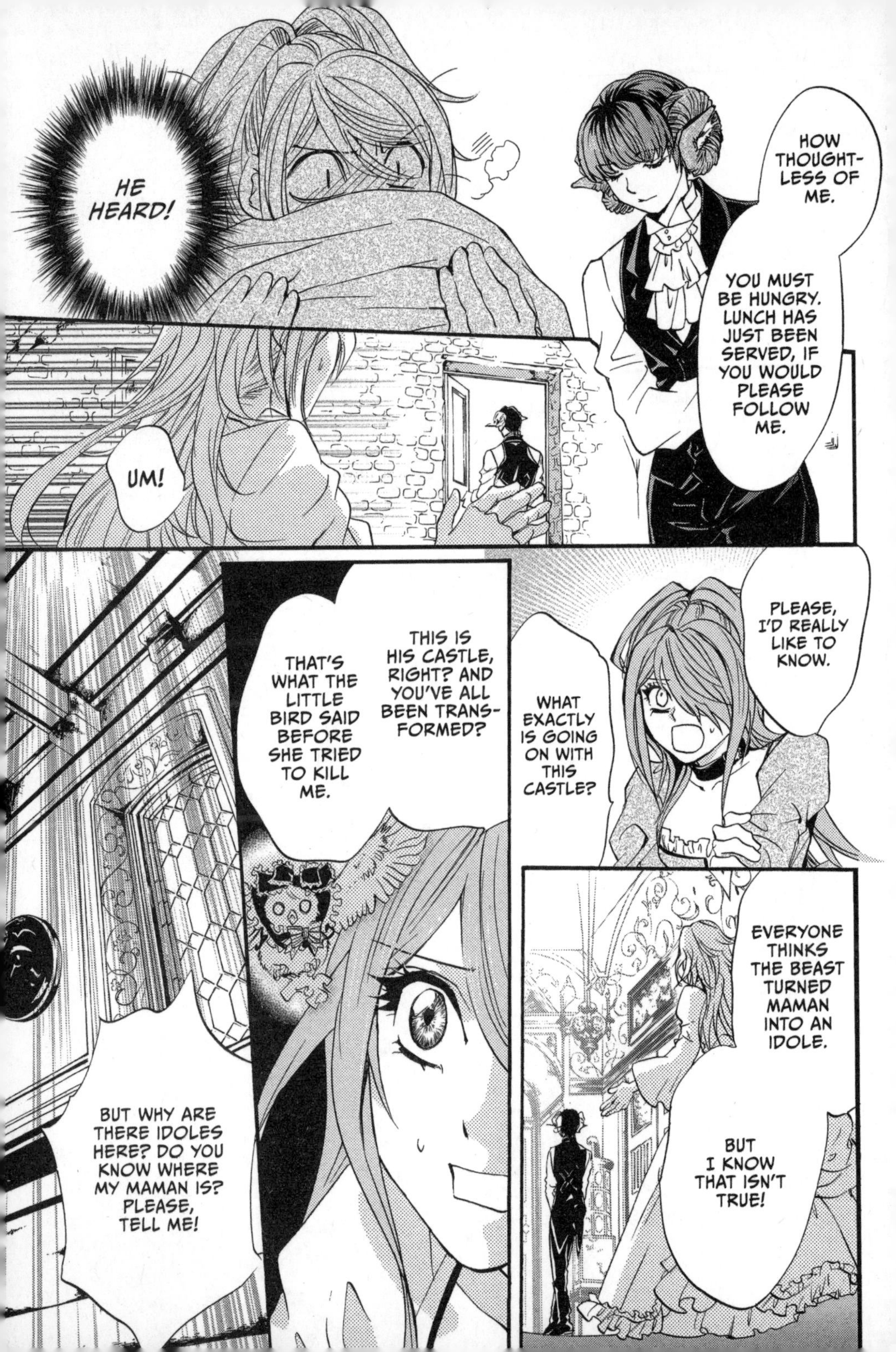
HOW THOUGHT-LESS OF ME.
YOU MUST BE HUNGRY. LUNCH HAS JUST BEEN SERVED, IF YOU WOULD PLEASE FOLLOW ME.
HE HEARD!
UM!
PLEASE, I'D REALLY LIKE TO KNOW.
WHAT EXACTLY IS GOING ON WITH THIS CASTLE?
THIS IS HIS CASTLE, RIGHT? AND YOU'VE ALL BEEN TRANS-FORMED?
THAT'S WHAT THE LITTLE BIRD SAID BEFORE SHE TRIED TO KILL ME.
EVERYONE THINKS THE BEAST TURNED MAMAN INTO AN IDOLE.
BUT I KNOW THAT ISN'T TRUE!
BUT WHY ARE THERE IDOLES HERE? DO YOU KNOW WHERE MY MAMAN IS? PLEASE, TELL ME!

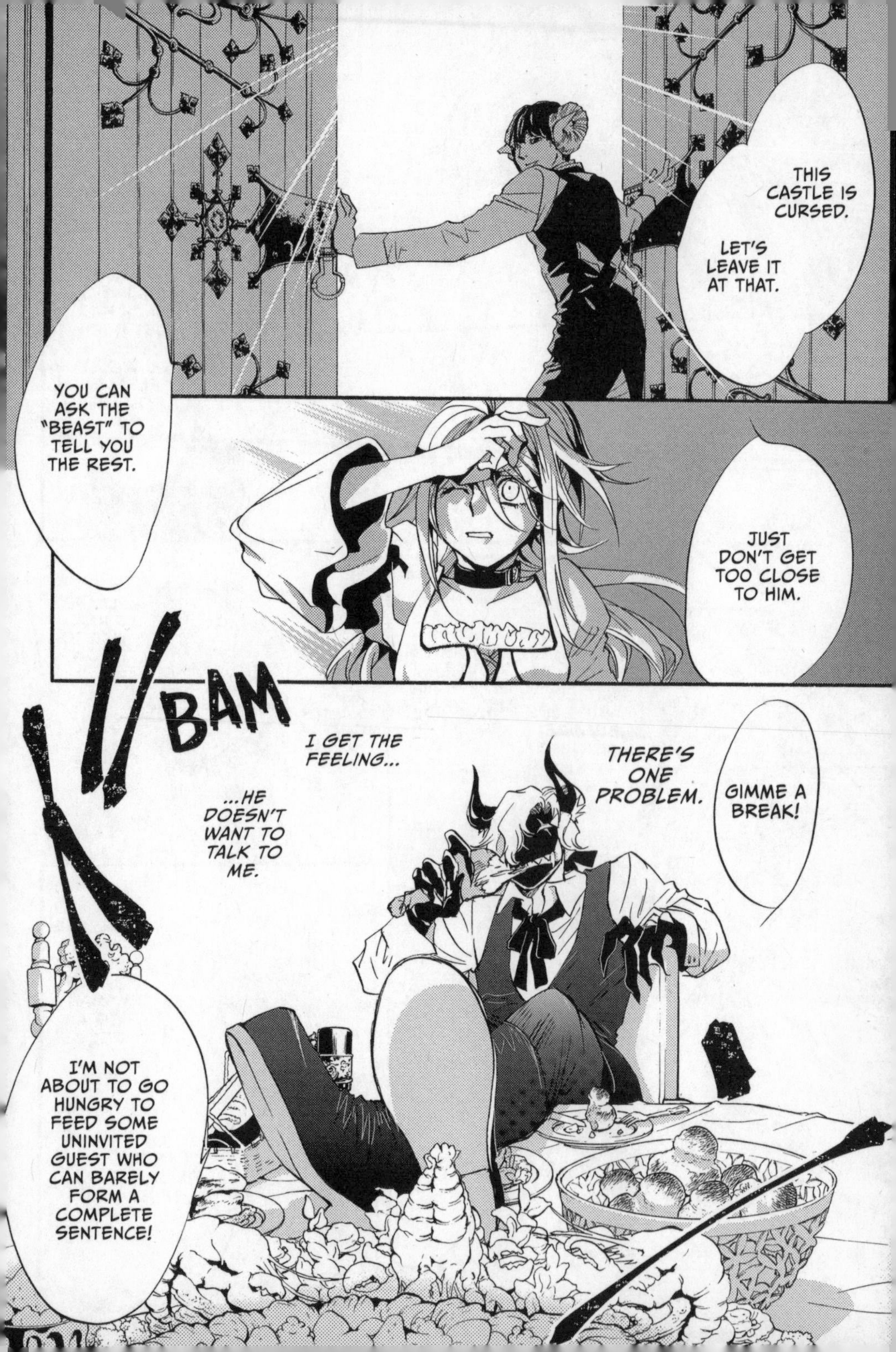
THIS CASTLE IS CURSED.
LET'S LEAVE IT AT THAT.
YOU CAN ASK THE "BEAST" TO TELL YOU THE REST.
JUST DON'T GET TOO CLOSE TO HIM.
BAM
GIMME A BREAK!
THERE'S ONE PROBLEM.
I GET THE FEELING...
...HE DOESN'T WANT TO TALK TO ME.
I'M NOT ABOUT TO GO HUNGRY TO FEED SOME UNINVITED GUEST WHO CAN BARELY FORM A COMPLETE SENTENCE!

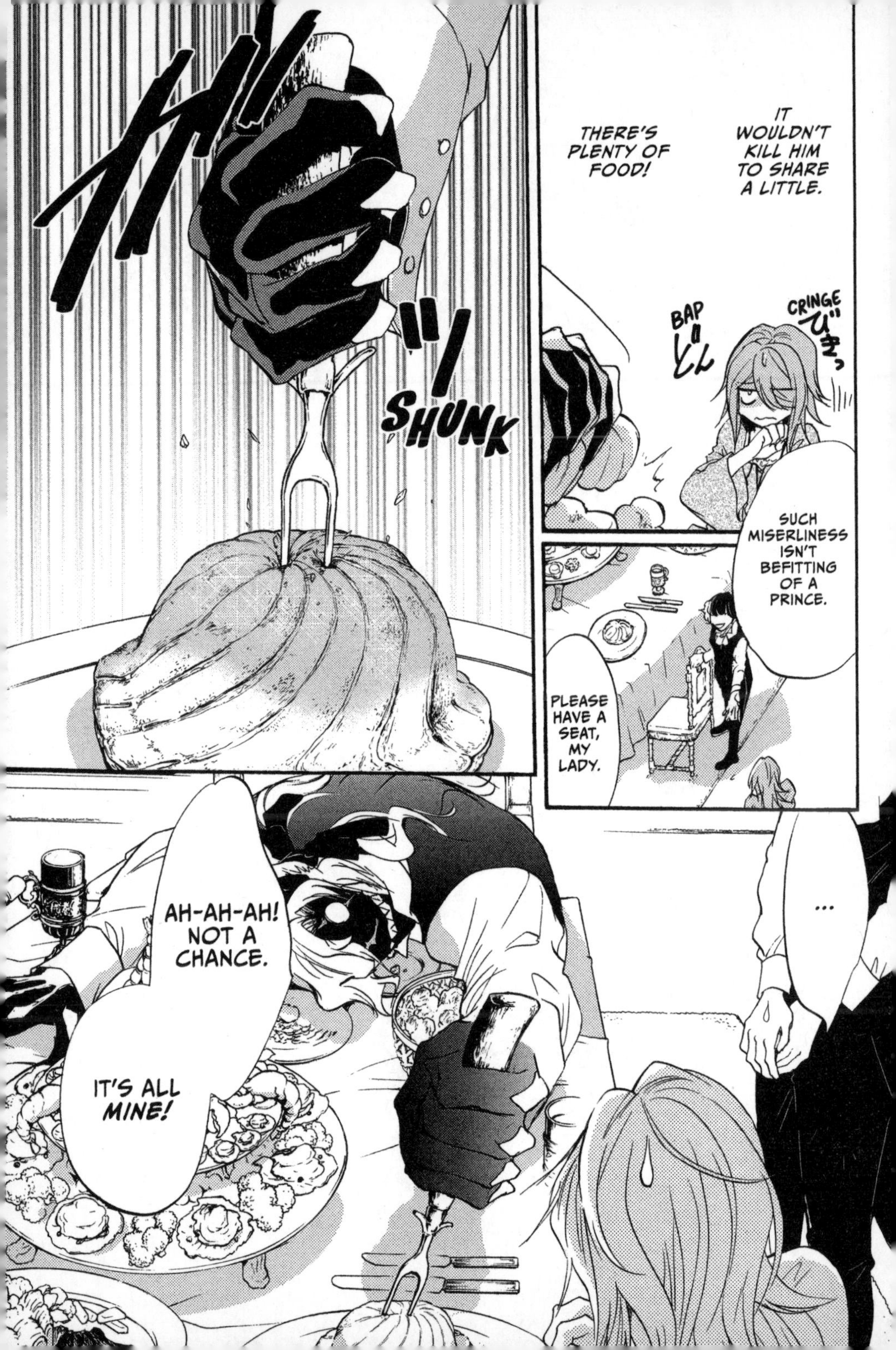
IT WOULDN'T KILL HIM TO SHARE A LITTLE.
THERE'S PLENTY OF FOOD!
CRINGE
BAP
SUCH MISERLINESS ISN'T BEFITTING OF A PRINCE.
PLEASE HAVE A SEAT, MY LADY.
SHUNK
...
AH-AH-AH! NOT A CHANCE.
IT'S ALL MINE!

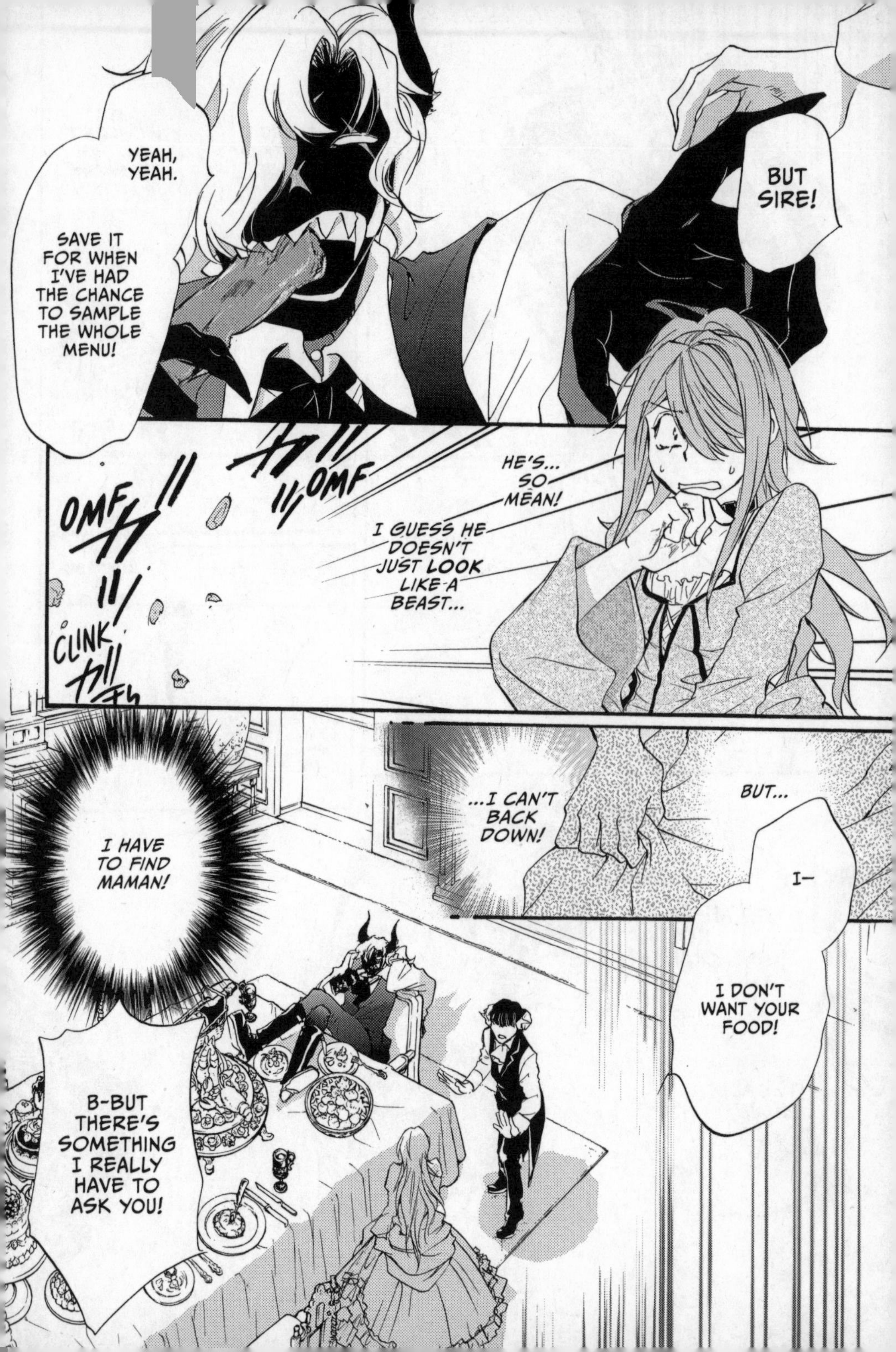
BUT SIRE!
YEAH, YEAH.
SAVE IT FOR WHEN I'VE HAD THE CHANCE TO SAMPLE THE WHOLE MENU!
HE'S... SO MEAN!
I GUESS HE DOESN'T JUST LOOK LIKE A BEAST...
OMF
OMF
CLINK
BUT...
I—
...I CAN'T BACK DOWN!
I HAVE TO FIND MAMAN!
I DON'T WANT YOUR FOOD!
B-BUT THERE'S SOMETHING I REALLY HAVE TO ASK YOU!

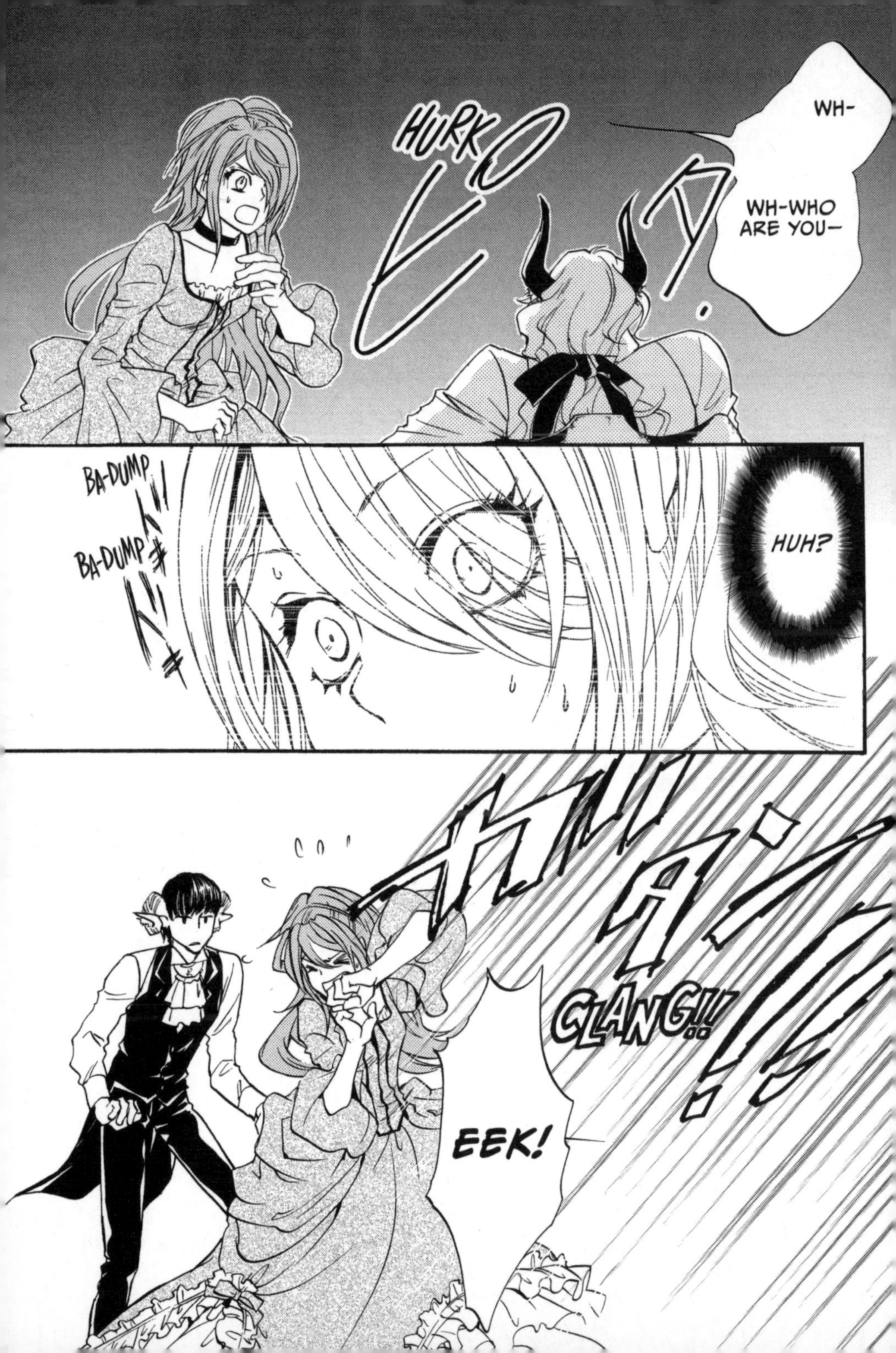
WH-
WH-WHO ARE YOU—
HURK
HUH?
BA-DUMP
BA-DUMP
CLANG!!
EEK!

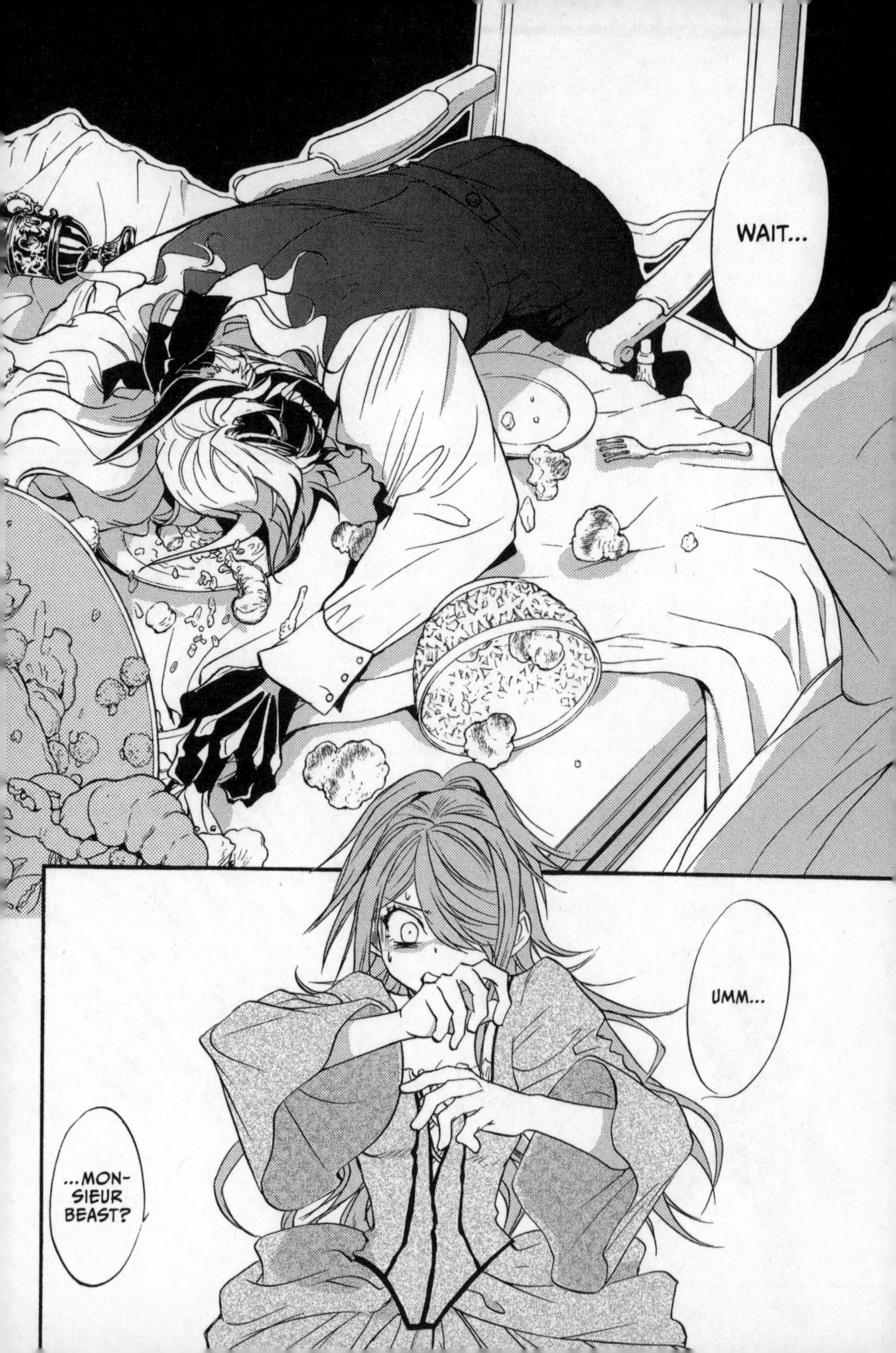
WAIT...
UMM...
...MON-SIEUR BEAST?

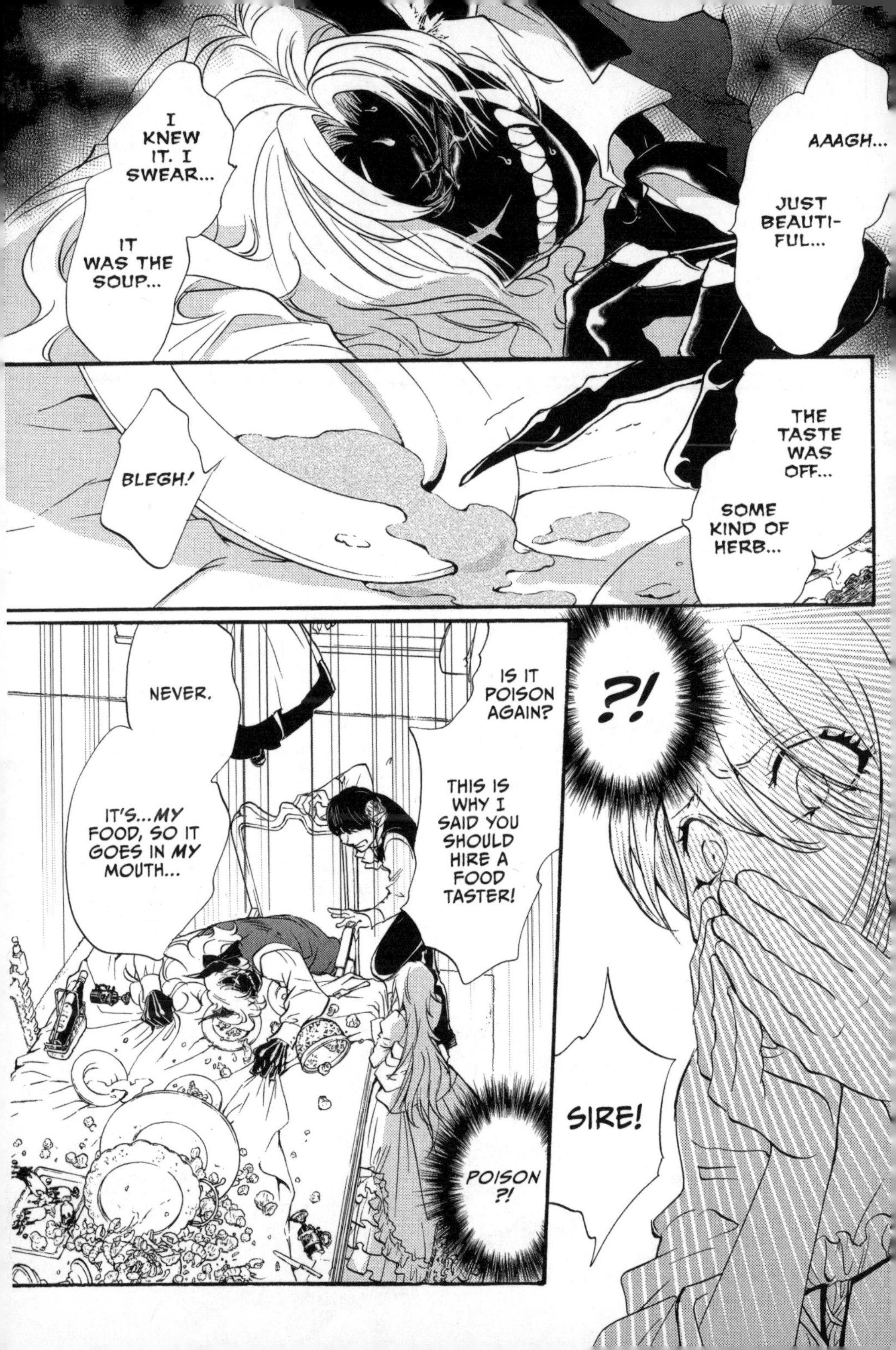
AAAGH...
JUST BEAUTIFUL...
I KNEW IT. I SWEAR...
IT WAS THE SOUP...
THE TASTE WAS OFF...
SOME KIND OF HERB...
BLEGH!
?!
SIRE!
POISON ?!
IS IT POISON AGAIN?
THIS IS WHY I SAID YOU SHOULD HIRE A FOOD TASTER!
NEVER.
IT'S...MY FOOD, SO IT GOES IN MY MOUTH...

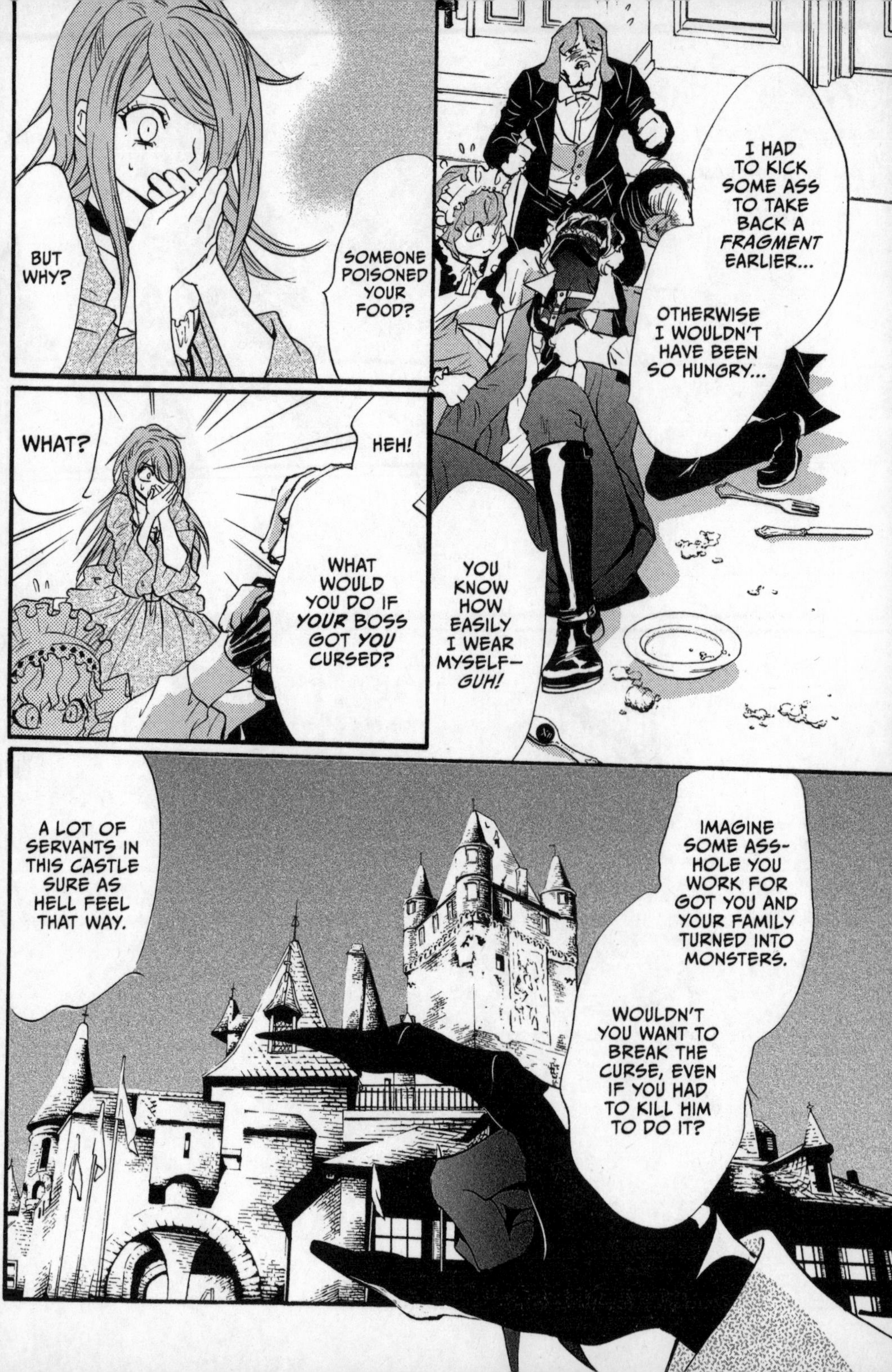
I HAD TO KICK SOME ASS TO TAKE BACK A *FRAGMENT* EARLIER...
OTHERWISE I WOULDN'T HAVE BEEN SO HUNGRY...
YOU KNOW HOW EASILY I WEAR MYSELF— *GUH!*
SOMEONE POISONED YOUR FOOD?
BUT WHY?
HEH!
WHAT?
WHAT WOULD YOU DO IF *YOUR* BOSS GOT *YOU* CURSED?
IMAGINE SOME ASS-HOLE YOU WORK FOR GOT YOU AND YOUR FAMILY TURNED INTO MONSTERS.
WOULDN'T YOU WANT TO BREAK THE CURSE, EVEN IF YOU HAD TO KILL HIM TO DO IT?
A LOT OF SERVANTS IN THIS CASTLE SURE AS HELL FEEL THAT WAY.

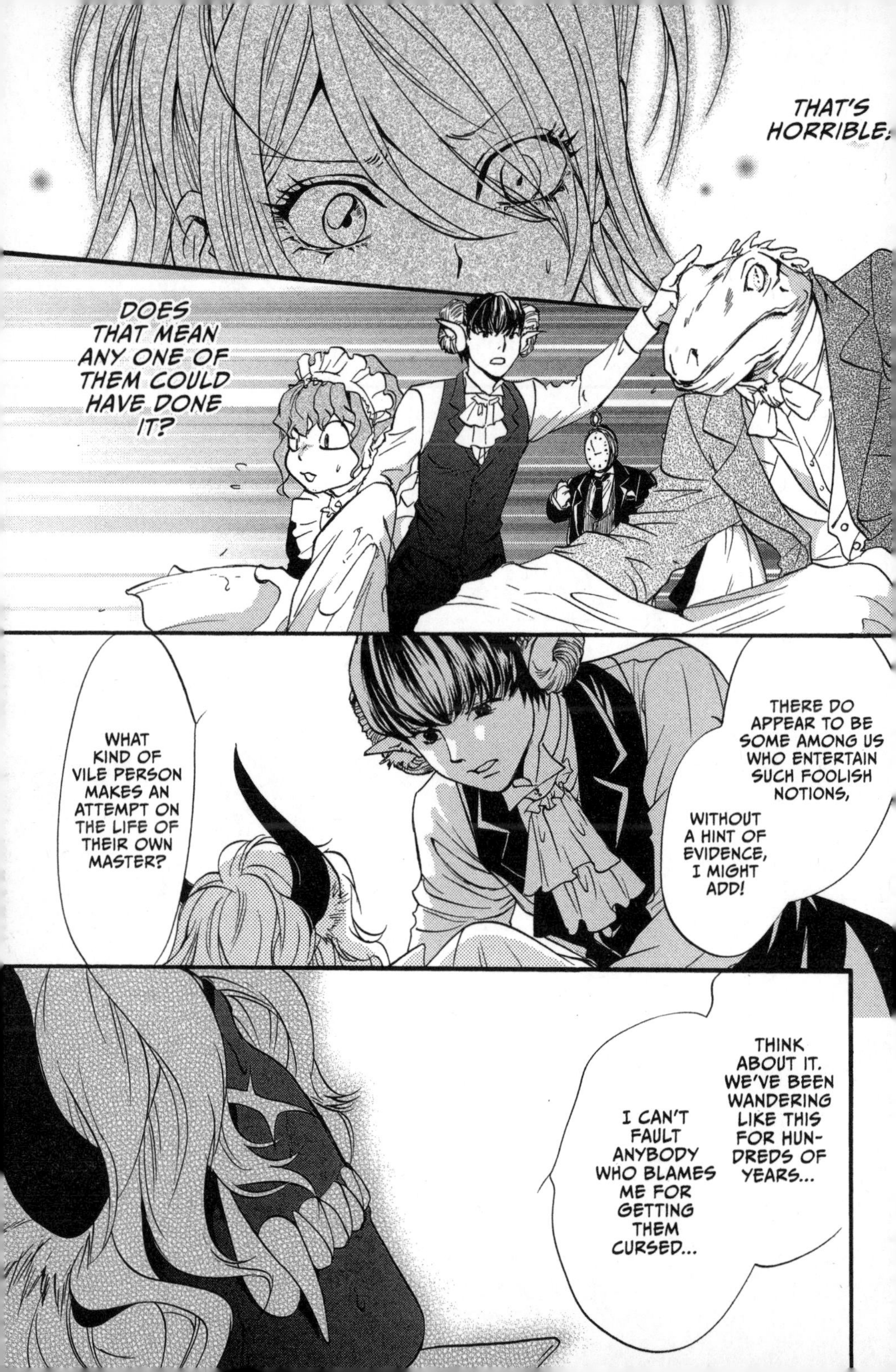
THAT'S HORRIBLE.
DOES THAT MEAN ANY ONE OF THEM COULD HAVE DONE IT?
THERE DO APPEAR TO BE SOME AMONG US WHO ENTERTAIN SUCH FOOLISH NOTIONS,
WITHOUT A HINT OF EVIDENCE, I MIGHT ADD!
WHAT KIND OF VILE PERSON MAKES AN ATTEMPT ON THE LIFE OF THEIR OWN MASTER?
THINK ABOUT IT. WE'VE BEEN WANDERING LIKE THIS FOR HUN-DREDS OF YEARS...
I CAN'T FAULT ANYBODY WHO BLAMES ME FOR GETTING THEM CURSED...

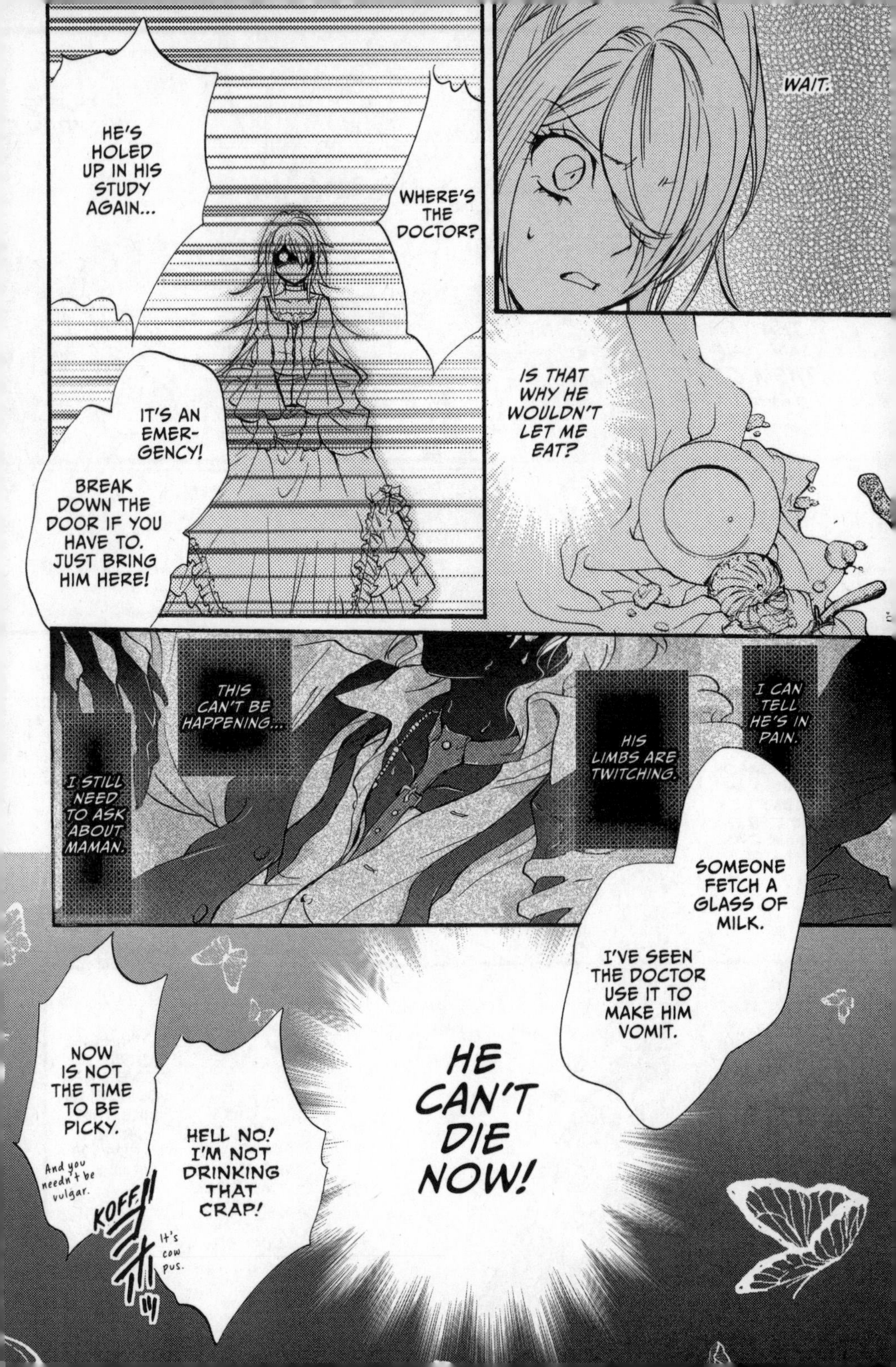
WAIT.
WHERE'S THE DOCTOR?
HE'S HOLED UP IN HIS STUDY AGAIN...
IS THAT WHY HE WOULDN'T LET ME EAT?
IT'S AN EMER-GENCY!
BREAK DOWN THE DOOR IF YOU HAVE TO. JUST BRING HIM HERE!
I CAN TELL HE'S IN PAIN.
HIS LIMBS ARE TWITCHING.
THIS CAN'T BE HAPPENING...
I STILL NEED TO ASK ABOUT MAMAN.
SOMEONE FETCH A GLASS OF MILK.
I'VE SEEN THE DOCTOR USE IT TO MAKE HIM VOMIT.
HE CAN'T DIE NOW!
HELL NO! I'M NOT DRINKING THAT CRAP!
It's cow pus.
NOW IS NOT THE TIME TO BE PICKY.
And you needn't be vulgar.
KOFF!!

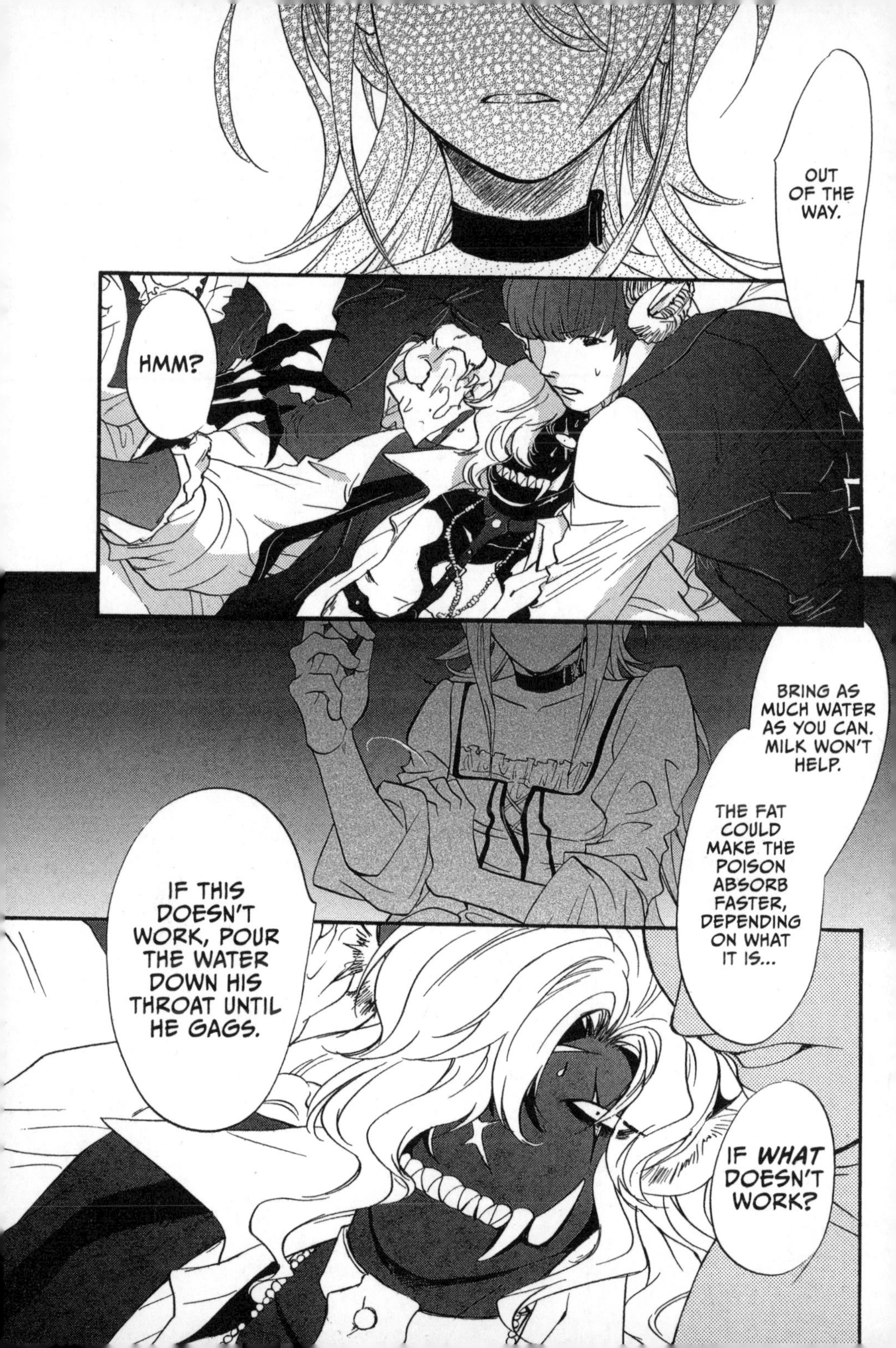
OUT OF THE WAY.
HMM?
BRING AS MUCH WATER AS YOU CAN. MILK WON'T HELP.
THE FAT COULD MAKE THE POISON ABSORB FASTER, DEPENDING ON WHAT IT IS...
IF THIS DOESN'T WORK, POUR THE WATER DOWN HIS THROAT UNTIL HE GAGS.
IF *WHAT* DOESN'T WORK?

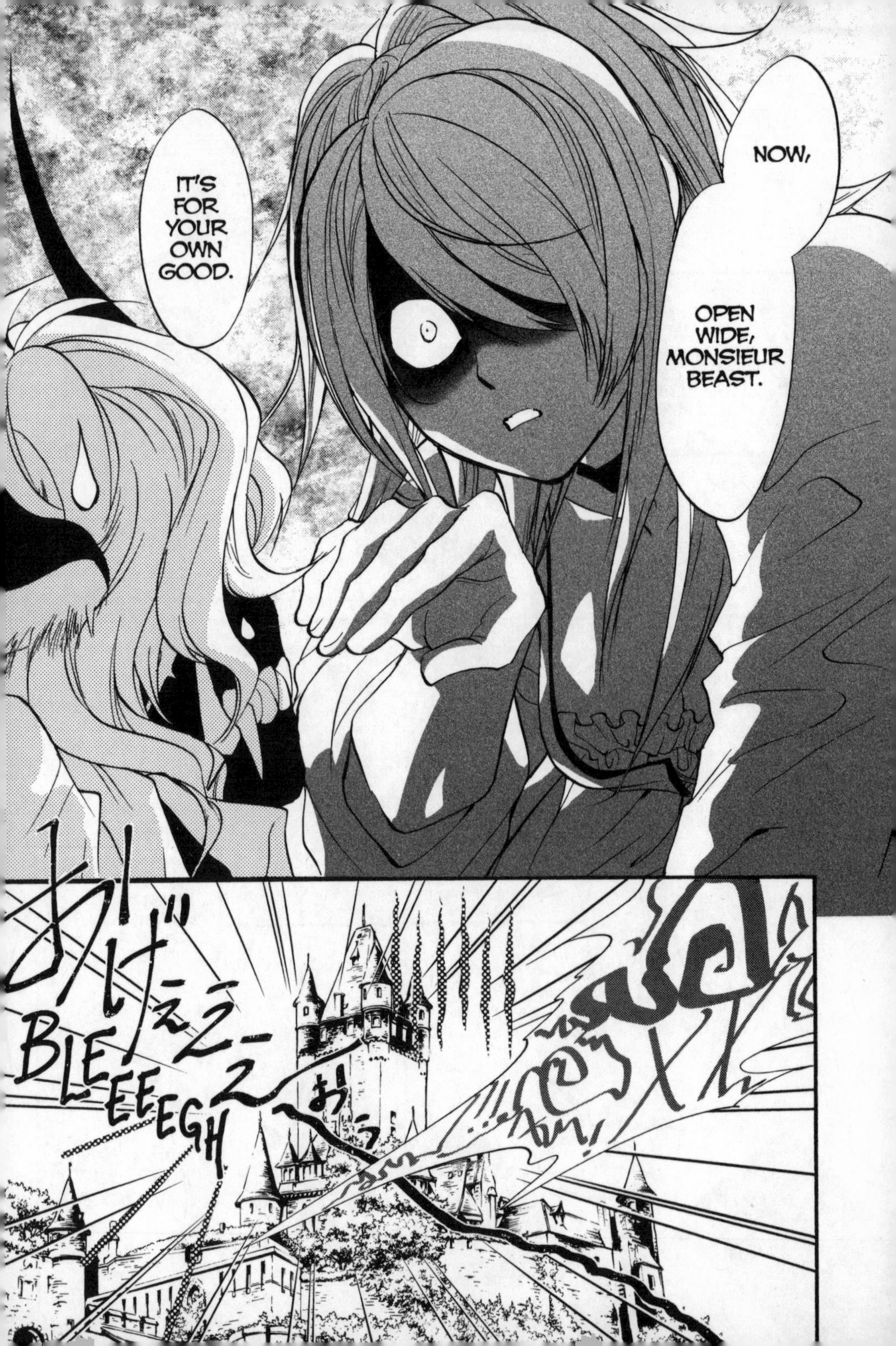
NOW,
OPEN WIDE, MONSIEUR BEAST.
IT'S FOR YOUR OWN GOOD.
BLEEEEGH

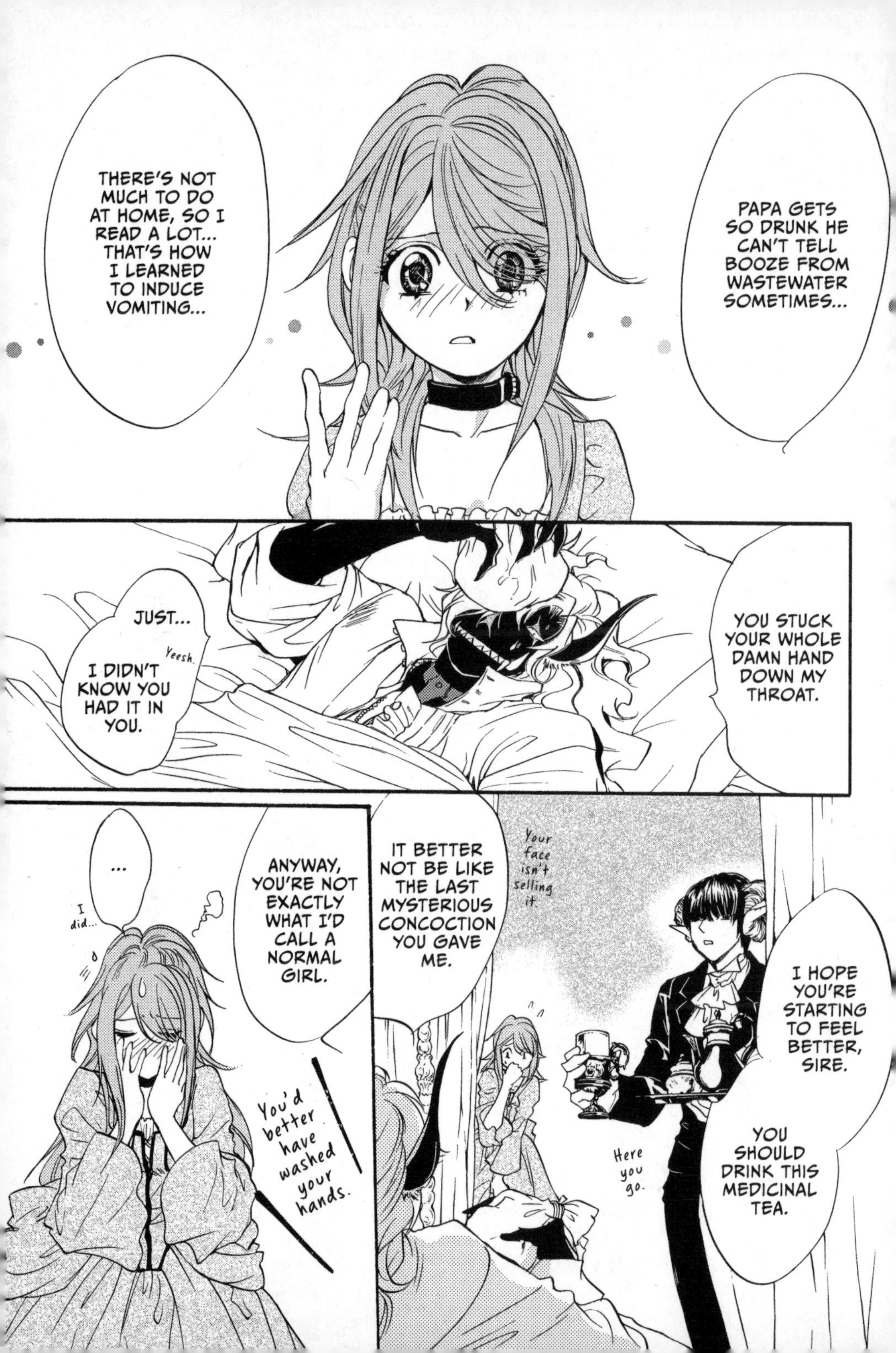
PAPA GETS SO DRUNK HE CAN'T TELL BOOZE FROM WASTEWATER SOMETIMES...
THERE'S NOT MUCH TO DO AT HOME, SO I READ A LOT... THAT'S HOW I LEARNED TO INDUCE VOMITING...
YOU STUCK YOUR WHOLE DAMN HAND DOWN MY THROAT.
JUST...
Yeesh.
I DIDN'T KNOW YOU HAD IT IN YOU.
I HOPE YOU'RE STARTING TO FEEL BETTER, SIRE.
YOU SHOULD DRINK THIS MEDICINAL TEA.
Here you go.
Your face isn't selling it.
IT BETTER NOT BE LIKE THE LAST MYSTERIOUS CONCOCTION YOU GAVE ME.
ANYWAY, YOU'RE NOT EXACTLY WHAT I'D CALL A NORMAL GIRL.
You'd better have washed your hands.
...
I did...

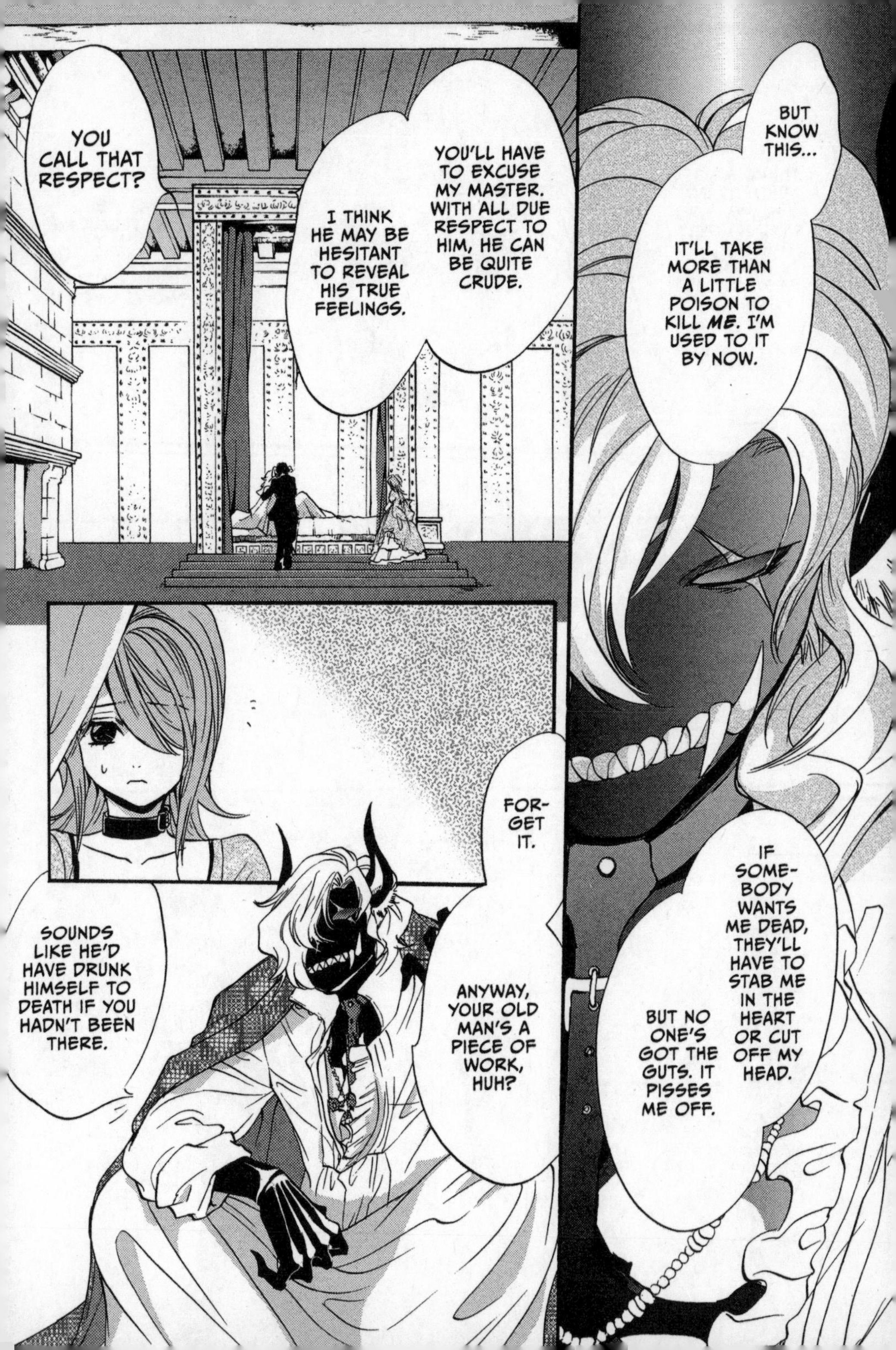
YOU CALL THAT RESPECT?
YOU'LL HAVE TO EXCUSE MY MASTER. WITH ALL DUE RESPECT TO HIM, HE CAN BE QUITE CRUDE.
I THINK HE MAY BE HESITANT TO REVEAL HIS TRUE FEELINGS.
FOR-GET IT.
ANYWAY, YOUR OLD MAN'S A PIECE OF WORK, HUH?
SOUNDS LIKE HE'D HAVE DRUNK HIMSELF TO DEATH IF YOU HADN'T BEEN THERE.
BUT KNOW THIS...
IT'LL TAKE MORE THAN A LITTLE POISON TO KILL ME. I'M USED TO IT BY NOW.
IF SOMEBODY WANTS ME DEAD, THEY'LL HAVE TO STAB ME IN THE HEART OR CUT OFF MY HEAD.
BUT NO ONE'S GOT THE GUTS. IT PISSES ME OFF.

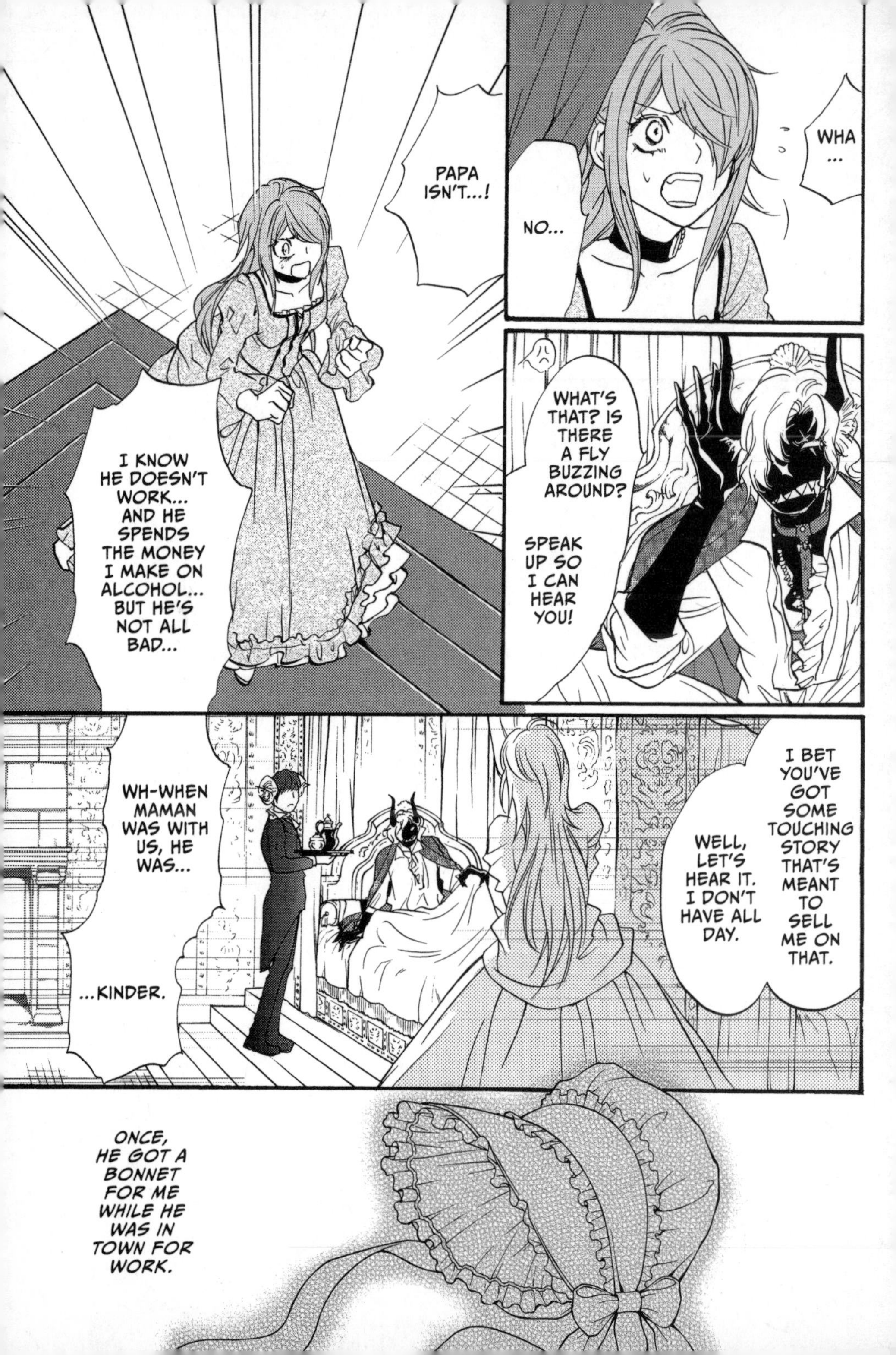
WHA...
NO...
PAPA ISN'T...!
I KNOW HE DOESN'T WORK... AND HE SPENDS THE MONEY I MAKE ON ALCOHOL... BUT HE'S NOT ALL BAD...
WHAT'S THAT? IS THERE A FLY BUZZING AROUND?
SPEAK UP SO I CAN HEAR YOU!
I BET YOU'VE GOT SOME TOUCHING STORY THAT'S MEANT TO SELL ME ON THAT.
WELL, LET'S HEAR IT. I DON'T HAVE ALL DAY.
WH-WHEN MAMAN WAS WITH US, HE WAS...
...KINDER.
ONCE, HE GOT A BONNET FOR ME WHILE HE WAS IN TOWN FOR WORK.

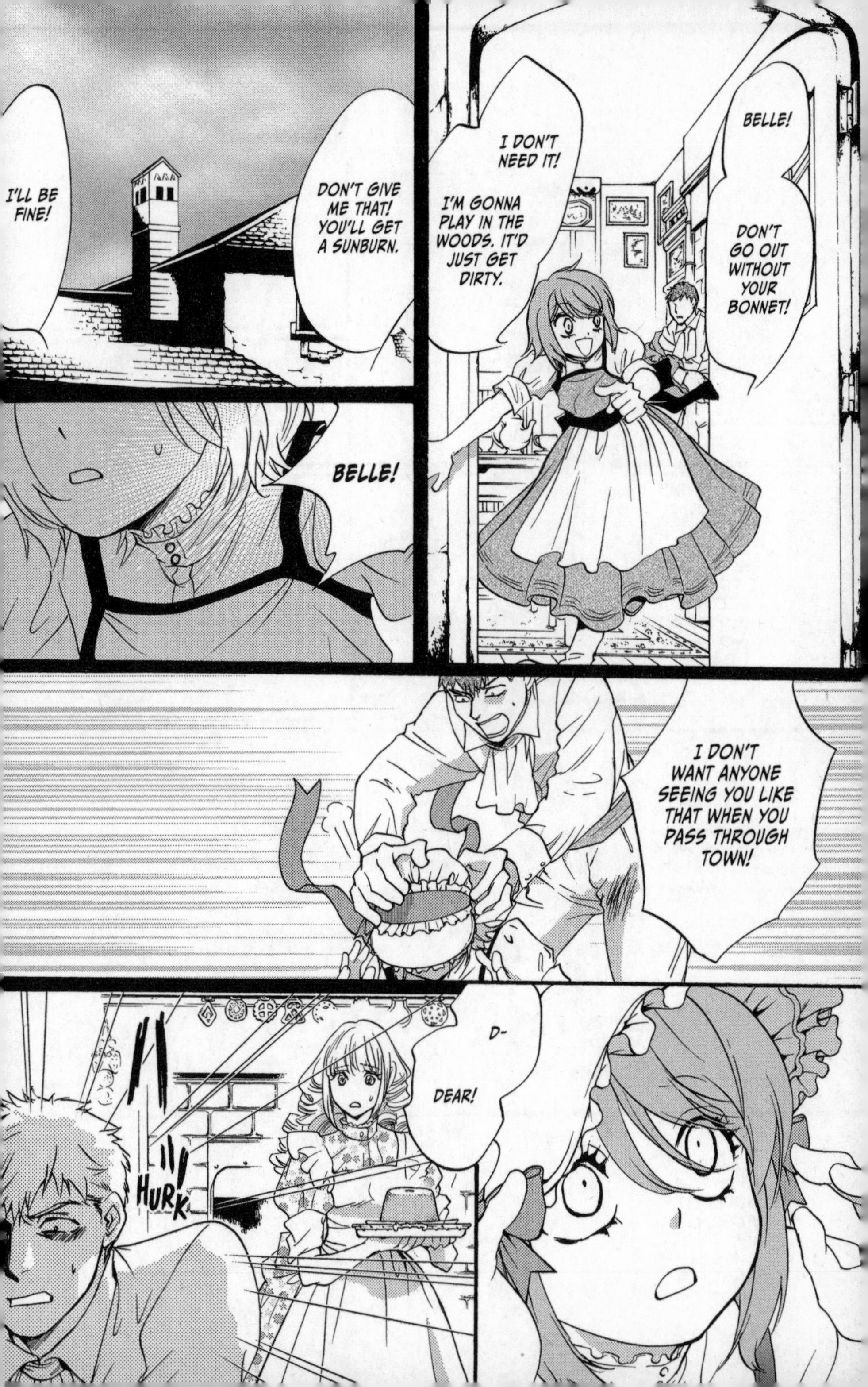
BELLE!
DON'T GO OUT WITHOUT YOUR BONNET!
I DON'T NEED IT!
I'M GONNA PLAY IN THE WOODS. IT'D JUST GET DIRTY.
DON'T GIVE ME THAT! YOU'LL GET A SUNBURN.
I'LL BE FINE!
BELLE!
I DON'T WANT ANYONE SEEING YOU LIKE THAT WHEN YOU PASS THROUGH TOWN!
D-
DEAR!
HURK

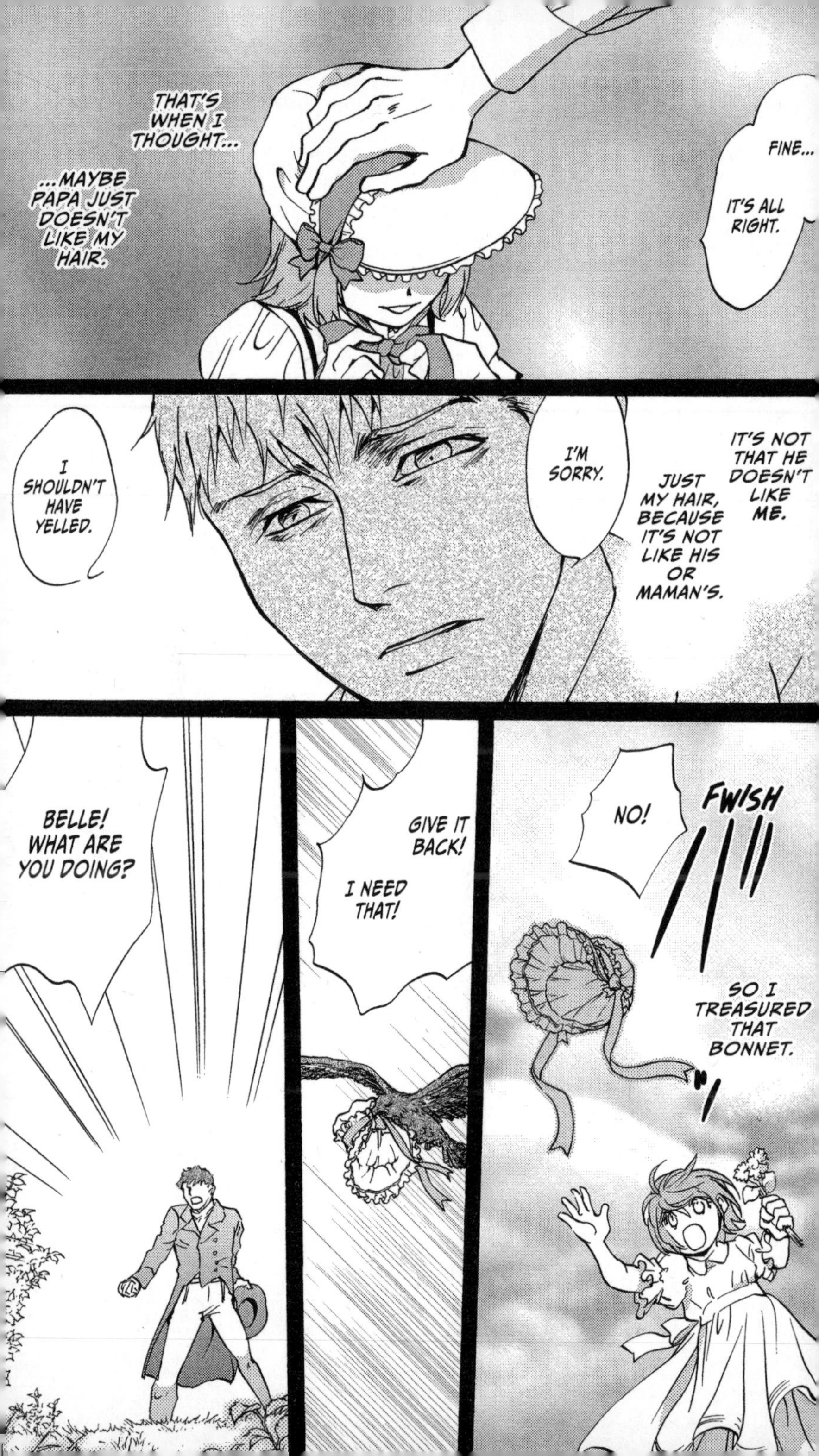
FINE...
IT'S ALL RIGHT.
THAT'S WHEN I THOUGHT...
...MAYBE PAPA JUST DOESN'T LIKE MY HAIR.
IT'S NOT THAT HE DOESN'T LIKE ME.
JUST MY HAIR, BECAUSE IT'S NOT LIKE HIS OR MAMAN'S.
I'M SORRY.
I SHOULDN'T HAVE YELLED.
SO I TREASURED THAT BONNET.
FWISH
NO!
GIVE IT BACK!
I NEED THAT!
BELLE! WHAT ARE YOU DOING?

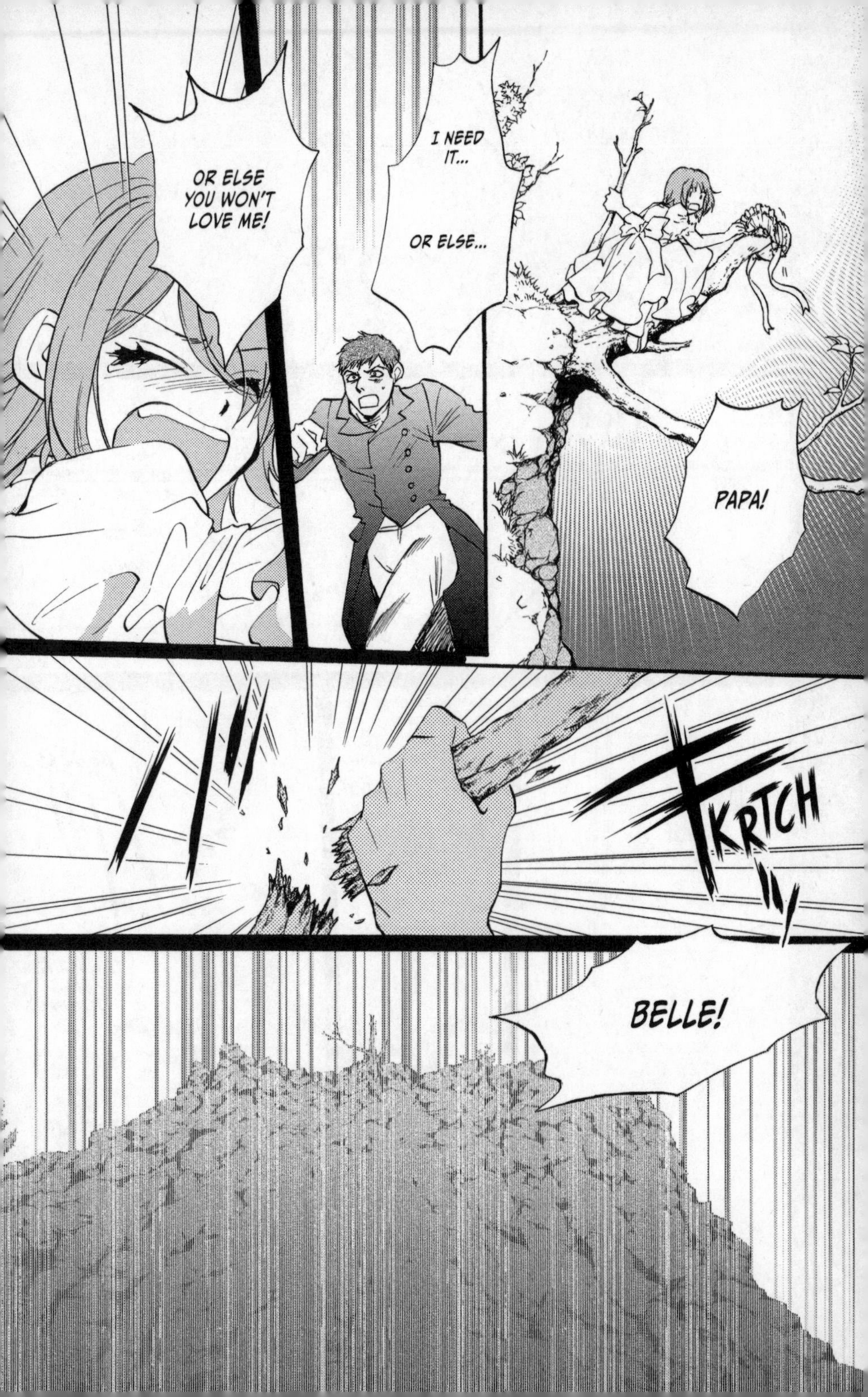
PAPA!
I NEED IT...
OR ELSE...
OR ELSE YOU WON'T LOVE ME!
KRTCH
BELLE!

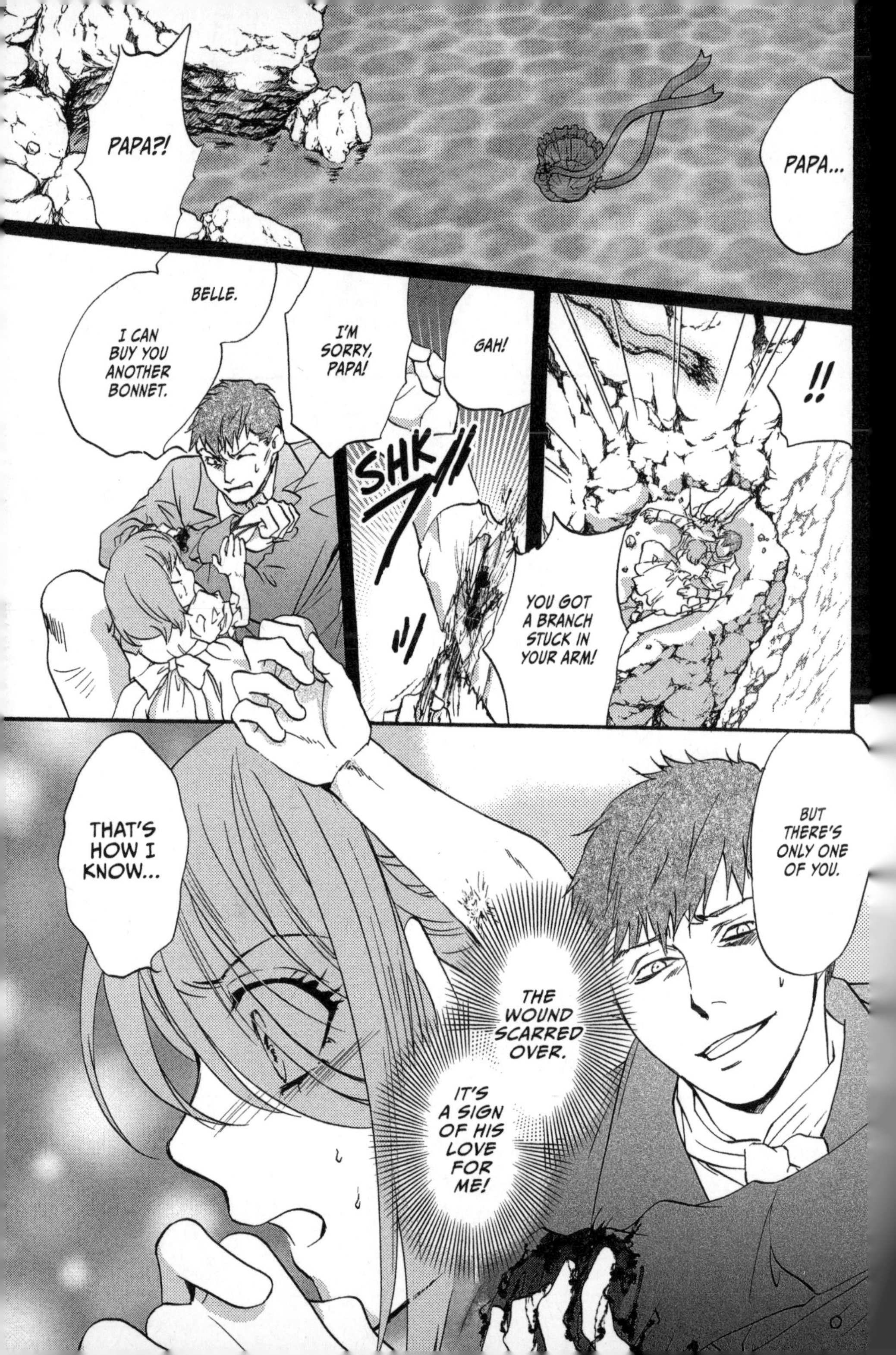
PAPA...
PAPA?!
!!
SHK
YOU GOT A BRANCH STUCK IN YOUR ARM!
GAH!
I'M SORRY, PAPA!
BELLE.
I CAN BUY YOU ANOTHER BONNET.
BUT THERE'S ONLY ONE OF YOU.
THE WOUND SCARRED OVER.
IT'S A SIGN OF HIS LOVE FOR ME!
THAT'S HOW I KNOW...

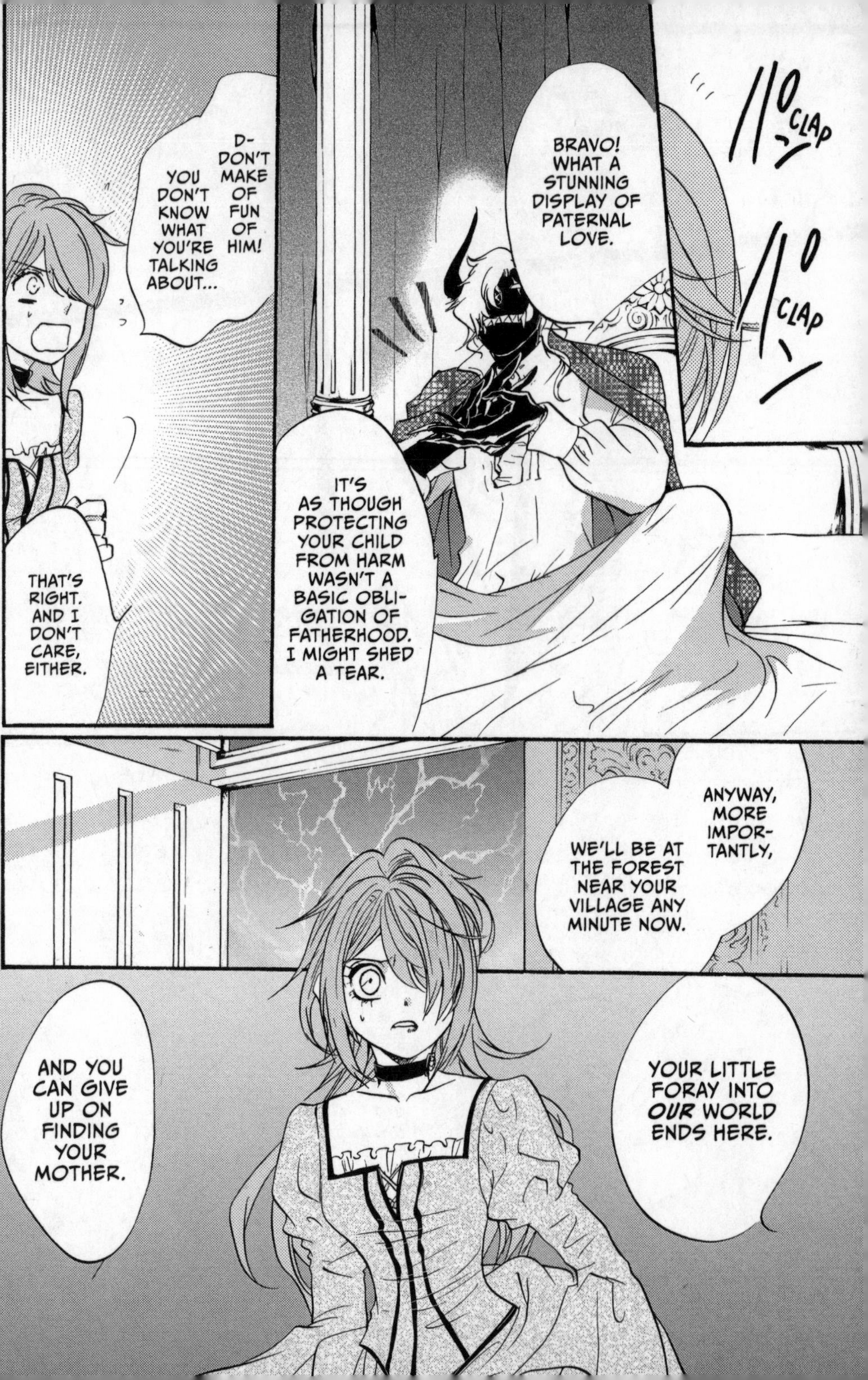
CLAP
CLAP
BRAVO! WHAT A STUNNING DISPLAY OF PATERNAL LOVE.
IT'S AS THOUGH PROTECTING YOUR CHILD FROM HARM WASN'T A BASIC OBLIGATION OF FATHERHOOD. I MIGHT SHED A TEAR.
D-DON'T MAKE FUN OF HIM!
YOU DON'T KNOW WHAT YOU'RE TALKING ABOUT...
THAT'S RIGHT. AND I DON'T CARE, EITHER.
ANYWAY, MORE IMPORTANTLY,
WE'LL BE AT THE FOREST NEAR YOUR VILLAGE ANY MINUTE NOW.
YOUR LITTLE FORAY INTO OUR WORLD ENDS HERE.
AND YOU CAN GIVE UP ON FINDING YOUR MOTHER.

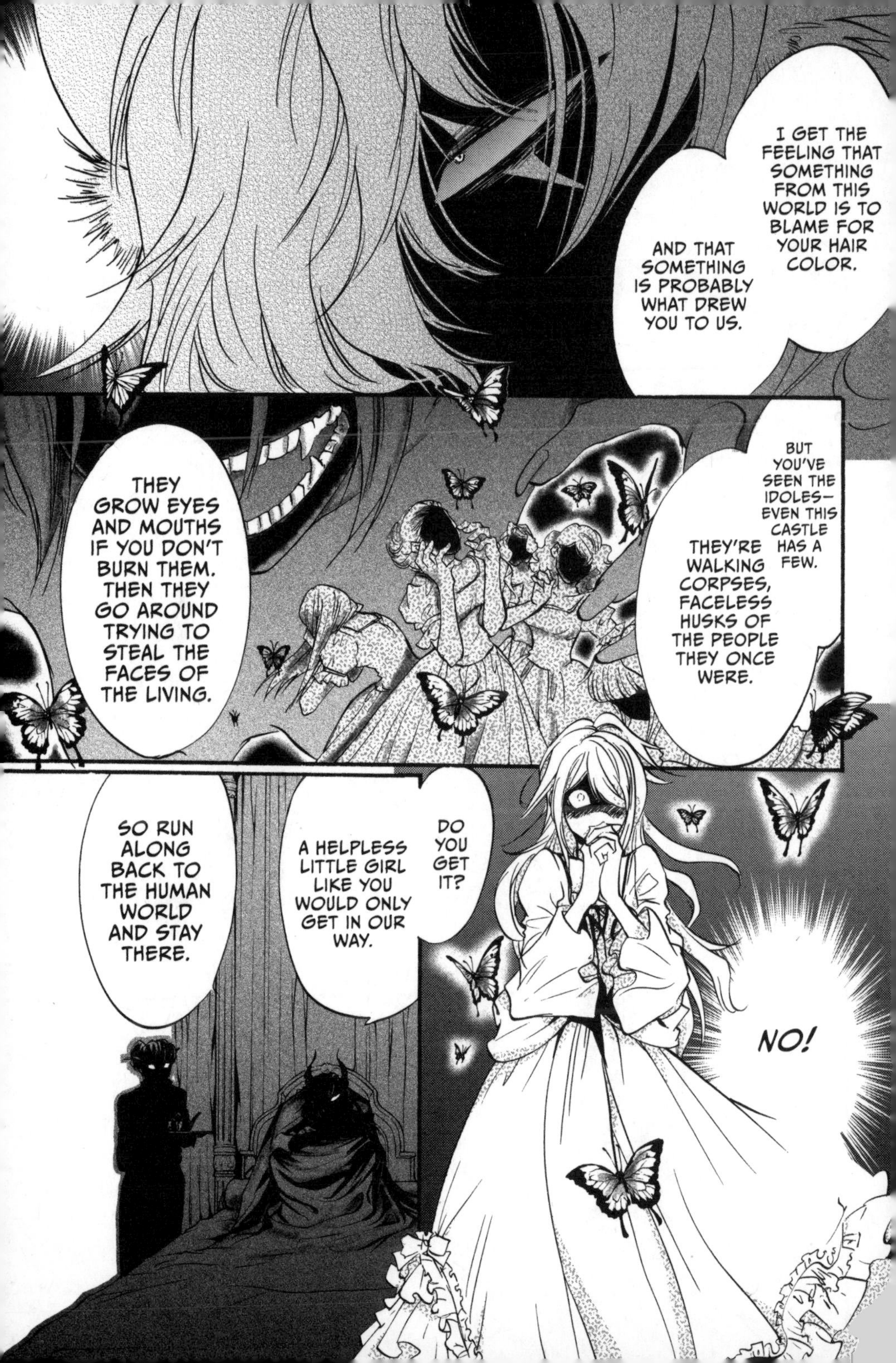
I GET THE FEELING THAT SOMETHING FROM THIS WORLD IS TO BLAME FOR YOUR HAIR COLOR.
AND THAT SOMETHING IS PROBABLY WHAT DREW YOU TO US.
BUT YOU'VE SEEN THE IDOLES—EVEN THIS CASTLE HAS A FEW.
THEY'RE WALKING CORPSES, FACELESS HUSKS OF THE PEOPLE THEY ONCE WERE.
THEY GROW EYES AND MOUTHS IF YOU DON'T BURN THEM. THEN THEY GO AROUND TRYING TO STEAL THE FACES OF THE LIVING.
NO!
DO YOU GET IT?
A HELPLESS LITTLE GIRL LIKE YOU WOULD ONLY GET IN OUR WAY.
SO RUN ALONG BACK TO THE HUMAN WORLD AND STAY THERE.

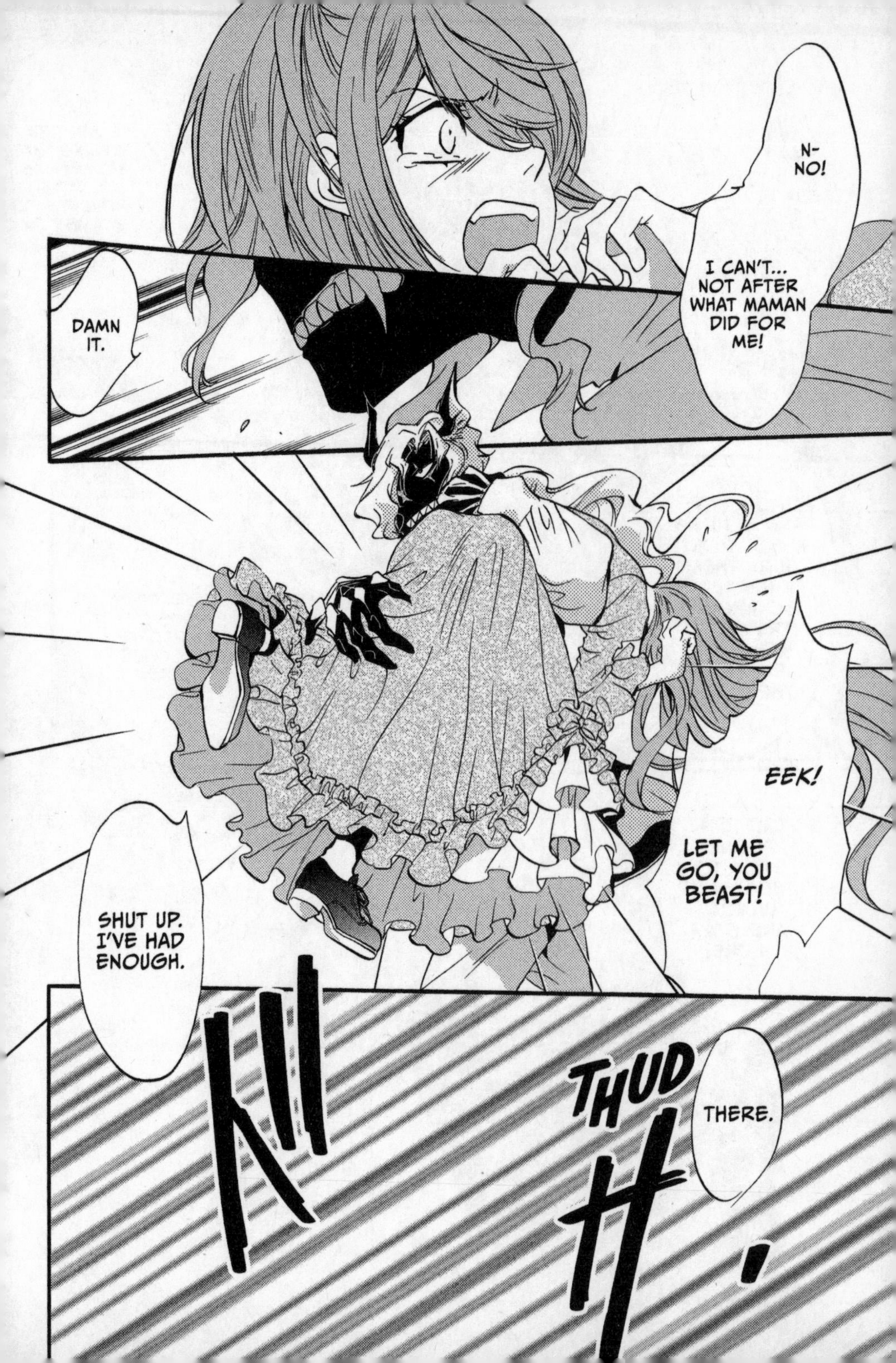
N-NO!
I CAN'T... NOT AFTER WHAT MAMAN DID FOR ME!
DAMN IT.
EEK!
LET ME GO, YOU BEAST!
SHUT UP. I'VE HAD ENOUGH.
THERE.
THUD

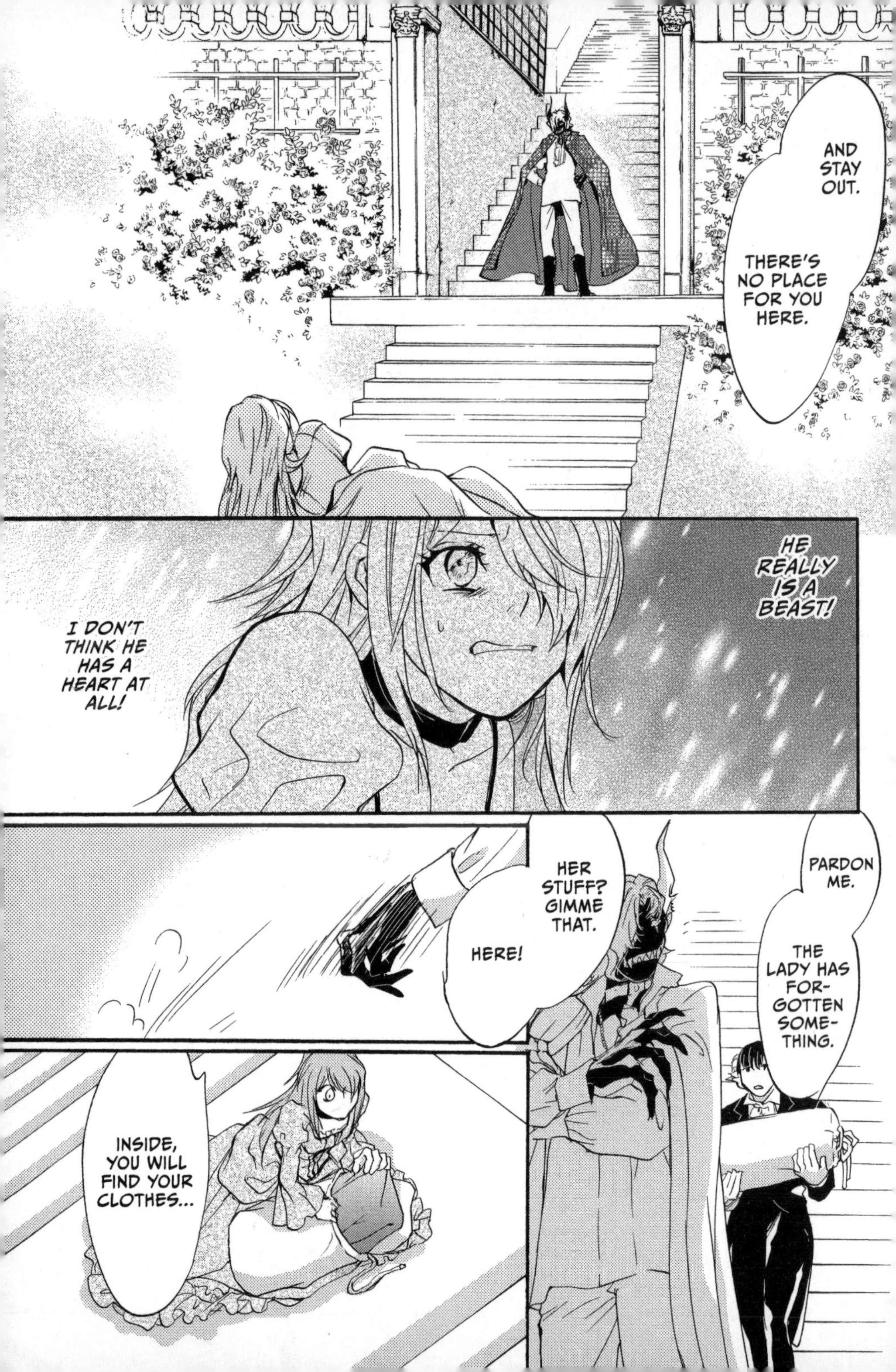
AND STAY OUT.
THERE'S NO PLACE FOR YOU HERE.
HE REALLY IS A BEAST!
I DON'T THINK HE HAS A HEART AT ALL!
PARDON ME.
THE LADY HAS FOR-GOTTEN SOME-THING.
HER STUFF? GIMME THAT.
HERE!
INSIDE, YOU WILL FIND YOUR CLOTHES...

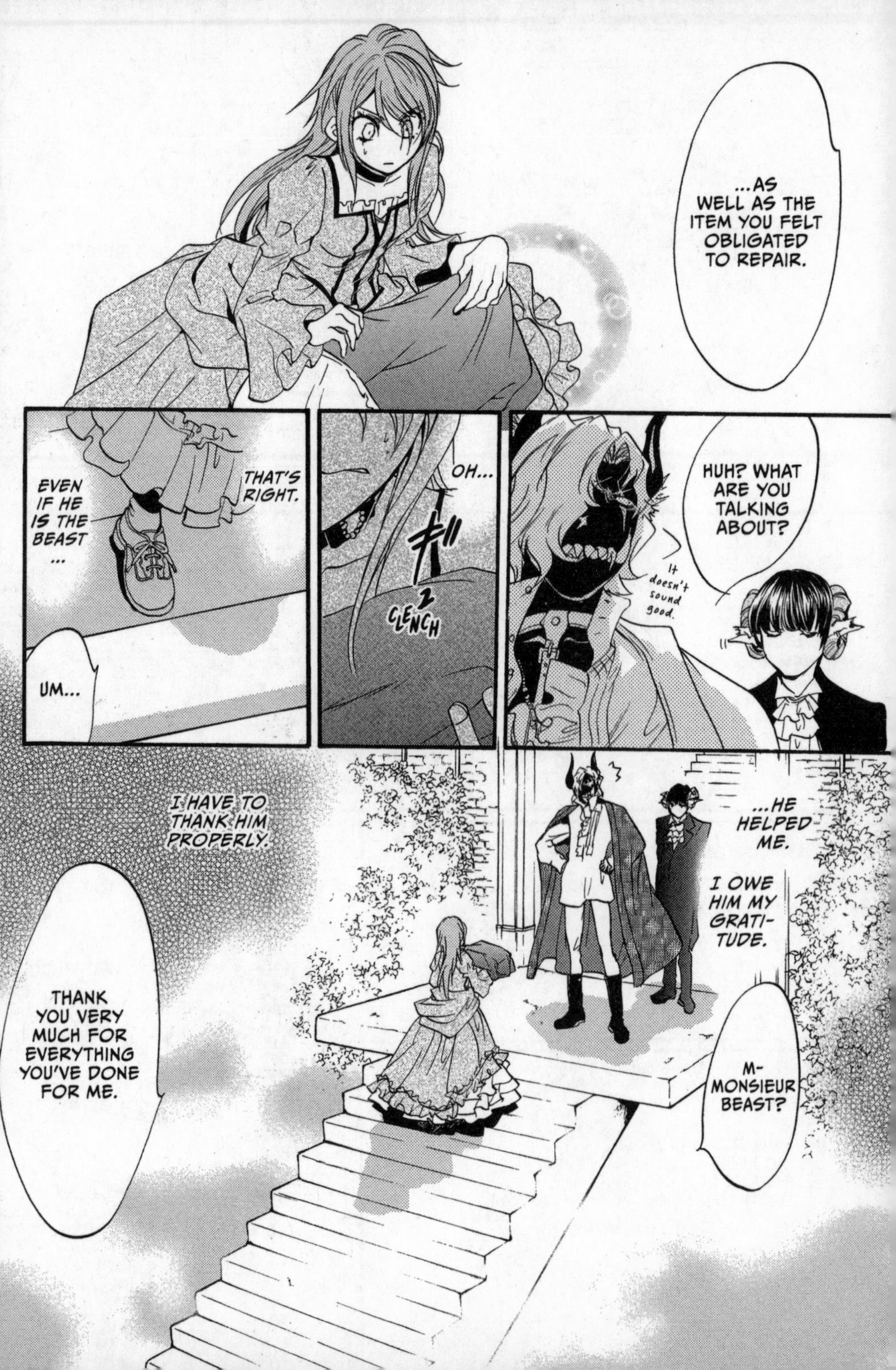
...AS WELL AS THE ITEM YOU FELT OBLIGATED TO REPAIR.
HUH? WHAT ARE YOU TALKING ABOUT?
It doesn't sound good.
OH...
CLENCH
THAT'S RIGHT.
EVEN IF HE IS THE BEAST ...
UM...
...HE HELPED ME.
I OWE HIM MY GRATI-TUDE.
M-MONSIEUR BEAST?
I HAVE TO THANK HIM PROPERLY.
THANK YOU VERY MUCH FOR EVERYTHING YOU'VE DONE FOR ME.

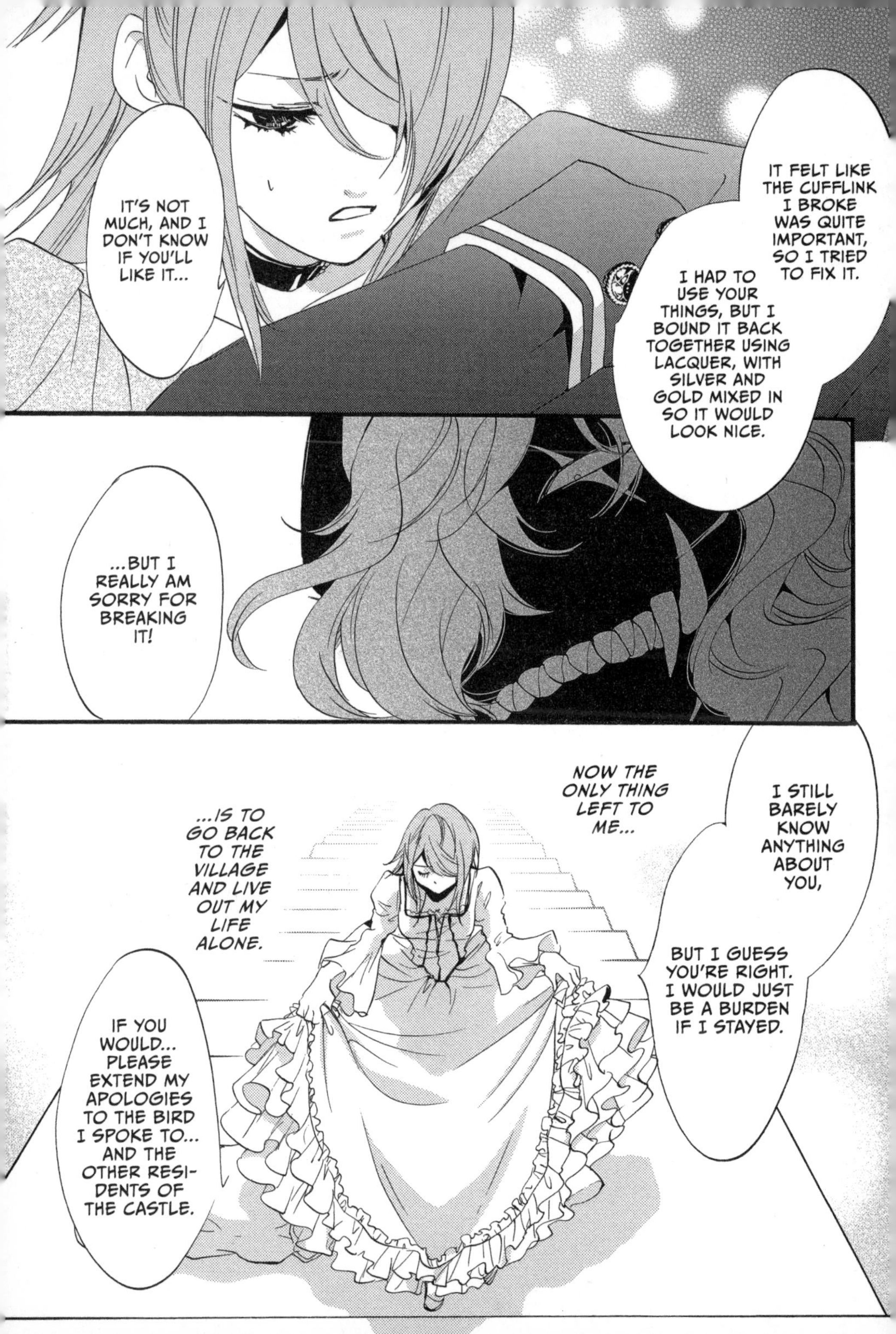
IT FELT LIKE THE CUFFLINK I BROKE WAS QUITE IMPORTANT, SO I TRIED TO FIX IT.
I HAD TO USE YOUR THINGS, BUT I BOUND IT BACK TOGETHER USING LACQUER, WITH SILVER AND GOLD MIXED IN SO IT WOULD LOOK NICE.
IT'S NOT MUCH, AND I DON'T KNOW IF YOU'LL LIKE IT...
...BUT I REALLY AM SORRY FOR BREAKING IT!
I STILL BARELY KNOW ANYTHING ABOUT YOU,
BUT I GUESS YOU'RE RIGHT. I WOULD JUST BE A BURDEN IF I STAYED.
NOW THE ONLY THING LEFT TO ME...
...IS TO GO BACK TO THE VILLAGE AND LIVE OUT MY LIFE ALONE.
IF YOU WOULD... PLEASE EXTEND MY APOLOGIES TO THE BIRD I SPOKE TO... AND THE OTHER RESI-DENTS OF THE CASTLE.

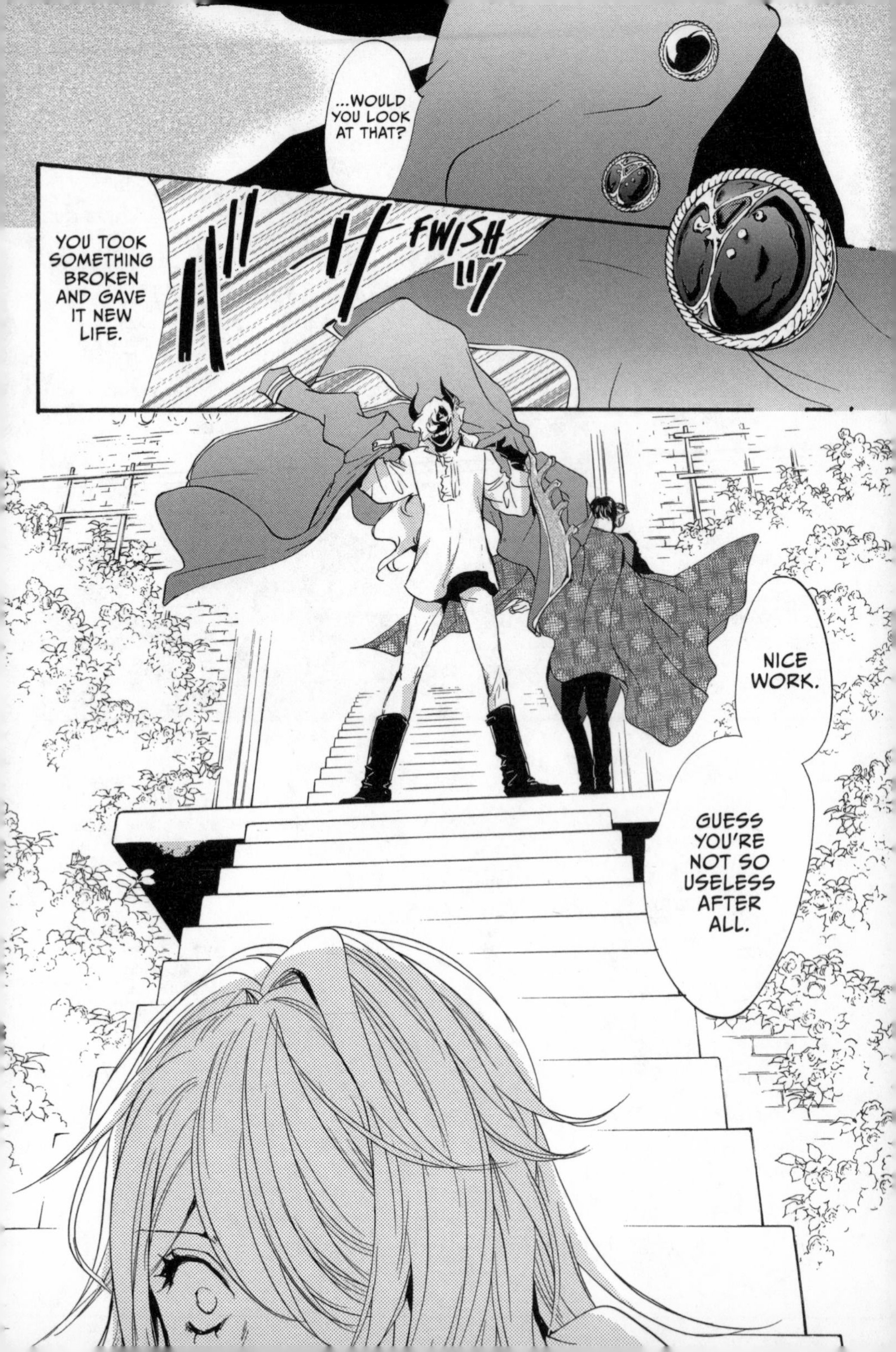
...WOULD YOU LOOK AT THAT?
YOU TOOK SOMETHING BROKEN AND GAVE IT NEW LIFE.
FWISH
NICE WORK.
GUESS YOU'RE NOT SO USELESS AFTER ALL.

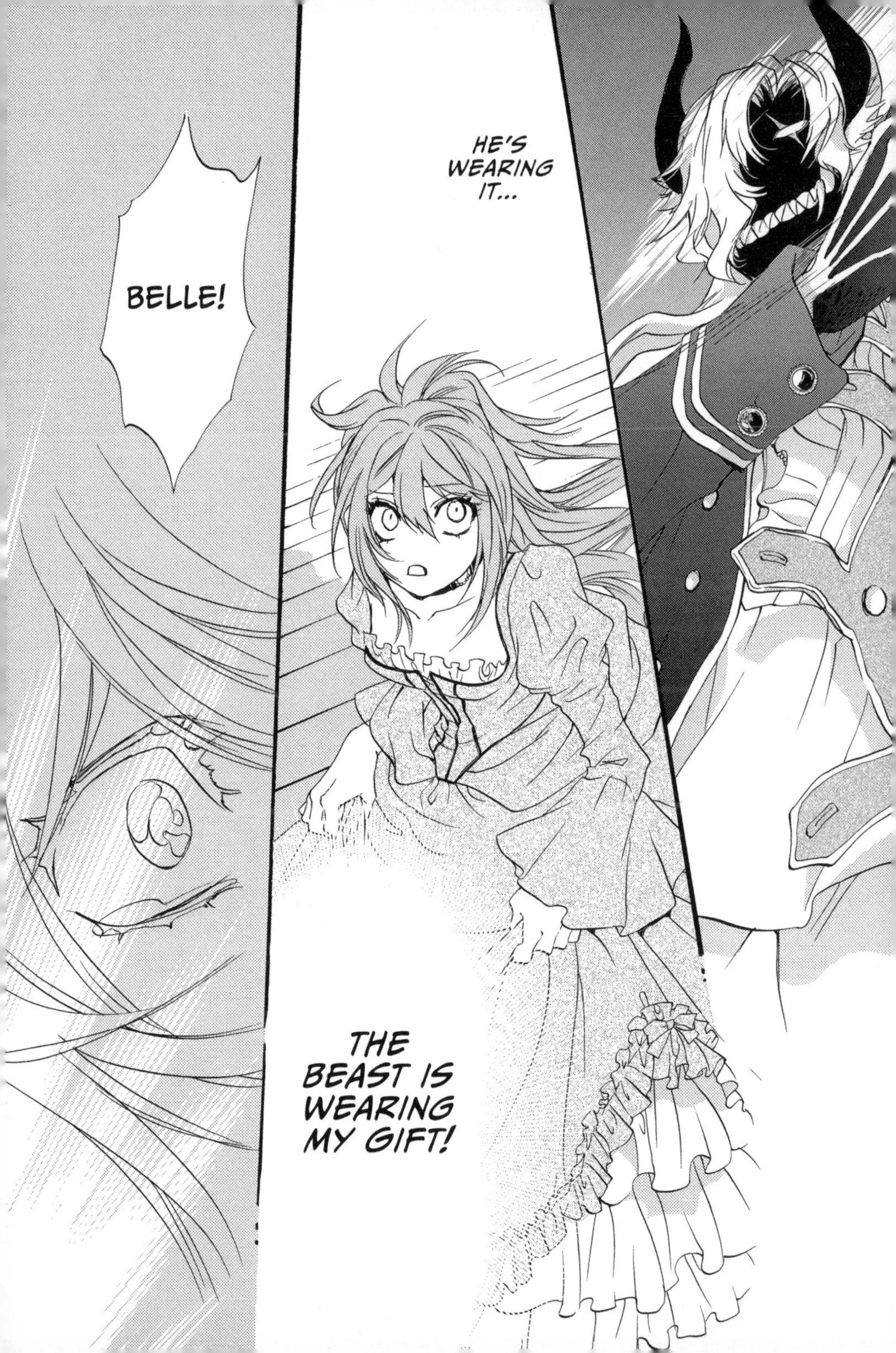
HE'S WEARING IT...
THE BEAST IS WEARING MY GIFT!
BELLE!

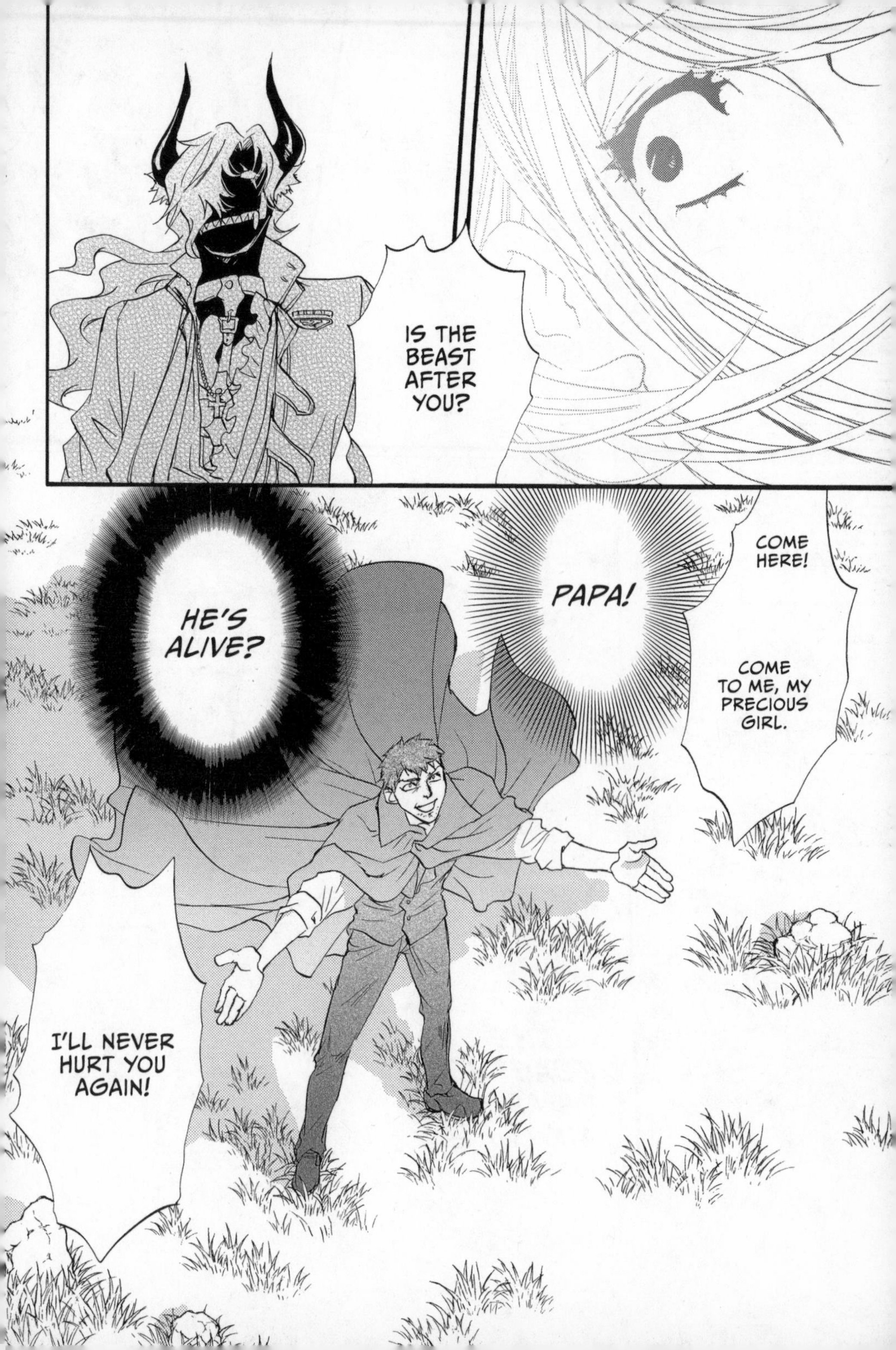
IS THE BEAST AFTER YOU?
COME HERE!
COME TO ME, MY PRECIOUS GIRL.
PAPA!
HE'S ALIVE?
I'LL NEVER HURT YOU AGAIN!

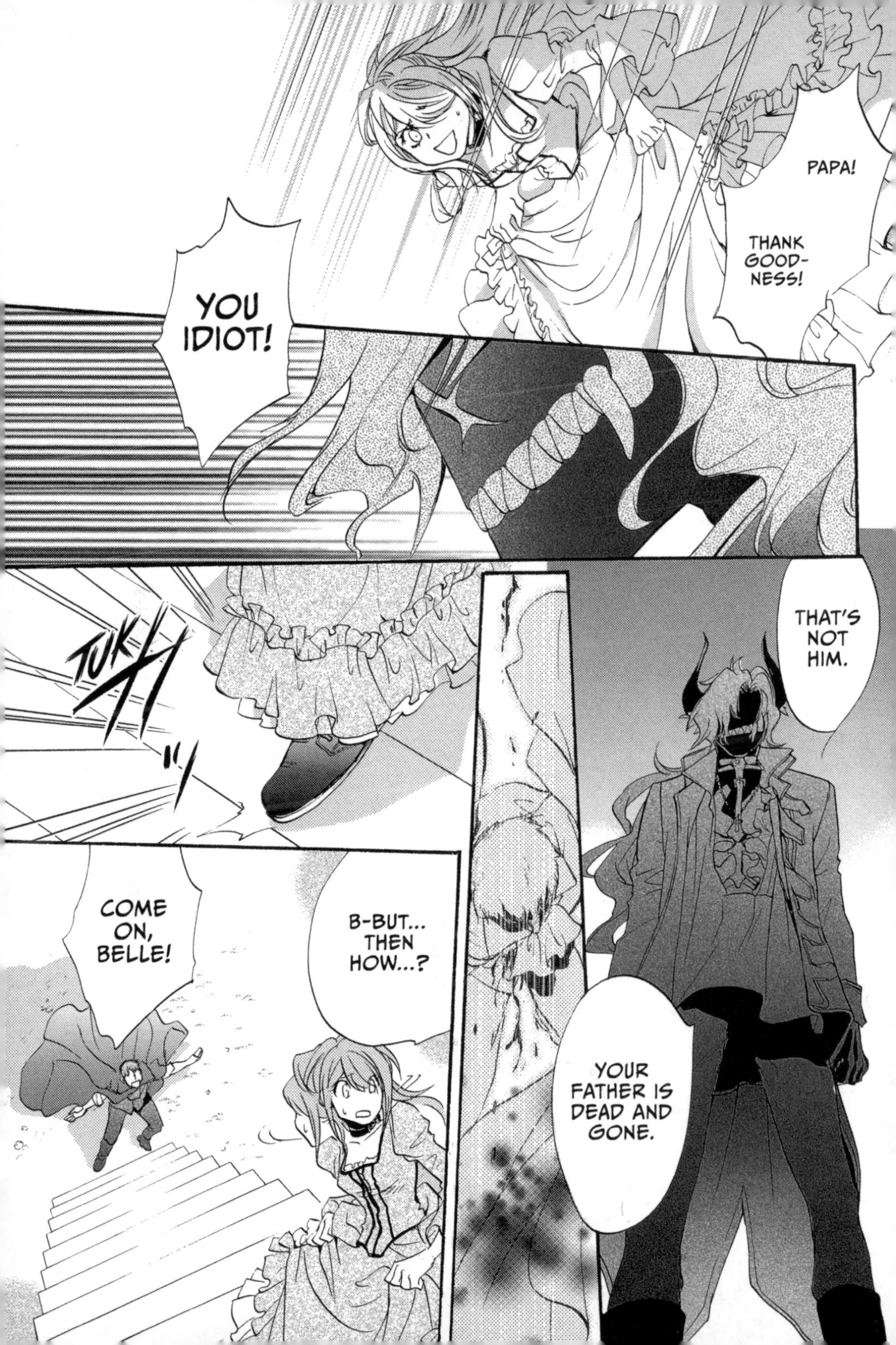
PAPA!
THANK GOOD-NESS!
YOU IDIOT!
THAT'S NOT HIM.
YOUR FATHER IS DEAD AND GONE.
TUK
B-BUT... THEN HOW...?
COME ON, BELLE!

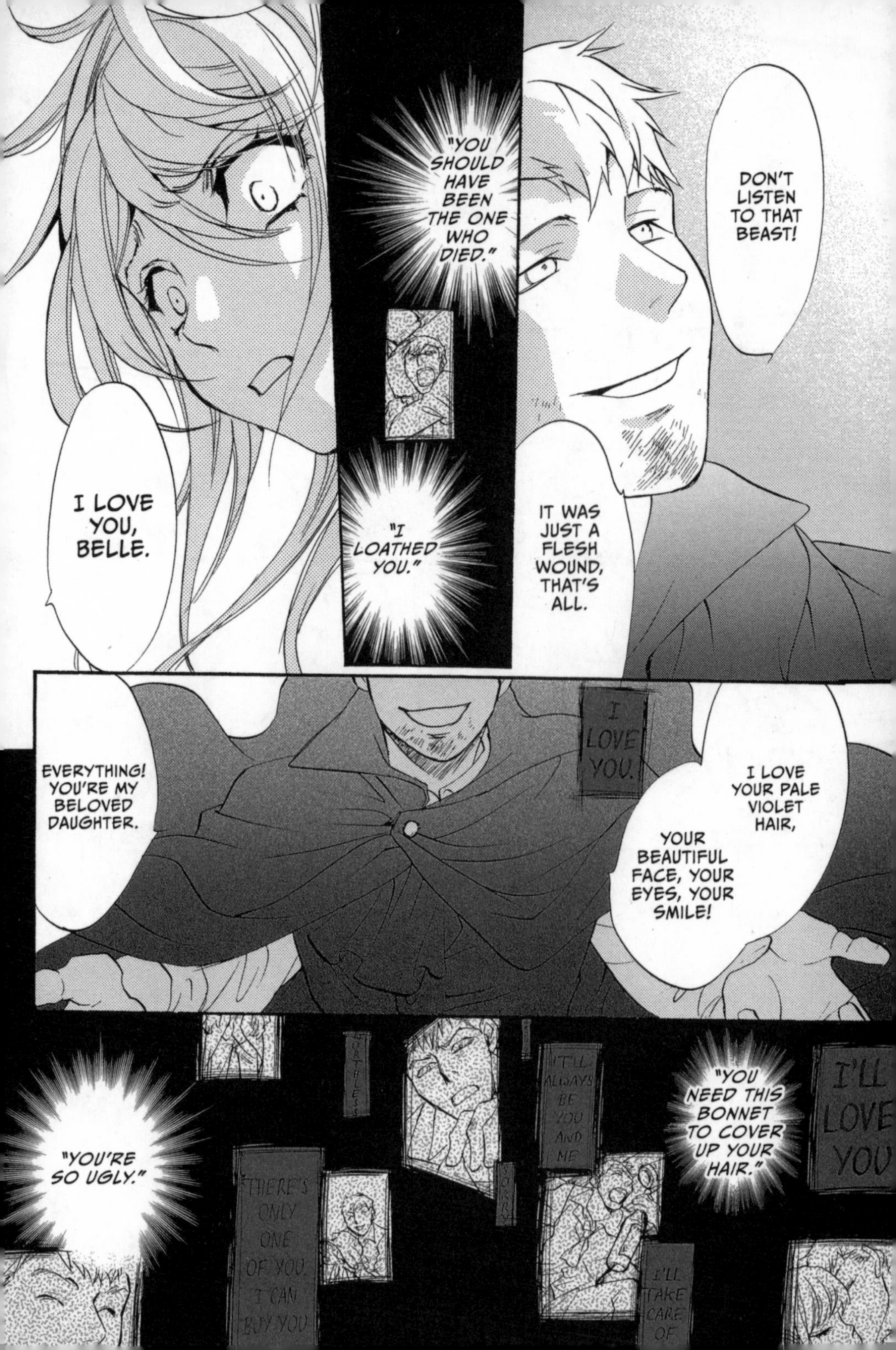
DON'T LISTEN TO THAT BEAST!
IT WAS JUST A FLESH WOUND, THAT'S ALL.
"YOU SHOULD HAVE BEEN THE ONE WHO DIED."
"I LOATHED YOU."
I LOVE YOU, BELLE.
I LOVE YOUR PALE VIOLET HAIR,
YOUR BEAUTIFUL FACE, YOUR EYES, YOUR SMILE!
I LOVE YOU.
EVERYTHING! YOU'RE MY BELOVED DAUGHTER.
I'LL LOVE YOU
"YOU NEED THIS BONNET TO COVER UP YOUR HAIR."
I'LL TAKE CARE OF
IT'LL ALWAYS BE YOU AND ME
SORRY
THERE'S ONLY ONE OF YOU. I CAN BUY YOU
"YOU'RE SO UGLY."

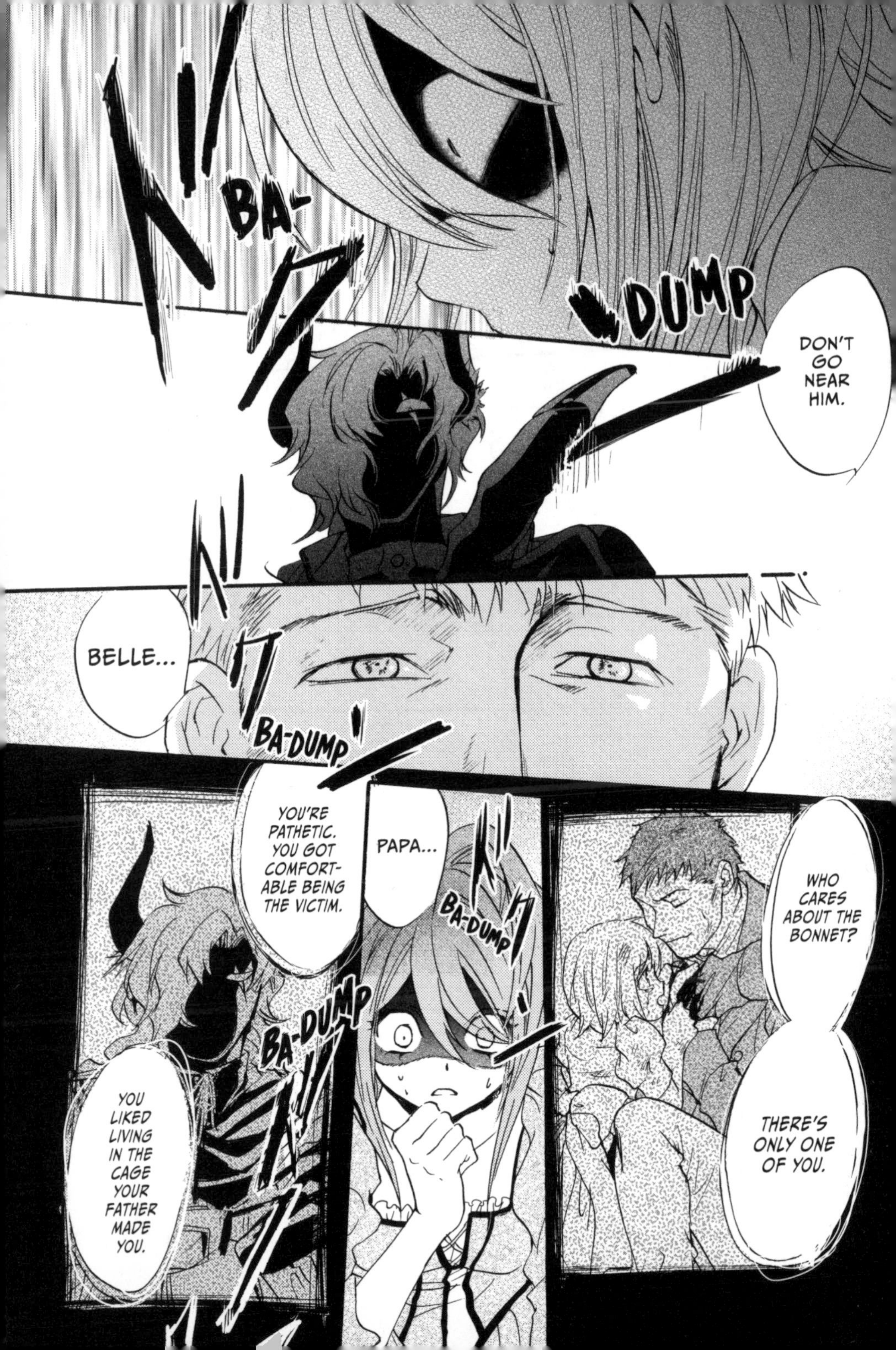
BA-
DUMP
DON'T GO NEAR HIM.
BELLE...
BA-DUMP
WHO CARES ABOUT THE BONNET?
THERE'S ONLY ONE OF YOU.
PAPA...
BA-DUMP
YOU'RE PATHETIC. YOU GOT COMFORT-ABLE BEING THE VICTIM.
BA-DUMP
YOU LIKED LIVING IN THE CAGE YOUR FATHER MADE YOU.

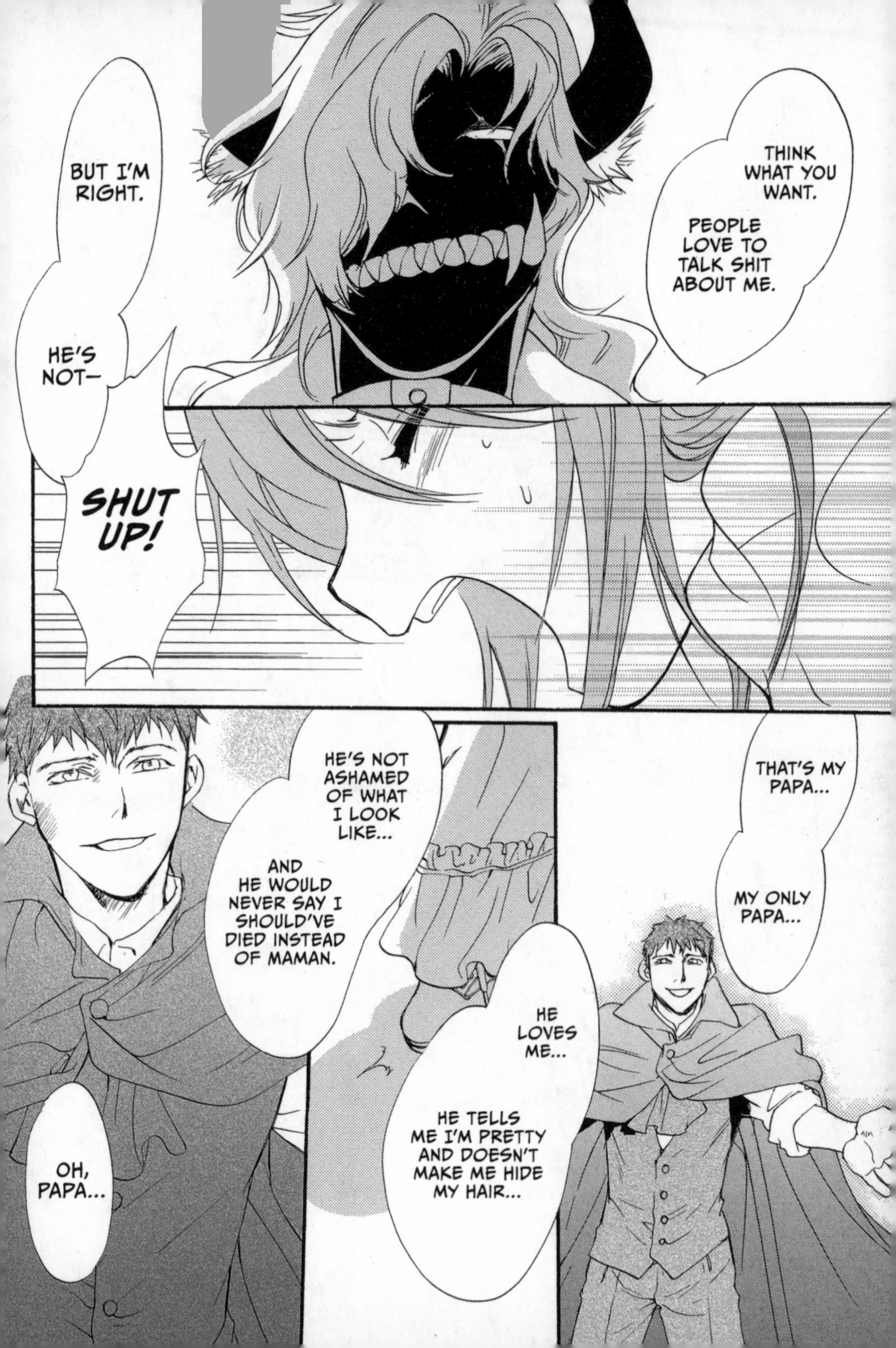
THINK WHAT YOU WANT.
PEOPLE LOVE TO TALK SHIT ABOUT ME.
BUT I'M RIGHT.
HE'S NOT—
SHUT UP!
THAT'S MY PAPA...
MY ONLY PAPA...
HE'S NOT ASHAMED OF WHAT I LOOK LIKE...
AND HE WOULD NEVER SAY I SHOULD'VE DIED INSTEAD OF MAMAN.
HE LOVES ME...
HE TELLS ME I'M PRETTY AND DOESN'T MAKE ME HIDE MY HAIR...
OH, PAPA...

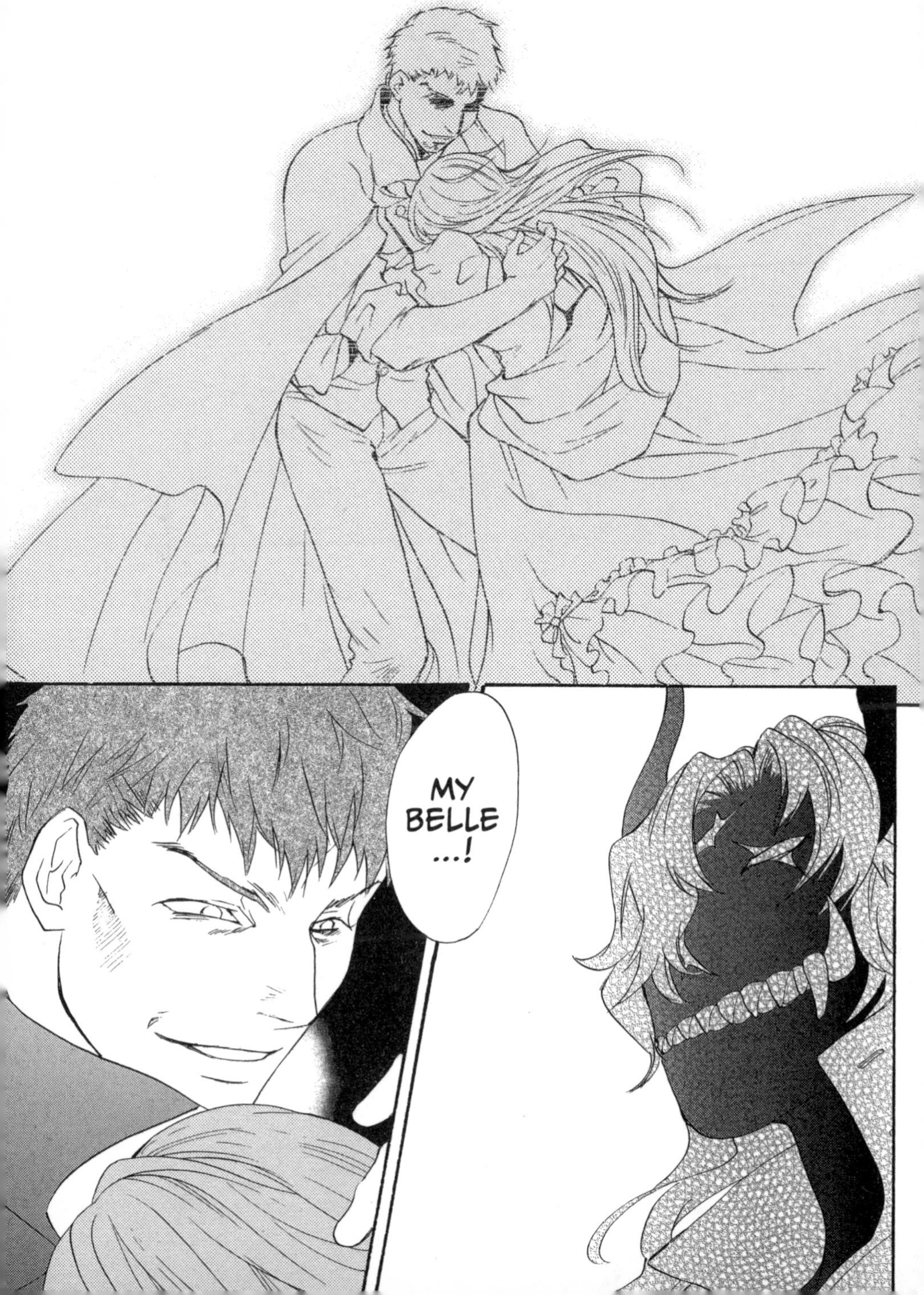
MY BELLE ...!

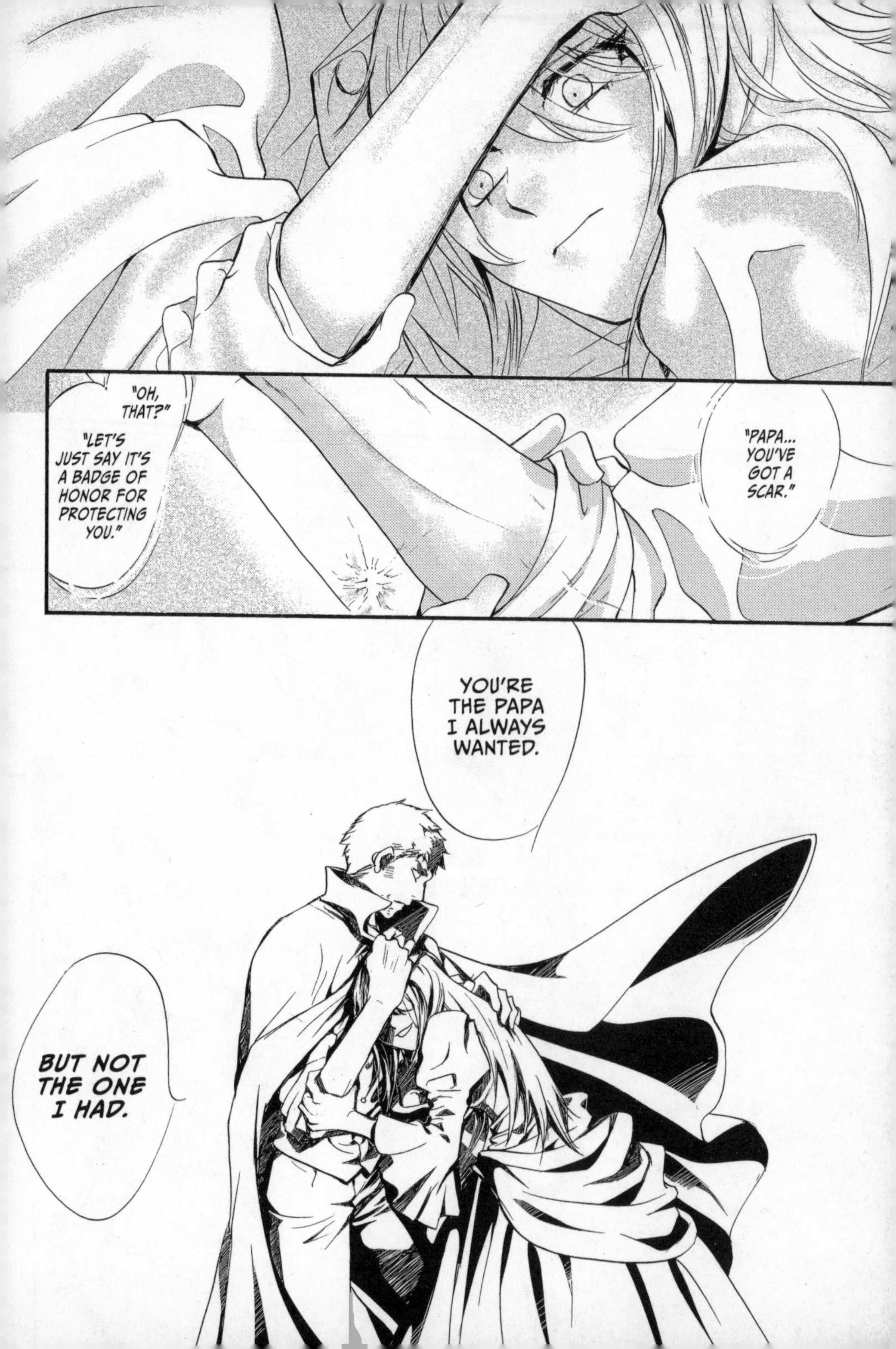
"PAPA... YOU'VE GOT A SCAR."
"OH, THAT?"
"LET'S JUST SAY IT'S A BADGE OF HONOR FOR PROTECTING YOU."
YOU'RE THE PAPA I ALWAYS WANTED.
BUT NOT THE ONE I HAD.

La belle et la bête

du paradis perdu

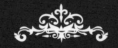

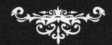

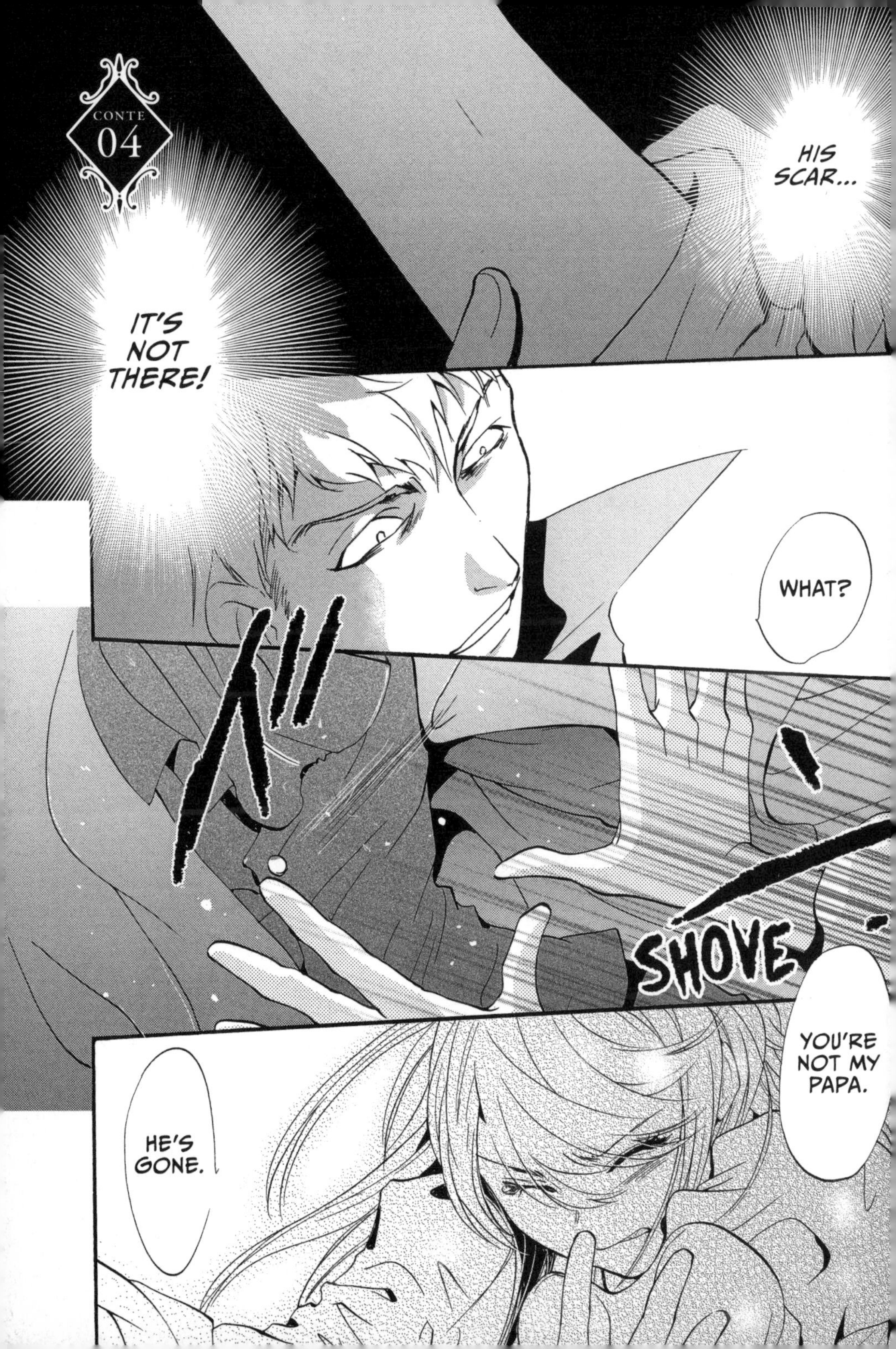
CONTE 04
HIS SCAR...
IT'S NOT THERE!
WHAT?
SHOVE
YOU'RE NOT MY PAPA.
HE'S GONE.

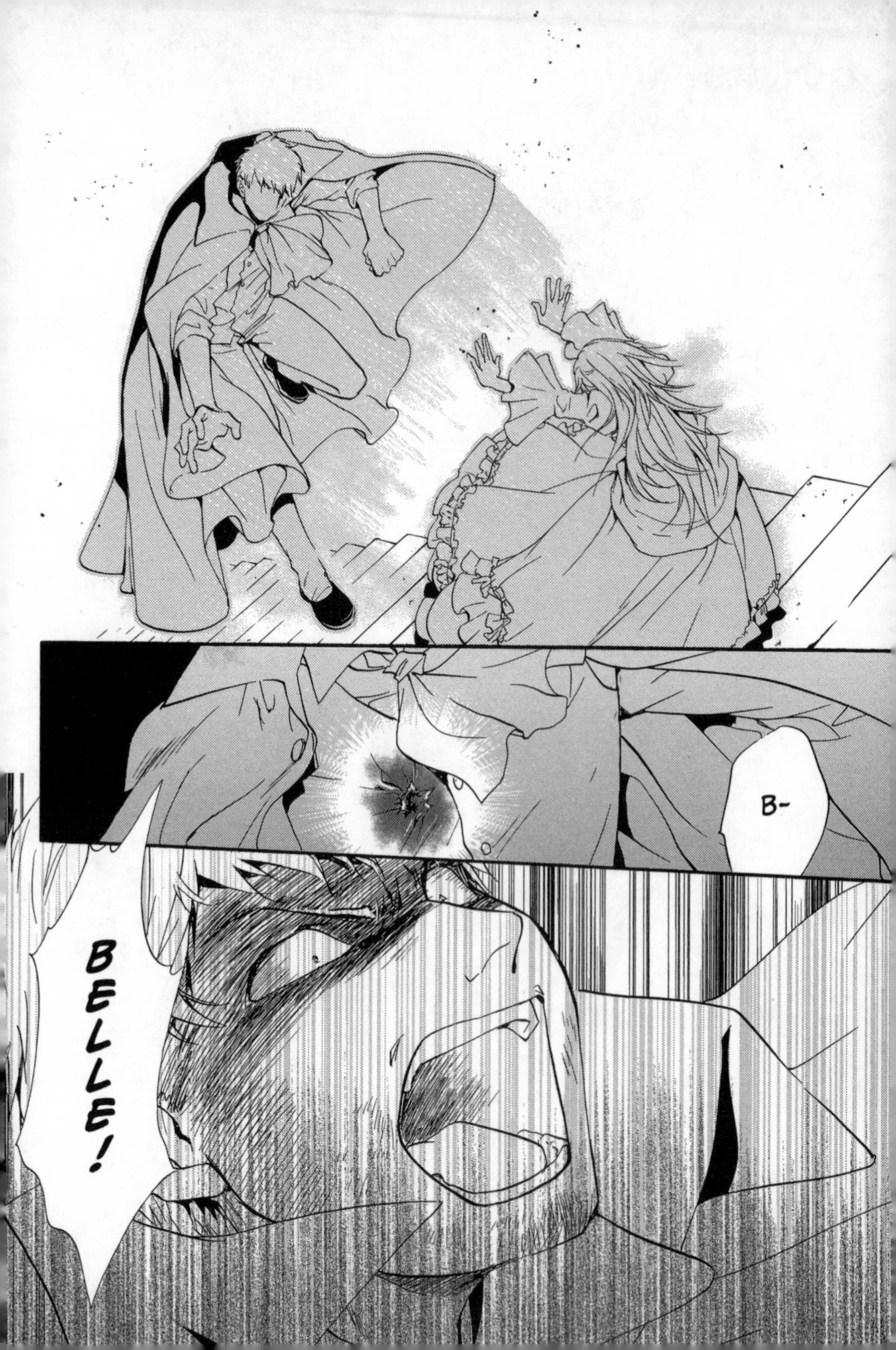
B-
BELLE!

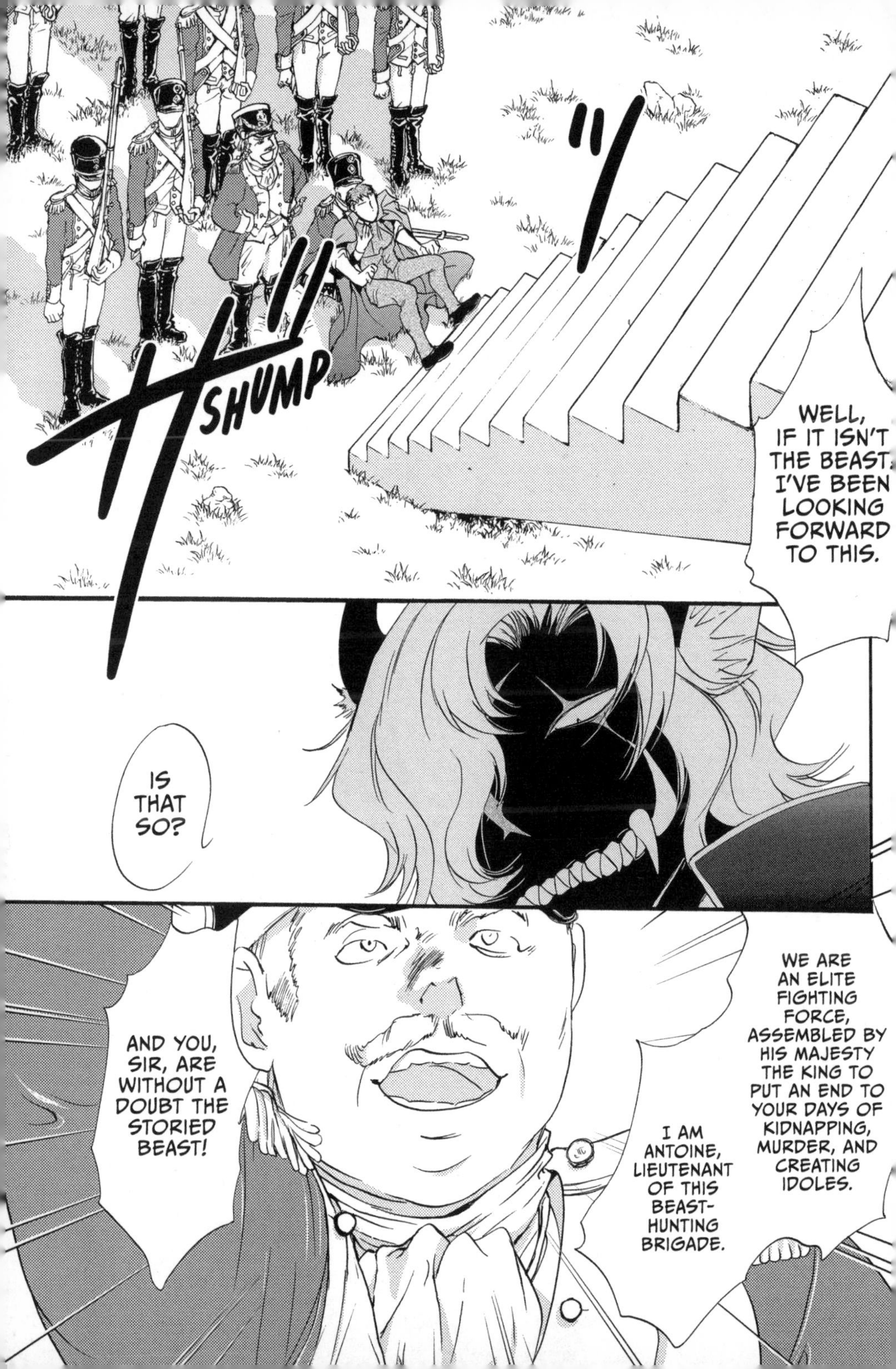
WELL, IF IT ISN'T THE BEAST. I'VE BEEN LOOKING FORWARD TO THIS.
SHUMP
IS THAT SO?
WE ARE AN ELITE FIGHTING FORCE, ASSEMBLED BY HIS MAJESTY THE KING TO PUT AN END TO YOUR DAYS OF KIDNAPPING, MURDER, AND CREATING IDOLES.
I AM ANTOINE, LIEUTENANT OF THIS BEAST-HUNTING BRIGADE.
AND YOU, SIR, ARE WITHOUT A DOUBT THE STORIED BEAST!

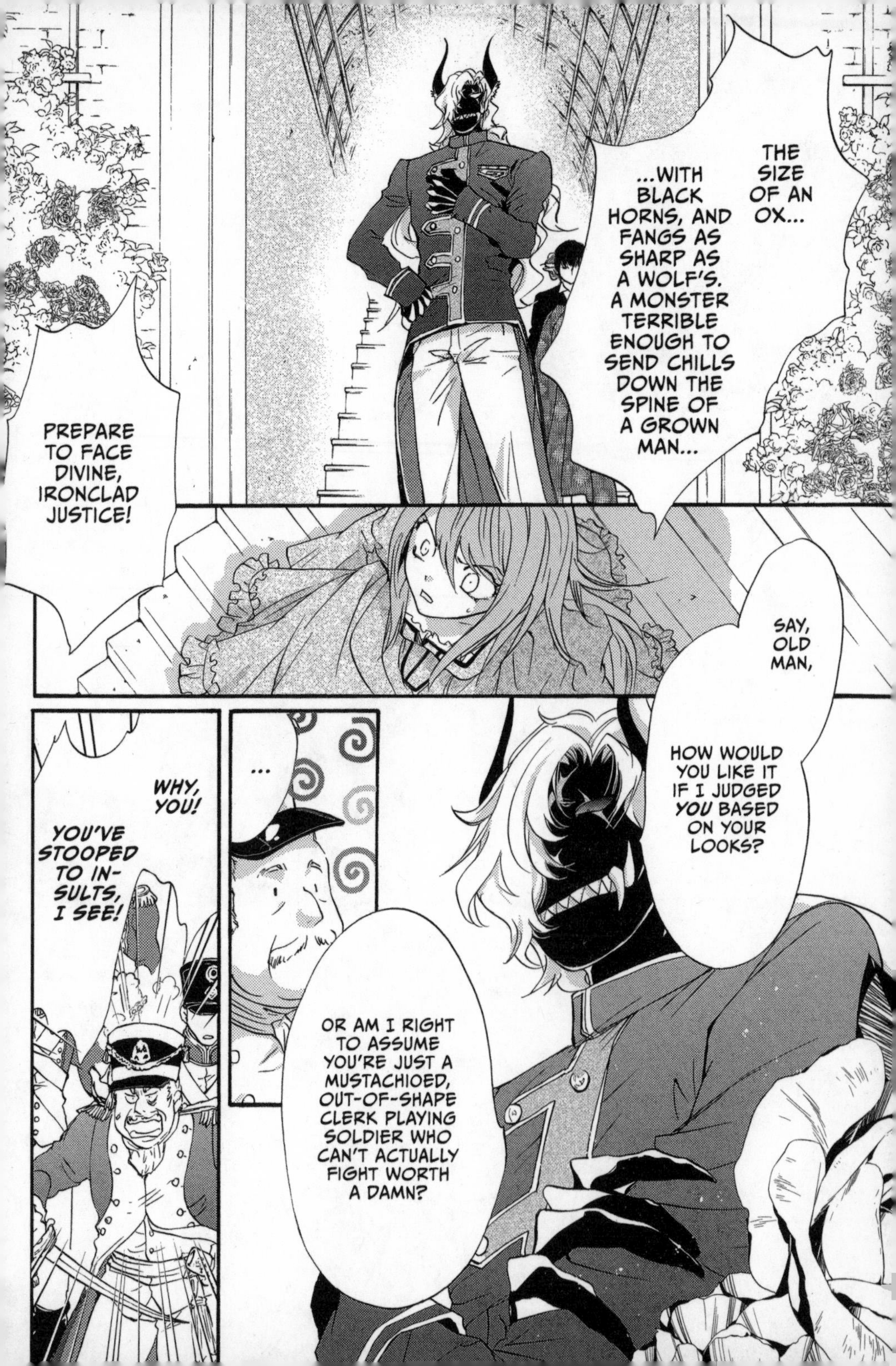
THE SIZE OF AN OX...
...WITH BLACK HORNS, AND FANGS AS SHARP AS A WOLF'S. A MONSTER TERRIBLE ENOUGH TO SEND CHILLS DOWN THE SPINE OF A GROWN MAN...
PREPARE TO FACE DIVINE, IRONCLAD JUSTICE!
SAY, OLD MAN,
HOW WOULD YOU LIKE IT IF I JUDGED YOU BASED ON YOUR LOOKS?
OR AM I RIGHT TO ASSUME YOU'RE JUST A MUSTACHIOED, OUT-OF-SHAPE CLERK PLAYING SOLDIER WHO CAN'T ACTUALLY FIGHT WORTH A DAMN?
...
WHY, YOU!
YOU'VE STOOPED TO IN-SULTS, I SEE!

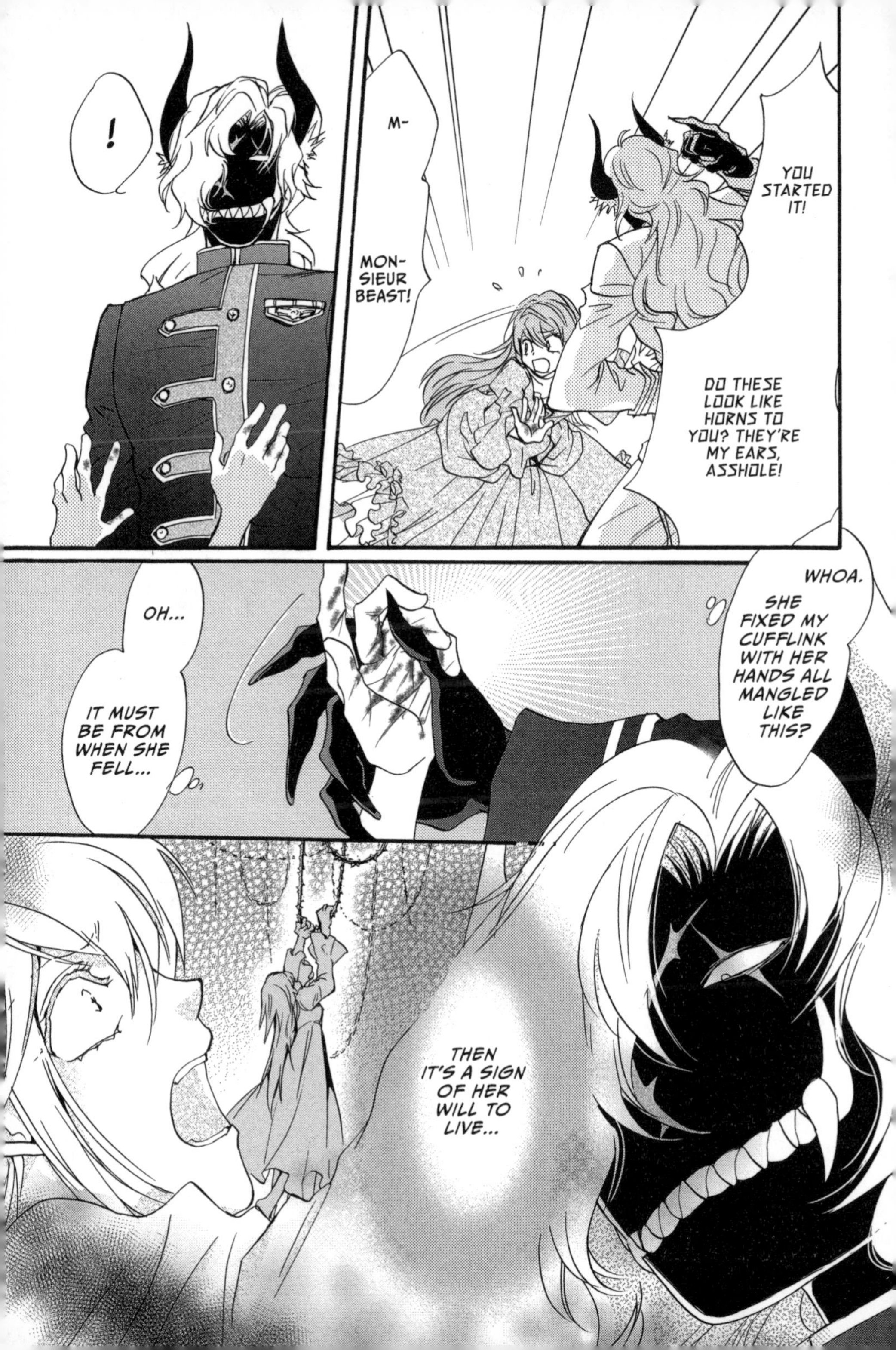
YOU STARTED IT!
DO THESE LOOK LIKE HORNS TO YOU? THEY'RE MY EARS, ASSHOLE!
M-
MON-SIEUR BEAST!
!
WHOA.
SHE FIXED MY CUFFLINK WITH HER HANDS ALL MANGLED LIKE THIS?
OH...
IT MUST BE FROM WHEN SHE FELL...
THEN IT'S A SIGN OF HER WILL TO LIVE...

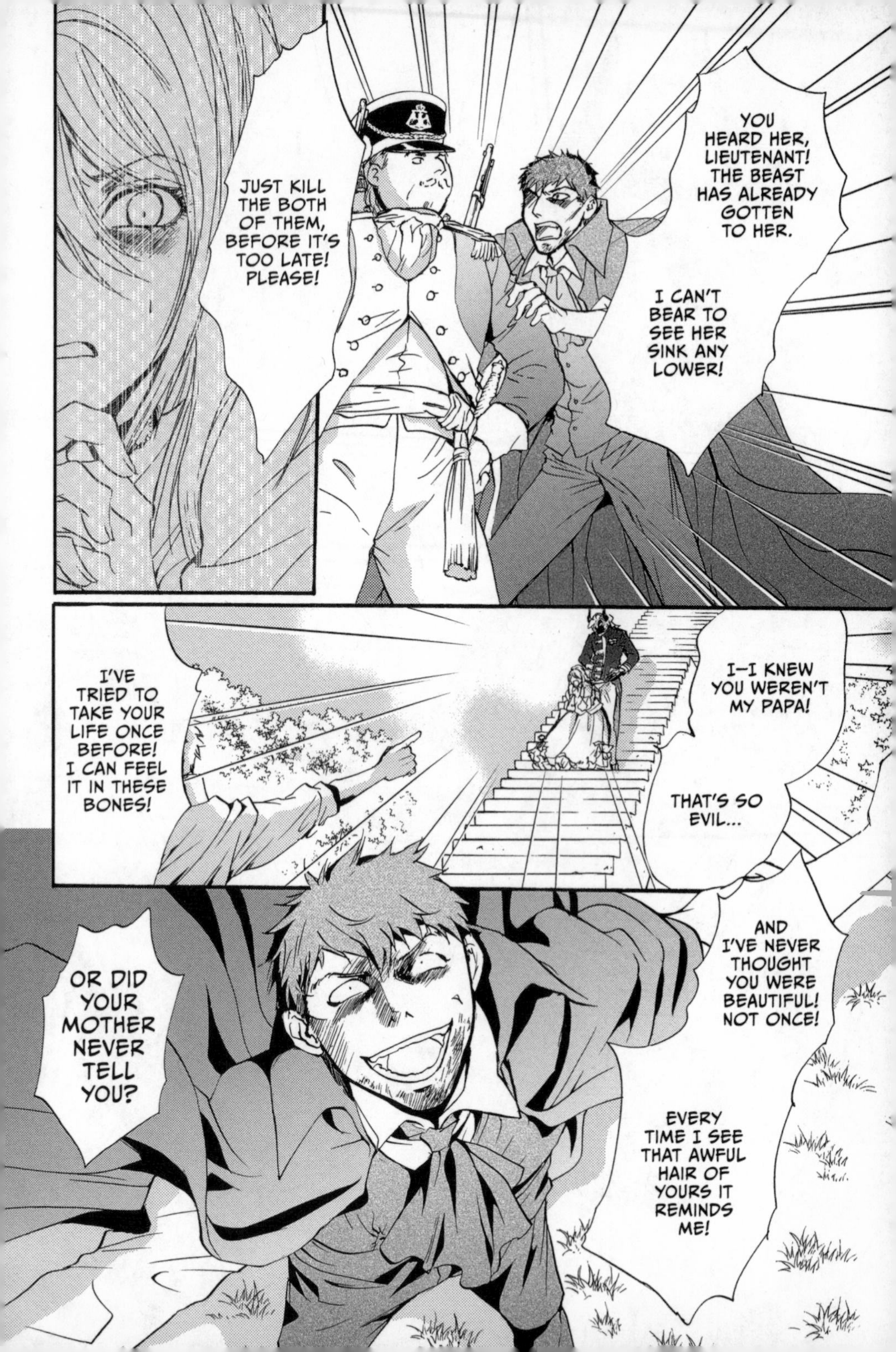
YOU HEARD HER, LIEUTENANT! THE BEAST HAS ALREADY GOTTEN TO HER.
I CAN'T BEAR TO SEE HER SINK ANY LOWER!
JUST KILL THE BOTH OF THEM, BEFORE IT'S TOO LATE! PLEASE!
I–I KNEW YOU WEREN'T MY PAPA!
THAT'S SO EVIL...
I'VE TRIED TO TAKE YOUR LIFE ONCE BEFORE! I CAN FEEL IT IN THESE BONES!
AND I'VE NEVER THOUGHT YOU WERE BEAUTIFUL! NOT ONCE!
EVERY TIME I SEE THAT AWFUL HAIR OF YOURS IT REMINDS ME!
OR DID YOUR MOTHER NEVER TELL YOU?

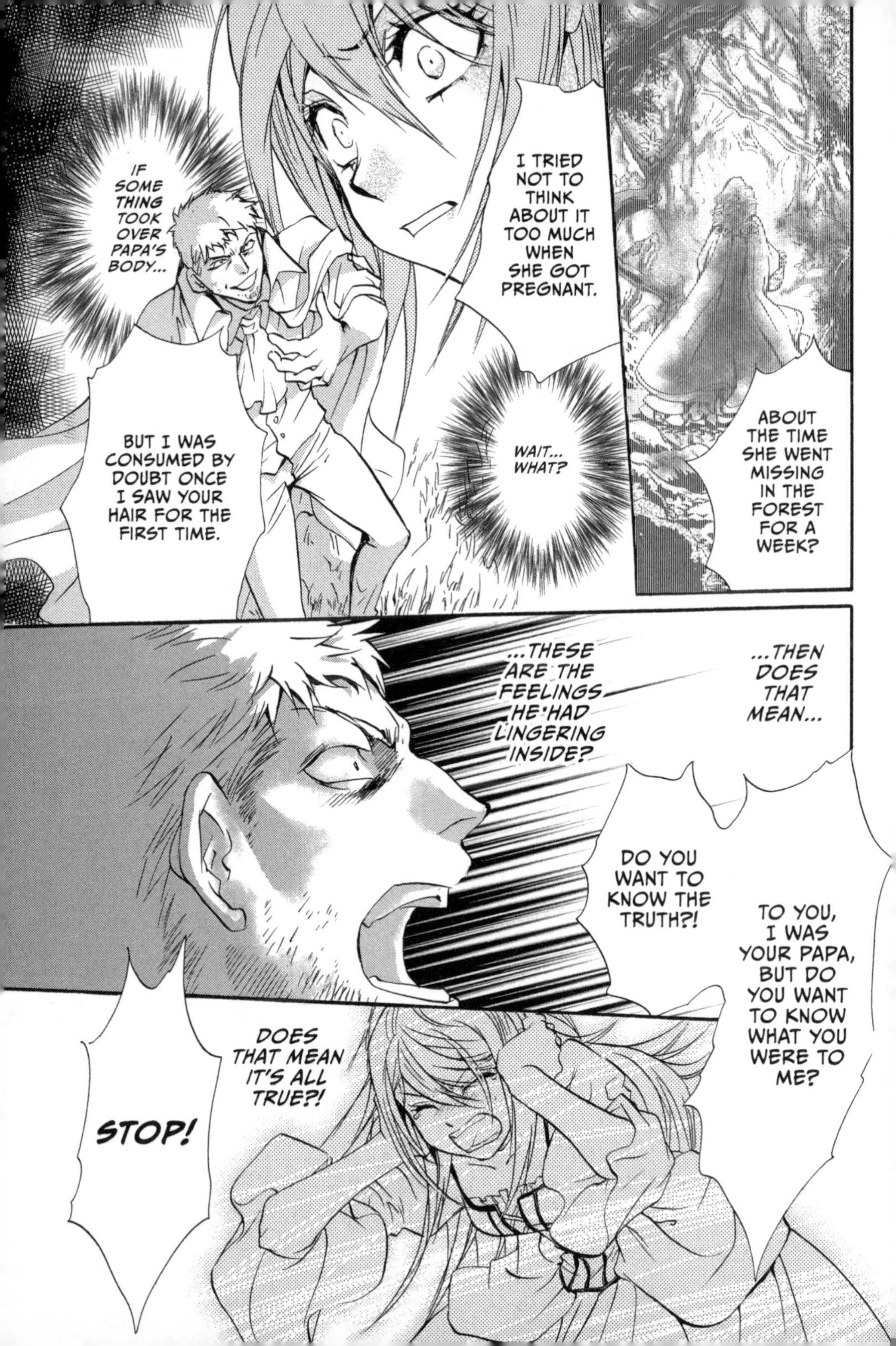
ABOUT THE TIME SHE WENT MISSING IN THE FOREST FOR A WEEK?
I TRIED NOT TO THINK ABOUT IT TOO MUCH WHEN SHE GOT PREGNANT.
IF SOME THING TOOK OVER PAPA'S BODY...
WAIT... WHAT?
BUT I WAS CONSUMED BY DOUBT ONCE I SAW YOUR HAIR FOR THE FIRST TIME.
...THEN DOES THAT MEAN...
...THESE ARE THE FEELINGS HE HAD LINGERING INSIDE?
TO YOU, I WAS YOUR PAPA, BUT DO YOU WANT TO KNOW WHAT YOU WERE TO ME?
DO YOU WANT TO KNOW THE TRUTH?!
DOES THAT MEAN IT'S ALL TRUE?!
STOP!

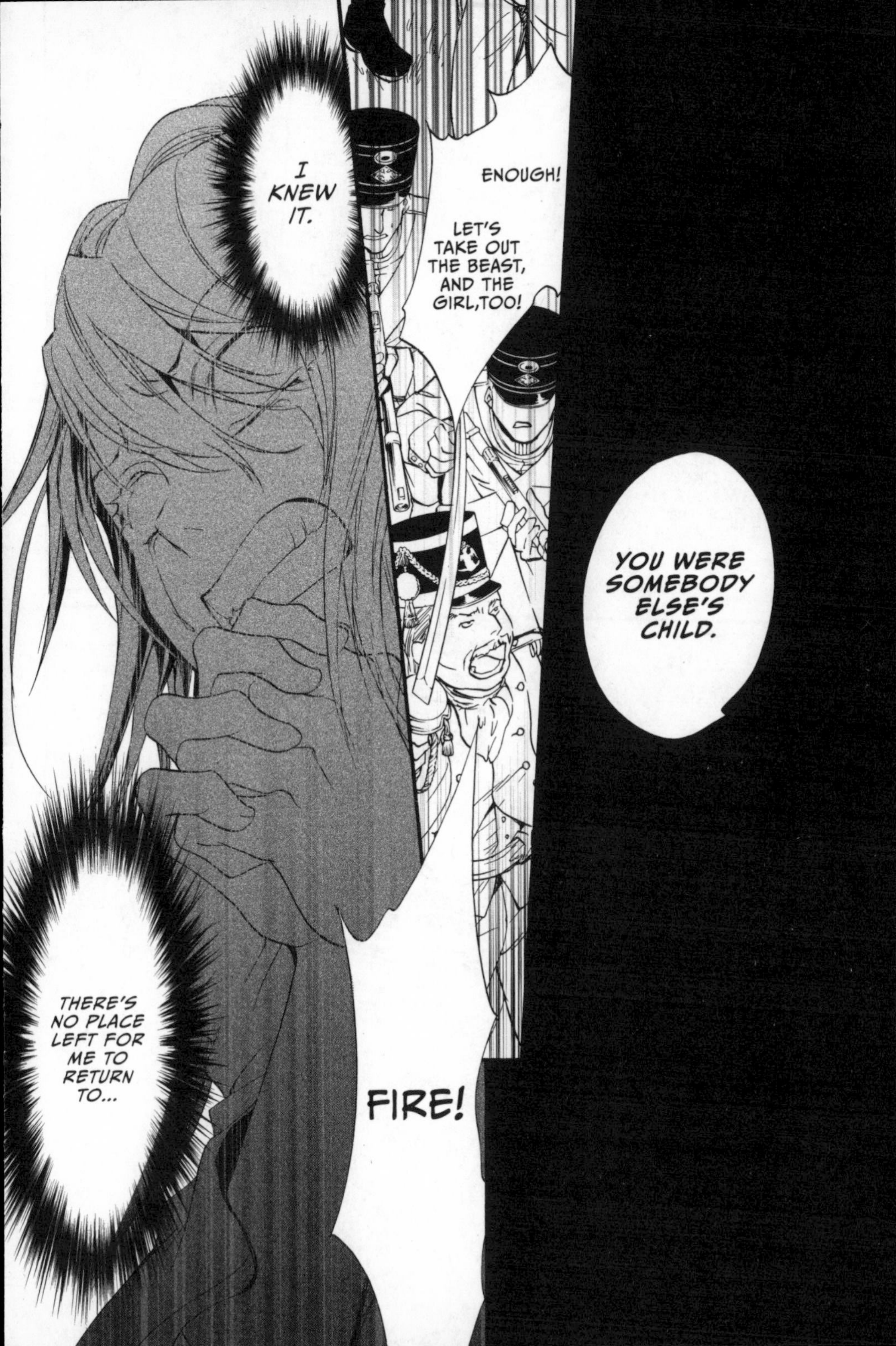
YOU WERE SOMEBODY ELSE'S CHILD.
ENOUGH!
LET'S TAKE OUT THE BEAST, AND THE GIRL,TOO!
I KNEW IT.
THERE'S NO PLACE LEFT FOR ME TO RETURN TO...
FIRE!

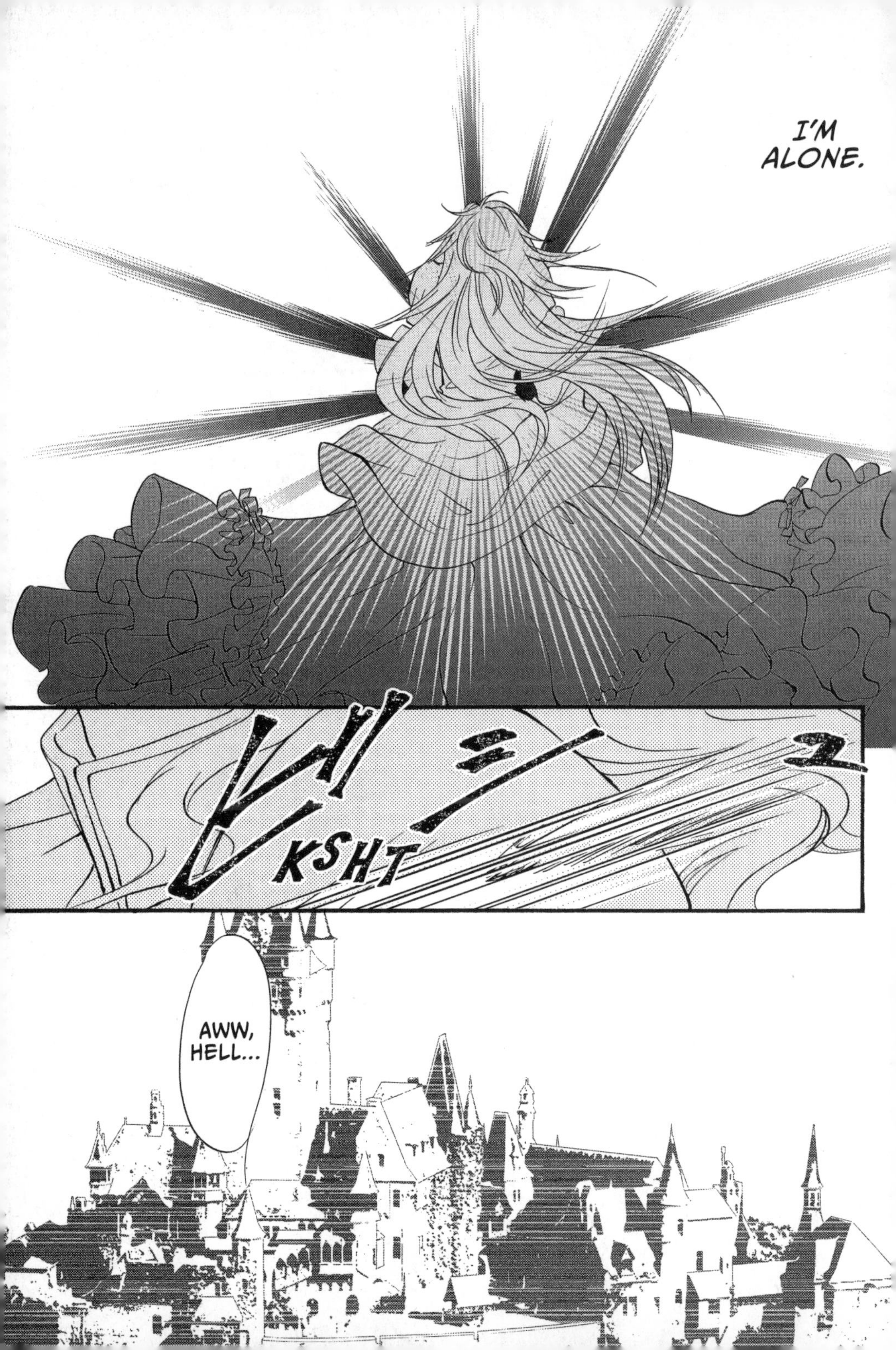
I'M ALONE.
KSHT
AWW, HELL...

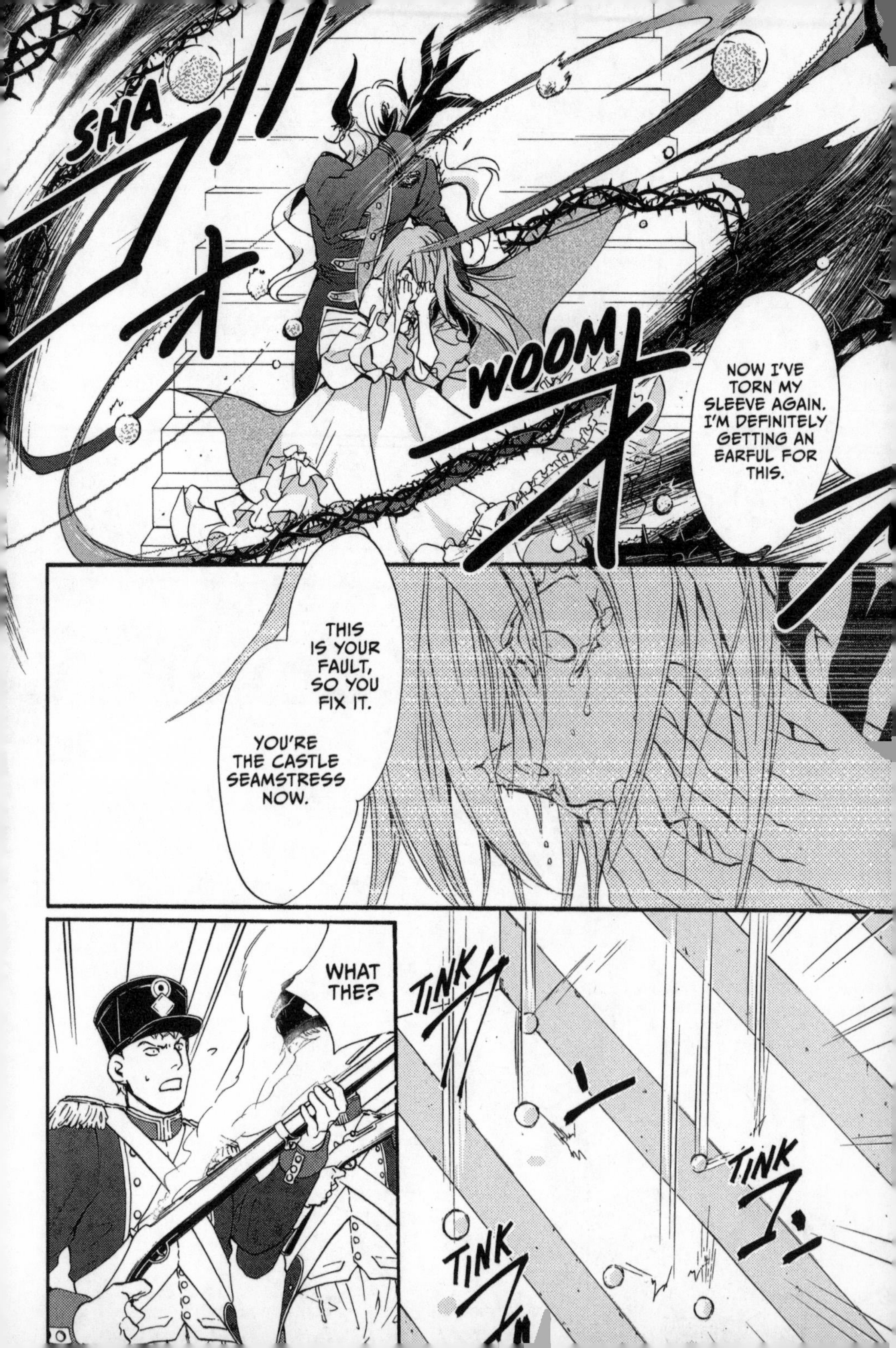
NOW I'VE TORN MY SLEEVE AGAIN. I'M DEFINITELY GETTING AN EARFUL FOR THIS.
WOOM
SHA
THIS IS YOUR FAULT, SO YOU FIX IT.
YOU'RE THE CASTLE SEAMSTRESS NOW.
TINK
TINK
TINK
WHAT THE?

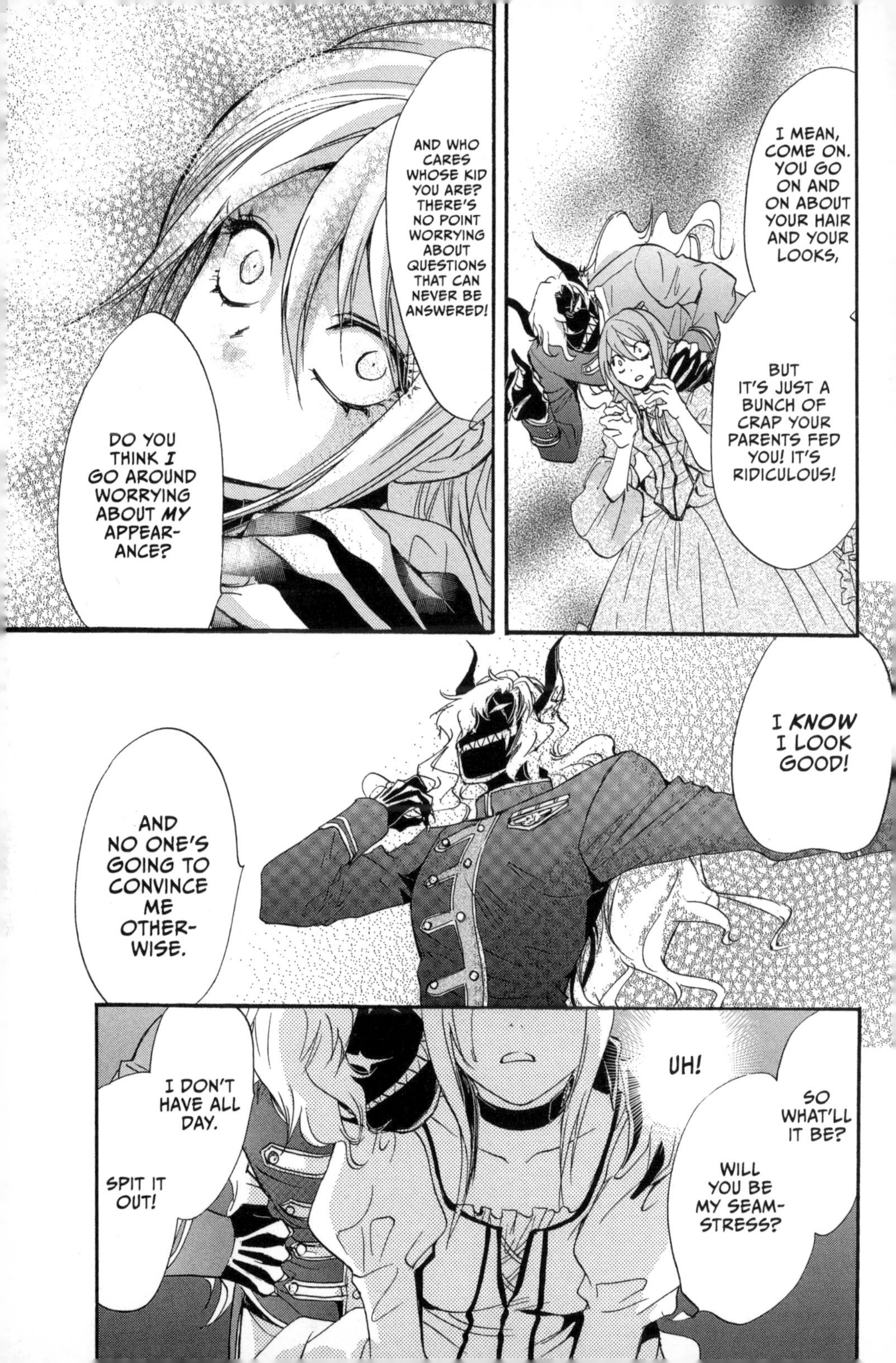
I MEAN, COME ON. YOU GO ON AND ON ABOUT YOUR HAIR AND YOUR LOOKS,
BUT IT'S JUST A BUNCH OF CRAP YOUR PARENTS FED YOU! IT'S RIDICULOUS!
AND WHO CARES WHOSE KID YOU ARE? THERE'S NO POINT WORRYING ABOUT QUESTIONS THAT CAN NEVER BE ANSWERED!
DO YOU THINK *I* GO AROUND WORRYING ABOUT *MY* APPEARANCE?
I *KNOW* I LOOK GOOD!
AND NO ONE'S GOING TO CONVINCE ME OTHERWISE.
SO WHAT'LL IT BE?
WILL YOU BE MY SEAMSTRESS?
UH!
I DON'T HAVE ALL DAY.
SPIT IT OUT!

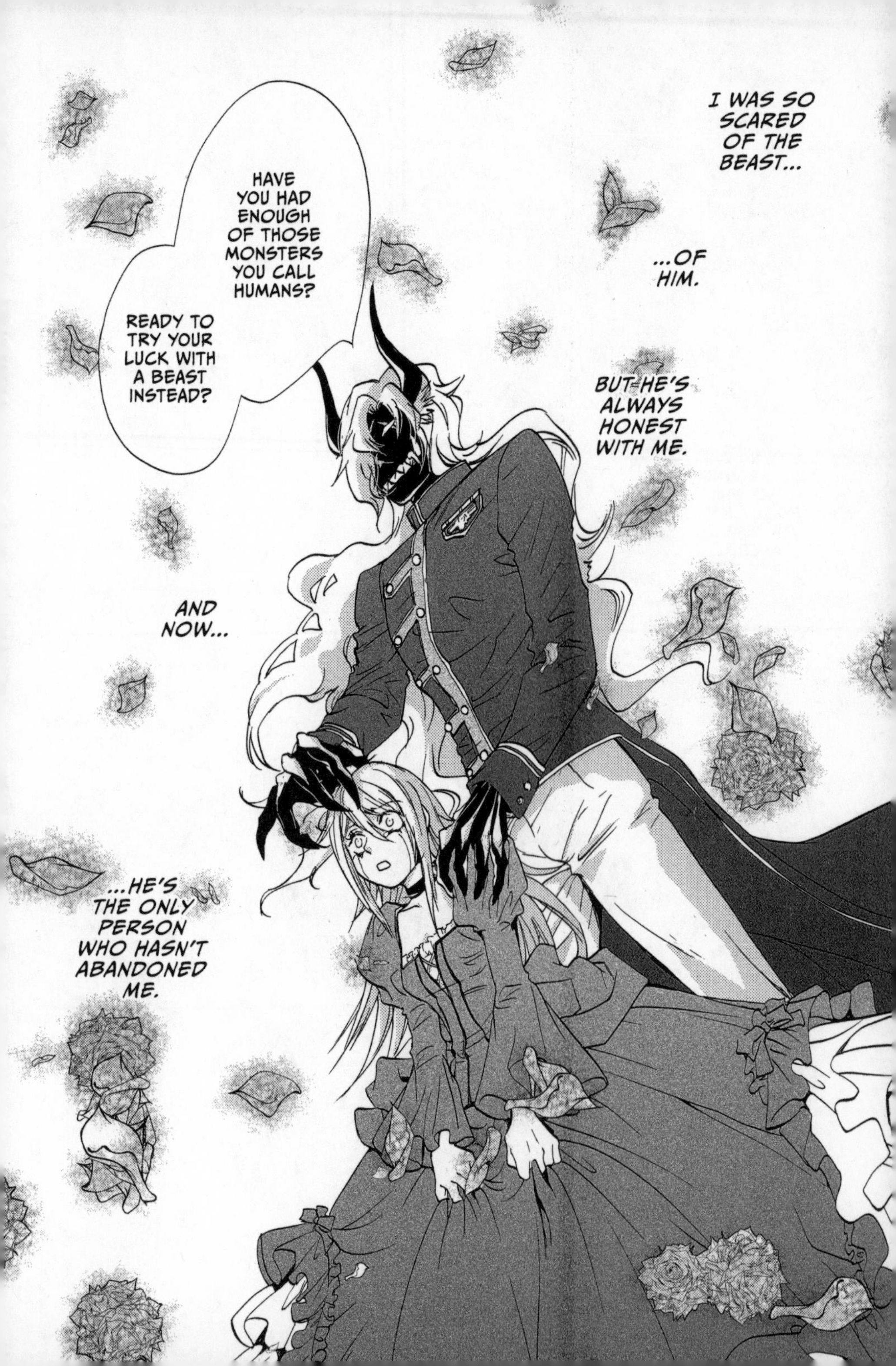
I WAS SO SCARED OF THE BEAST...
...OF HIM.
BUT HE'S ALWAYS HONEST WITH ME.
HAVE YOU HAD ENOUGH OF THOSE MONSTERS YOU CALL HUMANS?
READY TO TRY YOUR LUCK WITH A BEAST INSTEAD?
AND NOW...
...HE'S THE ONLY PERSON WHO HASN'T ABANDONED ME.

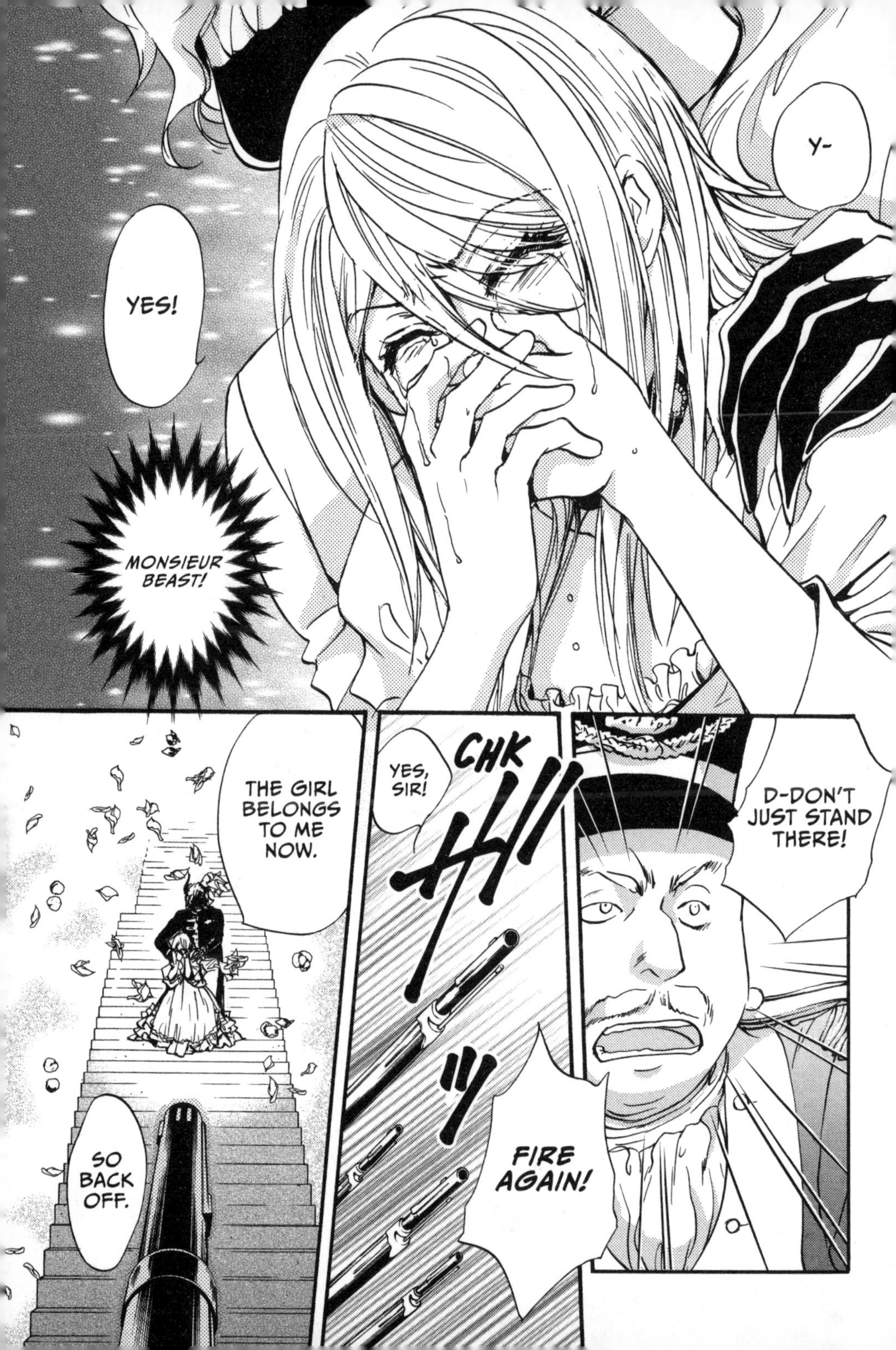
Y-
YES!
MONSIEUR BEAST!
D-DON'T JUST STAND THERE!
FIRE AGAIN!
CHK
YES, SIR!
THE GIRL BELONGS TO ME NOW.
SO BACK OFF.

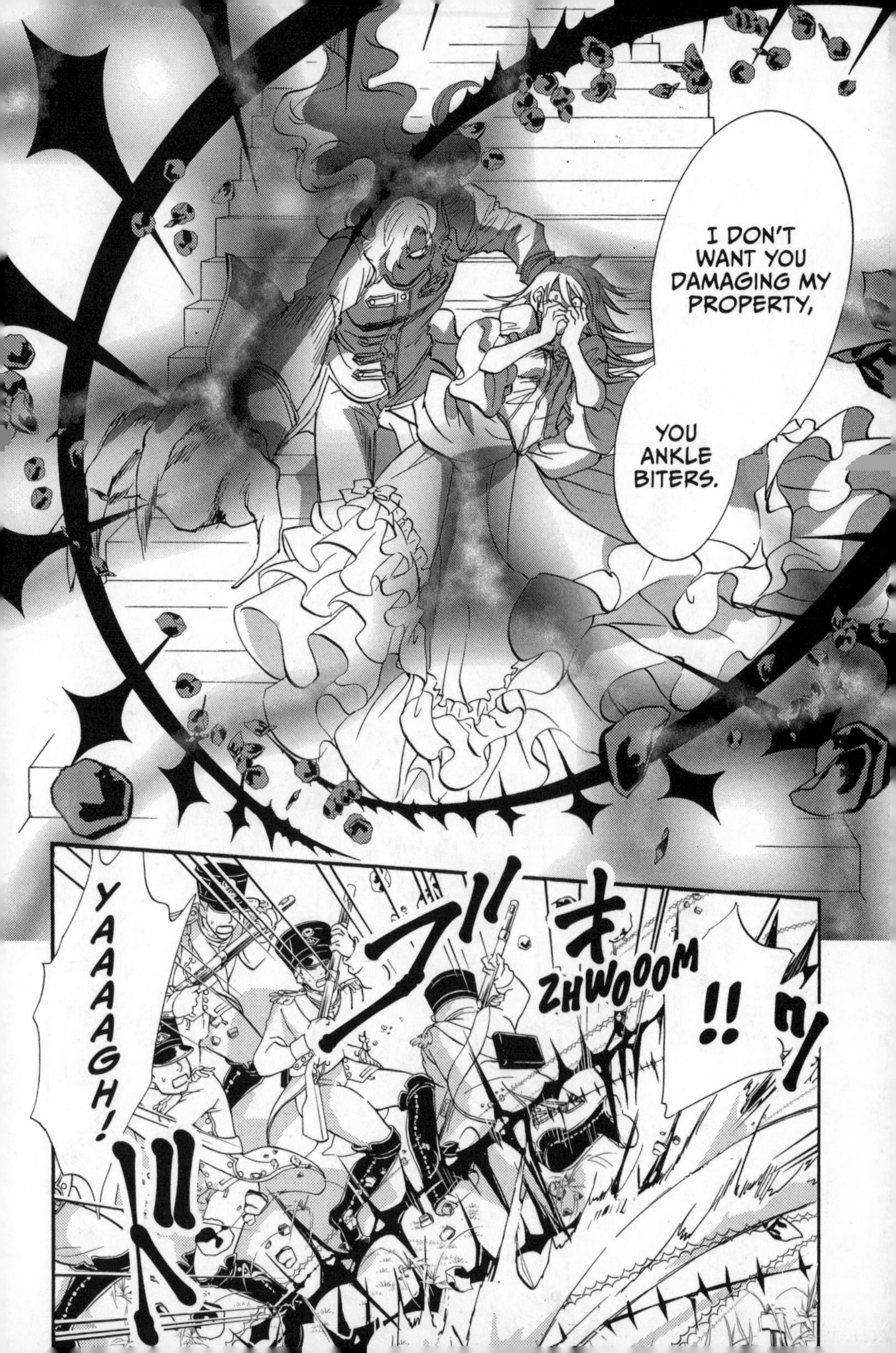
I DON'T WANT YOU DAMAGING MY PROPERTY,
YOU ANKLE BITERS.
ZHWOOOM!!
YAAAAAGH!

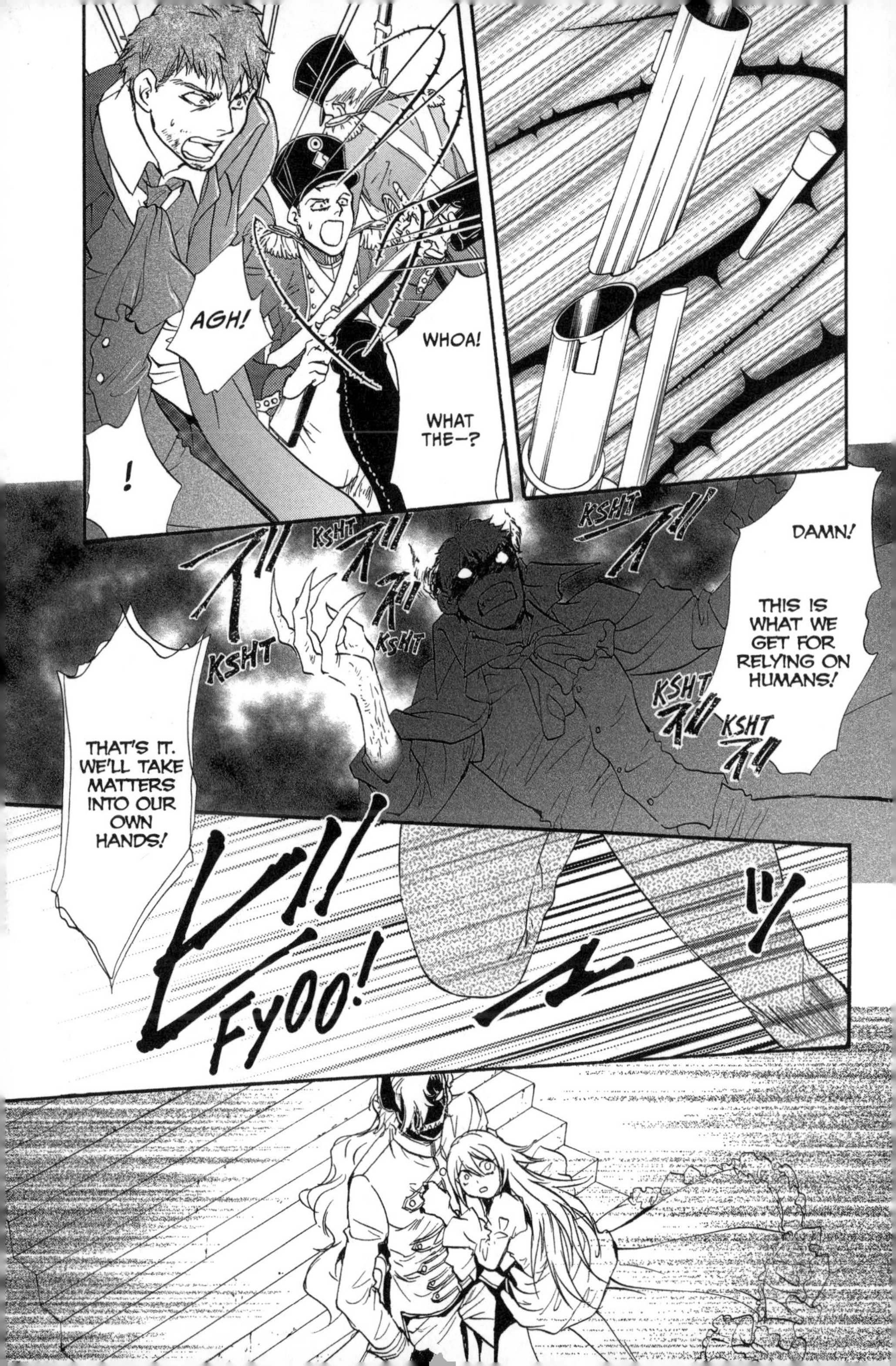
WHOA!
WHAT THE—?
AGH!
!
DAMN!
THIS IS WHAT WE GET FOR RELYING ON HUMANS!
KSHT
KSHT
KSHT
KSHT
KSHT
KSHT
THAT'S IT. WE'LL TAKE MATTERS INTO OUR OWN HANDS!
FYOO!

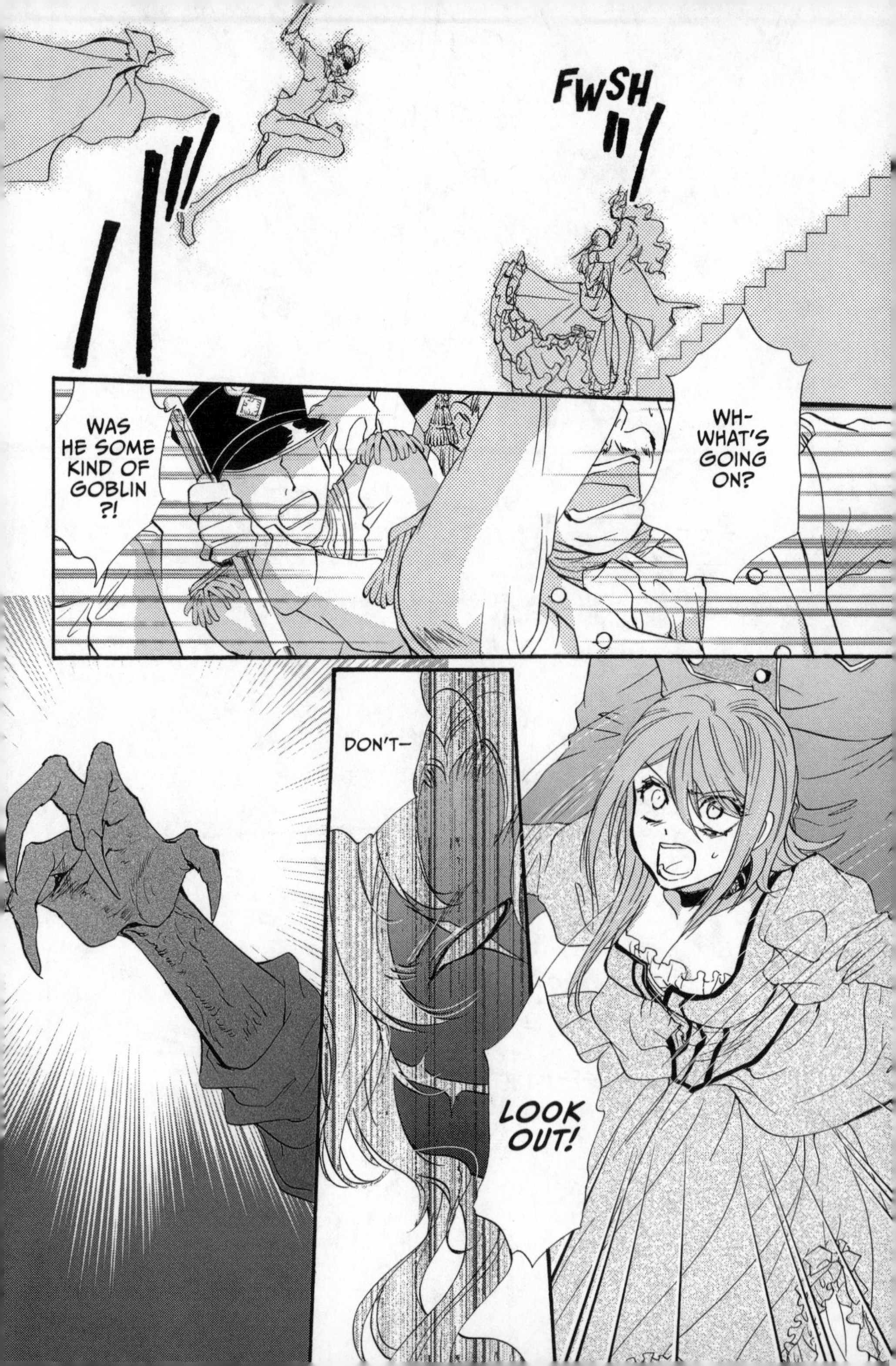
FWSH
WH-WHAT'S GOING ON?
WAS HE SOME KIND OF GOBLIN ?!
DON'T—
LOOK OUT!

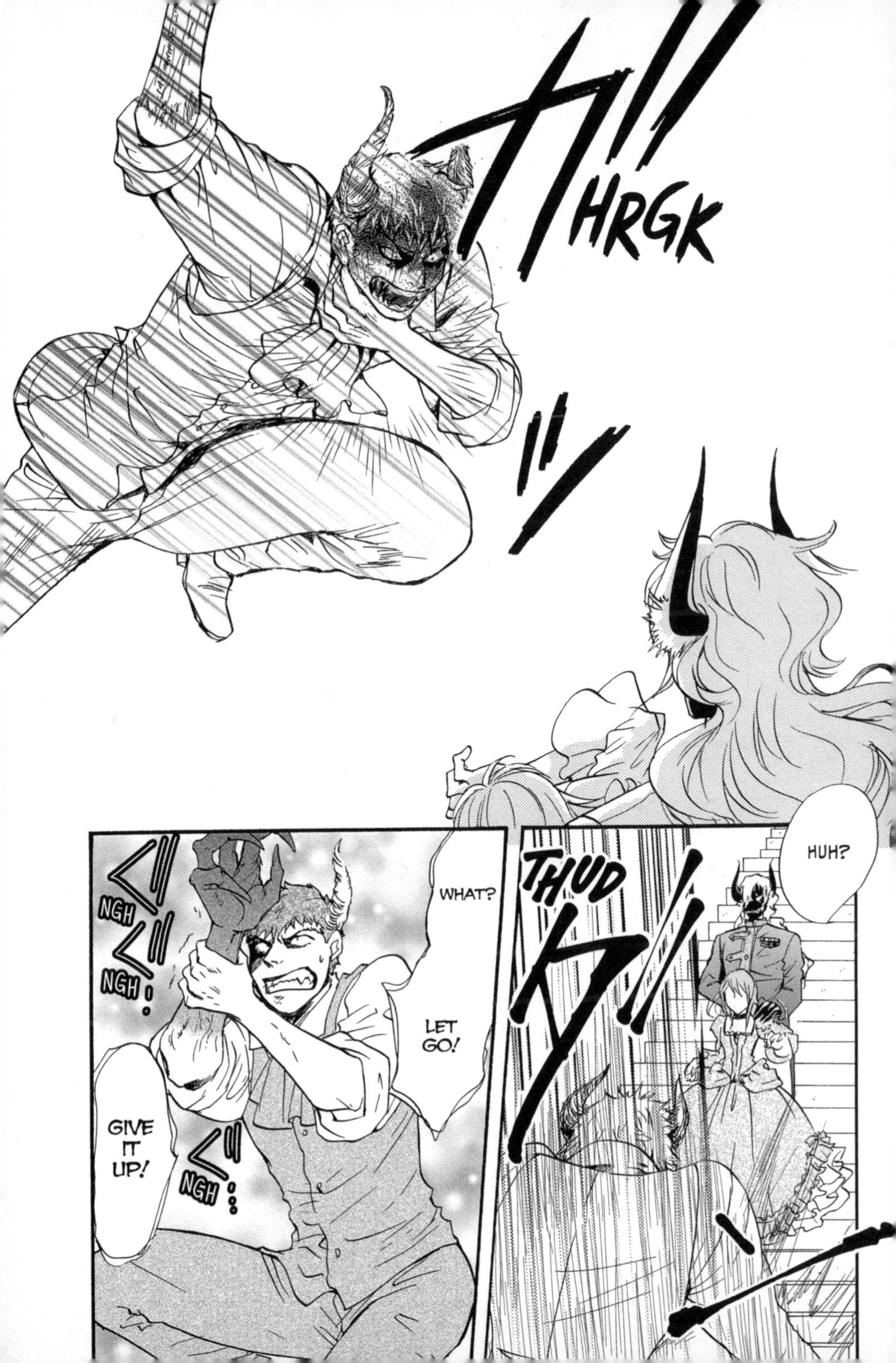
HRGK
HUH?
THUD
WHAT?
LET GO!
NGH NGH!
GIVE IT UP!
NGH...

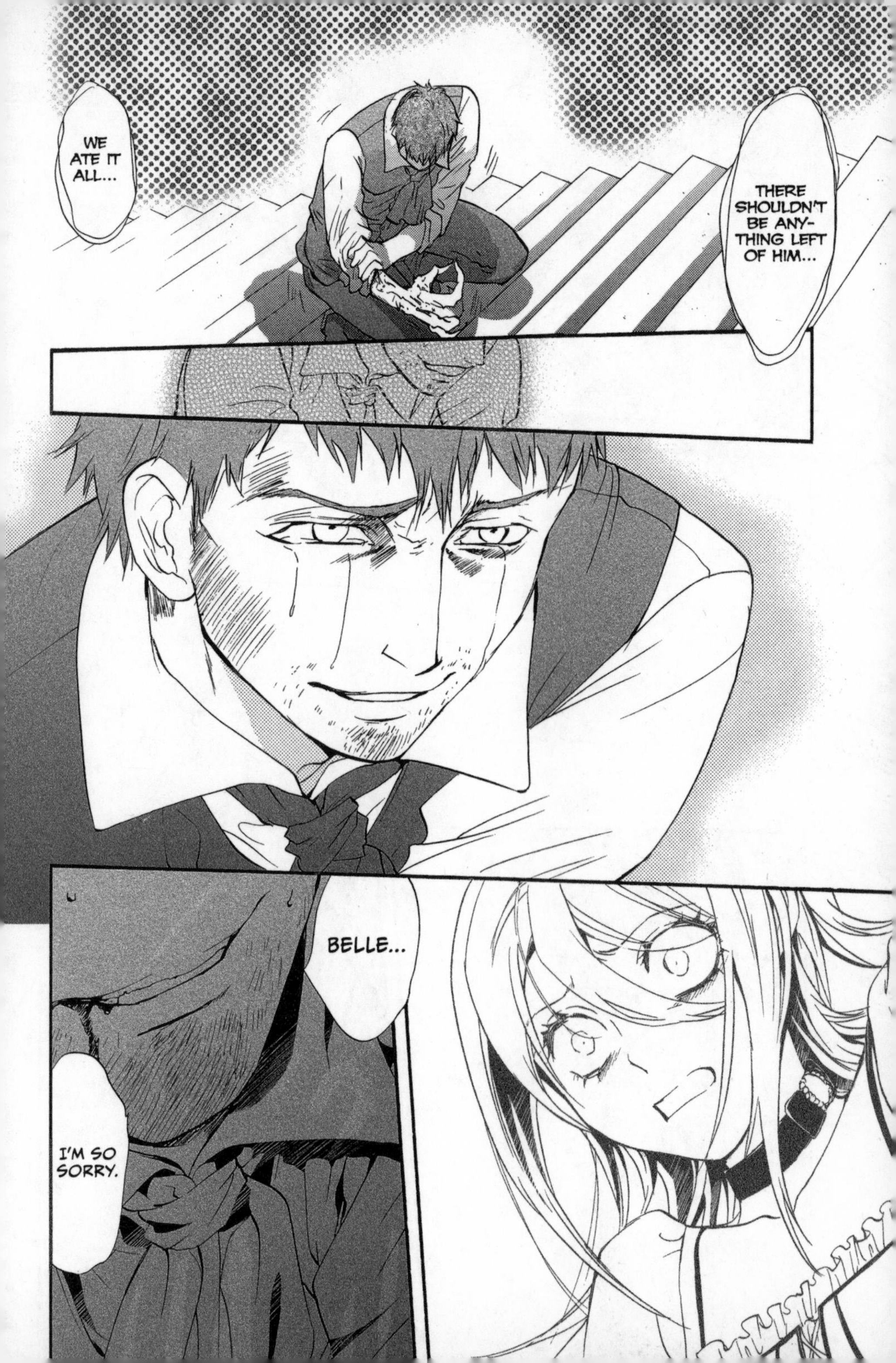
THERE SHOULDN'T BE ANY-THING LEFT OF HIM...
WE ATE IT ALL...
BELLE...
I'M SO SORRY.

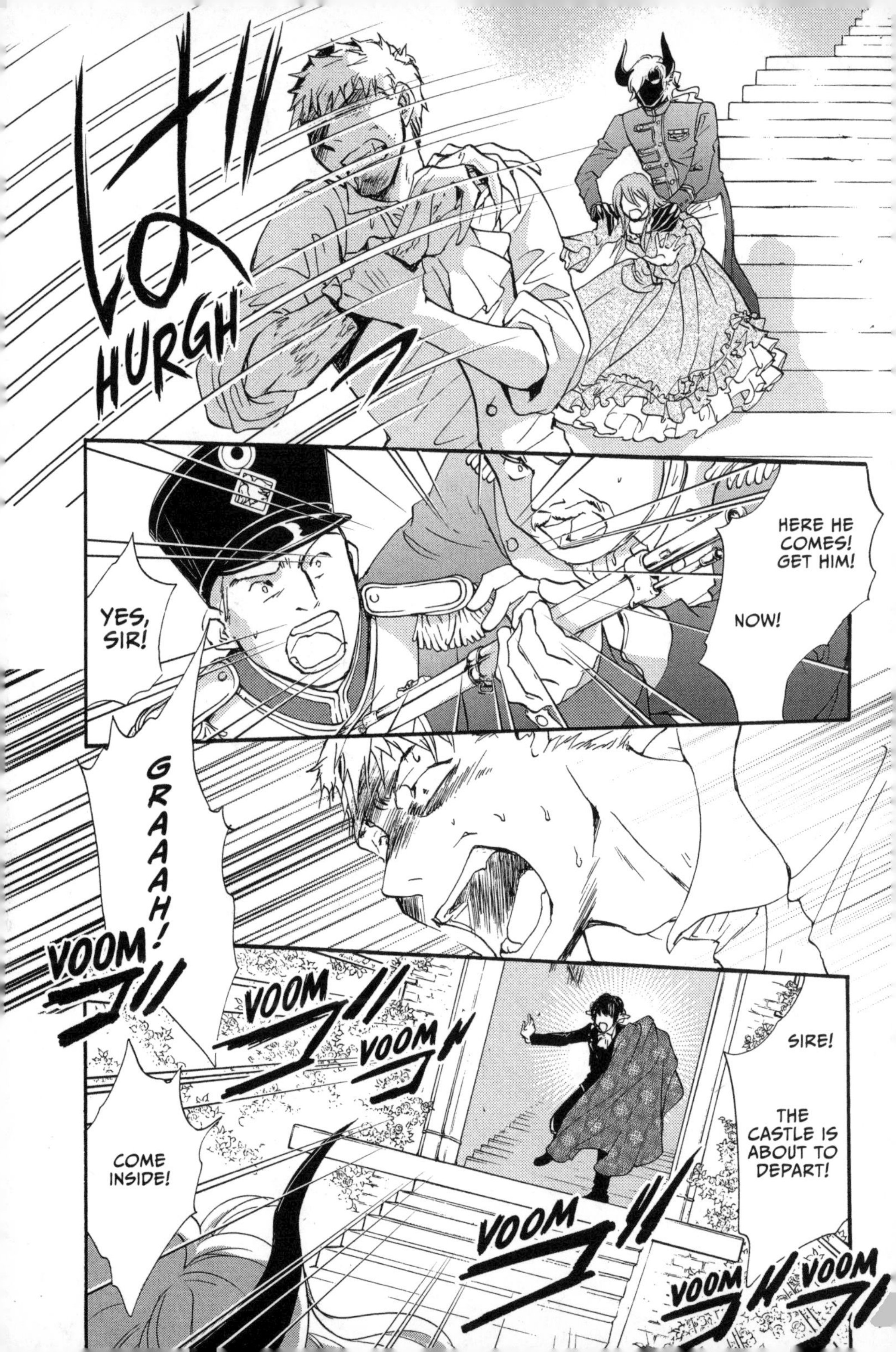
HURGH
HERE HE COMES! GET HIM!
NOW!
YES, SIR!
GRAAAAH!
SIRE!
THE CASTLE IS ABOUT TO DEPART!
VOOM
VOOM
VOOM
VOOM
COME INSIDE!
VOOM
VOOM

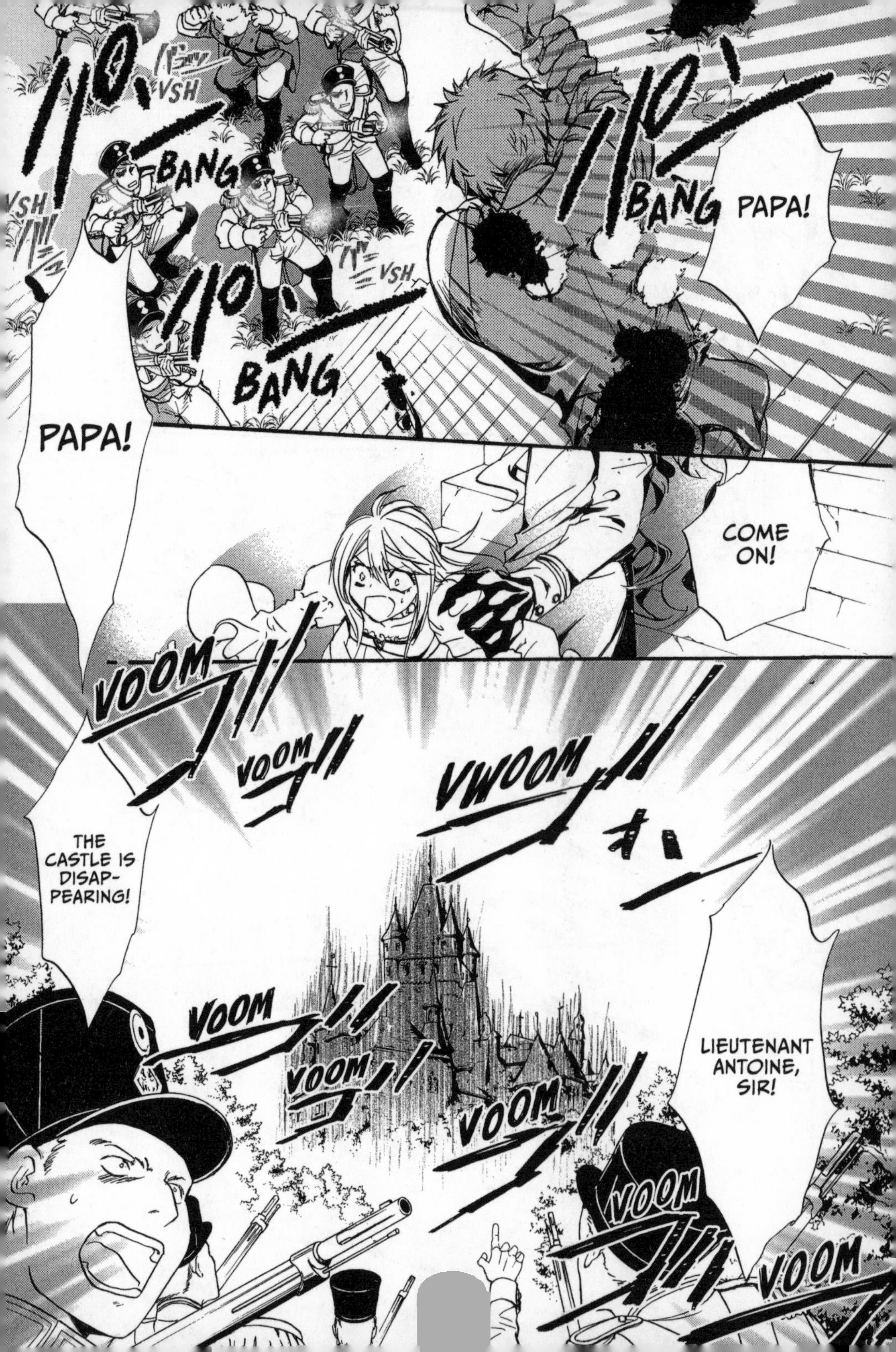
BANG
PAPA!
BANG
VSH
BANG
VSH
BANG
VSH
PAPA!
COME ON!
VOOM
VOOM
VWOOM
THE CASTLE IS DISAP-PEARING!
LIEUTENANT ANTOINE, SIR!
VOOM
VOOM
VOOM
VOOM
VOOM

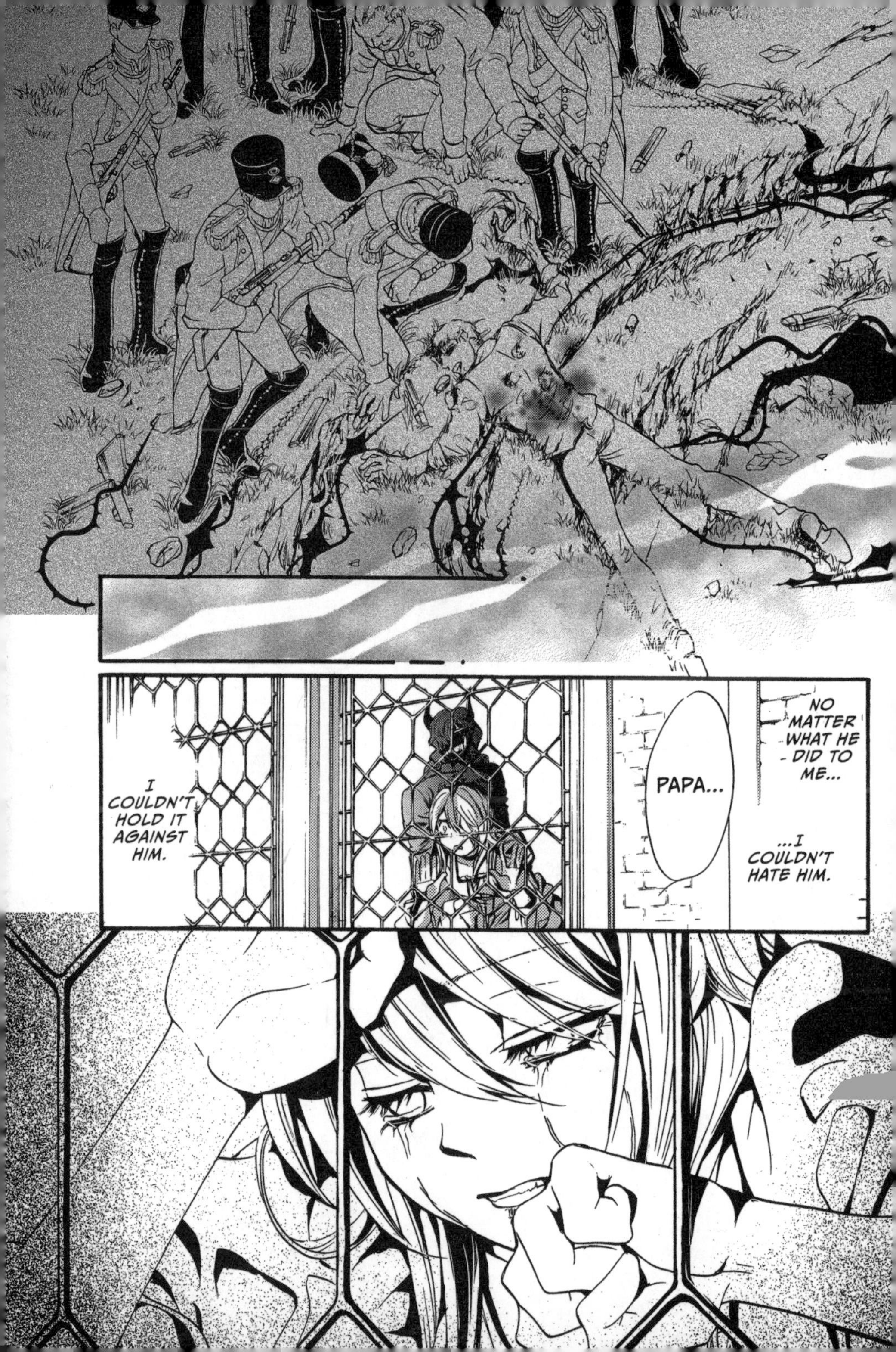
NO MATTER WHAT HE DID TO ME...
PAPA...
...I COULDN'T HATE HIM.
I COULDN'T HOLD IT AGAINST HIM.

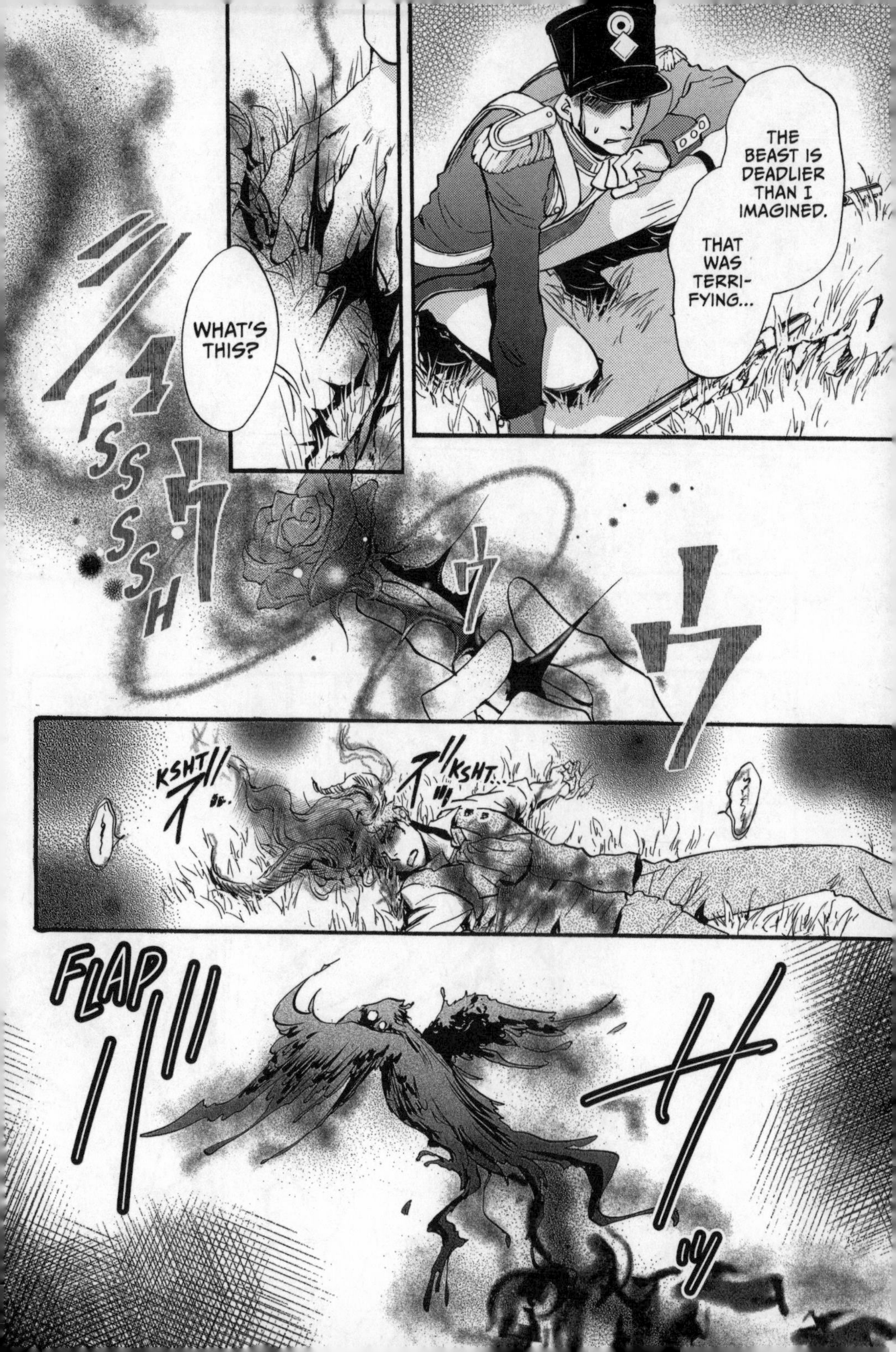
THE BEAST IS DEADLIER THAN I IMAGINED.
THAT WAS TERRI-FYING...
WHAT'S THIS?
FSSSSH
KSHT...
KSHT
FLAP

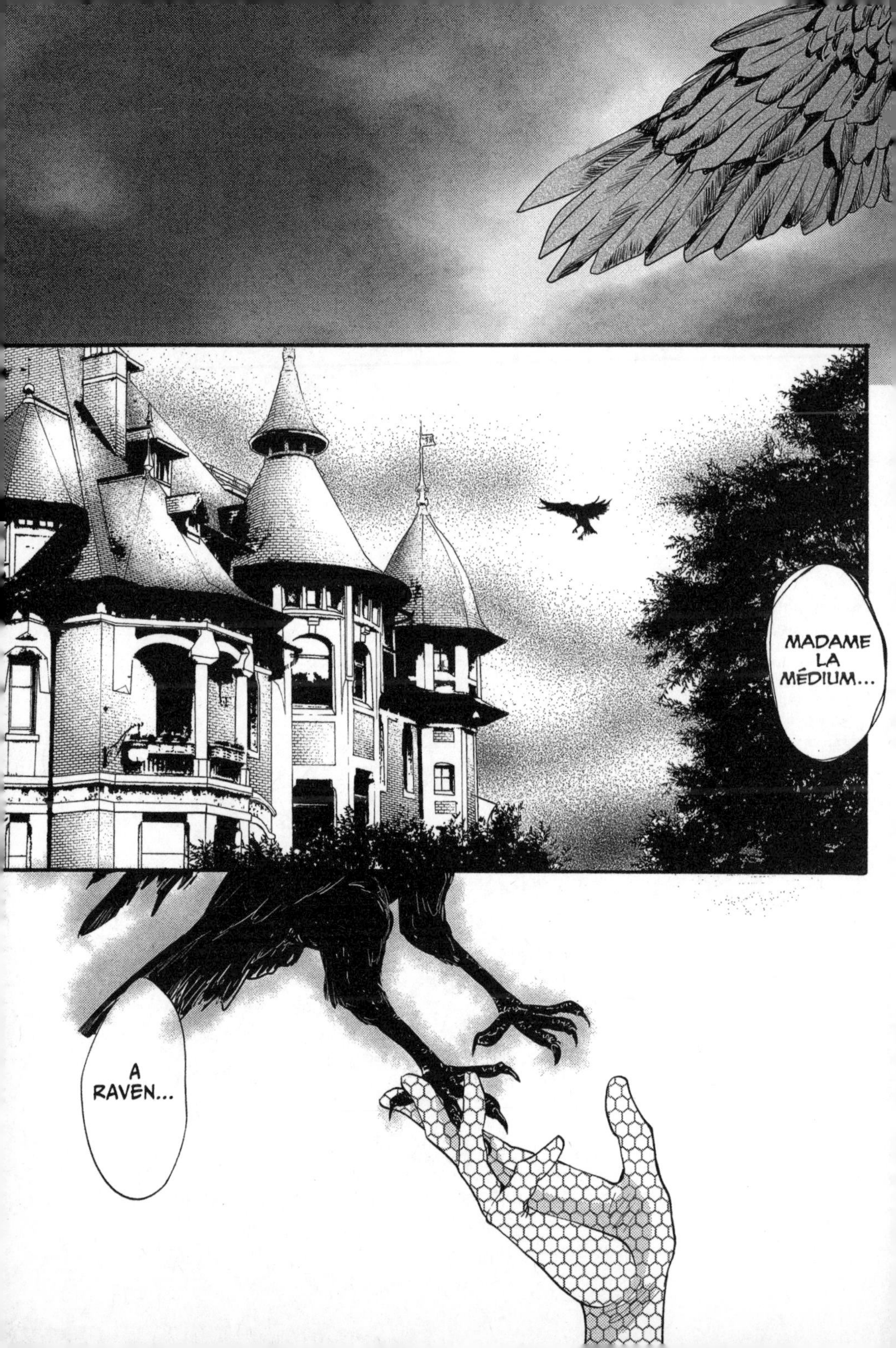
MADAME LA MÉDIUM...
A RAVEN...

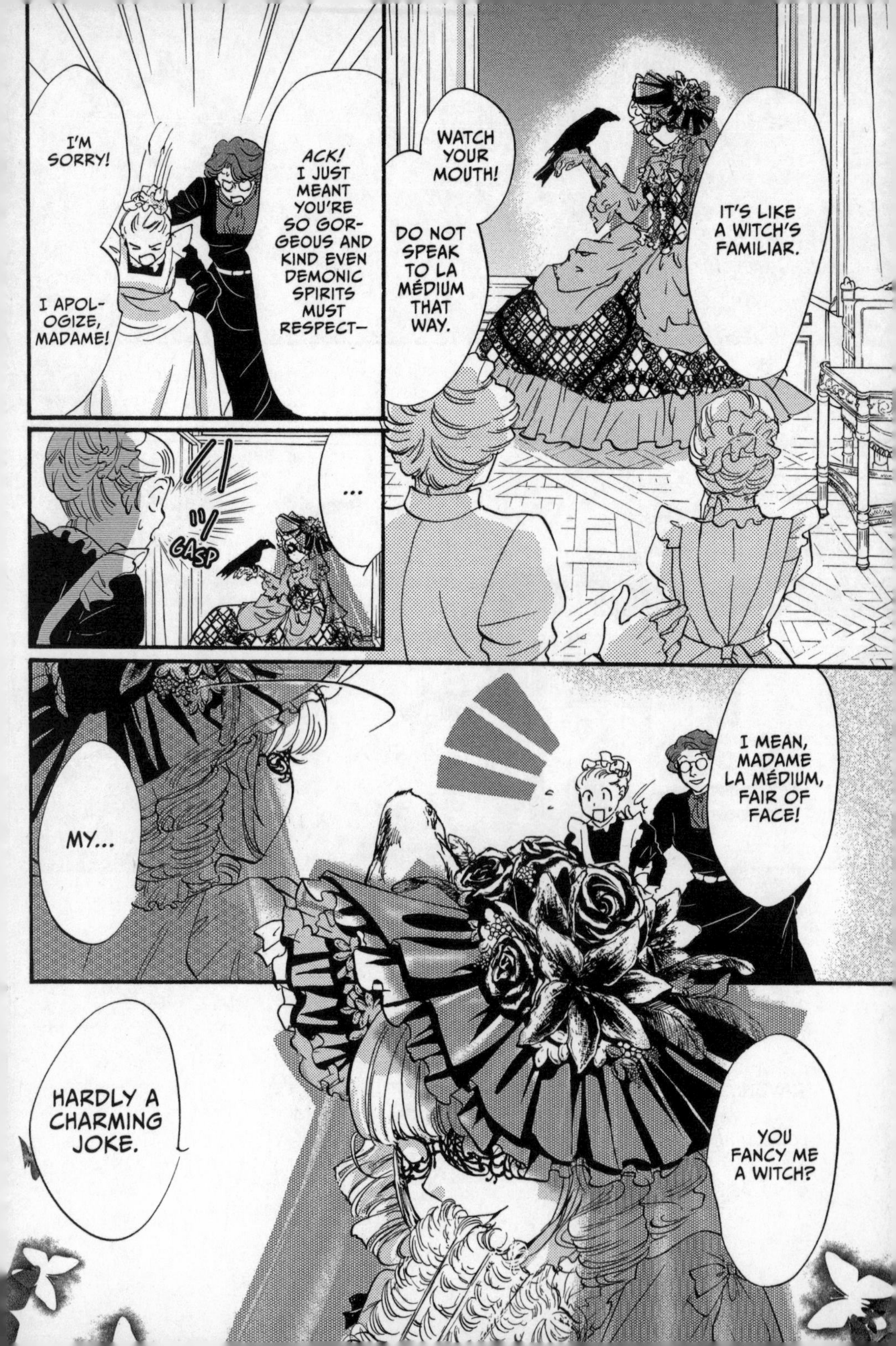
IT'S LIKE A WITCH'S FAMILIAR.
WATCH YOUR MOUTH!
DO NOT SPEAK TO LA MÉDIUM THAT WAY.
ACK! I JUST MEANT YOU'RE SO GORGEOUS AND KIND EVEN DEMONIC SPIRITS MUST RESPECT—
I'M SORRY!
I APOLOGIZE, MADAME!
...
GASP
I MEAN, MADAME LA MÉDIUM, FAIR OF FACE!
MY...
YOU FANCY ME A WITCH?
HARDLY A CHARMING JOKE.

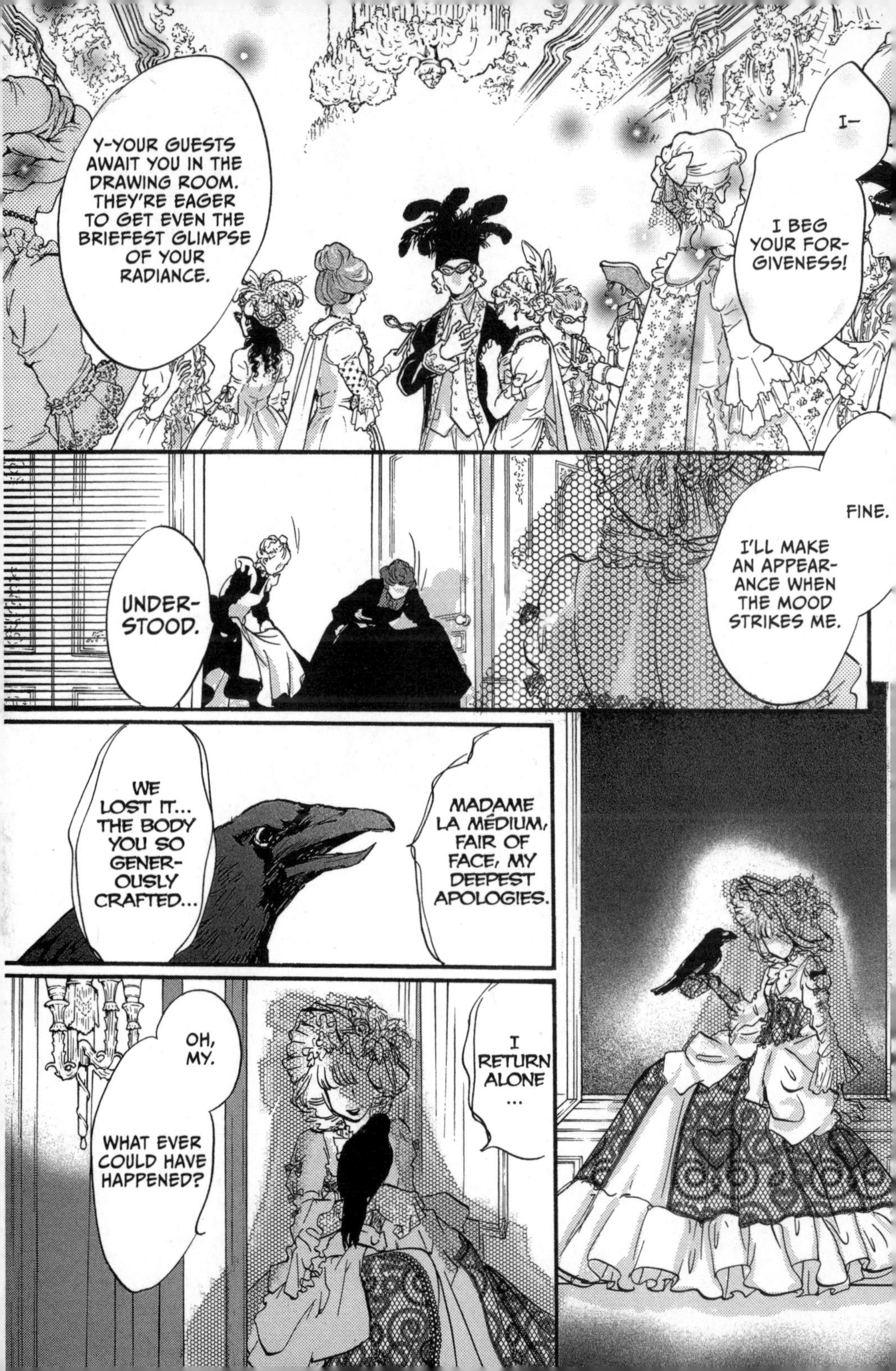
I—
I BEG YOUR FORGIVENESS!
Y-YOUR GUESTS AWAIT YOU IN THE DRAWING ROOM. THEY'RE EAGER TO GET EVEN THE BRIEFEST GLIMPSE OF YOUR RADIANCE.
FINE.
I'LL MAKE AN APPEARANCE WHEN THE MOOD STRIKES ME.
UNDERSTOOD.
MADAME LA MÉDIUM, FAIR OF FACE, MY DEEPEST APOLOGIES.
WE LOST IT... THE BODY YOU SO GENEROUSLY CRAFTED...
I RETURN ALONE...
OH, MY.
WHAT EVER COULD HAVE HAPPENED?

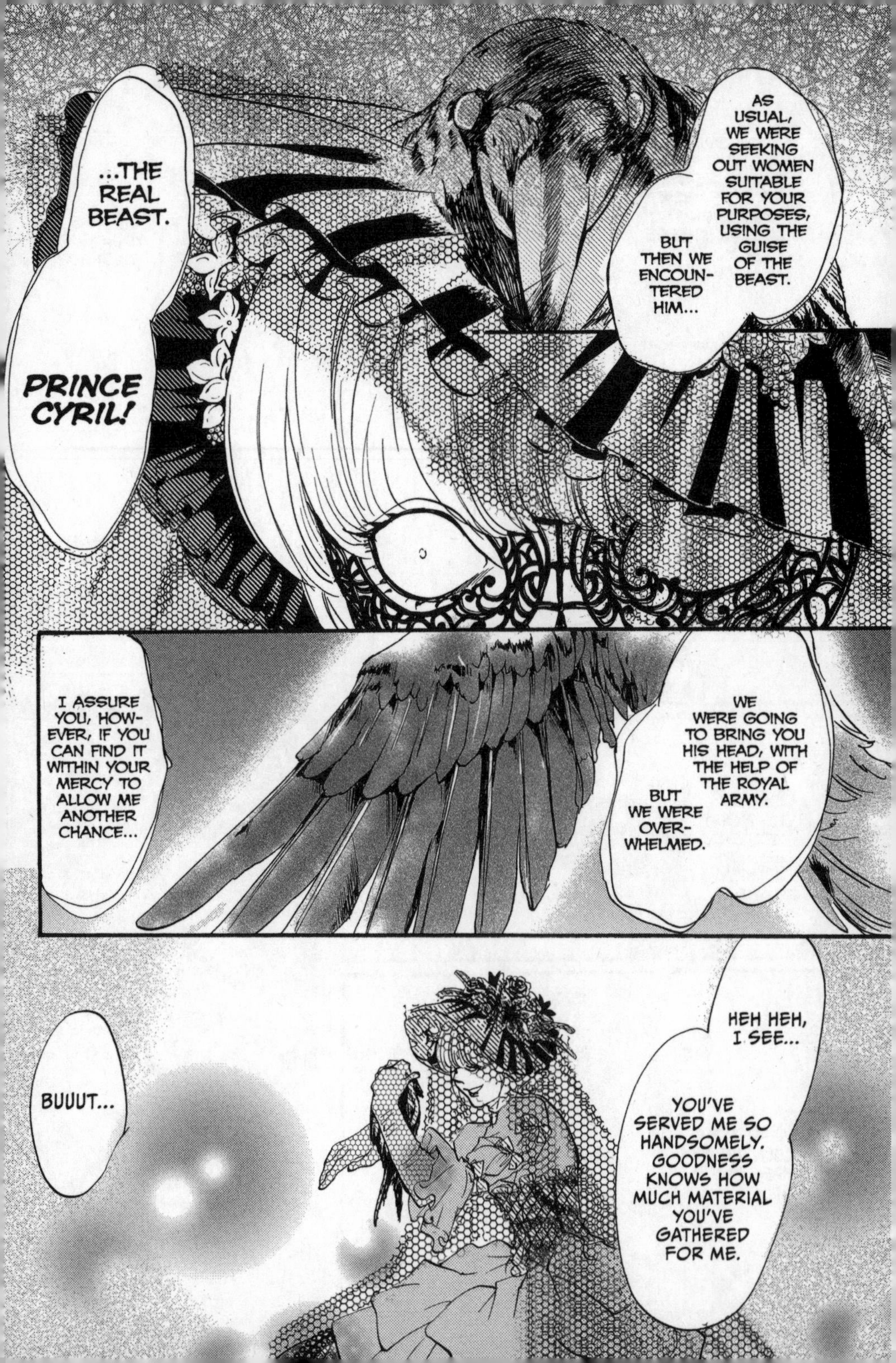
AS USUAL, WE WERE SEEKING OUT WOMEN SUITABLE FOR YOUR PURPOSES, USING THE GUISE OF THE BEAST.
BUT THEN WE ENCOUNTERED HIM...
...THE REAL BEAST.
PRINCE CYRIL!
WE WERE GOING TO BRING YOU HIS HEAD, WITH THE HELP OF THE ROYAL ARMY.
BUT WE WERE OVER-WHELMED.
I ASSURE YOU, HOW-EVER, IF YOU CAN FIND IT WITHIN YOUR MERCY TO ALLOW ME ANOTHER CHANCE...
HEH HEH, I SEE...
YOU'VE SERVED ME SO HANDSOMELY. GOODNESS KNOWS HOW MUCH MATERIAL YOU'VE GATHERED FOR ME.
BUUUT...

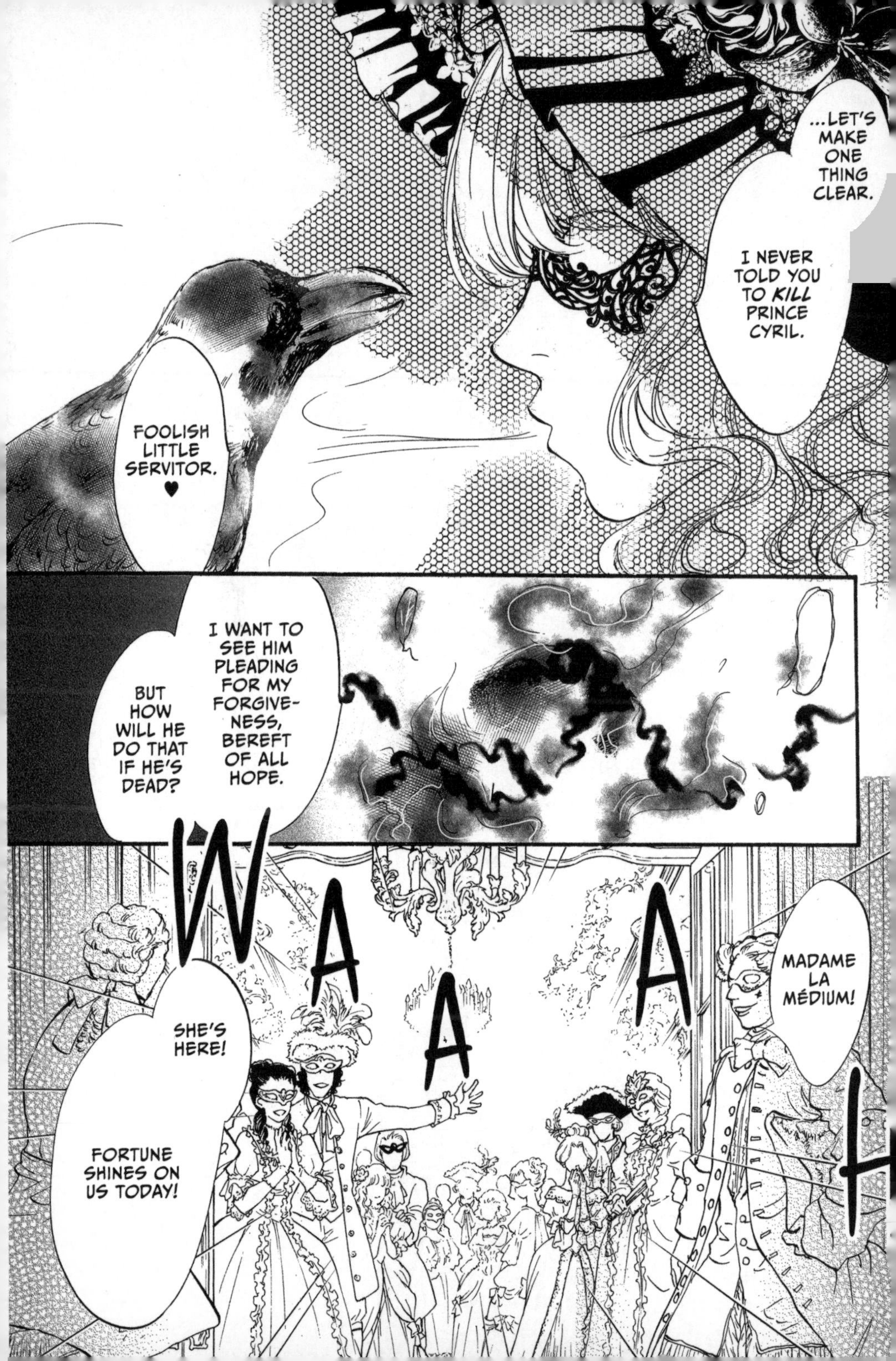
...LET'S MAKE ONE THING CLEAR.
I NEVER TOLD YOU TO *KILL* PRINCE CYRIL.
FOOLISH LITTLE SERVITOR. ♥
I WANT TO SEE HIM PLEADING FOR MY FORGIVE-NESS, BEREFT OF ALL HOPE.
BUT HOW WILL HE DO THAT IF HE'S DEAD?
MADAME LA MÉDIUM!
WAAAH
SHE'S HERE!
FORTUNE SHINES ON US TODAY!

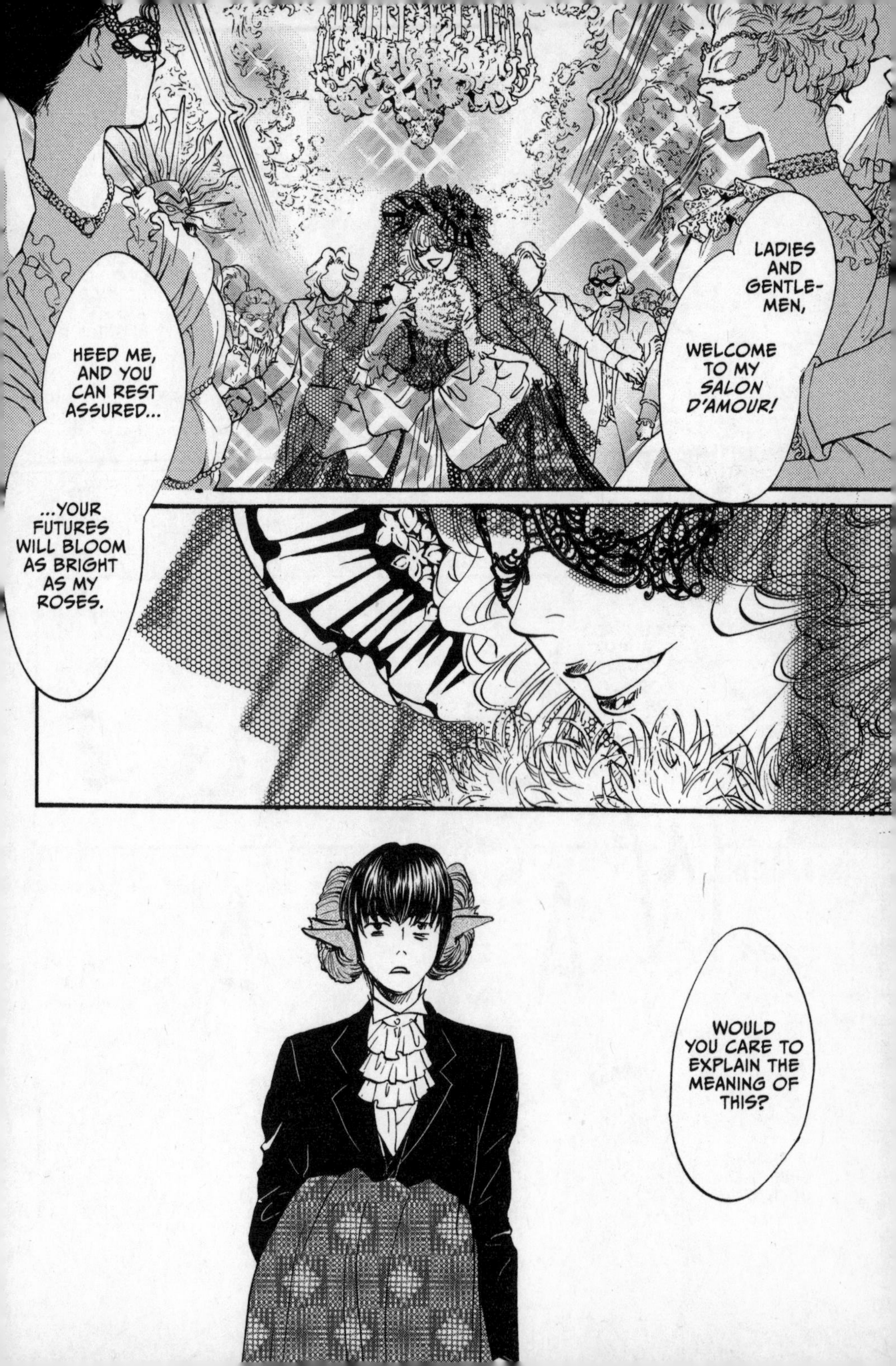
LADIES AND GENTLE-MEN,
WELCOME TO MY SALON D'AMOUR!
HEED ME, AND YOU CAN REST ASSURED...
...YOUR FUTURES WILL BLOOM AS BRIGHT AS MY ROSES.
WOULD YOU CARE TO EXPLAIN THE MEANING OF THIS?

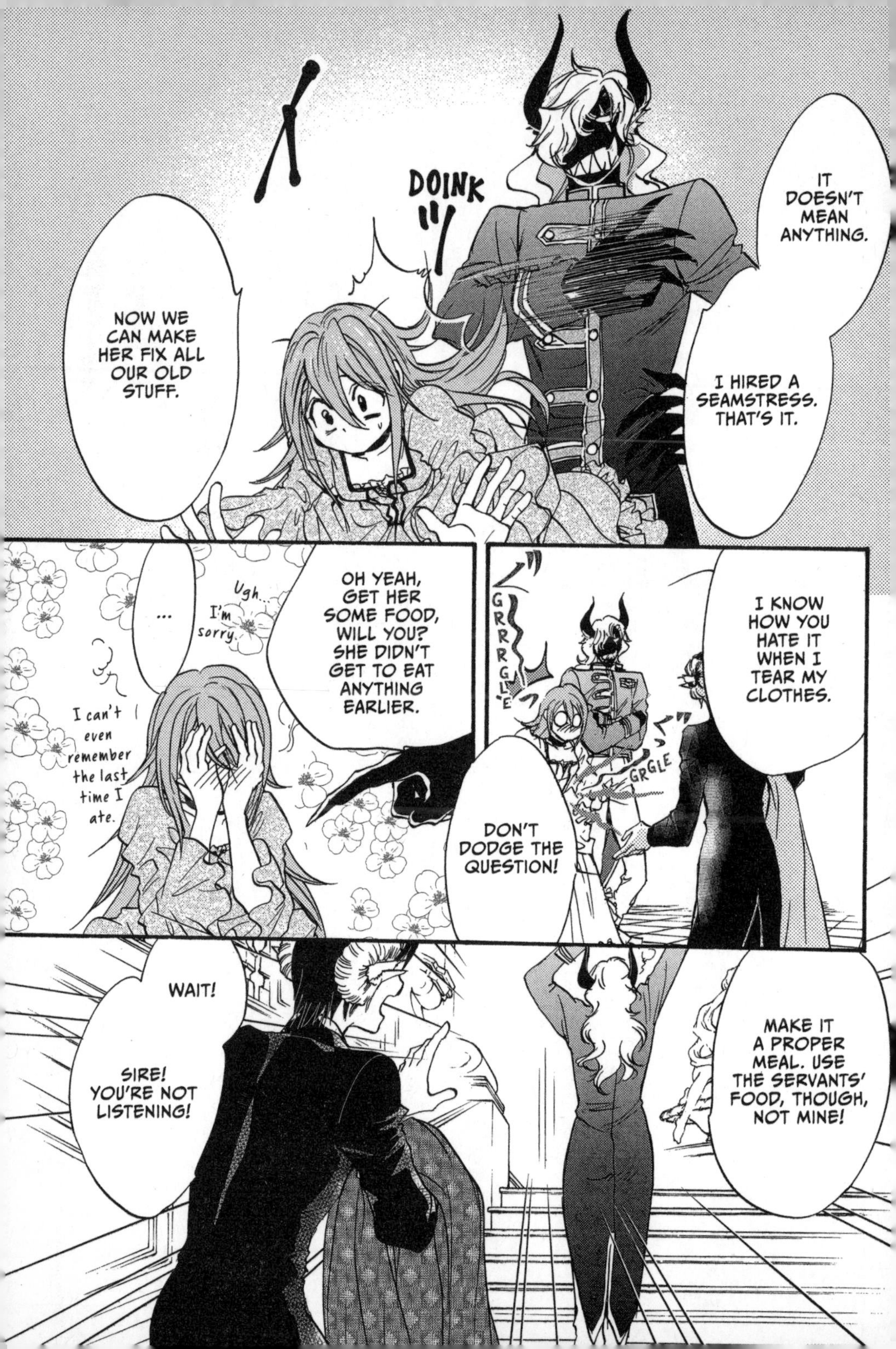
IT DOESN'T MEAN ANYTHING.
I HIRED A SEAMSTRESS. THAT'S IT.
DOINK
NOW WE CAN MAKE HER FIX ALL OUR OLD STUFF.
I KNOW HOW YOU HATE IT WHEN I TEAR MY CLOTHES.
GRRRGLE
GRGLE
DON'T DODGE THE QUESTION!
OH YEAH, GET HER SOME FOOD, WILL YOU? SHE DIDN'T GET TO EAT ANYTHING EARLIER.
Ugh... I'm sorry.
...
I can't even remember the last time I ate.
MAKE IT A PROPER MEAL. USE THE SERVANTS' FOOD, THOUGH, NOT MINE!
WAIT!
SIRE! YOU'RE NOT LISTENING!

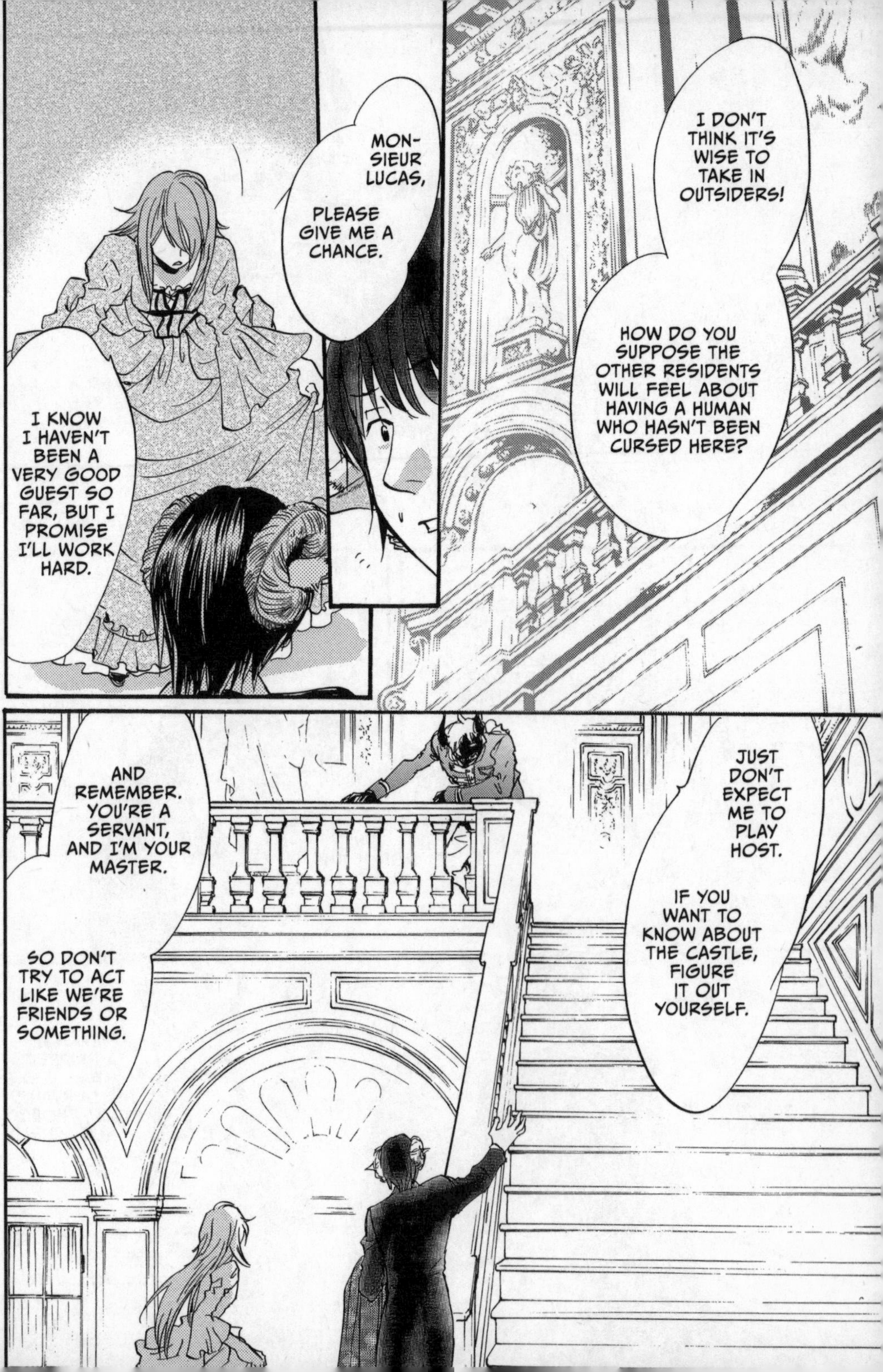
I DON'T THINK IT'S WISE TO TAKE IN OUTSIDERS!
HOW DO YOU SUPPOSE THE OTHER RESIDENTS WILL FEEL ABOUT HAVING A HUMAN WHO HASN'T BEEN CURSED HERE?
MON-SIEUR LUCAS,
PLEASE GIVE ME A CHANCE.
I KNOW I HAVEN'T BEEN A VERY GOOD GUEST SO FAR, BUT I PROMISE I'LL WORK HARD.
JUST DON'T EXPECT ME TO PLAY HOST.
IF YOU WANT TO KNOW ABOUT THE CASTLE, FIGURE IT OUT YOURSELF.
AND REMEMBER. YOU'RE A SERVANT, AND I'M YOUR MASTER.
SO DON'T TRY TO ACT LIKE WE'RE FRIENDS OR SOMETHING.

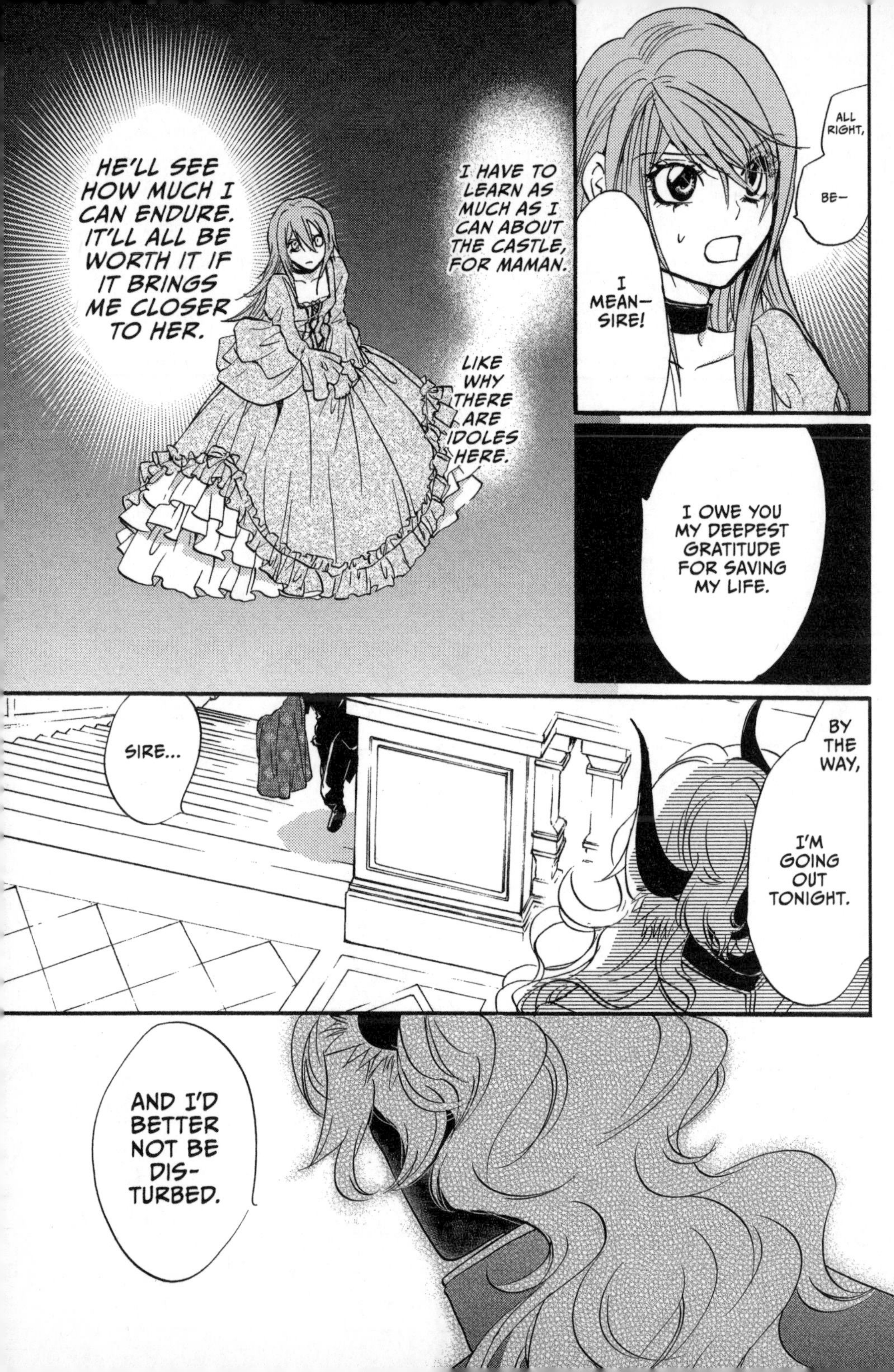
ALL RIGHT,
BE—
I MEAN— SIRE!
I OWE YOU MY DEEPEST GRATITUDE FOR SAVING MY LIFE.
I HAVE TO LEARN AS MUCH AS I CAN ABOUT THE CASTLE, FOR MAMAN.
LIKE WHY THERE ARE IDOLES HERE.
HE'LL SEE HOW MUCH I CAN ENDURE. IT'LL ALL BE WORTH IT IF IT BRINGS ME CLOSER TO HER.
BY THE WAY,
I'M GOING OUT TONIGHT.
SIRE...
AND I'D BETTER NOT BE DIS- TURBED.

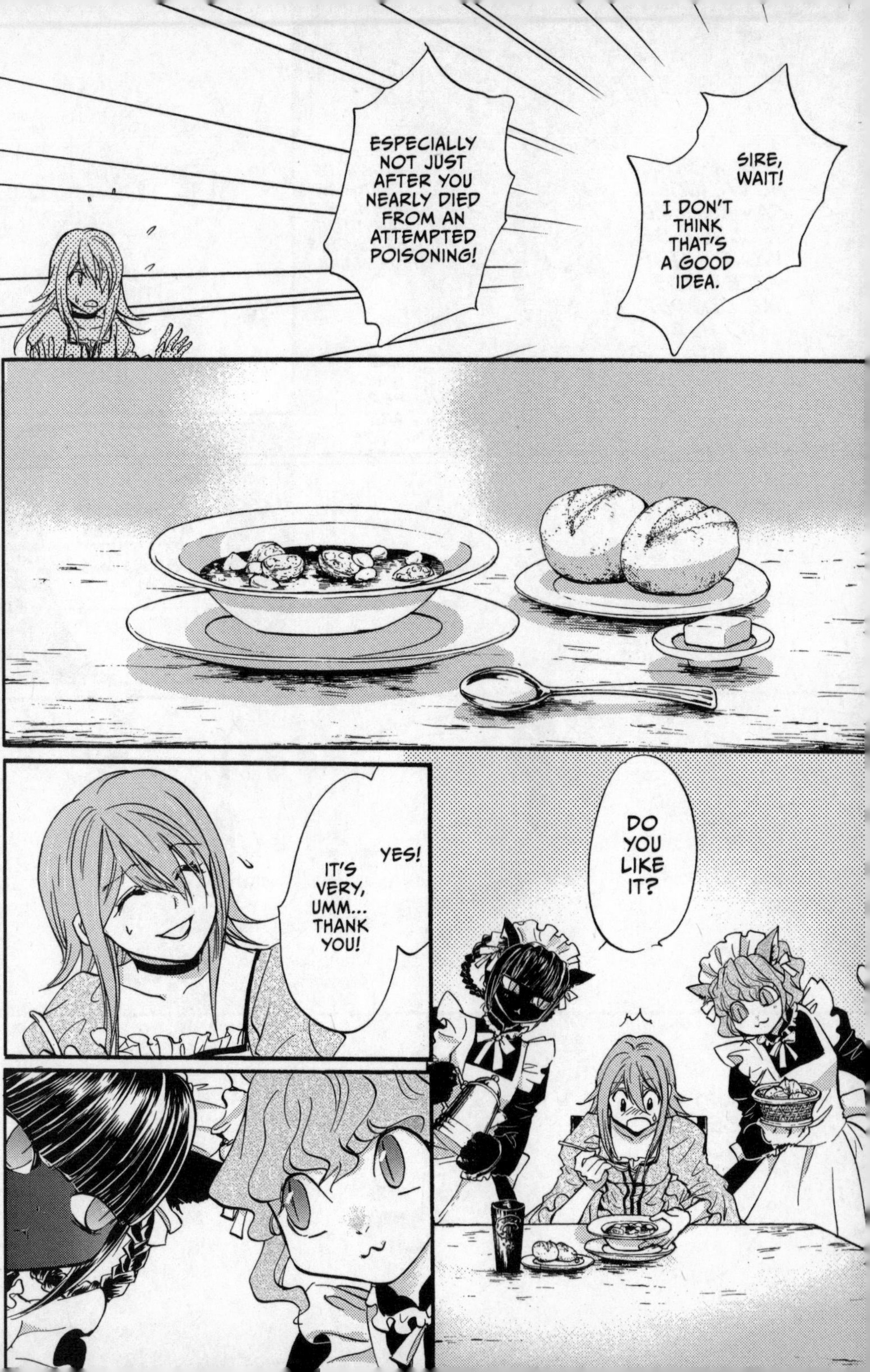
SIRE, WAIT!
I DON'T THINK THAT'S A GOOD IDEA.
ESPECIALLY NOT JUST AFTER YOU NEARLY DIED FROM AN ATTEMPTED POISONING!
DO YOU LIKE IT?
YES!
IT'S VERY, UMM... THANK YOU!

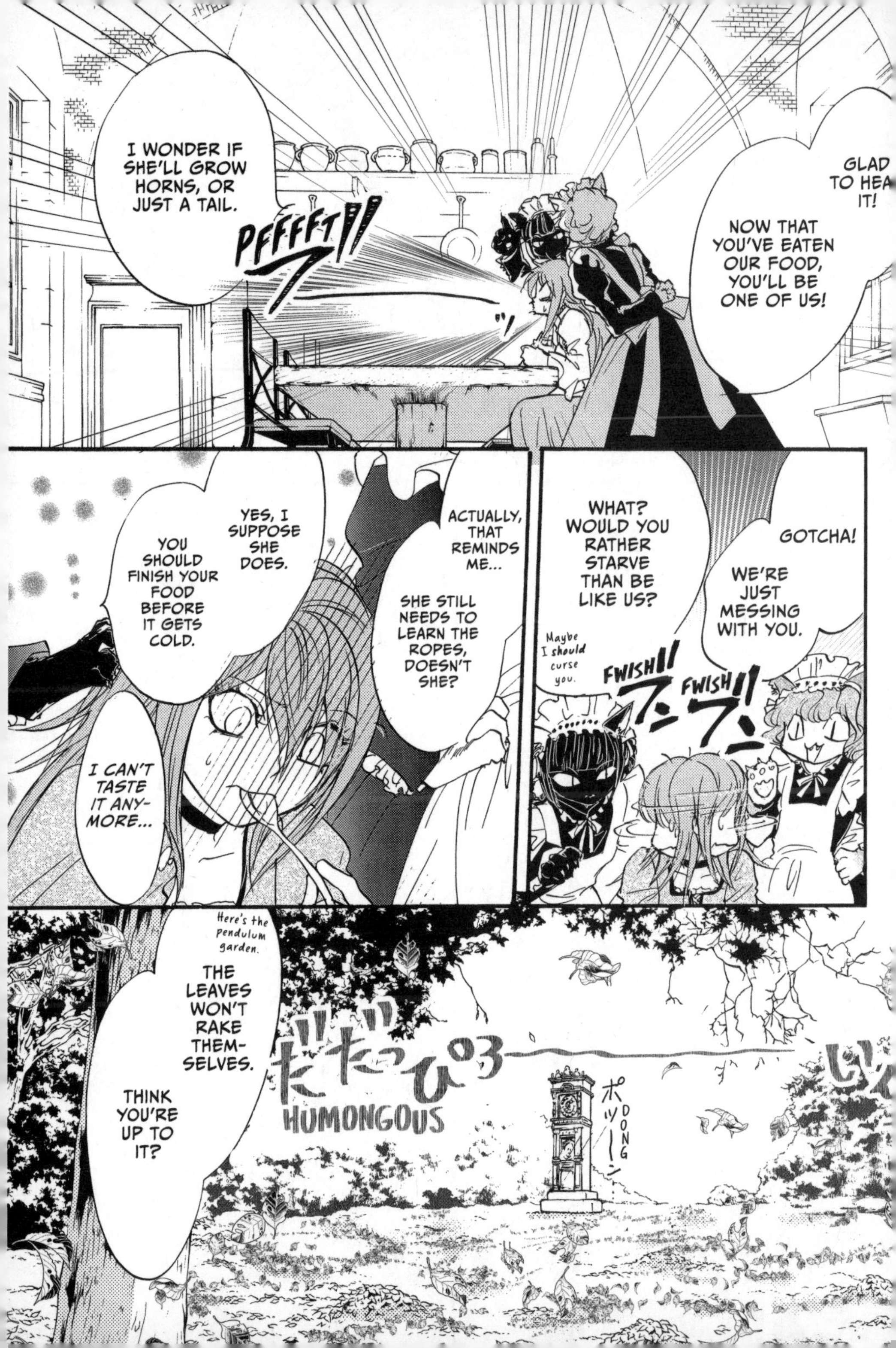
GLAD TO HEA IT!
NOW THAT YOU'VE EATEN OUR FOOD, YOU'LL BE ONE OF US!
PFFFFT!!
I WONDER IF SHE'LL GROW HORNS, OR JUST A TAIL.
GOTCHA!
WE'RE JUST MESSING WITH YOU.
WHAT? WOULD YOU RATHER STARVE THAN BE LIKE US?
FWISH!!
FWISH!!
Maybe I should curse you.
ACTUALLY, THAT REMINDS ME...
SHE STILL NEEDS TO LEARN THE ROPES, DOESN'T SHE?
YES, I SUPPOSE SHE DOES.
YOU SHOULD FINISH YOUR FOOD BEFORE IT GETS COLD.
I CAN'T TASTE IT ANY-MORE...
DONG
HUMONGOUS
Here's the pendulum garden.
THE LEAVES WON'T RAKE THEM-SELVES.
THINK YOU'RE UP TO IT?

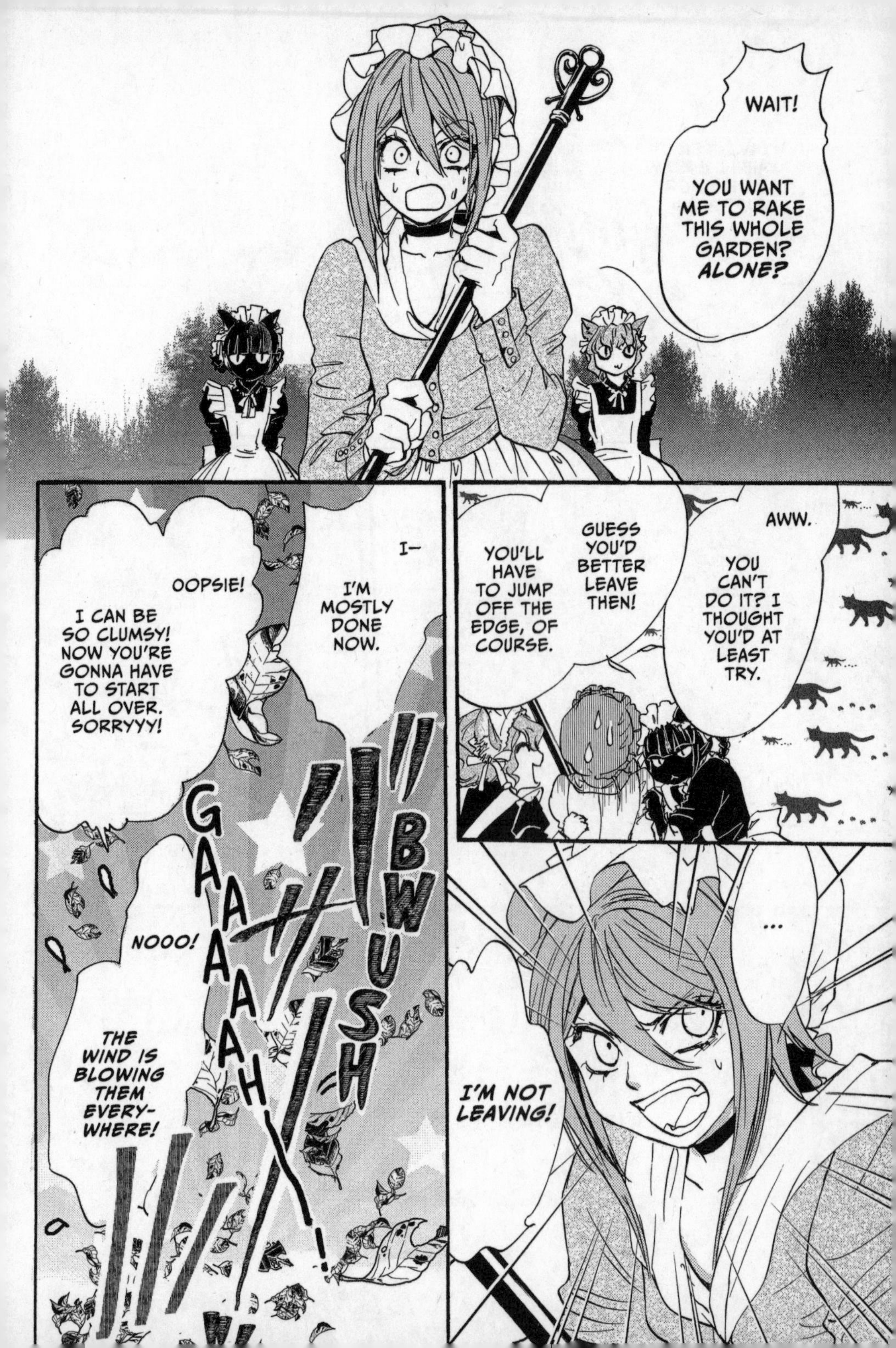
WAIT!
YOU WANT ME TO RAKE THIS WHOLE GARDEN? ALONE?
AWW.
YOU CAN'T DO IT? I THOUGHT YOU'D AT LEAST TRY.
GUESS YOU'D BETTER LEAVE THEN!
YOU'LL HAVE TO JUMP OFF THE EDGE, OF COURSE.
...
I'M NOT LEAVING!
I—
I'M MOSTLY DONE NOW.
OOPSIE!
I CAN BE SO CLUMSY! NOW YOU'RE GONNA HAVE TO START ALL OVER. SORRYYY!
BWUSH
GAAAAAH!
NOOO!
THE WIND IS BLOWING THEM EVERY-WHERE!

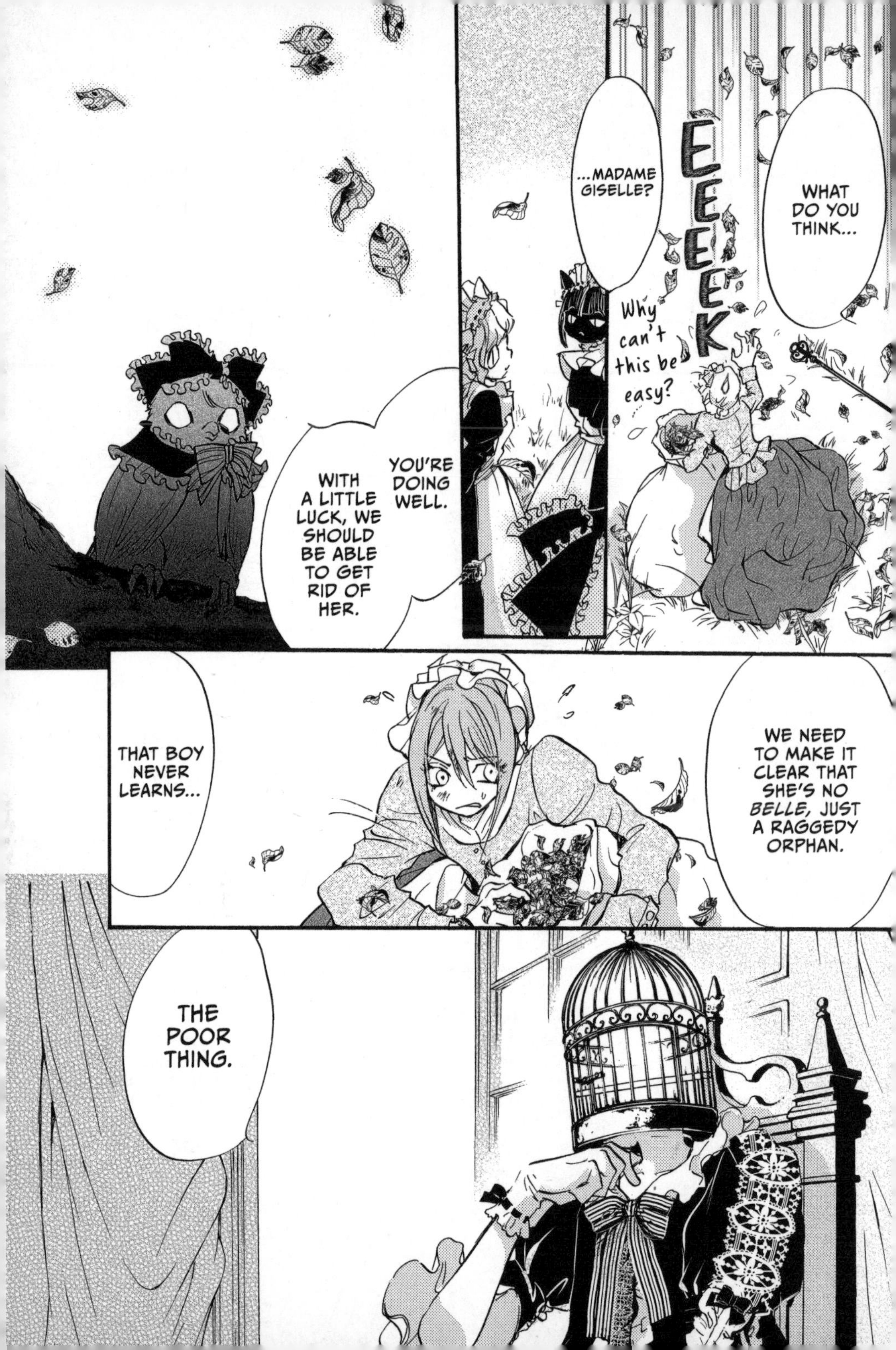
WHAT DO YOU THINK...
EEEEK
Why can't this be easy?
...MADAME GISELLE?
YOU'RE DOING WELL.
WITH A LITTLE LUCK, WE SHOULD BE ABLE TO GET RID OF HER.
WE NEED TO MAKE IT CLEAR THAT SHE'S NO *BELLE*, JUST A RAGGEDY ORPHAN.
THAT BOY NEVER LEARNS...
THE POOR THING.

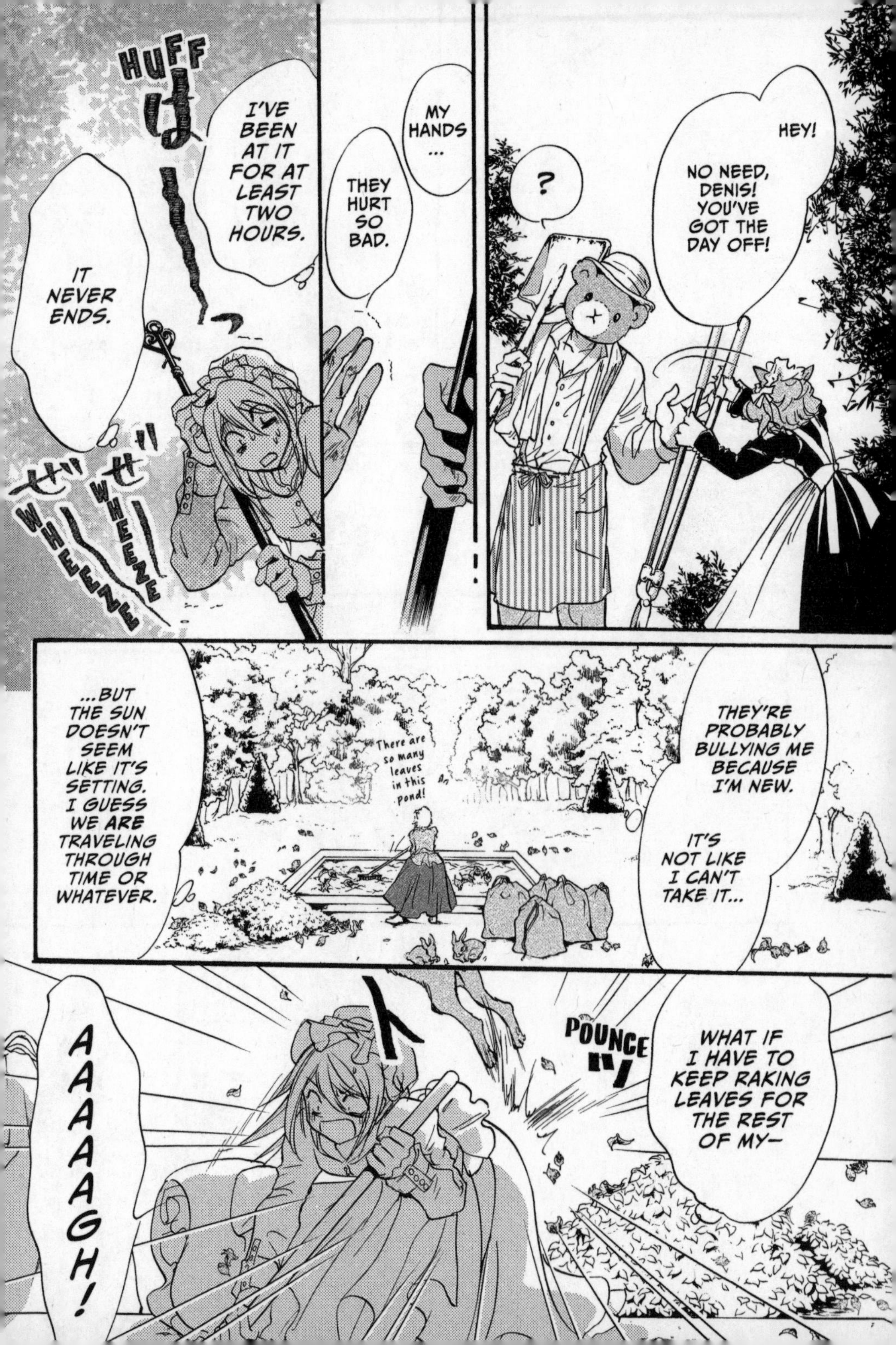
HEY!
NO NEED, DENIS! YOU'VE GOT THE DAY OFF!
?
MY HANDS ...
THEY HURT SO BAD.
HUFF
I'VE BEEN AT IT FOR AT LEAST TWO HOURS.
IT NEVER ENDS.
WHEEZE
WHEEZE
THEY'RE PROBABLY BULLYING ME BECAUSE I'M NEW.
IT'S NOT LIKE I CAN'T TAKE IT...
There are so many leaves in this pond!
...BUT THE SUN DOESN'T SEEM LIKE IT'S SETTING. I GUESS WE ARE TRAVELING THROUGH TIME OR WHATEVER.
WHAT IF I HAVE TO KEEP RAKING LEAVES FOR THE REST OF MY—
POUNCE
AAAAAAGH!

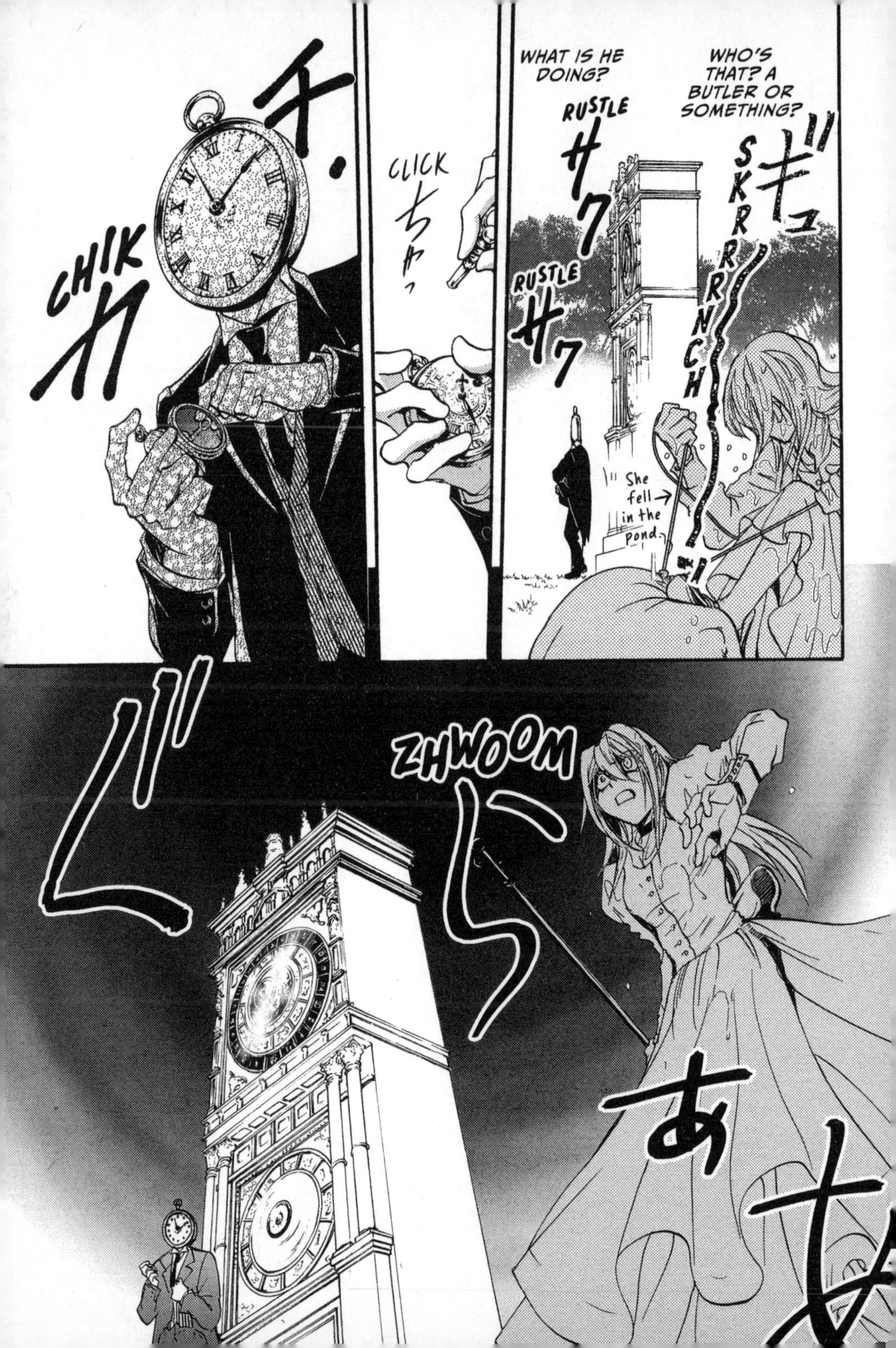
WHO'S THAT? A BUTLER OR SOMETHING?
SKRRRNCH
She fell in the pond.
WHAT IS HE DOING?
RUSTLE
RUSTLE
CLICK
CHIK
ZHWOOM

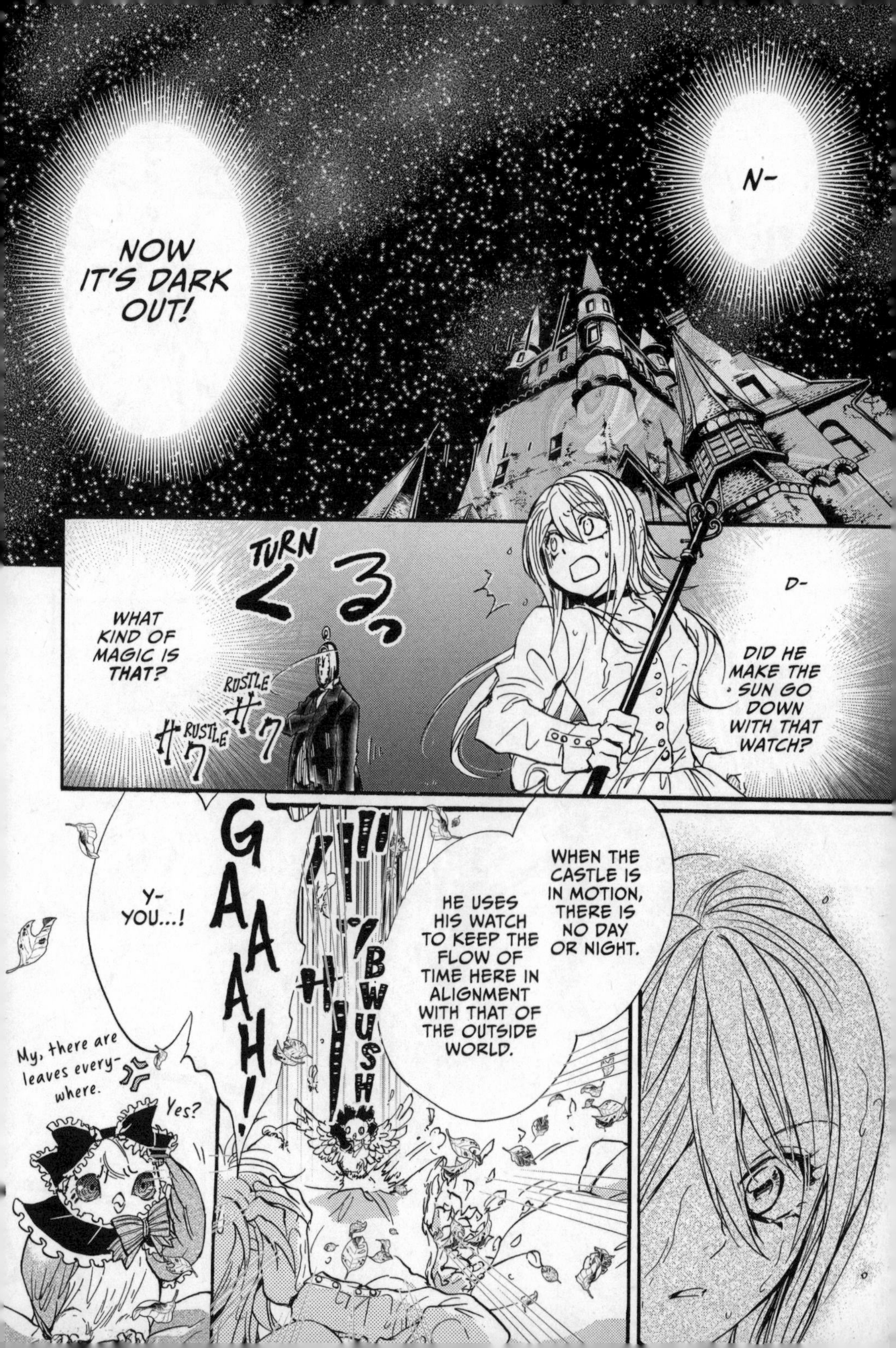
N-
NOW IT'S DARK OUT!
D-
DID HE MAKE THE SUN GO DOWN WITH THAT WATCH?
TURN
WHAT KIND OF MAGIC IS THAT?
RUSTLE
RUSTLE
WHEN THE CASTLE IS IN MOTION, THERE IS NO DAY OR NIGHT.
HE USES HIS WATCH TO KEEP THE FLOW OF TIME HERE IN ALIGNMENT WITH THAT OF THE OUTSIDE WORLD.
BWUSH
GAAAH!
Y- YOU...!
My, there are leaves every-where.
Yes?

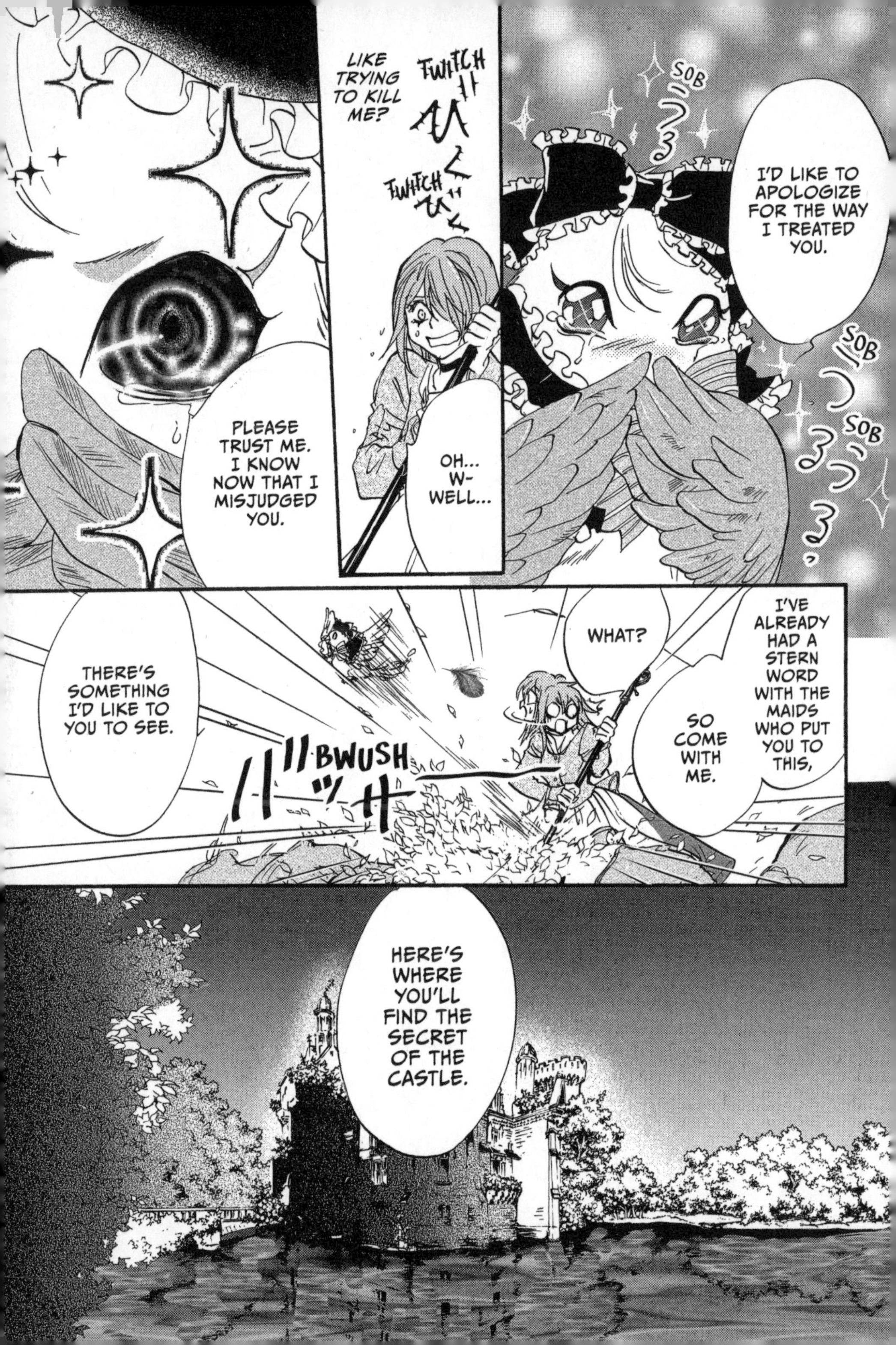
I'D LIKE TO APOLOGIZE FOR THE WAY I TREATED YOU.
SOB
SOB
SOB
LIKE TRYING TO KILL ME?
TWITCH
TWITCH
OH... W-WELL...
PLEASE TRUST ME. I KNOW NOW THAT I MISJUDGED YOU.
I'VE ALREADY HAD A STERN WORD WITH THE MAIDS WHO PUT YOU TO THIS,
SO COME WITH ME.
WHAT?
BWUSH
THERE'S SOMETHING I'D LIKE TO YOU TO SEE.
HERE'S WHERE YOU'LL FIND THE SECRET OF THE CASTLE.

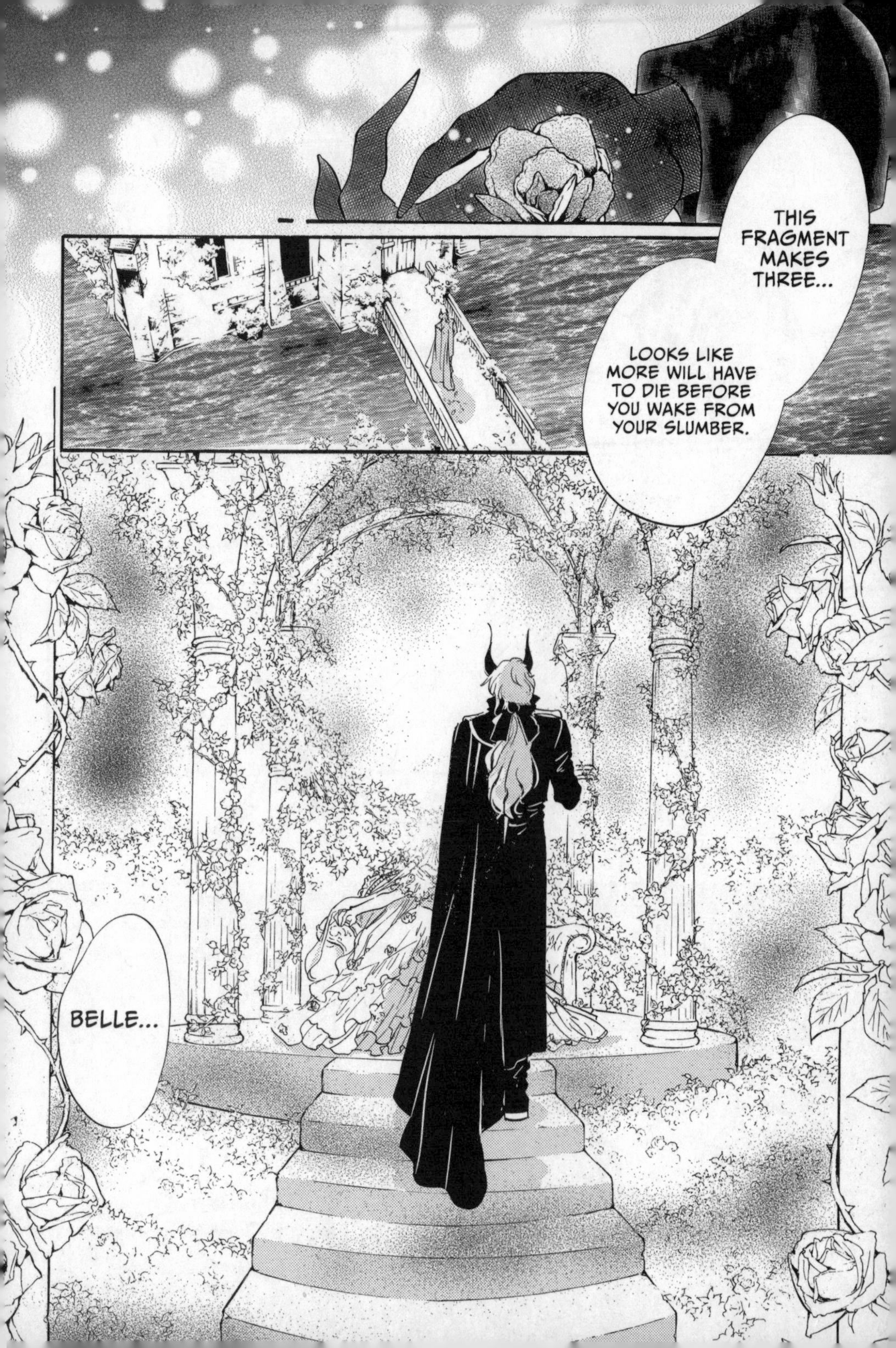
THIS FRAGMENT MAKES THREE...
LOOKS LIKE MORE WILL HAVE TO DIE BEFORE YOU WAKE FROM YOUR SLUMBER.
BELLE...

TO BE CONTINUED...

LA BELLE ET LA BÊTE

DU PARADIS PERDU

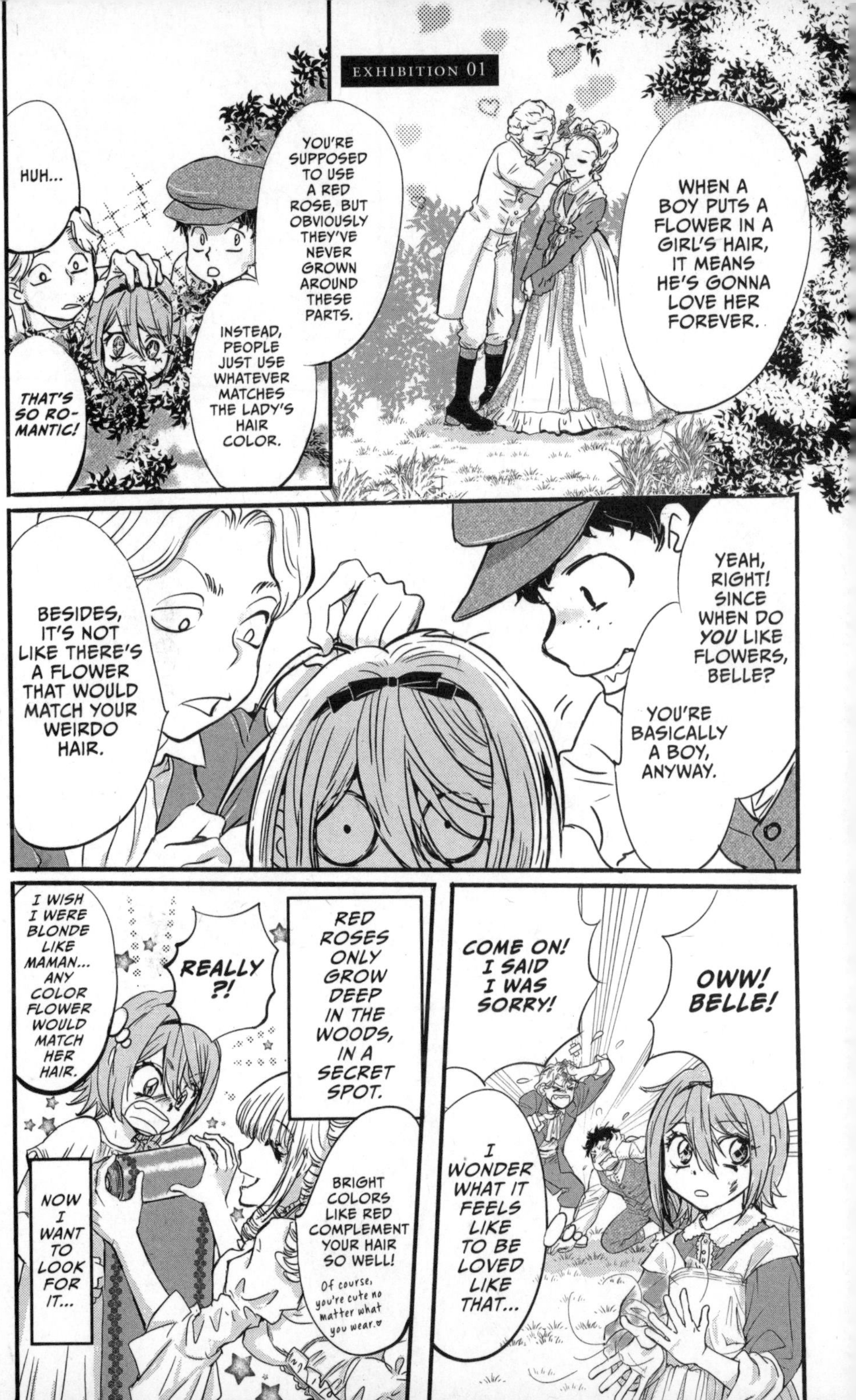
EXHIBITION 01
WHEN A BOY PUTS A FLOWER IN A GIRL'S HAIR, IT MEANS HE'S GONNA LOVE HER FOREVER.
YOU'RE SUPPOSED TO USE A RED ROSE, BUT OBVIOUSLY THEY'VE NEVER GROWN AROUND THESE PARTS.
INSTEAD, PEOPLE JUST USE WHATEVER MATCHES THE LADY'S HAIR COLOR.
HUH...
THAT'S SO RO-MANTIC!
YEAH, RIGHT! SINCE WHEN DO YOU LIKE FLOWERS, BELLE?
YOU'RE BASICALLY A BOY, ANYWAY.
BESIDES, IT'S NOT LIKE THERE'S A FLOWER THAT WOULD MATCH YOUR WEIRDO HAIR.
OWW! BELLE!
COME ON! I SAID I WAS SORRY!
I WONDER WHAT IT FEELS LIKE TO BE LOVED LIKE THAT...
RED ROSES ONLY GROW DEEP IN THE WOODS, IN A SECRET SPOT.
REALLY ?!
I WISH I WERE BLONDE LIKE MAMAN... ANY COLOR FLOWER WOULD MATCH HER HAIR.
BRIGHT COLORS LIKE RED COMPLEMENT YOUR HAIR SO WELL!
Of course, you're cute no matter what you wear.♡
NOW I WANT TO LOOK FOR IT...

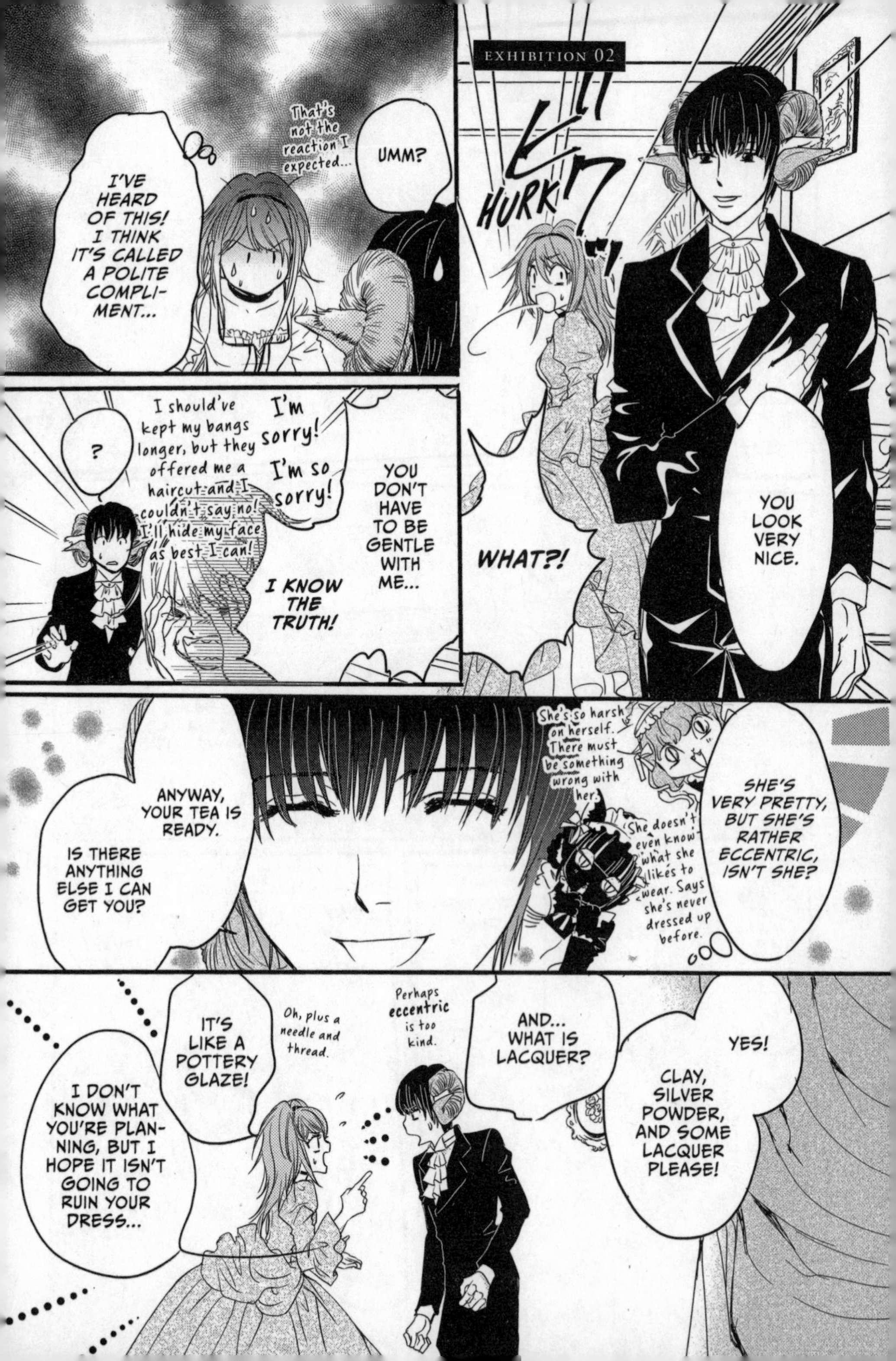
YOU LOOK VERY NICE.
HURK
WHAT?!
UMM?
That's not the reaction I expected...
I'VE HEARD OF THIS! I THINK IT'S CALLED A POLITE COMPLI-MENT...
YOU DON'T HAVE TO BE GENTLE WITH ME...
I KNOW THE TRUTH!
I'm sorry! I'm so sorry!
I should've kept my bangs longer, but they offered me a haircut and I couldn't say no! I'll hide my face as best I can!
?
SHE'S VERY PRETTY, BUT SHE'S RATHER ECCENTRIC, ISN'T SHE?
She's so harsh on herself. There must be something wrong with her.
She doesn't even know what she likes to wear. Says she's never dressed up before.
ANYWAY, YOUR TEA IS READY.
IS THERE ANYTHING ELSE I CAN GET YOU?
YES!
CLAY, SILVER POWDER, AND SOME LACQUER PLEASE!
AND... WHAT IS LACQUER?
Perhaps eccentric is too kind.
Oh, plus a needle and thread.
IT'S LIKE A POTTERY GLAZE!
I DON'T KNOW WHAT YOU'RE PLAN-NING, BUT I HOPE IT ISN'T GOING TO RUIN YOUR DRESS...

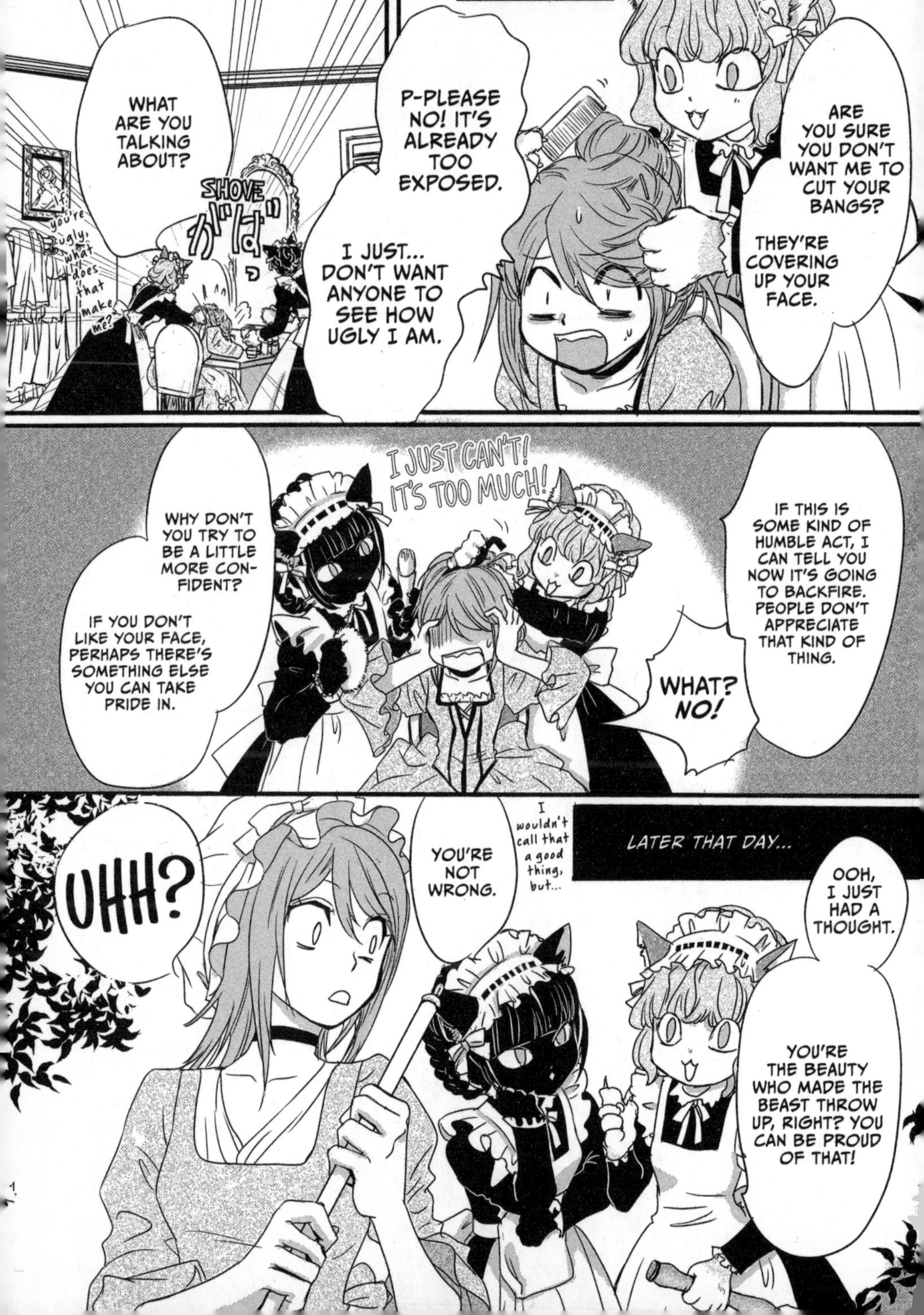
ARE YOU SURE YOU DON'T WANT ME TO CUT YOUR BANGS?
THEY'RE COVERING UP YOUR FACE.
P-PLEASE NO! IT'S ALREADY TOO EXPOSED.
I JUST... DON'T WANT ANYONE TO SEE HOW UGLY I AM.
WHAT ARE YOU TALKING ABOUT?
SHOVE
がばっ
If you're ugly, what does that make me?
IF THIS IS SOME KIND OF HUMBLE ACT, I CAN TELL YOU NOW IT'S GOING TO BACKFIRE. PEOPLE DON'T APPRECIATE THAT KIND OF THING.
WHAT? NO!
I JUST CAN'T! IT'S TOO MUCH!
WHY DON'T YOU TRY TO BE A LITTLE MORE CON-FIDENT?
IF YOU DON'T LIKE YOUR FACE, PERHAPS THERE'S SOMETHING ELSE YOU CAN TAKE PRIDE IN.
LATER THAT DAY...
OOH, I JUST HAD A THOUGHT.
YOU'RE THE BEAUTY WHO MADE THE BEAST THROW UP, RIGHT? YOU CAN BE PROUD OF THAT!
I wouldn't call that a good thing, but...
YOU'RE NOT WRONG.
UHH?

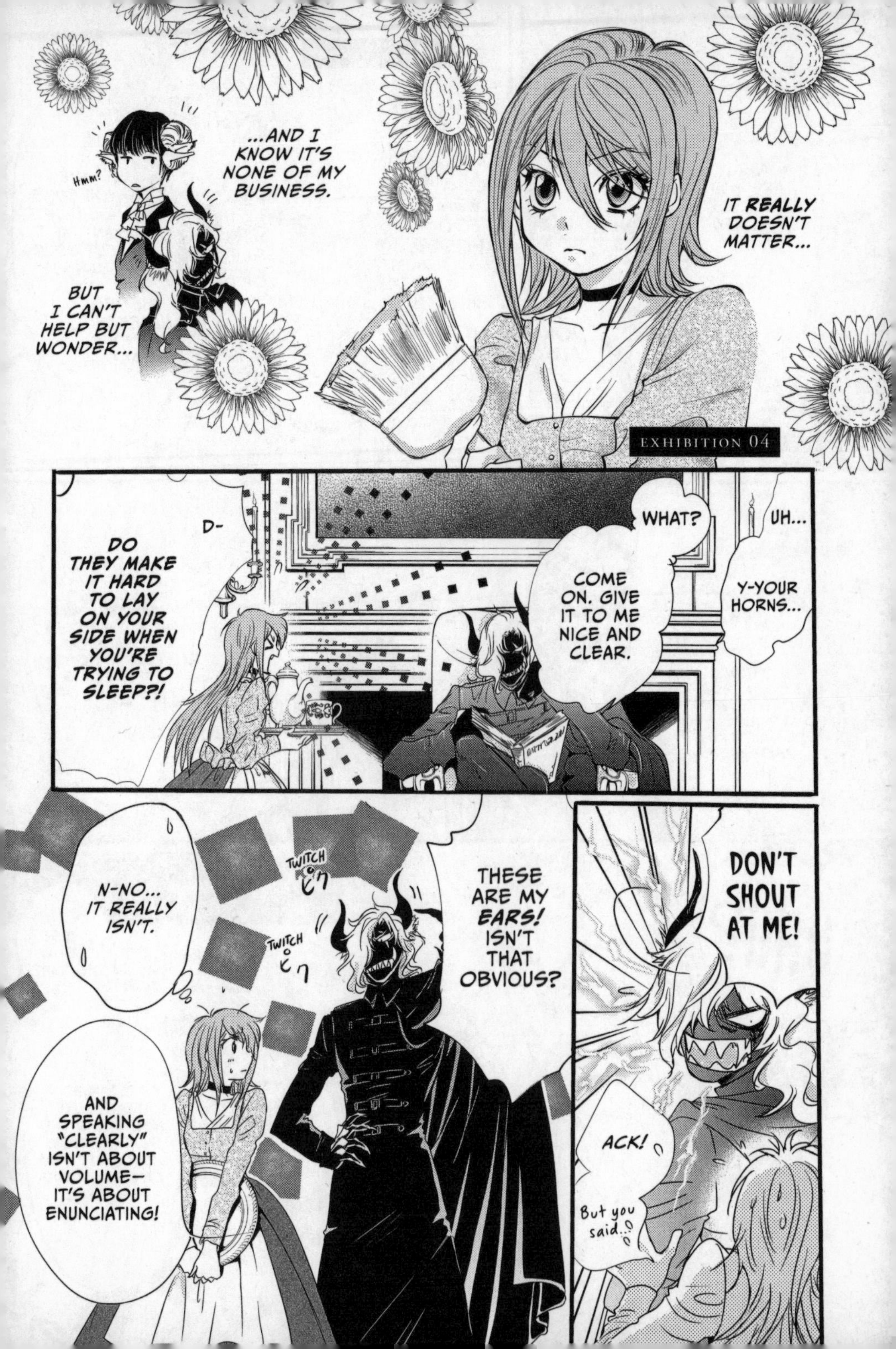
IT REALLY DOESN'T MATTER...
...AND I KNOW IT'S NONE OF MY BUSINESS.
Hmm?
BUT I CAN'T HELP BUT WONDER...
UH...
Y-YOUR HORNS...
WHAT?
COME ON. GIVE IT TO ME NICE AND CLEAR.
D-
DO THEY MAKE IT HARD TO LAY ON YOUR SIDE WHEN YOU'RE TRYING TO SLEEP?!
DON'T SHOUT AT ME!
ACK!
But you said...
THESE ARE MY EARS! ISN'T THAT OBVIOUS?
TWITCH
TWITCH
N-NO... IT REALLY ISN'T.
AND SPEAKING "CLEARLY" ISN'T ABOUT VOLUME— IT'S ABOUT ENUNCIATING!

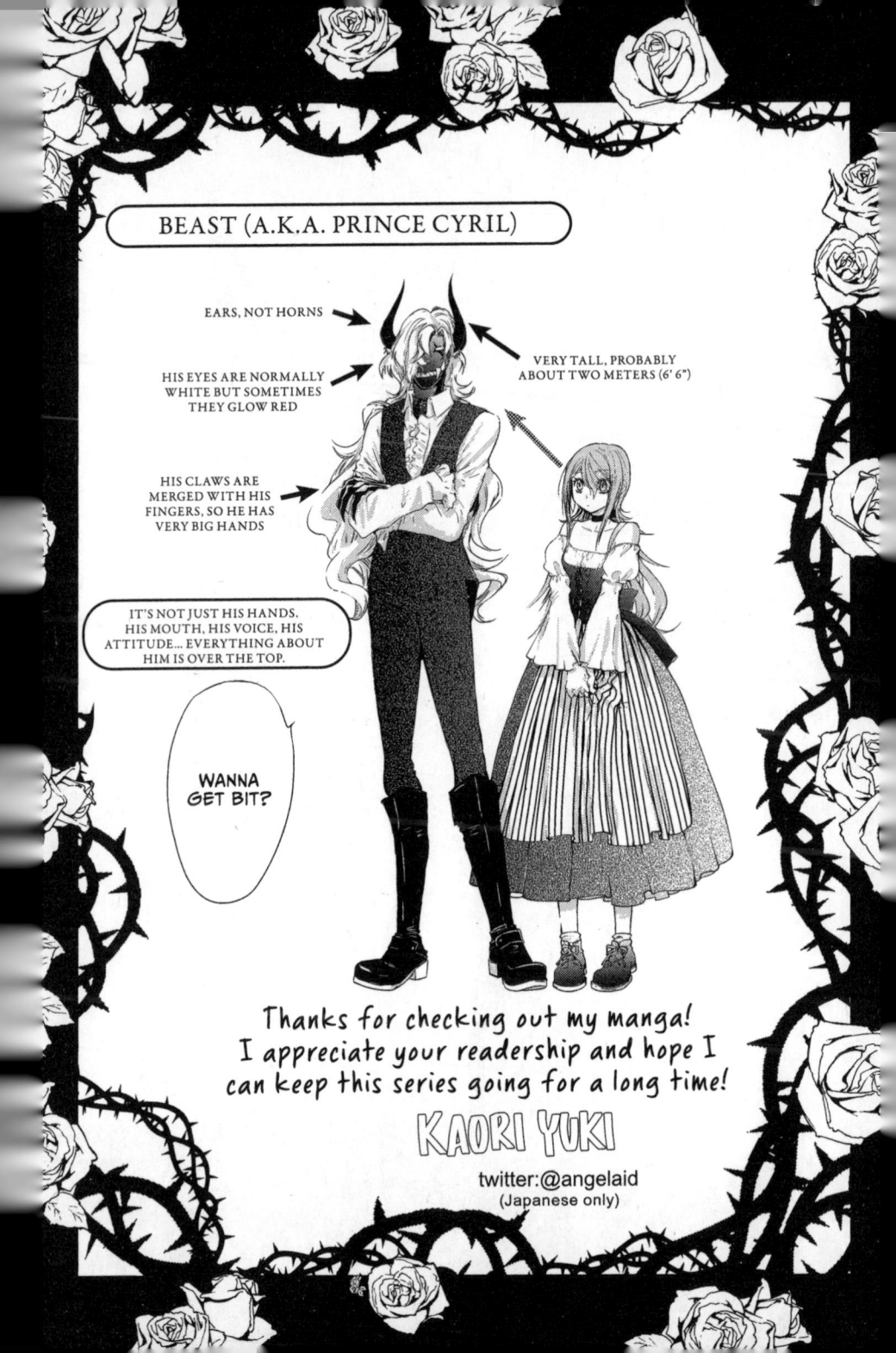

BEAST (A.K.A. PRINCE CYRIL)
EARS, NOT HORNS
VERY TALL, PROBABLY ABOUT TWO METERS (6' 6")
HIS EYES ARE NORMALLY WHITE BUT SOMETIMES THEY GLOW RED
HIS CLAWS ARE MERGED WITH HIS FINGERS, SO HE HAS VERY BIG HANDS
IT'S NOT JUST HIS HANDS. HIS MOUTH, HIS VOICE, HIS ATTITUDE... EVERYTHING ABOUT HIM IS OVER THE TOP.
WANNA GET BIT?

Thanks for checking out my manga!
I appreciate your readership and hope I can keep this series going for a long time!

KAORI YUKI

twitter:@angelaid
(Japanese only)

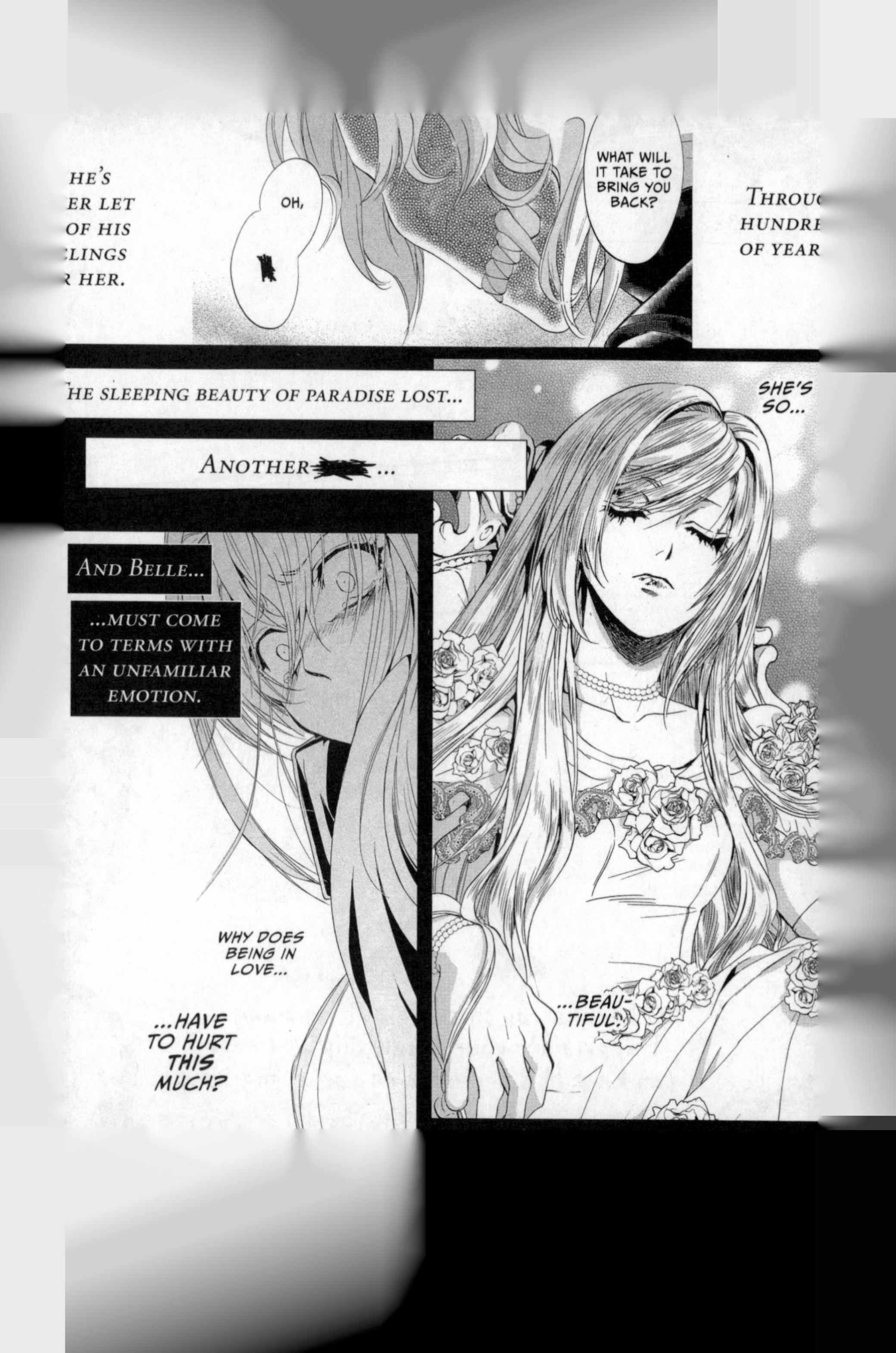
THROU
HUNDRE
OF YEAR
WHAT WILL IT TAKE TO BRING YOU BACK?
OH, [redacted]
HE'S
ER LET
OF HIS
LINGS
R HER.
SHE'S SO...
...BEAU-TIFUL.
HE SLEEPING BEAUTY OF PARADISE LOST...
ANOTHER [redacted]...
AND BELLE...
...MUST COME TO TERMS WITH AN UNFAMILIAR EMOTION.
WHY DOES BEING IN LOVE...
...HAVE TO HURT THIS MUCH?

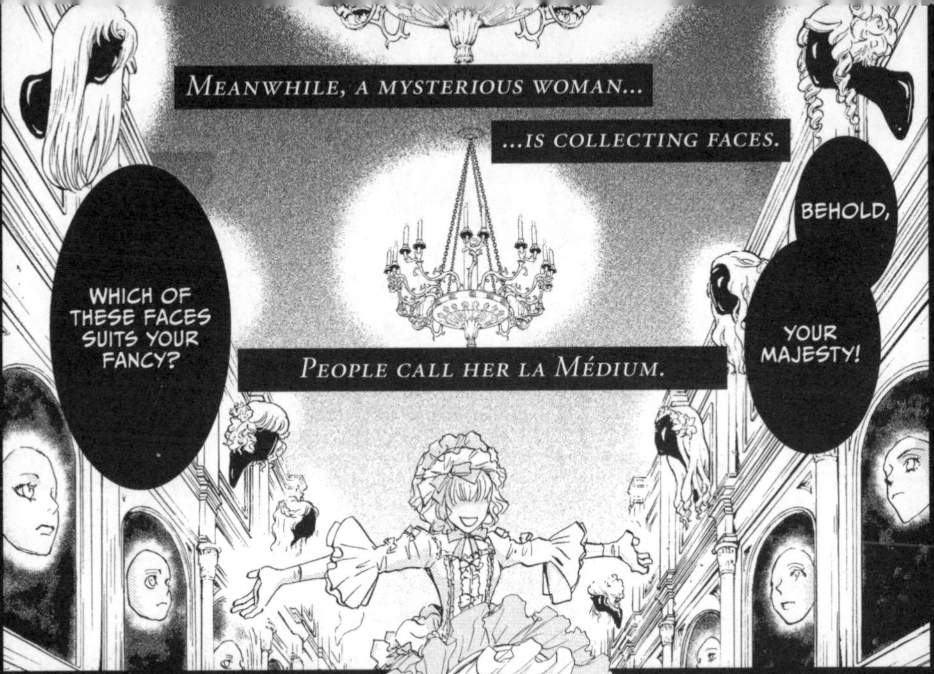
Meanwhile, a mysterious woman...
...is collecting faces.
Behold,
your majesty!
Which of these faces suits your fancy?
People call her la Médium.

And soon...

...she'll slither into Belle's and the Beast's lives!

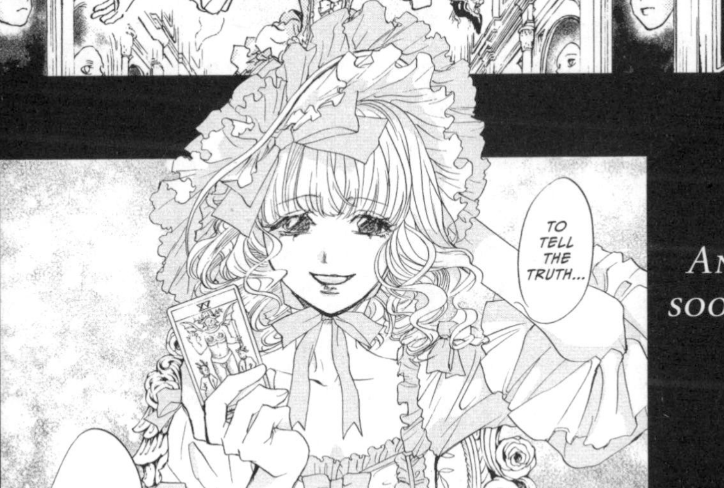
To tell the truth...
...I've even re-placed my own.

Beauty and the Beast of Paradise Lost 2

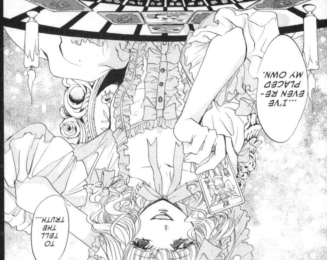

Beautifully seductive artwork and uniquely Japanese depictions of the supernatural will hypnotize CLAMP fans!

xxxHOLiC © CLAMP-ShigatsuTsuitachi CO.,LTD./Kodansha Ltd.
xxxHOLiC Rei © CLAMP-ShigatsuTsuitachi CO.,LTD./Kodansha Ltd.

Kimihiro Watanuki is haunted by visions of ghosts and spirits. He seeks help from a mysterious woman named Yuko, who claims she can help. However, Watanuki must work for Yuko in order to pay for her aid. Soon Watanuki finds himself employed in Yuko's shop, where he sees things and meets customers that are stranger than anything he could have ever imagined.

KC/
KODANSHA
COMICS

A Kodansha Comics Trade Paperback Original
Beauty and the Beast of Paradise Lost 1 copyright © 2020 Kaori Yuki
English translation copyright © 2021 Kaori Yuki

Published in the United States by Kodansha Comics, an imprint of
Kodansha USA Publishing, LLC, New York.

Publication rights for this English edition arranged through
Kodansha Ltd., Tokyo.

First published in Japan in 2020 by Kodansha Ltd., Tokyo
as *Rakuen no bijo to yaju, volume 1.*

ISBN 978-1-64651-250-8

Printed in the United States of America.

www.kodansha.us

9 8 7 6 5 4 3 2 1

Translation: Rose Padgett
Lettering: Phil Christie
Editing: Vanessa Tenazas
Kodansha Comics edition cover design by Phil Balsman

Publisher: Kiichiro Sugawara

Director of publishing services: Ben Applegate
Associate director of operations: Stephen Pakula
Publishing services managing editors: Alanna Ruse, Madison Salters
Production managers: Emi Lotto, Angela Zurlo
Logo and character art © Kodansha USA Publishing, LLC